The Cambridge Companion to Aphra Behn

Traditionally known as the first professional woman writer in English, Aphra Behn has now emerged as one of the major figures of the Restoration. During the 1670s and 1680s, she provided more plays for the stage than any other author, and greatly influenced the development of the novel with her ground-breaking fiction, especially *Love-Letters between a Noble-Man and his Sister*, and *Oroonoko*, the first English novel set in America. Behn's work straddles the genres: beside drama and fiction, she also excelled in poetry and she made several important translations from French libertine and scientific works. The chapters in this Companion discuss and introduce her writings in all these fields and provide the critical tools with which to judge their aesthetic and historical importance. The book also includes a full bibliography, a detailed chronology, and a description of the known facts of her life. The Companion will be an essential tool for the study of this increasingly important writer and thinker.

DEREK HUGHES is Professor of English Literature at the University of Aberdeen. In addition to many articles on Restoration drama and its background, he has published *Dryden's Heroic Plays* (1980), *English Drama, 1660–1700* (1996), and *The Theatre of Aphra Behn* (2001). He was the general editor of the six-volume *Eighteenth Century Women Playwrights* (2001), and has just completed an edition of early modern texts concerning slavery and America, which includes Behn's and Southerne's versions of *Oroonoko*. He is currently writing a book on representations of human sacrifice in literature and opera.

JANET TODD is the Francis Hutcheson Professor of English Literature at the University of Glasgow. She is a pioneer in the study of early women's writing; her books include *Women's Friendship in Literature* (1980), *The Sign of Angellica: Women, Writing and History* (1990) and the biographies, *The Secret Life of Aphra Behn* (1996), *Mary Wollstonecraft: A Revolutionary Life* (2000) and *Rebel Daughters: Ireland in Conflict 1798* (2003). She has edited the *Dictionary of British and American Women Writers* (1985), the complete works of Aphra Behn (1992–6) and, most recently, *The Collected letters of Mary Wollstonecraft* (2003). She is the general editor of the Cambridge edition of Jane Austen and co-editor of the journal *Women's Writing*.

THE CAMBRIDGE
COMPANION TO
APHRA BEHN

EDITED BY

DEREK HUGHES

University of Aberdeen

JANET TODD

University of Glasgow

PUBLISHED BY THE PRESS SYNDICATE OF THE UNIVERSITY OF CAMBRIDGE
The Pitt Building, Trumpington Street, Cambridge, United Kingdom

CAMBRIDGE UNIVERSITY PRESS
The Edinburgh Building, Cambridge, CB2 2RU, UK
40 West 20th Street, New York, NY 10011–4211, USA
477 Williamstown Road, Port Melbourne, VIC 3207, Australia
Ruiz de Alarcón 13, 28014 Madrid, Spain
Dock House, The Waterfront, Cape Town 8001, South Africa

http://www.cambridge.org

First published 2004

Printed in the United Kingdom at the University Press, Cambridge

Typeface Sabon 10/13 pt.   *System* LATEX 2$_\varepsilon$ [TB]

A catalogue record for this book is available from the British Library

Library of Congress cataloguing in publication data
The Cambridge companion to Aphra Behn / edited by Derek Hughes and Janet Todd.
p.   cm. – (Cambridge companions to literature)
Includes bibliographical references and index.
ISBN 0 521 82019 7 (hardback) – ISBN 0 521 52720 1 (paperback)
1. Behn, Aphra, 1640–1689 – Criticism and interpretation – Handbooks, manuals, etc.
2. Women and literature – England – History – 17th century – Handbooks, manuals, etc.
I. Hughes, Derek, 1944– II. Todd, Janet M., 1942– III. Series.
PR3317.Z5C36 2004 822'.4 – dc22 2004049740

ISBN 0 521 82019 7 hardback
ISBN 0 521 52720 1 paperback

CONTENTS

CONTENTS

CONTRIBUTORS

ROS BALLASTER is Fellow in English Literature at Mansfield College, Oxford University. Her book *Seductive Forms: Women's Amatory Fiction 1684–1740* was published in 1992. She has published a number of articles on seventeenth- and eighteenth-century women's writing and a book entitled *Fabulous Orients: Fictions of the East in Eighteenth-Century England*, is forthcoming in 2004.

HELEN M. BURKE is Associate Professor of English at Florida State University. She has published essays on Restoration and eighteenth-century British literature and drama, and is the author of *Riotous Performances: The Struggle for Hegemony in the Irish Theater, 1712–1784* (2003).

LINE COTTEGNIES is Professor of English Literature at the University of Paris 3 – Sorbonne Nouvelle. She is the author of a study of Caroline poetry, *L'Éclipse du regard: la poésie anglaise du baroque au classicisme 1625–1660* (1997) and she has been working on various aspects of seventeenth-century literature. She has recently co-edited with Nancy Weitz *Authorial Conquests: Genre in the Writings of Margaret Cavendish* (2003), and is currrently working on an edition of Shakespeare. She is also editor of an electronic journal specializing in early modern literature, www.etudes-episteme.com.

JOANNA LIPKING is editor of the Norton Critical Edition of *Oroonoko* and the author of essays treating Oroonoko's slave-trade and colonial backgrounds that appear in *Aphra Behn Studies* (1996) and *Aphra Behn (1640–1689): Identity, Alterity, Ambiguity* (2000). She teaches English at Northwestern University.

ROBERT MARKLEY is Professor of English at the University of Illinois and the editor of *The Eighteenth Century: Theory and Interpretation*. The author of four monographs and sixty articles in Restoration and eighteenth-century studies, cultural studies, and the cultural study of science, his books include *Two-Edg'd Weapons: Style and Ideology in the Comedies of Etherege,*

Wycherley, and Congreve (1988) and *Fictions of Eurocentrism: The Far East and the English Imagination, 1500–1730*, forthcoming.

JESSICA MUNNS is Professor of English Literature at the University of Denver. She has written widely on Restoration drama, and edits the journal *Restoration and Eighteenth-Century Theatre Research*. Her most recent book is *Gender, Power, and Privilege in Early Modern Europe* (2003), co-edited with Penny Richards; with Susan Iwanisziw she has just completed editing a selection of plays based on Behn's *Oroonoko*.

MARY ANN O'DONNELL is Professor of English and Dean of the School of Arts, Manhattan College. The second edition of her *Aphra Behn: An Annotated Bibliography of Primary and Secondary Sources* is due in 2004.

SUSAN J. OWEN is Reader in English Literature at the University of Sheffield. She has published articles on Behn in *Aphra Behn Studies* and the new Macmillan Casebook. Her extensive publications on Restoration drama include *Restoration Theatre and Crisis* (1996) and *Perspectives on Restoration Drama* (2002). She has edited the *Blackwell Companion to Restoration Drama* (2001) and A *Babel of Bottles: Drink, Drinkers and Drinking Places in Literature* (2000).

JACQUELINE PEARSON is Professor of English at the University of Manchester. She is the author of *The Prostituted Muse: Images of Women and Women Dramatists 1642–1737* (1988), an edition of Susanna Centlivre (Pickering 2001), and articles on Aphra Behn and other seventeenth- and eighteenth-century women writers. Her most recent monograph is *Women's Reading in Britain 1750–1835: a Dangerous Recreation* (1999).

LAURA J. ROSENTHAL is Associate Professor of English at the University of Maryland, College Park, and author of *Playwrights and Plagiarists in Early Modern England: Gender, Authorship, Literary Property* (1996). She is currently completing a manuscript entitled 'Infamous Commerce: Prostitution in Eighteenth-Century British Literature and Culture'.

SUSAN STAVES'S scholarly interests centre on English literature and history in the Restoration and eighteenth century, particularly on questions of how cultural ideologies are created and represented in various kinds of texts ranging from comedies to judicial opinions. She is the author of *Players' Scepters: Fictions of Authority in the Restoration* (1979) and *Married Woman's Separate Property in England, 1660–1833* (1990), and over thirty articles. With John Brewer, she has edited and contributed to *Early Modern Conceptions of Property* (1995) and with Cynthia Ricciardi she has edited

Elizabeth Griffith's *Delicate Distress* (1999). Her current book project is a literary history of women's writing in Britain from 1660 to 1789.

MELINDA S. ZOOK is Associate Professor of History at Purdue University. She is the author of *Radical Whigs and Conspiratorial Politics in Late Stuart England* (1999) and the co-editor of *Revolutionary Currents: Nation Building in the Transatlantic World* (2004). She is currently working on a book-manuscript on the political activism of dissenting women in Restoration England.

Except where otherwise stated, all citations from texts by Aphra Behn are taken from *The Works of Aphra Behn*, ed. Janet Todd, 7 vols. (London: Pickering; Ohio: Ohio State University Press, 1992–6). In the case of plays, the volume, act, scene, and line are provided parenthetically; for prologues and epilogues, volume and line numbers; and for poetry and prose, the volume and page. Dates of plays provided in brackets within the text refer to the first known performance unless otherwise stated. All dates are given in new style.

Aphra Behn Studies	*Aphra Behn Studies*, ed. Janet Todd (Cambridge: Cambridge University Press, 1996).
O'Donnell	Mary Ann O'Donnell, *Aphra Behn: An Annotated Bibliography of Primary and Secondary Sources* (New York: Garland, 1986).
Rereading Aphra Behn	*Rereading Aphra Behn*, ed. Heidi Hutner (London and Charlottesville: University Press of Virginia, 1993).
Todd	Janet Todd, *The Secret Life of Aphra Behn* (London: André Deutsch; New Brunswick: Rutgers University Press, 1996).

CHRONOLOGY

Mary Ann O'Donnell

Note: all dates are given in New Style.

1640   Long Parliament; impeachment of Archbishop William Laud and Thomas Wentworth, 1st Earl of Strafford.
        Probable date of Behn's birth as Eaffrey or Aphra, daughter of Bartholomew Johnson, a barber, and Elizabeth Johnson (née Denham), a wetnurse, in Harbledown, Canterbury. Baptised 14 December.

1641   Thomas Wentworth, 1st Earl of Strafford, executed.
        William Wycherley born.

1642   September. Theatres closed; Civil War begins.
        Isaac Newton, Thomas Shadwell born.

1644   Battle of Marston Moor gives parliamentary forces major victory.

1645   Archbishop Laud executed.

1647   The Scots surrender Charles I to Parliament; he later escapes to the Isle of Wight.
        John Wilmot, 1st Earl of Rochester, born.

1648   Second Civil War; Charles I captured.

1649   30 January Charles I executed.
        Commonwealth proclaimed.

1650   Anne Bradstreet's poems, *The Tenth Muse*, published.

1651   After his defeat at the Battle of Worcester, Charles II escapes capture by hiding in Boscobel Oak.
        Hobbes's *Leviathan* published.

1652   Thomas Otway born.

1653   Oliver Cromwell named Protector.
        Margaret Cavendish's *Poems and Fancies* and *Philosophicall Fancies* published.

1655	Lord Willoughby issues a prospectus to develop colonisation of Surinam.
1658	Oliver Cromwell dies; his son Richard assumes the role of Protector, 3 September.
1659	Protectorate dissolves.
1660	Charles II returns to London on his thirtieth birthday, 29 May.
	Theatres reopen. Two theatrical companies established: the King's Company, managed by Thomas Killigrew, and the Duke's, managed by William Davenant.
	Tatham's *The Rump* produced, Dorset Court, June; source of AB's *Roundheads*.
1661	Charles II crowned, 23 April.
	The Duke's Company moves into the Lincoln's Inn Fields theatre.
1662	Charles II marries Catherine of Braganza.
1663	King's Company moves into the Theatre Royal, Bridges Street, near Drury Lane.
	Katherine Philips' *Pompey* performed in Dublin; published.
	Delarivier Manley born.
	Abbé Paul Tallemant publishes his *Voyage de L'Isle d'Amour*.
	Probable date of AB's going to Surinam.
1664	Second Dutch War begins, December.
	Dryden and Sir Robert Howard's *The Indian Queen* produced Theatre Royal in Bridges Street, January; the feathers AB alleges to have brought back from Surinam were probably not used for this but rather for a revival.
	Katherine Philips' *Poems* published in unauthorized edition in January; Philips dies in June.
	Killigrew's *Collected Plays* published, including *Thomaso*.
	AB probably left Surinam by March.
	AB possibly begins the composition of *The Young King*.
1664–6	*Possible* marriage to a Mr Behn; *possible* death of same.
1665	Great Plague rages in London by June; theatres close on 5 June for sixteen months; court leaves London in July.
	La Rochefoucauld publishes the first authorized edition of his *Maximes* in Paris (unauthorized edition published in The Hague in 1664).
	Attempted murder in Antwerp of Anna Luisa van Mechelen by her sister Maria Theresa and her sister's husband

	Francisco di Tarquini (aka Prince Tarquin), a central event in AB's *The Fair Jilt*.
1666	Great Plague begins to abate thanks to brutal frosts of winter 1665–6.
	Court returns to London in February.
	Mary Pix (née Griffith), Mary Astell born.
	Attempted execution of Francisco di Tarquini in Antwerp, a central event in AB's *The Fair Jilt*, probably late May.
	Joseph Williamson draws up the 'Memorialls for Mrs Affora', July 1666, for AB to use on spying mission in Low Countries.
	AB goes to Bruges, then Antwerp, and makes contact with William Scot; sends a series of letters to Killigrew, Arlington, and Halsall and others detailing what she knows and asking for money; sinks deeply into debt; borrows £150 from Edward Botteler (or Butler).
	Great Fire of London, 2–6 September.
	Balthazar de Bonnecorse's *La Montre* published in Paris; revised edition, 1671.
1667	AB returns to London deeply in debt, probably in May; begins efforts to recoup personal losses incurred in service of the Crown.
	Dutch burn ships in the Medway.
	Treaty of Breda ends war with Dutch; gives Surinam to the Dutch in exchange for Manhattan Island, 21 July.
	First edition of Milton's *Paradise Lost*.
	Authorized edition of Katherine Philips' *Poems* and folio edition of her *Works* published.
	Margaret Cavendish publishes the *Life* of her husband, the Duke of Newcastle.
	'Widdow Behn' is referred to in a legal case related to the seizure of the ship, *Abraham's Sacrifice*.
	AB perhaps serves as copyist for Killigrew's King's Men.
1668	Deeply in debt, AB petitions the court to prevent her imprisonment for debt, probably in autumn; no evidence that she was ever in debtors' prison.
	William Davenant dies, April; his widow assumes charge of Duke's Company.
	Dryden named Poet Laureate; publishes his *Essay of Dramatick Poesie*.

Margaret Cavendish's *Playes Never Before Printed* published (adds to 1662 edition).

1670   Congreve born.

Probable year of Susanna Centlivre's birth.

Louise de Kéroualle, who becomes a powerful royal mistress, comes to England from France.

Behn's *The Forc'd Marriage* produced by the Duke's Company, September. The Duke's Company were to produce all Behn's plays until the two theatre companies merged in 1682. Milton's *Paradise Regained* and *Samson Agonistes* published.

The Forc'd Marriage published; produced again, 9 January.

The Amorous Prince produced, February; published.

Duke's Company moves to new playhouse in Dorset Garden, November.

The Rehearsal (King's Company, December) mocks *The Forc'd Marriage* among other plays.

AB publishes dedicatory poem to Edward Howard in *The Six Days Adventure*.

1672   Bridges Street Theatre destroyed by fire (January). King's Company moves temporarily to Lincoln's Inn Fields, recently vacated by the Duke's Company.

Declaration of Indulgence enacted.

AB probably serves as editor of *Covent Garden Drolery*.

James, Duke of York, marries Mary of Modena.

Margaret Cavendish, Duchess of Newcastle, dies.

The Dutch Lover produced in the new Duke's Theatre, Dorset Garden, February; published.

1674   End of war with Dutch.

King's Men move to new Theatre Royal in Drury Lane, March.

Second edition of Milton's *Paradise Lost*.

Death of Milton.

References by Roger Morrice suggest starting date of AB's relationship with John Hoyle as 1674–6.

1675   Work begins by Christopher Wren to restore St Paul's Cathedral.

Edward Phillips notices AB in *Theatrum Poetarum*.

La Rochefoucauld publishes the fourth edition of his *Maximes*, the edition mainly used by AB.

Publication in Paris of Tallemant's two 'Voyages', works used by AB.

1676   Artist John Greenhill dies; Behn eulogizes him in a poem.
Nathaniel Bacon raises a rebellion in Virginia; later used as central event of *The Widdow Ranter*.
Abdelazer produced, Duke's Theatre, Dorset Garden, 3 July.
The Town-Fopp produced, Duke's Theatre, Dorset Garden, licensed 20 September 1676.

1677   William of Orange marries Mary, daughter of James, Duke of York, and the late Ann Hyde, Duchess of York.
The Debauchee (attribution) produced at Duke's Theatre, Dorset Garden; licensed 23 February 1677; published.
Abdelazer published.
The Town-Fopp published.
The Rover produced, Duke's Theatre, Dorset Garden, 24 March; three issues published, the last issue with AB's name on the title page, licensed 2 July.
The Counterfeit Bridegroom (attribution) produced, Duke's Theatre, Dorset Garden, September 1677; licensed 4 October 1677.

1678   *Sir Patient Fancy* produced 17 January; published, licensed 28 January.
Popish Plot scare begins in September, with false allegations by Titus Oates about a planned Catholic coup.

1679   Catholic James, Duke of York, goes into exile.
First Exclusion bill introduced, May, to prevent James, Duke of York, from succeeding to the throne; Parliament dissolved.
Thomas Hobbes dies.
'Ephelia' praises AB in a poem addressed to 'Bhen' in *Female Poems on Several Occasions*.
Charles II taken ill; James summoned from exile in Brussels.
The Feign'd Curtizans produced, licensed 27 March; published.
The Young King produced September.

1680   Second Exclusion Bill rejected by the House of Lords, November.
James, Duke of York, returns to exile, in Scotland.
John Wilmot, Earl of Rochester, dies; his *Poems* published; *Burnet's Passages of the Life and Death of the Earl of Rochester* published.

Filmer's *Patriarcha* published (written between 1635 and 1642).

La Rochefoucauld dies.

William Howard, Viscount Stafford, executed as Catholic, 29 December; had met Behn on her spying mission.

AB's paraphrase/translation of 'Oenone to Paris' in *Ovid's Epistles*, edited by John Dryden.

Three of AB's poems published without attribution in Rochester's *Poems on Several Occasions*.

The Revenge (attribution) produced around June; published early July.

1681   Earl of Shaftesbury attempts to secure the Protestant succession by having Charles II's eldest illegitimate son, the Duke of Monmouth, declared heir to the throne; thwarted by King's dissolution of Oxford Parliament.

Confinement of Shaftesbury to the Tower on charge of high treason but indictment dismissed by a London Grand Jury.

Calderón de la Barca dies; his play *La Vida es sueño* (1635) is used in AB's *The Young King*.

James, Duke of York, returns from exile.

The Second Part of The Rover produced, January; published probably in June.

The False Count produced, probably in October; licensed 21 July; published December 1681 with the date 1682 on the title page.

The Roundheads produced December.

1682   The Duke's and King's Companies join to form the United Company, April.

Lady Henrietta Berkeley elopes with her brother-in-law Ford, Lord Grey September; Grey brought to trial November; this, along with Monmouth's Rebellion of 1685, forms the basis of *Love-Letters between a Noble-Man and his Sister*.

Gilbert Burnet warns Anne Wharton against AB, 'so abominably vile a woman'; Radcliffe accuses AB of having her plays written by a 'Greys Inn Lawyer'; Shadwell satirizes her in *The Tory Poets*, along with Otway, her 'Pimp'.

The Ten Pleasures of Marriage (unlikely attribution) published.

The Roundheads published February 1682.

Like Father, Like Son produced March 1682; only the
prologue and epilogue survive; adaptation of Randolph's *The
Jealous Lovers*.
*A Prologue by Mrs Behn to her New Play, Called Like
Father, Like Son* published, April.
The City-Heiress produced Duke's Theatre, Dorset Garden,
April; published.
Prologue [and Epilogue] *to Romulus and Hersilia* resulting in
warrant for arrest of AB and the speaker, Lady Slingsby,
August.

1683   Rye-House Plot to assassinate Charles II fails. The Earl of
Essex, Russell, and Algernon Sidney sent to the Tower;
Sidney and Russell executed; Ford, Lord Grey, escapes to the
continent.
Death of Shaftesbury and Thomas Killigrew.
AB's dedicatory poem to Creech, 'To the Unknown Daphnis'
published in the second edition of Creech's translation of
Lucretius' *De Natura Rerum*.
The anonymous *Romulus and Hersilia* published with AB's
prologue toned down and epilogue unchanged.
The Young King (produced 1679) published probably
November.

1684   Monmouth goes to Holland.
Publication of Rochester's *Valentinian* with prologue (and
probably epilogue) by AB; separate broadside publication of
these, February.
First part of *Love-Letters between a Noble-Man and his
Sister* published.
Poems upon Several Occasions published; contains *A Voyage
to the Isle of Love*.
Possible date of composition of *The Younger Brother*
(produced and published posthumously 1696).

1685   Charles II dies 6 February; theatres closed for ten weeks;
coronation of James II 23 April.
Earl of Argyll leads uprising in favour of Monmouth; Argyll
executed.
Monmouth's Rebellion June; put down at Sedgemoor;
Monmouth executed 15 July.
Publication of Montaigne's *Essays*, translated by AB's friend
Charles Cotton; 'Of Cannibals' used in *Oroonoko*.

Commendatory poem to Thomas Tryon published in his *The Way to Make All People Rich*.

A Pindarick on the Death of our Late Sovereign published February, with second edition and Dublin edition in the same year.

A Poem Humbly Dedicated to the Great Patern of Piety and Virtue Catherine Queen Dowager published in April; second edition published in Dublin.

A Pindarick Poem on the Happy Coronation of His Most Sacred Majesty James II and His Illustrious Consort Queen Mary, in two editions, May.

Second part of *Love-Letters between a Noble-Man and his Sister* published as *Love-Letters from a Noble-Man and his Sister*.

Miscellany . . . Together with Reflections on Morality, or Seneca Unmasqued (AB's translation of La Rochefoucauld) published.

1686   Fontenelle's *Entretiens sur la pluralité des mondes* and *Histoire des Oracles* published in Paris.

Anne Killigrew's *Poems* published.

The Luckey Chance produced by the United Company in Drury Lane April; licensed 23 April.

La Montre published.

1687   George Villiers, 2nd Duke of Buckingham, Edmund Waller, Charles Cotton, and Nell Gwyn, actress and mistress to Charles II, die.

Newton's *Principia* published.

John Hoyle accused of sodomy; verdict of *ignoramus*.

Langbaine notices AB's fifteen plays, identifying sources for nine, in *Momus Triumphans*.

Commendatory poem to Sir Francis Fane published in his play *The Sacrifice*.

Commendatory poem to Henry Higden published in his *Modern Essay on the Tenth Satire of Juvenal*.

The Emperor of the Moon produced, Dorset Garden, March; licensed 6 April, published.

The Luckey Chance published.

To the Most Illustrious Prince Christopher Duke of Albemarle on His Voyage to his Government of Jamaica published.

AB's translation of *Aesop's Fables* published with the 1666 Francis Barlow plates.

Third part of *Love-Letters between a Noble-Man and his Sister* published as *The Amours of Philander and Silvia*.

Writes to Edmund Waller's daughter-in-law after 21 October 1687 about her 'lame hand' and her impending death; includes poem on the death of Waller.

1688   *A Congratulatory Poem to Her Most Sacred Majesty on the Universal Hopes of all Loyal Persons for a Prince of Wales*, licensed 17 February; reissued in *Two Congratulatory Poems*; second edition, Edinburgh.

AB is vilified in an 'Epistle to Julian' as a harlot plagued by 'Poverty, Poetry [and] Pox'; Prior attacks her in 'A Session of Poets'.

Elegy for Waller published in the collection on his death February 1688.

Declaration of Indulgence April.

The Fair Jilt licensed 17 April; reissued in *Three Histories*.

A Poem to Sir Roger L'Estrange on His Third Part of the History of the Times; Relating to the Death of Sir Edmund Bury-Godfrey licensed 22 April.

Lycidus . . . Together with a Miscellany of New Poems licensed 13 May 1687 and probably published early 1688.

Second edition of *The Emperor of the Moon*.

Agnes de Castro licensed 24 May; reissued in *Three Histories*.

To Poet Bavius, published June.

10 June, birth of a son, James (later 'The Old Pretender') to the Catholic monarchs, James II and Mary of Modena, sets off succession crisis.

A Congratulatory Poem to the King's Most Sacred Majesty on the Happy Birth of the Prince of Wales, June; second edition and reissued as part of *Two Congratulatory Poems*.

Oroonoko; reissued in *Three Histories*.

November, the Protestant claimant, William of Orange, lands in England and moves on London.

December, Queen Consort Mary of Modena leaves England for France with the infant Prince. Glorious Revolution; flight of James II and supporters to France.

The History of Oracles published; reprinted in *Histories, Novels and Translations*, 1700.

	A Discovery of New Worlds published, includes 'The Translator's Preface'; reprinted in *Histories, Novels and Translations*, 1700.
1689	*A Congratulatory Poem to Her Most Sacred Majesty Queen Mary upon Her Arrival in England* published February.
	A Pindaric Poem to the Reverend Doctor Burnet on the Honour He Did Me of Enquiring after Me and My Muse published, probably in March.
	Coronation of William of Orange and Mary, daughter of James II, 11 April.
	AB dies, 16 April; buried in the east cloister of Westminster Abbey.
	Dryden loses Poet Laureateship to Shadwell.
	Robert Gould attacks AB in 'A Satyr against the Playhouse', included in his *Poems, chiefly consisting of Satyrs and Satyrical Epistles*.
	Nathaniel Lee laments her death in an elegy, and 'A Lady of Quality' mourns her passing in a broadside.
	Translation of the sixth book of Cowley's *Sylva*, the sixth book of Plants, in an edition supervised by Nahum Tate.
	The Lucky Mistake published.
	The History of the Nun, or The Fair Vow-Breaker published.
	The Widdow Ranter produced, Drury Lane, November.
	Dryden's prologue and epilogue to *The Widdow Ranter*, published separately, notes her ability to please and her portrayal of love.
1690	Locke's *Essay of Human Understanding* published.
	Reissue of *The Forc'd Marriage* (1671) published, 'As it is Acted at the Queens Theatre'.
	The Widdow Ranter published January, with an old and unrelated Shadwell prologue and epilogue.
1691	Gerard Langbaine publishes his *Account of the English Dramatick Poets*.
	Several previously unpublished AB poems printed in *The History of Adolphus*.
1692	Shadwell dies; Nahum Tate becomes Poet Laureate.
	John Hoyle, Gerard Langbaine, Nathaniel Lee die.
	The Lucky Mistake reissued in Bentley's Modern Novels.
	Several previously unpublished poems printed in *Miscellany Poems upon Several Occasions*.
1693	Mme de La Fayette dies.

Second edition of *Abdelazer* published.

Second edition of all three parts of *Love-Letters between a Noble-Man and his Sister*.

1694 Queen Mary dies; King William rules alone.

Mary Astell's *Serious Proposal to the Ladies* published.

Southerne's *The Fatal Marriage*, his adaptation of AB's *The History of the Nun*, produced, Drury Lane, February.

Second edition of all three parts of *Love-Letters between a Noble-Man and his Sister* reissued.

1695 Henry Purcell, Dorothy Osborne die.

Southerne's adaptation of AB's *Oroonoko* produced, Drury Lane, November or December.

New theatre company formed by Thomas Betterton, Anne Bracegirdle, and Elizabeth Barry in Lincoln's Inn Fields.

Catherine Trotter's dramatization *Agnes de Castro* produced, Drury Lane, December.

1696 *An Essay in Defense of the Female Sex* published; attributed to Judith Drake.

Delarivier Manley's first play, *The Lost Lover*, produced at Drury Lane, probably March, and *The Royal Mischief*, Lincoln's Inn Fields, March or April.

Mary Pix's first play, *Ibrahim*, presented at Drury Lane, probably in late April or early June.

The Younger Brother produced at Drury Lane, February; published in March with 'An Account of the Life of the Incomparable Mrs Behn'.

Two issues of *The Histories and Novels of the Late Ingenious Mrs Behn*, which includes 'The Life and Memoirs of Mrs. Behn. Written by One of the Fair Sex'.

1697 *The Rover* revived by His Majesties Servants, Little-Lincolns-Inn-Fields; second edition published.

The False Count reissued.

Possible revival of *The City-Heiress*.

Possible revival of *The Young King*.

Poems upon Several Occasions (1684) bound with 'Lycidus' (1688) reissued.

1698 Jeremy Collier's *A Short View of the Immorality and Profaneness of the English Stage* published.

Second edition of *The Roundheads*.

Second edition of *The City-Heiress*.

Second edition of *The Young King*.

Second edition of *The History of the Nun, or The Fair Vow-Breaker*.

Third edition of the 1696 *Histories and Novels*, *All the Histories and Novels*, with three additional titles and the greatly expanded 'History of the Life and Memoirs of Mrs Behn . . . By one of the Fair Sex' [no evidence of a 'second' edition].

The Unfortunate Bride, including 'The Unfortunate Happy Lady' and 'The Dumb Virgin' printed but not published.

The Wandring Beauty, including 'The Unhappy Mistake' printed but not published.

1699	Possible revival of *The Town-Fopp* March; second edition published.
	Fourth edition of *All the Histories and Novels*.
1700	Dryden dies 1 May; buried in Westminster Abbey.
	Reissue of the fourth edition of *All the Histories and Novels*. *Histories, Novels, and Translations Written by the Most Ingenious Mrs Behn*, probably issued as a companion volume to the reissued fourth edition of *All the Histories*. Includes *The Discovery of New Worlds* (retitled) with the 'Essay of Translated Prose', *The History of Oracles*, and the works printed but not published in 1698, *The Unfortunate Bride*, 'The Unfortunate Happy Lady', 'The Dumb Virgin', *The Wandring Beauty*, 'The Unhappy Mistake'.
1701	James II dies in exile.
1702	Publication of sixteen of AB's collected plays (omits *The Younger Brother* and the attributed plays).
1707	Two previously unpublished and several other poems in variant states printed in *The Muses Mercury*.
1717	*The Land of Love*, a revision and rearrangement of the *Voyage to the Isle of Love*.
1718	Letters allegedly written by AB to Mrs Price, to 'Philander', and to Hoyle, along with several poems in variant issues, published in *Familiar Letters of Love, Gallantry, and Several Occasions*.

I

MARY ANN O'DONNELL

Aphra Behn: the documentary record

When Aphra Behn first attracted public literary notice, it was in September 1670 with her first play, *The Forc'd Marriage*, which she published in 1671 with the epigraph, '*Va mon enfant! Prend ta fortune.*' Since the Duke's Company presented this as the opening play of their new season and Thomas Otway acted in it, we can assume that Behn's literary connections were formed before the staging of her first play. But tracing the convoluted path of Aphra Behn to this theatrical première is not simple.

Behn is a particularly hard person to pin down. Germaine Greer calls her 'a palimpsest; she has scratched herself out',[1] somehow avoiding notice in church or tax records, perhaps deliberately. Janet Todd underpins this when she notes that Behn 'has a lethal combination of obscurity, secrecy and staginess, which makes her an uneasy fit for any narrative, speculative or factual. She is not so much a woman to be unmasked as an unending combination of masks.'[2]

The closest we come to establishing a time and place for Behn's birth is in Harbledown, Kent, 14 December 1640, as Eaffrey Johnson, daughter of Elizabeth Denham and Bartholomew Johnson.[3] The name Johnson and the Kentish birthplace were noted in 1696 in the brief biographies published first in *The Younger Brother* and shortly thereafter in *Histories and Novels*. In these two documents, we have the skeleton of the biography: the voyage to Surinam, the marriage to Mr Behn, and the 'several Negotiations in Flanders' for Charles II. The name Johnson and the birthplace of Canterbury or Sturry have independent support in Col. Thomas Colepepper's manuscript 'Adversaria', where, after her death, he alludes to Behn's mother as having been his wetnurse.[4] Anne Finch, later Countess of Winchilsea, adds to the biography in marginalia in one of her manuscript poems, 'The Circuit of Apollo', where she sneered that Behn was 'Daughter to a Barber, who liv'd formerly at Wye a little market town (now much decay'd) in Kent.'[5]

The world into which Behn was born was rife with religious tension and political friction as the Civil War and the Stuart exile racked England. By

1642, the puritans had closed the theatres, and in January 1649 the King's head was severed in plain view of thousands who came to cheer or to weep. The kingdom fell to the protection of Oliver Cromwell and his roundheads, as the cavaliers and supporters of Charles II joined their new king in his exile on the continent. While Behn used cavaliers and Oliverians in her plays, most notably *The Roundheads* and the two parts of *The Rover*, and, while the theme of restoration runs through many of her other plays, she has left us no understanding of the impact of these angst-filled years on her youth.

The earliest biography, published with Behn's posthumously performed comedy *The Younger Brother* (February 1696), grew rapidly into the influential pieces published in the first and then the greatly augmented third editions of the *Histories and Novels*, and then into the standardized introduction to the fifth edition in 1705, the biography that was reprinted in later editions. Probably by Charles Gildon, since he signed the dedication, the sketch in *The Younger Brother* indicates that Behn went to Surinam with her father, mother, brother, and sisters (all information that could have been derived from *Oroonoko*), and that she suffered the 'loss of her Relations and Friends there', which 'oblig'd her to return to *England*'. Although the alleged death of the narrator's father could easily be derived from *Oroonoko*, it is absent in this account. The second 1696 version of her biography, in *Histories and Novels*, adds her father's relationship (not necessarily kinship) to Lord Willoughby, which afforded him the substantial post of 'Lieutenant-General of many Isles, besides the Continent of Surinam'.

While this voyage has less substantive evidence to support it than does her later spying mission, there is independent documentation of the Surinam stay. In sharp contrast to the floridly exaggerated early biographies, Behn leavens the highly romanticized details in *Oroonoko* with brutally graphic descriptions of the Surinam colony, including those of petty governmental officials from the early 1660s whose names would be unknown to Londoners of the late 1680s. In addition, her known political sympathies are somewhat distorted in her harsh portrayal of the royalist William Byam and her praise of Colonel George Martin, 'brother to *Henry Martin*, the great *Oliverian*', and a 'Man of great Gallantry, Wit, and Goodness, and whom I have celebrated in a Character of my New *Comedy*, by his own Name, in Memory of so Brave a Man'.[6] Several extant letters appear to refer to Behn and William Scot, son of Thomas Scot, Cromwell's Secretary of State for Intelligence, who was executed as a regicide in October 1660.[7] One letter from Byam to Sir Robert Harley in March 1664 alludes to 'Celadon'and 'Astrea', the code names used respectively by Scot and Behn in their later spying mission, leading to conjectures that Behn and Scot were in Surinam together, Behn as Scot's mistress.

Nothing supports the narrator's contention in *Oroonoko* that her father died during passage to Surinam. Equally, no evidence suggests that Behn and Scot knew one another before meeting in Surinam or were lovers in Surinam. If Behn's father moved his family to Surinam, it could have been in response to Lord Willoughby of Parham's Prospectus, which promised fifty acres per settler, with additional acreage for dependants.[8] Or 'Mr Johnson' could himself have been an agent of the King sent to check on the colony and its republican inhabitants shortly after the Restoration. Whatever the reason, Behn's stay in Surinam lasted somewhere between eighteen months and two and a half years. When her first play, *The Young King*, was eventually published in 1683, four years after the probable date of its belated première, Behn in her Preface refers to its 'Virgin-Muse' as 'an *American*', noting that it measured 'Three thousand Leagues of spacious Ocean . . . [and] visited many and distant Shores'. This suggests, somewhat mysteriously, that she spent more than just a few months in the Americas.

Somewhere between Behn's return from Surinam and her mission to the Low Countries comes her alleged marriage to Mr Behn, supposedly a London merchant of Dutch extraction, although the name is more frequently connected to Hamburg, Germany. Several candidates have been advanced, most notably Johan or John Behn, captain of the *King David*, a ship that plied the southern Atlantic trade route, but no documents so far confirm any marriage.[9] The closest evidence to a 'Mr Behn' appears in a May 1669 draft letter concerning the British seizure off the Irish coast of the *Abraham's Sacrifice*, a ship under the control of a Genoese captain. The letter refers to 'the factour, or the person that looks after the business of the Widow Behn,' suggesting Behn's marital status by this time and an involvement in the shipping business, and perhaps tying her to a Dutch or Hamburg merchant or the ship captain John Behn.[10] With plague so prevalent in England through the mid-1660s, 'Mr Behn' could well have expired by late 1665.

The records pick up again shortly after the outbreak of the Second Anglo-Dutch War in 1665 with the well documented spying mission that Behn undertook as an agent of the English government. She was sent by Joseph Williamson, aide to Secretary of State Henry Bennett, Lord Arlington, a connection perhaps made through Thomas Killigrew, groom of the bedchamber to Charles II and patentee of the King's Company, one of the two London theatrical companies. Her sailing companions to Flanders included William Howard, Viscount Stafford, and his son John, whose names reappear in her spying letters, and later in her writings.[11]

Behn arrived in Bruges with her brother and probably two others in late July 1666 with a fourteen-point list, 'Memorialls for Mrs Affora,' prepared by the Secretary of State's office, containing specific charges to lure William

Scot back to the English side with promises of a pardon and a considerable reward, and to gather information on the Dutch fleets and merchant ships and on possible operatives within the exiles living in Holland.[12] Her final extant letter is dated 26 December 1666, probably just before she returned to a London devastated by plague and fire.

The documents from her spying mission and several other surviving petitions afford the opportunity to hear the voice of Behn unfiltered by the literary modes and *personae* she later adopted.[13] From the beginning, we hear the voice of a young woman caught in an intrigue in which the spy-handlers at Whitehall could not keep their operatives in line or supply them with the means to perform their duties. Behn was shocked by the cost of living in Antwerp, the failure of Williamson's office to respond to her requests for assistance or for the speedy pardon of William Scot, one of the first promises she was given. Her problems were exacerbated by another English operative, Thomas Corney, who had been betrayed by William Scot the year before as Scot sought to ingratiate himself with Col. William Bampfield, a notorious turncoat in the service of the Dutch.[14] Behn and Scot met once, no more than twice, each fearful of crossing the border between Spanish Flanders, where Behn remained, and Holland, where Scot was by December in prison for debt. One month into her mission, Behn had already pawned some jewellery, but received no response to her increasingly urgent importunities first to Halsall, then to Killigrew, and finally to Arlington himself. By mid September, letters from her mother and 'S^r thomas'[15] made Behn realize how deeply in trouble she was, and she implored Killigrew to 'beleeue w^t you please: you shall find still this that how great a Child soeuer I am in other matters: I shall mind dilligently w^t I am now about', and begging 'for christ his sake S^r let me receaue no Ill opinion from his Maj:^{ty} who would giue my poore life to serue him in neuer so little a degree'.[16]

Behn's last document from the Flanders mission preserved in the Public Record Office, dated 26 December 1666, pleads for permission and money to return to London. She had warned the Home Office of the Dutch intention to attack the fleet in the Thames, a warning that was dismissed, and her mission was a failure.[17] Several other documents in the Public Record Office indicate Behn's return to London on £150 borrowed from a Mr Botteler or Butler, probably one of the Duke of Ormond's retinue, and even more insistent petitions demand redress. One indicates that she was to be taken to debtors' prison the following day, yet there is no evidence that this warrant was executed or that Behn ever spent any time incarcerated.

Between 1667 and 1670, the paper trail diminishes, but does not disappear. London was slowly rebuilding after war, plague, and fire, and the theatres regained the popularity they had enjoyed between the return of Charles II in

1660 and the devastation. Thomas Killigrew held one of the two patents for theatrical productions and directed the King's Company while Sir William Davenant held the patent for the Duke's Men. They vied through the early part of the decade to hire the most popular actors and attractive actresses, women having been allowed full participation in theatrical productions by order of the King, and then to have the newest theatres and the best stage machinery.

In the two years before the production of her first play in 1670, Behn seems to have been associated with Dryden and the Howards in Killigrew's King's Company, as scribe and perhaps as adapter of old plays, since the appetite for these revisions was voracious. There are few scribal copies of plays and prompt-books extant, but one of these, the prompt-book for Edward Howard's unsuccessful *A Change of Crownes*, may be in Behn's hand.[18] Her petitions and letters from Flanders show a clear hand and spelling sufficient to the scribal task, as does her later commonplace book.[19] Howard soon shifted to Davenant's company; Behn probably changed companies at the same time, since in the same year that she published her first play, she also wrote a dedicatory poem to Edward Howard for the publication of *The Six Day's Adventure*.

Her first staged work, *The Forc'd Marriage*, was quickly followed by *The Amorous Prince* (February 1671), the first definitely and the second probably serving her well with the third-night receipts that provided the playwright's remuneration. In 1672, she probably edited *The Covent Garden Drolery*, a compendium of popular songs, prologues, and epilogues from the theatre, additional evidence of her closeness to literary London.

Following the failure of her third play, *The Dutch Lover* (February 1673), Behn disappeared from the records for three years. We can speculate that she was travelling, perhaps again as an agent for the Crown, or that she had found protection with a lover. A recently recovered contemporary reference in Roger Morrice's 'Entering Book' suggests that Behn began a relationship with John Hoyle at about this time.[20] The bisexual Hoyle figures throughout Behn's writings. In an early piece, 'Our Cabal,' he appears aloof, accompanied by 'Mr Ed. Bed.,' whose description ('His Beauty Maid; but Man, his Mien') echoes the depiction of the androgynous 'fair Clarinda' in one of her most famous poems. Significantly her first dedication does not appear until her eighth play, *The Feign'd Curtizans*, with its fulsome praise of the real courtesan Nell Gwyn, suggesting that prior to this Behn had no need to court favour with patrons.

Behn returned to the stage by July 1676 with her only tragedy, *Abdelazer*, a brilliant revision of the early seventeenth-century play *Lust's Dominion*, perhaps by Dekker and others. Shortly thereafter came *The Town-Fopp*

(September 1676) and, by March of the following year, her great success *The Rover*. With *The Rover*, Behn drew charges of plagiarism, since she drew heavily from *Thomaso*, an unproduced drama by her old spy-master and employer Thomas Killigrew, and she defended herself in a feisty postscript.

With the popularity of *The Rover*, Behn secured her theatrical reputation, but the times were not conducive to a prosperous theatre. In 1673, James, Duke of York and heir presumptive to the crown, made public his Catholicism and married the Catholic princess Mary of Modena. This second marriage raised fears that a male heir would displace his Protestant daughters, Mary and Anne, from the succession, and create a perpetual Catholic dynasty. Fears of this led, between 1678 and 1681, to parliamentary moves to exclude James from the succession and replace him by Charles II's eldest illegitimate son, James, Duke of Monmouth. With this political turmoil, Behn's dramas become increasingly political, satirizing the emerging anti-royalist Whigs as greedy, sexist 'cits', especially in her great London plays, *Sir Patient Fancy*, *The Roundheads*, and *The City-Heiress*. In these, Behn explores the recurrent themes of forced marriage between a handsome woman and the classic *senex amans*, revealing the hypocrisy of the puritanical, impotent old bourgeois merchant who would seek to block the rightful heir, always a loyalist cavalier, from his rightful possessions. In these plays, Behn explored issues of women's right of self-determination, the tyranny of patriarchy, and the use of masquerade and carnival to re-normalize the world. Behn's darker side also emerges in this period, most notably in 1681 with *The Second Part of The Rover*, which she dedicated to James, Duke of York, whom she had supported throughout the Exclusion Crisis.

In August 1682, Behn's attack on the Whigs and Monmouth in the Epilogue to *Romulus and Hersilia* led to a warrant for the arrest of Behn and Lady Slingsby (formerly Mary Lee), the actress who delivered the Epilogue. There is, however, no evidence of the warrant's execution, and the offending epilogue was published virtually unchanged early the following year with the play.

From August 1682 to early 1684, Behn disappeared from the scene, emerging to publish a prologue to the late Earl of Rochester's *Valentinian* in February 1685 and shortly thereafter her first published foray into fiction, the first part of the *Love-Letters between a Noble-Man and his Sister*. In the last four years of her life, Behn occupied herself predominantly with fiction, translation, and poetry, writing only four more plays, two of which were staged posthumously.[21]

In 1684, she published *Poems upon Several Occasions*, a major compendium of her pieces dating back as early as the 1670s. Two later collections, *Miscellany* in 1685 and a miscellany added to *Lycidus* in 1688, mix her poems with works by many others, including the Earl of Rochester, Thomas Otway, Sir George Etherege, the Earl of Dorset, Mrs Taylor, and Anne Wharton. The highly charged political events of the time gave opportunity for publishing poems on the death of Charles II, the mourning of Queen Catherine, the coronation of James II, Queen Mary of Modena's pregnancy and delivery, and at the very end of her life poems to Sir Roger L'Estrange, Gilbert Burnet, and the new Queen Mary II, daughter of James II, who, with her husband William of Orange, ascended the throne on her father's exile.

Behn's fiction has the same political and satirical edginess as her plays. *Love-Letters between a Noble-Man and his Sister* is a remarkable *roman à clef* focusing simultaneously on Monmouth's rebellion and the incestuous relationship between Ford, Lord Grey of Werke, and his wife's sister, and written in three parts as the real-life story was unfolding. In 1688, with *The Fair Jilt* and *Oroonoko*, and a translation of *Agnes de Castro*, Behn's development of the narrator's voice, one of her major contributions to the evolution of the novel, gained full maturity. In some of the narrator's self-reflexive assertions, we may be hearing Behn's voice telling us that she was once intended for a convent, that she visited Venice, that she was sent by Charles II into Flanders as a spy, that she witnessed the slave rebellion in Surinam, that she donated some South American flies to 'His Majesty's *Antiquaries*' and brought back to London Indian feathers used in a production of *The Indian Queen*.[22]

While in most of her poetry and fiction, her voice must be seen as filtered through a *persona*, we can hear some of her voice in her prefaces and dedications and in her political poems. With the failure of her third play, *The Dutch Lover*, Behn retaliated with a detailed preface to the 'Good, Sweet, Honey Sugar-Candied Reader'. Here, between complaints about the staging of her play, she humorously limns the playhouse fop who condemned her play, '*God damn him, for it was a womans*'. In this same piece, Behn gives some insight into her literary theory, preferring Shakespeare to Jonson, and noting that plays are meant to entertain rather than educate. Another brief insight into Behn's literary models comes in the dedication 'To Lysander' of *Seneca Unmasqued*, where she praises '*that unstudied, and undesigned way of writing (tho not so approved of by the Learned) which is used by a Courtier who has Wit, as that of the late Lord* Rochester *and present Lord* Mulgrave'. After praising '*those little chance things of Sir* Carr. Scroope', Behn delivers her highest praise for the '*Charming and Incomparable Mr* Dryden'. Such moments of personal intervention in her writing are rare.

Addressing Henry Howard, later Duke of Norfolk, in the dedication of *The City-Heiress* in 1682, Behn praises him for voting '*Not guilty*' in the trial of his uncle, William Howard, Viscount Stafford, a Catholic lord executed during the height of the Popish Plot, the same William Howard who with his son John had accompanied her to Flanders at the start of her spying mission. In her dialogue 'Pastoral to Mr. Stafford', printed in 1685, Behn praises Stafford's son John for a translation from Virgil, but devotes close to a quarter of the poem to the execution of Stafford (I, 64). Again, in Spring 1688, the year before her death, in her *Poem to Sir Roger L'Estrange on His Third Part of His History of the Times: Relating to the Death of Sir Edmund Bury-Godfrey*, she deplores the frenzy that led to the Popish Plot and openly mourns the death of the Catholic Stafford, who 'like a *God*, dy'd to redeem *Our Faith*' (I, 82). Shortly thereafter, the dedication to *Oroonoko* to Lord Maitland contained a passage that almost certainly linked Behn to Catholicism, a passage that was deleted while the work was still in press, surviving in one known copy (III, p. 55 and note). To Henry Howard, Duke of Norfolk, she devotes a section of the *Pindarick Poem on the Happy Coronation of His most Sacred Majesty James II*, calling him '*Mæcena* of my *Muse*, my *Patron* Lord' (I, p. 217).

According to the documentary record, the last four years of her life were marked by poverty and illness. In August 1685, she pledged the proceeds of her next play as collateral for a debt of £6 she owed Zachary Baggs,[23] and she also begged Jacob Tonson for an additional £5 for her *Poems upon Several Occasions*. When she sent her elegy on the poet Waller to Abigail Waller, his daughter-in-law, she appended a letter with a postscript noting her 'Lame hand scarce able to hold a pen.'[24] Impelled by poverty and defying her increasing debilitation, Behn saw her greatest literary output in the period between 1684 and her death.

The difficulties Behn encountered as a woman writer also impinge, especially toward the end of her life. In *The Luckey Chance*, she tells the dedicatee, Lawrence Hyde, Earl of Rochester, that this play is '*the Product of a Heart and Pen, that always faithfully serv'd that Royal Cause*', while in the Preface, she answers charges of bawdry, comparing her scenes to other plays by contemporaries, and concluding that 'such Masculine Strokes in me, must not be allow'd'. In this same Preface, she notes that she will be 'kinder to my Brothers of the Pen, than they have been to a defenceless Woman' (VII, pp. 215–17). Although she had been charged with plagiarism and bawdry, Behn, in fact, was less vilified than most of her contemporaries, especially Dryden. As she grew more famous, the hacks of the period attacked. In the widely circulated poem 'The Session of Poets', Behn is mocked for appealing to Apollo for the laurels, with allusion to her 'Black Ace' (pudenda) and her advanced age.[25] Alexander Radcliffe alleged that a '*Greys Inn* Lawyer', her 'Friend in Bosom', either John Hoyle or Edward Ravenscroft, was the author of her plays.[26] Thomas Shadwell denounced Otway as her Pimp, while 'An Epistle to Julian' called her a harlot plagued by 'Poverty, Poetry, Pox'.[27] The hack Robert Gould, nettled by her success, is probably the author of the oft-quoted lines denouncing 'Sapho, Famous for her Gout and Guilt': 'For *Punk* and *Poesie* agree so pat, / You cannot well be *this*, and not be *that*'.[28] In 'The Journey to Parnassus', another classic 'sessions-of-poets' poem, Apollo rejects her for her lasciviousness and her plagiarism, adding that 'since her Works had neither Witt enough for a Man, nor Modesty enough for a Woman, she was to be look'd upon as an Hermaphrodite, & consequently not fit to enjoy the benefits & Priviledges of either Sex, much less of this Society.'[29]

Yet the commonplace book she kept with others between 1685 and her death shows that these attacks are gentle compared to the routine vilifications of courtiers and actors of the time.[30] And many of her contemporary writers, among them Thomas Otway, Nahum Tate, Jacob Tonson, and Thomas Creech, wrote in her support, and Nathaniel Lee mourned her death in a broadside. John Dryden, who published, and praised, her paraphrase 'Oenone to Paris' in his *Ovid's Epistles* in 1680, wrote a prologue and epilogue to *The Widdow Ranter*, recalling Behn's ability to portray love and asking the audience to accept this 'orphan' play of a dead writer.[31]

In one of her earliest statements in her own voice, in 1678 in her preface 'To the Reader' to *Sir Patient Fancy*, Behn described herself as one 'forced to write for Bread and not ashamed to owne it' (VI, p. 5). The same pride and unflinching self-understanding come through in all her direct statements. As she was dying, she completed a translation of the last book of Abraham Cowley's *Six Books of Plants*. At the point that Cowley is considering the laurel tree, the leaves of which adorn the brows of conquerors and poets, Behn allows her voice to break through, acknowledging the break with the marginal notation 'The Translatress in her own Person speaks' (I, p. 325). Noting the fame of Katherine Philips, 'Orinda', as a poet, Behn seeks to be honoured with her, when she interpolates:

Among that number, do not me disdain,
Me, the most humble of that glorious Train.
I by a double right thy Bounties claim,
Both from my Sex, and in *Apollo*'s Name:
Let me with *Sappho* and *Orinda* be
Oh ever Sacred Nymph, adorn'd by thee;
And give my Verses Immortality.

Despite attempts in the nineteenth and early twentieth century to damage her reputation and denigrate her literary importance, the works of Aphra

Behn are read more widely and presented in theatres more often today than at any time except during her life. She wrote about what concerned her – politics, sexual freedom, imbalances in the power structure. She spoke to her late seventeenth-century audiences with power and vigour in a voice no less powerful and vigorous than she addresses us with today. That is her major accomplishment.

NOTES

1 'Roundtable', in *Aphra Behn (1640–1689): Identity, Alterity, Ambiguity*, ed. Mary Ann O'Donnell, Bernard Dhuicq, and Guyonne Leduc (Paris: L'Harmattan, 2000), p. 282.
2 Todd, p. 9.
3 Duffy, *The Passionate Shepherdess: Aphra Behn 1640–1689* (London: Cape, 1977), p. 20; Jane Jones, 'New Light on the Background and Early Life of Aphra Behn', in *Aphra Behn Studies*, pp. 310–20; Todd, p. 14.
4 British Library MS Harl. 7588.
5 Quoted in Todd, p. 13. The manuscript is in the Folger Library.
6 *Oroonoko* in *Works*, III, pp. 97, 111. The play to which Behn refers, *The Younger Brother*, was produced and published posthumously.
7 Harrison Platt, 'Astrea and Celadon: An Untouched Portrait of Aphra Behn', *PMLA*, 49 (1934), 544–59.
8 Reprinted in Joanna Lipking's Norton Critical edition of *Oroonoko* (New York, 1997), pp. 101–3.
9 Henry A. Hargreaves, 'A Case for Mr. Behn', *Notes and Queries*, 207 (1962), 203–5.
10 James Fitzmaurice, 'Aphra Behn and the *Abraham's Sacrifice* Case', *Huntington Library Quarterly*, 56 (Spring 1993), 319–26.
11 It is not clear how Behn came to make these court connections. The extant manuscripts of her spying mission, preserved in the Public Record Office, have been published by W. J. Cameron in *New Light on Aphra Behn* (Auckland: University of Auckland Press, 1961).
12 PRO SP 29/172, no. 81.I
13 In addition to the documents reproduced by Cameron, Peter Beal calendars the remaining PRO petitions and other Behn manuscripts in the second volume of his *Index of English Literary Manuscripts* (London, 1987), pp. 1–6.
14 This is the same Bampfield involved with Anne Murray, later Lady Halkett, in her attempts to assist James, Duke of York, to escape from England in 1648.
15 Sir Thomas has not yet been identified. Behn implies a closeness to him, adding that he 'is selldom in towne'. There is the possibility that Behn refers to Thomas Colepepper.
16 PRO SP 29/172, no. 14. Quoted in Cameron, pp. 61–4.
17 The Dutch did, in fact, sail up the Thames and destroy much of the British fleet in June 1667.
18 This manuscript is currently under study by Mary Ann O'Donnell.
19 For an examination of Bod. MS Firth c.16, see, Mary Ann O'Donnell, 'A Verse Miscellany of Aphra Behn: Bodleian Library MS Firth c.16', in *English*

Manuscript Studies ed. Peter Beal and Jeremy Griffiths (Oxford, 1989), vol. II, pp. 189–227.

20 P. A. Hopkins, 'Aphra Behn and John Hoyle: A Contemporary Mention, and Sir Charles Sedley's Poem on His Death', *Notes & Queries*, 239 (June 1994), 176–85.

21 Her last plays were *The Emperor of the Moon* and *The Luckey Chance*, along with *The Widdow Ranter* and *The Younger Brother*, these latter performed and published posthumously.

22 The convent reference appears in *The History of the Nun*; the Venice visit in 'The Dumb Virgin'; the spy mission is noted in *The Fair Jilt*. The last three references are found in *Oroonoko*.

23 Baggs was a functionary in the Theatre Royal and later its treasurer. His father had held the lease on Dorset Garden before his death in the 1670s.

24 Letter and poem are now in the possession of the Pierpont Morgan Library. For reproduction of the postscript, see O'Donnell, 'A Verse Miscellany'.

25 *Poems on Several Occasions by the Right Honourable, The E. of R.* (Antwerp, 1680).

26 *The Ramble*: *An Anti-Heroick Poem* (London, 1682).

27 *The Tory Poets*: *A Satyr* (London, 1682); 'An Epistle to Julian' [1688?] British Lib. MS Harleian 7317, fol. 58*. Reprinted in part in *The Works of Aphra Behn*, ed. Montague Summers, 6 vols. (London, 1915), I, p. lvii.

28 *A Satyrical Epistle to the Female Author of a Poem call'd Silvia's Revenge &c.* (London, 1691).

29 *A Journal for Parnassus, Now Printed from a Manuscript circa 1688* ed. Hugh MacDonald (London, 1973).

30 See O'Donnell, 'A Verse Miscellany'.

31 This prologue and epilogue were printed separately and are not the pieces usually printed with the play, which were Dryden's pieces from a much earlier Shadwell play. For the text of the prologue and epilogue expressly written for *The Widdow Ranter*, see Autrey Nell Wiley, *Rare Prologues and Epilogues, 1642–1700* (London: Allen and Unwin, 1940).

2

SUSAN STAVES

Behn, women, and society

Advocates for dramatically different ideologies about women's nature and women's appropriate function in society clashed with one another in Aphra Behn's lifetime. Although some of these ideologies claimed to be traditional, none of them was simply so. Behn's plays, fiction, and poems raise acute questions about these ideologies and make it clear that she found none of them entirely satisfactory. Here I will consider three of these clashing ideologies: first, the Church of England religious ideology, at once the dominant ideology of Behn's society and the one with which she had the least sympathy; second, an economic and legal ideology; and third, the libertine ideology, the one that Behn in many ways found attractive, but one that seemed to work better for men than for women. Each of these ideologies had very different understandings of what the value of women was and I will conclude with a discussion of Behn's inventive exploration of the problem of women's value. Although the majority of women in Behn's society belonged to the labouring and yeoman classes – toiling in agriculture, in work like the spinning of wool, in domestic service, or as the daughters or wives of small farmers – these sorts of women are not important characters in Behn's works, so I will focus here mainly on women from the higher social classes who are her principal concern.

The Church

It would be difficult to discern from Behn's writings that the dominant ideology during the period when she wrote was that of the Church of England. Churches in Behn's plays and fiction, usually Roman Catholic churches on the continent, typically appear as places where men and women discover their lovers and make assignations, not places of devotion. Her wits display their cleverness in blasphemy. Nevertheless, the overwhelming majority of Behn's English contemporaries belonged to the Church of England and respected its religion. Most of the writing published by Behn's female contemporaries was religious writing, much of it by dissenting women, notably the Quakers, but some by pious Church of England women, like Susanna Hopton, who in 1673 published her *Daily Devotions, Consisting of Thanksgivings, Confessions, and Prayers*. . . . The unpublished diaries, letters, and poems of most women of this period testify to their intense and serious religious devotion.

Most Englishmen and women learned about God's plan for women from Anglican preachers and from the Church's interpretation of the Bible. Those who were educated and reasonably devout read sermons and books like the Revd Richard Allestree's *Whole Duty of Man* (1658, 1659) and *The Ladies Calling* (1673). Women learned that God had created them as creatures with souls and that they had duties to worship God and to attend to the health of their souls. They learned, as Behn's Lady Galliard in *The City-Heiress* (1682) says (in one of the rare moments in Behn when a character expresses a religious idea), that however secretly they might sin, 'Heaven will know't.' (Wilding, the rake who is trying to seduce her promptly responds: 'Hell and the Devil! I'll hear no more / Of this Religious stuff, this Godly nonsense', VII: 4.1.179, 197–98.) According to the Church, God had instituted marriage for the benefit of mankind and the good order of society. A husband had a sacred duty to love and support his wife, the wife a sacred duty to love and obey her husband. The wife's duty to obey, Allestree explained, was 'the mulct that was laid upon the first woman's disobedience to God, that she (and all derived from her) should be subject to the husband.'[1] Husband and wife were enjoined 'to be fruitful and multiply', and, when they became parents, were required to nurture and to instruct the children who might be born to them. In an age when maternal and infant mortality rates were high, the Church had a special rite for women who had safely given birth, the Churching of Women. The woman came into church so that the clergyman could offer prayers of thanksgiving for her having survived childbirth, for God's gift of the child, and for the child's physical and spiritual welfare.

The Church also taught that daughters and sons had a religious obligation to honour and obey their parents. Because of the radical challenges during the Civil Wars to hierarchies both political and domestic, the Restoration Church of England often stressed that proper observances of hierarchy in the family and in the state were interdependent. In the important matter of a daughter's marriage, most clergy and most decent people were inclined to consider that the daughter had an obligation to heed her parents' advice, but that, in the end, either the daughter or the parents ought to have a right to veto an unacceptable suitor. To cite Allestree again, 'as the Daughter is neither to anticipate, nor contradict the will of her Parent, so (to hand the

balance even) I must say she is not obliged to force her own, by marrying
where she cannot love; for a negitiveness in the cause is sure as much the
child's right as the Parent's . . . 'tis Love only that cements the hearts, and
where that union is wanting, 'tis but a shadow, a carcass of marriage'.[2]

As a state church, the Church of England had ecclesiastical courts that
exercised some jurisdiction over certain matters of morality and marriage.
The Church valued pre- and post-marital chastity in both men and women,
although, in the absence of effective contraception, the fact that women
could become pregnant from pre-marital intercourse made them easier to
identify as fornicators. With variable degrees of vigilance in different local-
ities, the Church courts proceeded against fornicators, exacting fines and
public penance in church as the price of forgiveness. Church courts entertained claims for the annulments of marriages and granted divorces from
bed and board, or what we would call separations, to husbands or wives
who could demonstrate that a spouse was guilty of adultery or cruelty. It
was to these courts that Behn characters like Bellmour and Diana in *The
Town-Fopp* (1676) would have to go to get an annulment (although, like
those of other Restoration dramatists, Behn's representations of canon law
are often inaccurate).[3]

Poor relief was parish based, supported by local poor rates, and administered by local overseers. Bartholomew Johnson, believed to be Behn's father,
a barber, served as an Overseer of the Poor for a parish in Canterbury.[4]
In case of need, everyone had a legal right to subsistence from his or her
local parish, entitlement to food, shelter, and medical care. Among the most
important duties of parish officers was to attend to the support of illegitimate, abandoned, or otherwise needy infants and children. Then as now,
the cost of supporting children born outside of marriage and of women with
dependent children was a significant expense for taxpayers. Parish officers
were often successful in identifying fathers of illegitimate children, sometimes persuading them to marry, or, failing that, requiring them to pay child
support. Then as now, dislike for having to pay for the consequences of other
people's sexuality significantly fuelled public hostility to sexual adventures
outside of marriage.

Behn gives a very hostile glimpse of the Church's Poor Law system in 'The
Adventure of the Black Lady' (1698), where the genteel heroine Bellamora
has become pregnant in the country, then flees to London in hopes of having
her child secretly. She loses most of her money in London and thus becomes
an object of interest to the local authorities. The Poor Law system was local,
the Act of Settlement (1662) allowing Justices of the Peace to remove poor
newcomers to a parish if a complaint were filed within 40 days; London

officials were especially concerned about the influx of rural poor becoming an added burden to London ratepayers. Charges would include the immediate expenses for medical care of poor women bearing children and the long-term expense of the parish's subsequent obligation to provide for an illegitimate child who would gain a settlement by being born in the parish. Thus, when neighbours to the house where Bellamora prepares to deliver her child hear of her presence, they report it to the authorities, and, the narrator relates, 'the Vermin of the Parish (I mean, the Overseers of the poor, who eat the Bread from 'em) [began] to search for a young Black-hair'd Lady . . . which was either brought to bed, or just ready to lie down' (III, p. 320). From Behn's classist point of view the idea of the Poor Law touching any genteelly born person represents a terrible derogation. In this story, happily for the heroine, her fiancé and seducer, one Fondlove, is possessed of a good estate and is glad to marry her once he learns where she is and that she is about to have his child. In fact, intercourse between engaged couples followed by pregnancy and marriage before the child was born was not uncommon in the period, demographers estimating that about twenty per cent of brides were pregnant at the time of marriage. Actual illegitimacy rates in this period were very low, just below two per cent.[5] In 'The Adventure of the Black Lady', when the officials come to find Bellamora, Fondlove has rescued her and she has gone out to shop 'for several pretty Businesses that Ladies in her Condition want' (III, p. 320).

Economic and legal

From the theological perspective, marriage was a spiritual union and a fundamental unit of God's plan for the social order. But the ease with which the Church permitted couples to contract marriage simply by the exchange of vows in the present tense conflicted with a more worldly economic and legal ideology that understood women as instruments for the transmission and increase of family property. Contemporary intellectuals correctly believed that primogeniture, the inheritance of family fortunes by eldest sons, was crucial to maintaining sufficient wealth in upper-class families to allow them to maintain their distinction from the lower social ranks doomed to labour. Had family property been evenly divided among all children, it would have become progressively dispersed into amounts too small to constitute an aristocratic or gentry estate. Although by Behn's day strict primogeniture at common law had been modified by pre-nuptial 'settlements' that typically provided portions – smaller shares of family property – for younger sons and for daughters, the distinction between the heir and 'the rest' continued to be crucial to the maintenance of the upper classes. Todd usefully describes Behn as a 'pseudo-aristocrat', that is, a person not born into the upper-classes, 'but one who had internalized their view and images and who aimed to support their privilege and pretension and to enjoy and serve their culture'.[6] As a 'pseudo-aristocrat', Behn vehemently supports the entitlements of upper-class men to substantial property by inheritance or marriage, although, like many literary texts, hers often support the pretensions of younger sons over elder ones. Contradictorily, with equal vehemence, she denounces marriage for money as virtual prostitution. Behn's identification with the upper classes and her willingness to use romance modes expressive of upper-class ideology are undermined by her sharp sense of a need for money to support leisure and status, a sense oddly akin to that of the City merchants her Tory politics drive her to satirize.

Older statutes continued to criminalize attempts at gaining heiresses' property by marrying them as forms of theft from the woman's family, as Behn notices in *The City-Heiress*. Despite primogeniture, in the absence of sons, a daughter or daughters became heiresses to the family property at common law; wills or family settlements might also name women heiress. The forcible abduction of an heiress, 'maid, widow, or wife', against her will, 'for lucre', in order to marry or to rape her, commonly called 'stealing an heiress', was a felony.[7]

In *The City-Heiress*, Wilding, the Tory rake protagonist, has impoverished himself by lavish spending and provoked his Whig City uncle, Sir Timothy Treat-all, to disinherit him. One of his schemes is to elope with Charlot, heiress to the newly dead Sir Nicholas Gettall, a woman with a fortune of £3,000 a year. He proposes to get back into his uncle's good graces by boasting of this coup and asks to stash Charlot at the uncle's house. Sir Timothy as a City Whig fomenting sedition against the King is the chief butt of Behn's satire in the play; evil-mindedly, he thinks of getting his nephew hanged 'for seducing and most feloniously bearing away a young City-Heiress' (VII: 3.1.143–4), while marrying her himself to beget another heir. Not trusting Sir Timothy with a property so valuable as Charlot, Wilding takes the precaution of substituting Diana, the mistress he has been keeping for three years, for the heiress. As written, the statute protects a man who has the heiress's consent, but Behn was correct to think that its real point was to protect the family property and that women who might have given some degree of consent could be induced by family members to say that they had not. Believing that he is talking to Charlot, although he is really talking to Diana, Sir Timothy attempts to persuade her to marry him and brushes aside her protests that she has already pledged her 'Faith and Troth' to Wilding.

SIR TIMOTHY Faith and Troth! We stand upon neither Faith nor Troth in
the City, Lady. I have known an Heiress married and bedded, and yet with
the advice of the wiser Magistrates, has been unmarried and consummated
anew with another, so it stands with our Interest; . . . . Nay, had you married
my ungracious Nephew, we might . . . have hang'd him for a Rape.

DIANA What, though he had my consent?

SIR TIMOTHY That's nothing, he had not ours.   (VII: 3.1.174–82)

(Sir Timothy seems to overlook the fact that the statute, unusually, also made
knowing accessories to stealing an heiress guilty of felony as well, although
perhaps he counts on his City connections to help him avoid indictment.
When Diana points out that his marrying her would seem to be the same
offence as Wilding's doing so, Sir Timothy tells her that a City jury would
never indict him – as a City jury had refused to indict the Whig leader, the Earl
of Shaftesbury.) Behn uses Diana's rather plaintive little question to underline
her sense that, when it comes to women's fortunes, the legal system is likely
to give more weight to patriarchal economic interests than to the desires of
the woman. At the end of *The City-Heiress*, although Charlot's discoveries
that Wilding has two mistresses have challenged her illusions about him as
a lover, she still professes to love him. Charlot knows elopement has ruined
her reputation, and decides to bestow herself and her fortune on Wilding in
marriage.

Conventional wisdom held that marriages between people of similar social
rank and fortune were most suitable; often, however, marriages like these
were not possible. The bride's portion, invested, was supposed to make her
roughly 'self-supporting' should she become a widow by throwing off enough
income to fund her widow's jointure. (A jointure was a provision of land or
income made in the prenuptial agreement or elsewhere for the wife should she
survive her husband.) Unfortunately, families often 'impaired' their estates
by over-spending: fathers might indulge in building houses they could not
afford, fathers or sons, and even mothers, could gamble or spend too much
money on jewels. Impaired estates could drive families to seek to recoup their
fortunes by marriage. Younger sons, perennially afflicted with small portions,
or worse, unpaid portions, were especially tempted to look to marriage with
a woman of fortune as the only way to secure a capital sum sufficient to
produce an income that would allow them to remain among the ranks of the
leisured, governing classes.

Many of Behn's rake heroes are younger sons who see marriage with a
rich woman, or, sometimes, being kept by a rich woman, as the only way
to maintain the social rank of their birth family. For example, Hazard at
the beginning of *The Widdow Ranter* (1689) explains what drove him to

Virginia and why he is willing to plot to marry (or be kept by) Madame Surelove or to consider marrying the rich Widow Ranter:

> Ill Company, and that Common Vice of the Town, Gaming, soon run out my Younger Brothers Fortune . . . My Elder Brother, an Errant Jew, had neither Friendship, nor Honour enough to Support me, but at last was mollified by perswasions and the hopes of being for ever rid of me, sent me hither with a small Cargo to seek my fortune, –   (VII: 1.1.39–45)

Hazard, however, does not intend to trade. As he says indignantly when other colonists ask how he intends to support himself, 'I was not born to work Sir' (VII: 1.1.230).

Brides' families might also seek to advance themselves economically and socially by negotiating marriages based on parlaying whatever advantages they could bring to the table, not only the notorious exchange of money for higher social status, but an array of possible advantages including political or professional connections or ownership of particular pieces of land that might have special attractions for the groom's family. Perceived defects in prospective spouses might be repaired by infusions of more cash. Behn makes a mordant joke in *Sir Patient Fancy* (1678) when the puritanical but avaricious knight, fearing that his daughter is no longer a virgin, laments: 'oh she's debaucht – her reputation's ruin'd, and she'le need a double Portion' (VI: 4.3.25–7).

Playwrights, including Behn, like to show attempted 'forced marriages', in which parents, uncles, brothers or guardians, often for financial reasons, insist on a child's marrying someone that child strenuously dislikes; in comedy, lovers typically outwit these attempts. Behn is attracted to Spanish and Italian settings in part because the English supposed parents and guardians there were conspicuously coercive. She evokes English Protestant sympathy for her continental heroines like Florinda and Hellena in *The Rover* (1677) or Marcella and Cornelia in *The Feign'd Curtizans* (1679), who try to avoid both forced marriage and forced confinement in convents. Florinda's brother, Don Pedro, tells her she should be pleased to marry old Don Vincentio, rich from trade in Africa, because of his possession of an ancient estate and because of 'the Joynture he'l make you' (V: 1.1.72). Hellena, for once on the same page as contemporary theologians and moralists, who railed against marriages prompted by avarice rather than love, exclaims, 'such a Wedlock would be worse than Adultery' (V: 1.1.118–19). An amusing, extreme case of a father hoping to raise his family through his daughter's marriage is that of Dr Baliardo in Behn's farce, *The Emperor of the Moon* (1687). Obsessed with telescopes that permit him to observe the moon and convinced that a superior race of beings lives there, the doctor succumbs to a plot of his daughter's lover, who convinces him that the Emperor of the Moon wishes to marry his daughter.

Although most comedy supposes that love rather than practical economic considerations animates girls' choices, historical evidence suggests that even unmarried women could find the economic advantages of a proposed marriage more important than sentiment. Behn is unusual in presenting some women who marry for money as at least partly sympathetic. With only a small fortune herself, bereft of other means of support, Leticia Bredwell in *The Luckey Chance* (1686) marries old alderman Sir Feeble Fainwould, not loving or even liking him, indeed, despite her disgust for that 'nautious thing . . . an old Man turn'd Lover' (VII: 1.3.55–6). When her former suitor, Bellmour, with whom she exchanged promises of marriage, but who she was told had died, proves very much alive, she pleads for his understanding: 'remember I was poor and helpless. / And much reduc'd, and much impos'd upon' (VII: 2.2.49–50). Later we learn that Leticia first resisted Sir Feeble's temptation of a jointure of £500 a year, only succumbing to his proposals after he – falsely – gave her news that Bellmour had been hanged in Holland. Julia, the other female protagonist in this comedy, has married another alderman, a rich banker, Sir Cautious Fulbank. She rather sharply instructs her young lover, Gayman, who has impoverished himself giving her extravagant presents, 'Love's a thin Dyet, nor will keep out Cold' (VII: 4.1.36). At the end of the play, Leticia has conveniently avoided consummating her marriage with Sir Feeble; he has been sufficiently terrorized that he turns Leticia, along with jewels he has given her, over to her lover. Julia is not quite so fortunate, yet her husband's avaricious willingness to pay a gambling debt to Gayman by permitting Gayman to have intercourse with her is offered as justification for Julia's outrage at her husband and her refusal to sleep with him any longer. Julia's husband tells Gayman, 'If I dye Sir – I bequeath my Lady to you – with my whole Estate' (VII: 5.2.386–7).

On the one hand, Behn vehemently attacks the immorality of forced marriages and her heroines vigorously express the loathsomeness of being forced to marry a rich old man as no better than rape. She shows the power of patriarchal legal and economic systems to ride roughshod over women's desires. On the other hand, especially in her city comedy, a low mimetic mode, she is exceptionally alert to the economic dilemmas of women who lack money to live at what to them is an acceptable social standard and surprisingly sympathetic both to Tory rakes and to female characters who jettison the scruples of conventional morality in order to get money for themselves. When she writes more in the mode of romance, as in 'The Wandring Beauty' (1700), she offers a more traditional plot of a virtuous young woman, Arabella Fairname, who walks away from her gentry family rather than be forced to marry old Sir Robert Richland. Arabella works as a servant for several years before being rewarded with marriage to the rich and virtuous Sir Lucius Lovewell. But, reading the whole body of Behn's work, one gets the sense that Behn thought real women could almost never count on good fortune like Arabella's and that, given the power of patriarchal coercion and an economic and legal system often inimical to the interests of women, and given economic difficulty, real women might be excused for resorting to less high-minded ways of shifting for themselves.

Libertinism

The ideology to which Behn was most attracted was that of libertinism, the seventeenth-century revival of classical Epicurean hedonism that first came to England from France. Royalists like the playwright William Wycherley and, most importantly, King Charles II himself, imbibed French libertinism when they were in exile on the continent during the interregnum. Erudite French libertinism, like that of Pierre Gassendi, cultivated atomism, was anti-Aristotelian and moderately sceptical, but did not attack Christianity or conventional morality. Philosophically, libertinism made the senses a primary source of knowledge and stressed the reality of the material world over what it saw as the illusory character of ideals. Royalist English libertinism like the Earl of Rochester's and Behn's celebrated the authority of nature over that of what it debunked as religious superstition and argued for the value of physical pleasure in present time. Thus Behn in her poem 'The Golden Age' imagines a time when lovers could satisfy their sexual desires:

> Not kept in fear of Gods, no fond Religious cause,
>   Nor in Obedience to the duller Laws.
>   Those Fopperies of the Gown were then not known,
>   Those vain those Politick Curbs to keep man in,
> Who by a fond mistake Created that a Sin;
> Which freeborn we, by right of Nature claim our own.
>
> (I, p. 33)

The materialism of the English philosopher Thomas Hobbes also seemed to support libertinism, although Hobbes was not interested in justifying sexual hedonism. Royalist libertinism engaged in an aggressive transvaluation of values, itself becoming a quasi-religion in which blasphemy became both a pleasure and a duty and what conventional morality regarded as vices (fornication, adultery, drunkenness, gambling, and sometimes sodomy) became virtually obligatory rituals. Libertinism was an upper-class, coterie philosophy, not one its devotees ever intended the common people should adopt. In the Restoration context, libertinism offered a critique of puritanism. Indeed, royalist libertinism often asserted that chastity was impossible and that puritanism was no more than hypocrisy. Behn enjoyed and translated the witty maxims of the French duke, La Rochefoucauld, one of which declared: 'If we can resist our Passions, 'tis more from the weakness of them than our own Vertues' (IV, p. 59). Also, in the English context, particularly as the King himself seemed to embrace libertinism, libertinism – somewhat illogically – attached itself to loyalty to monarchy.

While libertinism authorized women's free enjoyment of sexual pleasure, a serious problem for Behn was that libertinism was a masculinist ideology. It was hostile to marriage or any other long-term commitment, typically figured women as provided by nature for men's pleasure, and sometimes did not scruple to resort to violence to gratify male desire. Inheriting from courtly love the idea that passion flourished only outside of marriage, libertinism regarded marriage as a betrayal of the good. In glorifying present sexual pleasure, it countenanced sexual practices that had fewer problematic consequences for men than for women. (Barring the non-trivial threats of venereal disease, social disgrace, or even criminal prosecution for sodomy or rape.) Unlike the Church, libertinism was not concerned with the reproductive capacities of women, with pregnancy, or with the protection of children.

For Behn, who was drawn to the libertine critique of religion and morality, and who wrote and socialized in libertine circles, a central problem was to work out the sharply different consequences of libertinism for women. Her libertine men insist that passion has reality only in the present, that desire is so fleeting that lovers cannot promise constancy. Yet, in a world where male violence toward women is endemic and where women lack genteel ways of supporting themselves, women require reliable male protectors. And Behn's women yearn for constant love. One of her songs inventively and elegantly, if unconvincingly, turns the fickleness of a male lover into consolation for the deserted and distressed Aminta:

> The softest love grows cold and shy,
>   The face so late ador'd,
> Now unregarded passes by,
>   Or grows at last abhor'd;
> All things in Nature fickle prove,
>   See how they glide away;
> Think so in time thy hopeless love
>   Will die, as Flowers decay
>   (I, p. 169)

As Behn represents them, male desire and female desire differ. Male libertine desire focuses narrowly on the pleasure of sexual intercourse in the present moment; it is a desire for conquest and the experience of power as well as for sexual orgasm. Hence, it is excited by resistance, heightened by woman's fear, and diminished by successful enjoyment. Wilding, one of Behn's darker rakes, articulates what thrills him about the prospect of illicit intercourse with Lady Galliard:

> The stealths of Love, the Midnight kind admittance,
> The gloomy Bed, the soft-breath'd murmuring Passion;
> Ah, who can guess at Joys, thus snatcht by parcels!
> The difficulty makes us always wishing,
> Whilst on thy part, Fear still makes some resistance;
> And every Blessing seems a kind of Rape.
>
> (VII: 1.1.341–6)

Female desire, in contrast, represented as soft, melting, yielding, wants protracted courtship. It entails an experience of powerlessness, and is coloured by fear of disgrace and dread of abandonment. For the woman, the experience of desire is simultaneously proof that she is desirable, threat to her separate identity, and exciting because it has the power to destroy. Behn's amorous women also eroticize male violence, finding themselves drawn to men who draw their swords on the slightest provocation and men who do not scruple to use force to grab and 'ruffle' women.

Libertinism construes sexual appetite not only as natural but also as irresistible. As it exalts physical lovemaking as the source of highest pleasure, so, especially in amorous fiction and verse, it exalts lovers as superior people, nobler than those prudent, cowardly, or cold beings who decline invitations to love. From a modern feminist point of view, there is an unhappy coincidence between this libertine exaltation of lovemaking as irresistible and the misogynist belief that women are incapable of controlling their own sexuality. Some of Behn's most memorable women characters are those – like Angellica in *The Rover*, La Nuche in *The Second Part of the Rover* (1681), and Lady Galliard in *The City-Heiress* – who struggle to resist libertine seduction and their own desires only to yield, not with simple rapture, but with despair over their own powerlessness.

Lady Galliard is perhaps the best-developed example of Behn's representation of the pathos of the female lack of self-control. There is no ordinary reason why Wilding should not marry Lady Galliard, a rich widow who wants to marry him, yet he argues that illicit love between them will be not only more exciting than matrimony, but more noble:

Beauty shou'd still be the Reward of Love,
Not the vile Merchandize of Fortune,
Or the cheap Drug of a Church-Ceremony.
. . . All the desires of mutual Love are vertuous.
(VII: 4.1.165–7, 174)

When Wilding affects to believe that Lady Galliard does not love him unless she demonstrates it by having illicit intercourse, then threatens to leave her, she submits, pleading, 'My Reason's weary of the unequal strife; / And Love and Nature will at last o'ercome' (VII: 4.1.262–3). One way to read the inequality of which she complains would be to say that she finds her reason unequal to her passion; yet, because the scene entails her attempting to counter Wilding's arguments with her own, the line also seems to invite the reading that she finds her own female reasoning powers weaker than his male capabilities. 'Pity my Weakness, and admire my Love', she murmurs (VII: 4.1.279). Once Lady Galliard is 'undone', she vows never again to yield, but almost immediately her agitated distress and rage reattract Wilding, who theatrically threatens to kill himself with his sword if she will not revoke her vow. Lady Galliard can only sigh and say, 'I confess I am but feeble woman' (VII: 4.1.418). Behn allows her a respectable husband at the end, but she has to witness Wilding decide to marry the virgin heiress and she clearly still yearns for him. As Elizabeth Howe has pointed out, Behn used Elizabeth Barry, famous as a tragic actress, as Lady Galliard to represent a new kind of 'tragic mistress', capable of suffering and pathos.[8]

The value of women

Behn was seriously interested in the problem of what the 'value' of women was in her society and experiments with dividing and isolating elements of conventional female value. While theological and aristocratic ideologies – including libertinism – attempted to resist the idea that female worth could be expressed as monetary value, the newer economic ideology suggested that any thing or any one might have a market value expressible in pounds. Behn's version of a maximally desirable woman simultaneously possesses beauty, the power to evoke desire in men, wealth, and wit. (Behn is not much interested in other qualities other contemporaries would have found essential to desirable femininity: modesty, housekeeping skill, charity, fertility, or self-control.) In a variation of aristocratic romance, when Behn represents the body of her maximally desirable woman, she offers an erotic fusion between a beautiful female body and an opulent display of wealth in the form of sumptuous fabrics and dazzling jewels. Consider, for example, her description of Miranda in *The Fair Jilt* (1688): 'she turn'd up her Veil, and discover'd to his View the most wond'rous Object of Beauty he had ever seen, dress'd in all the Glory of a young Bride; her Hair and Stomacher full of Diamonds, that gave a lustre all dazling to her brighter Face and Eyes' (III, p. 22). Such descriptions emphasize the great wealth possessed by the woman, but they do not descend to numerical quantification of its market value. Trying to dissuade the courtesan La Nuche in *The Second Part of the Rover* from following an impulse to give her love away for free, the old bawd Petronella in a more realistic vein reminds her: 'Do you not daily see – fine Cloathes, rich Furniture, Jewels and Plate are more inviting than Beauty unadorn'd: be old, diseas'd, deform'd, be any thing, so you be rich and splendidly attended, you'l find yourself Lov'd and Ador'd by all' (VI: 4.1.369–72). But even Petronella does not entirely believe in the power and desirability of opulent wealth alone; she steals La Nuche's jewels and money in hopes of again setting herself up as a courtesan, but she also buys the mountebank's magic elixir in hopes of restoring her own youth and beauty.

Behn, however, repeatedly imagines efforts to disaggregate the value of a woman, raising questions about the relative value of its supposedly constituent elements, and, sometimes, playing with moves to quantify their market value. Her most obvious move, perhaps, is to break apart female beauty and female wealth. Mordantly, in *The Second Part of the Rover*, she offers two fabulously rich Jewish female 'monsters' from Mexico, one a Giant, the other a Dwarf (neither has a proper name); each is worth £100,000. Men find both women's bodies disgusting, anti-Semitism heightening their disgust. The giant is especially frightening; a timorous Featherfool has to be coaxed up a ladder so that he can kiss her. Nevertheless, four male characters scheme to court and marry them, and two ultimately do. In an odd bit of comic business, Featherfool and Harlequin sneak up on the Giant while she is sleeping, creep close to steal the pearl necklace she is wearing, then eat the pearls one by one, supposedly to hide their theft. This seems a vivid emblem of the male desire to incorporate the woman's wealth.

Debate over whether or how one could set economic value on parts of female value prompts some of Behn's most intricate and intriguing dialogue. The courtesan Angellica in *The Second Part of the Rover* has set a price of 1,000 crowns a month as her fee. She explains that she has concluded that men are inconstant and resolved 'that nothing but Gold, shall charm my heart' (V: 2.1.129–30). Men's mocking her, she says, does not displease her, since 'their wonder feeds my vanity, and he that wishes but to buy,

gives me more Pride, than he that gives my Price, can make my pleasure'
(v: 2.1.115–17). Once he desires her, the rake hero Willmore launches a
moral condemnation of Angellica's offer to exchange 'love' for money. While
the moral condemnation may sound odd coming from the mouth of a libertine, he argues a point of libertine morality according to which an exchange
of sexual pleasure for sexual pleasure is a legitimate transaction, whereas
marrying for money or selling sex for money is not.

Willmore's exploration of the legitimacy of the exchange Angellica proposes becomes more original as he considers the possibilities of fractionating
her value:

> I grant you, 'tis [the rental price] set down, a Thousand Crowns a month –
> pray how much may come to my Share for a Pistole. – Bawd take your black
> Lead and Sum it up, that I may have a Pistols worth of this vain gay thing, and
> I'll trouble you no more.   (v: 2.1.305–8)

When Moretta insists that only 'the whole piece' is for sale, he replies:

> 'Tis very hard, the whole Cargo or nothing – Faith Madam, my Stock will not
> reach it, I cannot be your Chapman [i.e., man who trades] – Yet I have Country
> Men in Town, Merchants of Love like me; I'll see if they'll put in for a Share,
> we cannot lose much by it, and what we have no use for, we'll sell upon the
> *Frydays* Mart at – *Who gives more?* [at auction] I am studying Madam how
> to purchase you, tho' at present I am unprovided of Money.   (v: 2.1.311–17)

There is a certain logic to the proposition that, if a month's sexual enjoyment
of a woman is available for purchase, then she should be willing to sell ten
minutes at a lesser price. Yet a function of this is to remind us that the status
and desirability of women is supposed to be related to the exclusivity of the
terms upon which they can be purchased: a woman who is available to only
one man in marriage for her entire life is supposed to be the most valuable;
a woman who negotiates long-term arrangements, like the exclusive kept-
mistresses of the seventeenth century or now, more valuable than the woman
who can be bought by a limited clientele for a night; who are in turn more
valuable than the women out on the street prepared to turn short tricks for all
comers. Willmore's consciousness is affected by the late seventeenth-century
financial revolution in which new forms of commodification, especially the
creation of shares, fractional interests, and contingent and future interests
were strange novelties. English shipping, for instance, crucial to the growth
of trade and empire, operated by allowing investors to pool resources so
that they could buy fractional shares in ships; eights, sixteenths, or thirty-
seconds were bought by groups of male friends like those Willmore proposes
as sharers in Angellica. Auctions were also common in trade and in the sale of

houses, household goods, and art in this period when people struggled with change from a traditional regime of 'just price' to a new capitalist regime of 'market value'.

Does a woman lose her value and become undesirable if she is unchaste? Behn's representations of male desire for courtesans in *The Rover* and in *The Feign'd Curtizans* remind her audiences that the idea that only female chastity can evoke male desire cannot be true. Behn's male libertines typically insist that they prefer a mistress to a 'dull wife'. On the other hand, a few male characters profess that whores lack the power to evoke desire. Behn explores the language used to speak of unchaste women. Some of this language, like 'mercenary jilt', 'strumpet', 'crack', or 'cheap whore' is stigmatizing, yet some of it, like 'courtesan', seems glamorizing. In *The Feign'd Curtizans*, where no actual professional courtesan ever appears, but where three young women pretend to be courtesans, glamorous foreign names for prostitutes themselves seem to have the power to arouse male desire. Pietro describes his success in pimping his supposed courtesan to Sir Signal Buffoon, reporting that when he told him 'that no Man lives here without his Inamorata', the 'very word . . . so fir'd him, that he's resolv'd to have an Inamorata whatever it cost him' (VI: 1.1.144–6). (Part of the attraction is the knowledge that other men have been attracted to the woman in question.) Later we find Sir Signal eager for a walk so that he can see the courtesans, 'the *bona roba*'s, the *inamorata*'s, and the *Bell ingrato's*' (VI: 1.1.267–8). Flirting with blasphemy, Cornelia, designed for a nun but determined to pretend to be a courtesan, tells her sister that 'Curtizan' is 'a Noble title and has more *Votaries than Religion*' (VI: 2.1.65–6). The principal libertine rake in this play, Galliard, insists that what is merely a stigmatizing name cannot lessen the desirability of a beautiful woman: 'Love is Love, where ever beauty is, / Nor can the Name of whore, make beauty less' (VI: 3.1.220–1).

Galliard's friend, Sir Harry Fillamour, however, praises constancy and says that a courtesan is simply a 'Whore', who 'filthily exposes all her Beautys to him can give her most, not Love her best' (VI: 1.1.57–8). The action of the play tests Fillamour's belief that an unchaste woman would necessarily also be undesirable. Marcella, the woman he loves, pretends to be the courtesan Euphemia. When Fillamour finds Euphemia desirable, Marcella writes a letter summoning him back to Viterbo, where she is supposed to be. In the supposed apartment of the courtesan, Fillamour is disoriented to find that it does not seem at all sordid, that it 'rather seems th' Apartment of some Prince, / Then a Receptickle for lust and shame' (VI: 4.1.3–4). (That courtesans might seem at home in royal apartments should not have seemed surprising to an audience in the days of Charles II, notorious for indulging himself in mistresses, some of whom could be met in the royal palaces.)

Fillamour makes an effort to say that 'Euphemia', '*richly and loosely dressed*', is beautiful and tempting but ought to repent. Marcella replies with words that seem close to Behn's own view:

> Virtue itself's a dream of so slight force,
> The very fluttering of Love's wings destroys it,
> Ambition, or the meaner hope of interest, wakes it to nothing,
> In men a feeble Beauty, shakes the dull slumber off –
>
> (VI: 4.1.40–3)

Fillamour claims that good men will not respect whores, but that they revere innocent women. Little in Behn's textual world seems to support this proposition. The power of Euphemia's beauty so threatens to 'melt' Fillamour that he flees her immediate presence, but cannot bring himself to leave for Viterbo. In the end, Behn relents and allows both Marcella and Sir Harry to retain their chastity and to marry, but not before having demonstrated that an innocent woman can be indistinguishable from a 'whore' and that even a professed constant lover is not immune to the temptations of apparently vicious beauty.

From at least some modern feminist perspectives, there is something sad about Behn characters like Lady Galliard and all the other women 'too feeble' to resist the importunities of fickle and perfidious rakes. Early feminists like Mary Astell were soon to tell women that they were not so feeble and that they had the rational capacity to resist such lovers' blandishments. So many of Behn's comedies and fictions show us women who abandon moral scruples either for what they think is love or because they can think of no better ways to survive economically. Sometimes Behn is fascinated with and at least a bit sympathetic to the woman, however villainous, trapped and driven by love's 'Tyrannick power'; at other times, she exposes the conjoint power of love and poverty to embolden women to act to provide for themselves despite conventional morality. Her anger at contemporary men's exploitation of women and at the unfairness of contemporary theological, moral, economic, and legal systems towards women seems expressed in a kind of compensatory rough justice that exempts characters like Lady Fancy or Lady Fulbank or Lady Galliard from the punishments they would be apt to suffer in more conventional plots by male writers. Behn's endings in works like these are strained, even sour, conspicuously lacking the festivity more typically associated with comedy. How far Behn's critiques of the position of women in her society were constrained by the literary forms in which she wrote – forms that her critiques, up to a point, stretched – and how far they were limited by her own inability to imagine alternative, less misogynist constructions of womanhood, we will never know.

NOTES

1 [Richard Allestree], *The Ladies Calling. In Two Parts. By the Author of the Whole Duty of Man, the Causes of the Decay of Piety, and the Gentleman's Calling* (Oxford, 1673), p. 175. Wing Film.

2 Allestree, *Ladies Calling*, pp. 162, 166.

3 See Gellert Spencer Alleman, *Matrimonial Law and the Materials of Restoration Comedy* (Philadelphia: n.p., 1942).

4 Todd, p. 15.

5 J. A. Sharpe, *Early Modern England: A Social History, 1550–1760* (London: Arnold, 1997, 2nd edn), p. 43; E. A. Wrigley, R. S. Davies, J. E. Oeppen, R. S. Schofield, *English Population History from Family Reconstruction* (Cambridge: Cambridge University Press, 1997), p. 219.

6 Todd, p. 224.

7 3 Hen. VII, c.2. Should the woman have consented to an original elopement, but then withdrawn her consent before rape or forcible marriage, the statute also applied. 4 & 5 Phil. & Mar. 58 punished taking away a girl under sixteen without her parents' or guardians' consent to 'deflower' or marry her with fine and imprisonment and provided that the abductor, should he have married the girl, would forfeit all her lands to her family during his life.

8 Elizabeth Howe, *The First English Actresses: Women and Drama, 1660–1700* (Cambridge: Cambridge University Press, 1992), p. 135. As Howe points out, Barry played Hellena in *The Rover*, rather than Angellica, but she also played the seduced Corina in *The Revenge* and La Nuche in *The Second Part of the Rover*.

3

DEREK HUGHES

Aphra Behn and the Restoration theatre

The Restoration theatre gave women an unprecedented public presence and identity. Actresses for the first time appeared on the public stage. Although they were the objects of lust, gossip, seduction, and (occasionally) assault, they also excited admiration through their talent, and some – such as Mary Betterton – enjoyed long and distinguished careers without any hint of scandal. The theatre also gave women other forms of prominence. In February 1663, Katherine Philips' translation of Corneille's *La Mort de Pompée* was performed in Dublin; her translation of Corneille's *Horace*, completed after her death by Sir John Denham, was performed at court in 1668 and at the King's Company's Bridges Street theatre in 1669. In 1668 Sir William Davenant's widow Mary assumed temporary managership of the Duke's Company, during the minority of her sons.[1] In 1669 the King's Company staged Frances Boothby's *Marcelia*: the first original play by a woman to reach the public stage. And, in 1670, Aphra Behn emerged as the first British woman to make a living as a creative writer, with her tragicomedy *The Forc'd Marriage*, performed in September 1670 by the Duke's Company, the more successful and adventurous of the two companies. Two plays by Elizabeth Polwhele, *The Faithful Virgins* and *The Frolicks*, may also have been performed in 1670–1. Behn thus made her début at a time when the stage was evidently quite open to women writers; yet only she went on to make a career as a dramatist. After 1671, no other woman is known to have had a play professionally staged until 1695, six years after Behn's death, when a period of cutthroat theatrical competition produced a demand for new writers, creating an opportunity which six women dramatists had seized by the end of the century.

Behn's status as the first British woman to earn her living as a creative writer might make her seem a vulnerable and marginal figure, and it is easy to quote misogynist satire mocking her. One often cited satirist is Robert Gould, who attacked Behn on several occasions, and in his *Satyrical Epistle* wrote:

For *Punk* and *Poesie* agree so pat
You cannot well be *this*, and not be *that*.[2]

Later, he approvingly quoted the Earl of Rochester's observation that '*Whore's the like Reproachful Name / As Poetress [sic]*'.[3] These passages are regularly produced as evidence of the woman writer's marginal and despised status.[4] It is, however, far less often mentioned that even Gould warmly admired Katherine Philips; indeed, the lines just quoted immediately precede a tribute to Philips. Gould objected to women who wrote dirty plays; he did not object to women who wrote.

Although Behn did not have a play staged until 1670, she was in fact only the third fully professional dramatist, male or female, to establish herself since the reopening of the theatres in 1660, for the stage in the 1660s had been dominated by gentlemen amateurs (such as the Earl of Orrery), who were now bowing out. Her predecessors as emergent professionals were John Dryden and Thomas Shadwell. In the preface to her old-fashioned and unsuccessful comedy *The Dutch Lover* (February 1673), which had been overshadowed by Shadwell's more forward-looking *Epsom-Wells* (December 1672), she jostles for position with Dryden and Shadwell, without naming either. She gently mocks the bombast of Dryden's heroic plays and mounts a more severe attack on Shadwell, evidently piqued that his inferior talent had judged the moment so well, and that she had judged it so badly. At this early stage of her career, she does not see herself as a face in a crowd, but as competing for top place in a threesome.

Moreover, in the years from 1670 to her death in 1689 Behn had at least eighteen new plays performed (some other, anonymous, plays have also speculatively been attributed to her). During that same period, Dryden and Thomas Durfey had fourteen premières; no man had more. In these two decades, therefore, Behn had twenty-five per cent more new plays put on than any male competitor, and she seems to have been regarded as a safe pair of hands in a crisis. During the season of 1677–8, the two companies put on twelve or thirteen new comedies. There were some spectacular failures in the spring of 1678 (including Behn's *Sir Patient Fancy*), and no known successes in the season. The companies seem to have burned their fingers with comedy, and in the following season only one new comedy was staged. It was by Behn: *The Feign'd Curtizans* (by March 1679). From late 1678 to 1681, England was gripped by political crisis; during this period, the demand for comedy dropped, but it revived in 1681–2, when eight new comedies were staged. Of these, no less than four were by Behn.

On three occasions Behn's prefaces – to *The Dutch Lover* (1673), *Sir Patient Fancy* (1678), and *The Luckey Chance* (1686) – lament the failure or disappointing reception of the play, and attribute it to prejudice against the woman writer, particularly the woman writer who claimed the male privilege of bawdiness. We have no grounds for doubting the particular instances of hostility that she documents, such as the '*long, lither, phlegmatick, white, ill-favour'd, wretched Fop*', who announced to his neighbours '*that they were to expect a woful Play, God damn him, for it was a womans*' (v, p. 162). Yet, as has partially been seen, there were other factors at work. *The Dutch Lover*, a play of intrigue and mistaken identity among the Spanish gentry, followed a pattern which had been popular in the previous decade, but was now stilted and old-fashioned in comparison to Shadwell's recent hit, an important stage in the evolution of genteel sex comedy. As already mentioned, *Sir Patient Fancy* was one casualty out of several in the 1677–8 season, and (despite Behn's complaints of a specific prejudice against female bawdy), it is possible that there was a general reaction against the increasing sexual frankness of comedy.[5] It is a measure of Behn's status that she alone should have had a comedy staged in the following season, but she briefly became more cautious. *The Feign'd Curtizans* is daring enough, in showing two gentlewomen masquerading as prostitutes, but (unlike *Sir Patient Fancy* and its predecessor, *The Rover*) it avoids consummated sex. In the preface to *The Luckey Chance* (probably April 1686), Behn again complained about a double standard in judging bawdy plays. Yet the prefatory material to the next two sex comedies, Sir Charles Sedley's *Bellamira* (May 1687) and Thomas Durfey's *A Fool's Preferment* (March/April 1688), also complained of audience squeamishness. 'I am very unhappy', Sedley wrote, 'that the Ice that has borne so many Coaches and Carts, shou'd break with my Wheelbarrow.'[6] Sex comedy, both by women and men, had palled; the fashion was for farce, and Behn obliged in her next play, the highly successful *Emperor of the Moon* (March 1687).

In turning to farce, as in retreating from sex comedy in *The Feign'd Curtizans*, Behn acknowledges that she has been the victim of changing fashion, not entrenched misogyny. Although at times caught out by the changing marketplace, Behn responded to its vagaries with supreme creativity. Following the merger of the two companies in 1682, there was a disastrous slump in the demand for new plays. Having had four new plays performed in the season of 1681–2, Behn lived to see only two further premières of her work: of *The Luckey Chance* (1686) and *The Emperor of the Moon* (1687).[7] During this crisis, Thomas Otway died in poverty, perhaps of starvation. Behn, by contrast, creatively diversified, becoming a pioneer in realistic short fiction (of which *Oroonoko* is the most famous example), and also in longer narrative forms: *Love-Letters between a Noble-Man and his Sister* is judged by many to be the first English novel.

No other late seventeenth-century writer was as resourceful and diversely inventive.

Behn and the development of the repertory

The stereotyped image of Restoration comedy was for a long time of a witty, urbane, London-based comedy, probably containing illicit sex; a form of comedy which started with the arrival of Charles II, a witty, urbane king dedicated to illicit sex, and continued in a largely steady state until the moral campaign against the stage which gathered force during the 1690s, in the reign of William III. In fact, the Restoration theatre changed almost year by year, and Behn's career responded to its changes.

The principal topic of Restoration drama during its first decade was the Restoration itself. Play after play portrayed a cycle of usurpation and providentially restored authority, though by the mid-1660s some dramatists were tactfully critical of royal amorousness. The leading genre was one that was appropriate to portraying the sequence of calamity and regeneration: tragicomedy.[8] There was at first, however, no dominant mode of comedy. Social comedy set in London did not start to establish itself until 1668, and comedy was quite often located in the subplots of serious plays. The leading actors of the King's Company, Charles Hart and Nell Gwyn, inspired Dryden and others to portray couples who fenced in witty, sexually daring dialogue (sometimes in the subplots of tragicomedies, such as Dryden's *Secret Love*, January 1667), but comedies did not contain consummated sex until long after Nell Gwyn had left the stage for Charles II's bed. It is unsurprising, therefore, that Behn's first three plays were tragicomedies in name or fact: *The Young King* (not performed until, probably, 1679), *The Forc'd Marriage* (September 1670), and *The Amorous Prince* (February 1671). *The Young King* is an ambivalent treatment of the theme of Restoration, in which an attempt at female rule yields to renewed patriarchy, and an initially sexually aggressive prince is tamed into kingship and monogamy. *The Amorous Prince* takes up the delicate theme of royal sexuality, portraying the reform of a ruler who is initially a cynical and unscrupulous seducer. It does, with unprecedented daring, start with the immediate aftermath of a seduction, but this is a crime to be atoned, not a pleasure to be repeated.

The development of drama in the 1670s presents a paradox. There was increasing public suspicion of Charles II and his authoritarian, Catholic brother James (later, briefly, James II). In the disastrous Third Dutch War of 1672–4, Charles had allied himself with Louis XIV against Protestant Holland. And his French mistress, Louise de Kéroualle, Duchess of Portsmouth, was deeply unpopular. Kings in serious drama were now rarely restored heroes, and sometimes sexually voracious and oppressive tyrants (e.g. in Thomas Otway's *Don Carlos*, June 1676, or Nathaniel Lee's *Mithridates*, February 1678). Behn's one tragedy *Abdelazer* (June/July 1676) is rather more indulgent to royal amorousness, but nevertheless portrays a royal court disrupted by a king's obsession with a married woman. Yet, in comedy, sexual attitudes progressively became freer. The seduction which takes place just before the start of *The Amorous Prince* is deplored, rectified by marriage, and distanced by the foreign setting (the court of Florence) and the romance genre. In *Epsom-Wells*, by contrast, Shadwell portrayed adultery in contemporary and realistically represented metropolitan society, though the adulterers are subordinate and unappealing characters. The first high-profile play to portray sex between its leading characters was William Wycherley's *The Country-Wife* (January 1675), whose hero, Horner, pretends that he has been emasculated during a VD cure, and – apparently not a threat to the men – gains easy access to all the women in town. Sex thus definitively reaches the stage a full fifteen years after it had reached Charles II's court.

The Country-Wife is complex in its portrayal of the relationship between sexual instinct and the restrictions of social existence, but it is not complex in its portrayal of sex itself, which is simple fun. There is no exploration of the emotional complexities of seduction, infidelity, and rejection. Nor did the play produce an instant surge of imitations. Once sex had been staged, however, the way was open for a more emotionally and psychologically searching portrayal of sexual experience. This came in a play of fourteen months later (only the second sex comedy since *The Country-Wife*): Sir George Etherege's *The Man of Mode* (March 1676), which *does* portray the emotional complexity of sex. Its hero, Dorimant, is a charming, dispassionately observed seducer, who enjoys giving pain to women, and succeeds. In contrast to *The Country-Wife*, this play had an immense impact, though mainly in provoking reaction. Comedy grew darker, and there was a sequence of plays featuring Dorimant-like seducers, who (unlike their original) are portrayed with unambiguous severity; the playwrights' sympathies are always with the women on whom the seducer preys. It is in the aftermath of *The Man of Mode* that Behn wrote *her* first sex comedy, *The Rover* (March 1677). The hero, Willmore, is a woman's-eye view of the Dorimant-figure; but it is important to remember that male writers were also critically recreating him.

The complications in the history of sex comedy do not, however, end there. Demand for comedy dropped following the failures of the 1677–8 season, and the commencement of the Exclusion Crisis (1678–81), during which fears of a Catholic coup produced ultimately unsuccessful attempts to exclude

James from the succession. Behn retreated from sex comedy in *The Feign'd Curtizans*, and her next two plays were tragicomedies: *The Young King* was retrieved from the bottom drawer and (probably) staged in 1679, and she then adapted Marston's *The Dutch Courtesan* as *The Revenge* (January–April 1680). *The Second Part of The Rover* (c. January 1681) is only the second new sex comedy for three years; like its predecessor, Otway's *The Souldiers Fortune* (June 1680), it shows a continuing darkening in the portrayal of sexual desire and betrayal. In the wake of the royalist triumph in the political crisis, there was a flurry of often cheerful politicized comedies about the sexual humiliation of elderly opposition figures by young royalists (1681–3); of these the best (and least cheerful) is Behn's *The City-Heiress* (April 1682). But then the theatres merged, the market for new plays diminished, farce became fashionable, and new sex comedies were rare and unsuccessful for the remainder of the decade. So the comedy of adultery and seduction occurs very sporadically, in separated clusters, each different in character and impetus from the others. In Behn's career, we see her carefully, if not always successfully, aiming at the constantly moving target of audience taste.

It is often claimed that Restoration comedy by male authors was macho in its sexual attitudes and exploitative in its treatment of women. As already indicated, however, comedies after *The Man of Mode* show considerable sympathy for the actual or intended victims of seducers: examples are Thomas Durfey's *Trick for Trick* (March 1678) and Otway's *Friendship in Fashion* (April 1678). Moreover, one striking feature of this period is a protofeminist drama by men that is far more starry-eyed in its optimism about women's capacities than Behn ever is. The heroine of Thomas Durfey's *Madam Fickle* (November 1676), for example, is a linguistic virtuoso, shifting vocal styles and dialects in order to baffle and deceive a number of rather dim, male supremacist suitors. Her antitype is Sir Arthur Oldlove, an antiquarian who collects obviously fake historical relics: Sir Gawain's skull, Sir Lancelot's sword, Pompey the Great's breeches, the tears of that patron saint of anti-feminist writing, St Jerome. (In his *Epistle against Jovinian*, St Jerome had recycled some antifeminist satire by an earlier writer, Theophrastus, and this was often re-used: for example, by Chaucer in *The Wife of Bath's Prologue*.) These are relics of a totally male-dominated past, but it is now a past without a narrative: merely a clutter of meaningless things. The power of narrative has passed to the woman; and, during the play, St Jerome's tears are spilt.

Durfey thus shows women liberating themselves by equalling or surpassing men in language. Behn never does this, in part because she doubts whether language is the real key to power. The social domination of men is grounded upon their capacity for violence. *The Rover* is full of male violence, against women and against other men, though women are normally the cause. At one point, a woman attempts violence, when the prostitute Angellica threatens her faithless lover Willmore with a pistol. She lacks the killer instinct, however, and cannot pull the trigger.[9]

Actors and actresses

One area in which Behn was at a disadvantage in comparison with leading male writers was her initial lack of patrons. Shadwell enjoyed the patronage of the Duke of Newcastle. Dryden's plays frequently appeared with dedications to leading members of the nobility. Not, however, until the publication of her ninth play, *The Feign'd Curtizans*, did Behn find a dedicatee: Nell Gwyn. Gwyn had never acted in a Behn play; she retired from the stage a few months after Behn's début, and in any case worked for the rival King's Company. Given Behn's previous lack of patrons, it would be risky to read too much into her eventual choice here, but it is appropriate that someone who had catered so sensitively for the capabilities of her actors and actresses should, uniquely, have chosen such a dedicatee.

We know nothing about the casting process, though it is probable that authorial advice was sought, and clear that experienced dramatists such as Behn often wrote with the talents of particular players in mind.[10] Inevitably, the players differed vastly in their versatility. Some tended to be typecast: Elinor Leigh, who specialized in ageing beauties and (less frequently) mature temptresses, and specialist comic actors, such as the mercurial Antony Leigh (Elinor's husband), the heavy, wooden Cave Underhill, and James Nokes, whose talent was for fatuous pusillanimity. At the other extreme was Thomas Betterton, the leading actor of the Duke's company and the greatest actor of his age, who had a huge range, perhaps lacking only a talent for light-touch buffoonery (his chief comic role was Sir Toby Belch). His Behn roles included the villainous Abdelazer and the principled Belvile in *The Rover*. They did not, as one might perhaps have expected, include the glamorous, bone-headed Willmore in *The Rover*. That part was taken by the company's other leading man, William Smith, who had a lighter touch than Betterton, having created the part of the foppish butterfly, Sir Fopling Flutter, in *The Man of Mode*. If Betterton lacked Smith's gift for light foolery, he could combine sexual magnetism with cold ruthlessness, as in the part of Etherege's Dorimant. No comic role more fully exploits this combination than that of the glamorous, unscrupulous Wilding in *The City-Heiress*.

Behn's plays are by no means relentlessly dark, but they can explore the darker side of male sexuality, and at some time or other she calls on the most menacing register of her actors. For example, one of Antony Leigh's lines was sexually unconventional or over-enthusiastic old men: a voyeuristic homosexual pimp in Otway's *The Souldiers Fortune*, a flagellant foot-fetishist in his *Venice Preserv'd*. Leigh's talents are used fairly innocuously in the part of Sir Patient Fancy, but far less so in Sir Anthony Meriwill in *The City-Heiress*: in part an endearingly roistering character, but also one who takes a voyeuristic delight in the sexual harassment and humiliation of women. Cave Underhill tended to be chosen when comic parts required a dimension of menace or violence: he was, accordingly, cast as the would-be rapist Blunt in *The Rover*.

In her use of actresses, Behn tended to work against caricature and stereotyping, and to go for depth. For example, she had no use for Elinor Leigh's superannuated beauties, and made little use of this otherwise popular actress. A part that one might expect to have gone to Elinor Leigh was Lady Knowell, the middle-aged learned lady in *Sir Patient Fancy*, based on two dessicated female pedants in Molière's *Les Femmes savantes*. Leigh took the part of one of the learned ladies in a later and closer adaptation of Molière's play, Thomas Wright's *The Female Vertuoso's* (1693), but in Behn's play the part went to Ann Marshall Quin, who generally played commanding beauties (such as Angellica in *The Rover*). The casting ensures that the role is given depth and complexity. Another actress with a definite (though not exclusive) line was Elizabeth Currer, who excelled as scheming, manipulative women, such as the prostitute Aquilina in *Venice Preserv'd*. The names of some of her parts tell their own story: Betty Frisque, Madam Tricklove, Jenny Wheedle. Behn, however, never wrote such parts for her, and generally created roles of some sensitivity, such as the unhappily married Lady Fancy in *Sir Patient Fancy*: based, to be sure, on a scheming, manipulative wife in Molière's *Le Malade imaginaire*, but given a dignity and attractiveness lacking in the original. Even further from the Jenny Wheedles is the virginal teenager Ariadne in *The Second Part of The Rover*: chaste, yet fascinated by the whore La Nuche and even mistaken for her, in a way that suggests a fundamental unity of desire with her social antitype.

A distinctive Behn character is the assertive yet tragically vulnerable woman, such as the Queen Mother in *Abdelazer* and Angellica in *The Rover*. Both were played by actresses with a track record in commanding, tragic roles, Mary Lee and Ann Marshall Quin. (Mary Betterton, who excelled both in commanding and vulnerable roles, was reserved by Behn for the latter.) In her later career Behn wrote her commanding, tragic parts for Elizabeth Barry, the greatest actress of the period. Barry had started her career with sprightly roles, such as Hellena in *The Rover*, but quickly moved to passionate, sensual victims, such as Monimia in Otway's *The Orphan* (1680), who kills herself after unwittingly committing incest. She continued to play such roles into the 1690s, but increasingly also took the part of the wilfully unchaste woman. At some stage, probably quite early, she took over the part of Angellica, and she created the equivalent role of the prostitute La Nuche in *The Second Part of The Rover*. Behn seems to have taken the lead in exploring the sensual extremes of Barry's talent. Prior to La Nuche, she had created the part of the prostitute Corina in *The Revenge*, a revision of Marston's *The Dutch Courtesan* which shows a great deal of compassionate empathy with the prostitute. This is Barry's first recorded role of this nature. Her later roles include Lady Galliard in *The City-Heiress*, a fiercely moral woman who is seduced by two men in a single night, and Lady Fulbank in *The Luckey Chance*, who resembles Otway's Monimia in being betrayed into unchastity through a bedroom trick. Behn's interest in commanding yet victimized women predates Barry's growth into such roles, but she wrote her most complex roles of this kind for Barry, and in doing so extended Barry's range. The actress and the author each stretched the other. However fortuitous, it is appropriate that Behn's first dedication should have been to an actress.

Behn and the resources of the theatre

Behn wrote for the Duke's Company, until the merger of 1682. Her earliest plays were produced at its Lincoln's Inn Fields theatre: a converted tennis court, which was the first English theatre to have changeable scenery. In 1671, the company moved to the Dorset Garden theatre, which was the late seventeenth-century theatre best equipped for ambitious stage spectacle.

Scene changes were effected by shutters running in grooves, placed in sets of perhaps three, by matching wings, also set in grooves, and borders (suspended at the top of the scenic area).[11] Probably at Lincoln's Inn Fields (and certainly at later theatres) two sets of shutter grooves were called for, sufficiently far apart for the first set to draw and reveal characters in front of the second.[12] Aphra Behn was especially fond of such 'discovery scenes'. The rear shutters could also be drawn, to reveal a three-dimensional scene, or to create a 'long' scene using the whole depth of the stage, such as the 'long street' which is used both in *The Rover* and *Sir Patient Fancy*. In addition to the scenic space, however, there was an apron stage in front of the proscenium arch, with one or two doors on either side,[13] on which most acting took place. The forestage could be used as a neutral scenic space, in which change of place could occur without change in the scene behind it: characters could, for example, pass from room to room, or from the house to the street, simply by leaving through one door and returning through another, without any change of scenery.[14]

Behn only used the full resources of Dorset Garden once, in her spectacular musical farce *The Emperor of the Moon* (March 1687), but from the outset she had a remarkable gift for exploiting the visual resources of the stage, especially in order to examine the different ways in which men and women control space. This skill is evident even in her first play to reach the stage, *The Forc'd Marriage* (September 1670). The heroine of the play (Erminia) is, against her will, given by the king in marriage to a military hero, who grows jealous at her obvious love for someone else and apparently murders her. The first thing we see is the male domination of public space; a ritual of masculinity – of soldiers after a victory – in which all the important male characters are on stage. There is not a woman in sight, despite the fact that the climax of the ritual is the rewarding of the victorious hero with the woman's hand.

Women can never establish equivalent ceremonial control of public space. When they try to enact a ceremony – of mourning for the apparently dead Erminia – it is disrupted by fighting men. As always, order is conditional on male violence. More strikingly, this disrupted female gathering is followed by the one occasion on which women do command the stage in a ceremony. Behn takes the aesthetically risky course of having the reputedly dead heroine appear to various characters as a ghost (in which guise she fills even strong men with terror). As spirit she stages a ceremony, presenting her unwanted husband with, apparently, a prophetic dream of his future: of the woman he is truly destined to marry, and the victories he is to win. In this masque, men and women appear as Glory and Honour, Mars and Pallas, and Fortune. Women appear as the equals of men, even in the representation of war, but they can only do so because they seem disembodied. They are removed from that hierarchy of physical strength which determines their inferiority in a warrior culture.

Behn is interested not only in space but in boundaries between different kinds of space. The doors and balcony in the proscenium arch assume a recurrent symbolic importance, the door in particular being an important focus of attention. Men pass through doors, even batter them down, with ease, but boundaries present women with far more difficulty. In *The Amorous Prince*, women never go outside dressed as women. The only woman to negotiate the outside world – with some difficulty – does so dressed as a young man. Women are repeatedly seen framed in windows or doors but they cannot step through the frame: there is an invisible barrier between them and the outside world. In the final scene, they confront their lecherous ruler in the guise of prostitutes (a recurrent figure in Behn). In an earlier scene, the pictures of the supposed prostitutes are distributed in the street, but only their images are allowed outside, not they themselves.

Boundaries are similarly important in *The Rover*. The prostitute Angellica first appears framed in her balcony: an object of desire, but inhabiting an enclosed, separate world whose illusions of power are destroyed when Willmore goes through her door and wins her love. Her portraits are displayed outside her door, but when she passes in the flesh into the outside world she finds betrayal and disillusionment from witnessing Willmore's infidelity. The chaste heroine Florinda communicates with her lover Belvile, of whom her brother disapproves, from a window. When she tries to elope with him, standing outside the garden gate, she is approached by Willmore, who tries to rape her. Later, escaping from her brother, she passes through an open door into a house, occupied by the foolish Blunt, who is smarting with misogynous rage because he has been cheated by a prostitute. She is locked behind an interior door, and in due course most of the male cast – less constricted by boundaries – force their way through the house door and (not knowing the identity of the imprisoned woman) clamour for sex outside the door behind which she is concealed. Boundaries for women are places of great danger: one may find a rapist on either side of the door. Men, however, assault and force doors with ease.

Behn also exploits another boundary: the scenic shutter. The drawing and closing of the shutters means that the audience can be confronted with spaces of radically different sizes. Act 2 scene 1 of *The Rover* is in 'The Long Street'; that is, all the shutters have been drawn to reveal the full depth of the stage. There can thus be a vivid contrast between indoor enclosure and the perilous wide spaces of the public world. But the drawing of the shutters can also be used to reveal a character in a space (and state) which contrasts radically with that of the previous scene. As in some of the door and balcony episodes, the drawing of the shutters creates the initial spectacle of a character *framed*, as when, in *Sir Patient Fancy*, the scene

> *Draws off, and discovers* LADY FANCY *in her Night-gown, in a Chamber as by the dark.*   (3.2.83b–c)

Lady Fancy is a young woman, married to an impotent old man, and she is here expecting her very first night with her lover. She is, apparently, on a point of transition and change. But things go wrong. A little later, there is another discovery: the scene

> *Changes to* LADY FANCY's *Bed-chamber, discovers her as before;* LODWICK *as just risen in disorder from the Bed: buttoning himself and setting himself in order; and noise at the door of unlatching it.*   (VI: 3.2.189c–e)

Her husband is at the door; and, to make matters worse, Lodwick is not the man she loves. She has slept with the wrong man by mistake.

It has been pointed out that Aphra Behn is particularly fond of such discovery scenes.[15] Most of them simply ensure scenic continuity, and are neither sexual nor even necessarily private: in *Abdelazer* '*the Scene draws off and discovers both the Armies, which all fall on and make the main Battell*' (v: 4.240b–c). Of their nature, however, these scenes emphasize a juxtaposition between different kinds of space, and those which show a woman in a state of vulnerable undress do generally place her on a traumatic boundary, pre- or post-seduction. In addition, they emphasize one extreme in her oscillation between the complementary vulnerabilities of the private and public female selves. Lady Fancy is seemingly on the edge of a moment of sexual liberation in a totally private space. It is wrecked, not only by the arrival of her husband at her door, but by the fact that an unwanted sexual opportunist has entered her room, and indeed her. As always, boundaries mean little to men.

As well as particular moments of revelation, Behn also exploits large-scale visual structures. After the defeat of the Exclusion movement in 1681, she – like other dramatists – wrote political sex comedies, one of which, *The City-Heiress*, shows the sexual humiliation of a senile Whig by a vigorous young Tory.[16] The Tory is the rakish and impoverished Tom Wilding; the Whig, his uncle, the opposition politician Sir Timothy Treat-all (a caricature of the Whig leader, the Earl of Shaftesbury). In a plot taken from Middleton's *A Mad World My Masters*, Wilding and his friends infiltrate Sir Timothy's house in disguise and terrorize and burgle him. In another plot, Wilding deceives and seduces the vulnerable widow Lady Galliard, leaving her an easy prey to his friend Sir Charles Meriwill, who has hitherto been deferential to the point of terror, but who now turns up drunk and browbeats her into a second surrender, and into marriage.

The heroes' conduct has received diverse assessments from critics. Some express discomfort; others, enthusiasm.[17] The issue may possibly be resolved if we *visualize* the sequence and structure of the play. At 11 o'clock, Wilding and his accomplices assemble to carry out their burglary, with 'Habits and Vizards' (vii: 3.1.537). At 12 o'clock, however, he has another appointment, with Lady Galliard. So he takes time off from the burglary to perform the seduction, and then carries on burgling. The seduction is an interlude in a burglary. Each starts on the hour, an hour apart. Wilding's triumphant mastery of Lady Galliard's body, dressed only in night-clothes (she has been '*discover'd in an undress at her Table*', vii: 4.1.0b; emphasis added), is mirrored in the next scene by the overpowering of Sir Timothy's senile body, also in its night-clothes. The vizards and disguises worn during the burglary act as a touchstone for the histrionics and lies with which Wilding accomplishes the seduction.

Yet more disturbing is the second seduction of Lady Galliard, by the hitherto respectful but now drunkenly aggressive Sir Charles. How did Sir Charles get drunk? He did so at Sir Timothy's house, by forcing the anti-royalist villain to kneel in front of his own guests and drink Charles II's health, and by drinking along with him. A ritual of loyal toasts to the King gives this timid Tory the courage to be a sexual tyrant, and (in more mirroring) the manhandling of Sir Timothy's body is replicated in that of Lady Galliard's (the stage directions specify that Sir Charles is to *pull* each of them: VII: 3.1.230b, 4.1.473). And the wheel comes full circle after Sir Charles has possessed Lady Galliard, in a second ritual of loyal toasts. '*Undrest*' (VII: 5.1.338b) (i.e. displaying his sexual triumph), he comes onto Lady Galliard's balcony, throws money to a group of musicians, and bids them 'drink the Kings Health, with my Royal Master's the Duke' (VII: 5.1.339–40). This is a gesture both of loyalty and (given what his undress reveals to the world) of sexual triumph. Indeed, the serenaders have been sent by Sir Charles's voyeuristic uncle to celebrate his sexual victory. What had been sequential – a ritual of political loyalty and an episode of sexual domination – are now fused into a single image.

We need waste no sympathy on Sir Timothy, but the overall pattern is troublesome. Alone, the burglary and (perhaps) the seduction might be acceptable. They become unsettling when the seduction is sandwiched in the middle of the burglary and is so visibly paralleled with it. It is similarly unsettling when the two counterbalancing sets of loyal toasts to Charles II are chronologically and causally bound together by the intervening link of the second seduction. Once the visual structure of the play is followed, Behn's virile and energetic Tory heroes become distinctly problematic. Implicitly, Behn makes a point that recurs throughout her work: that the systems of authority that she supports in the state are oppressive when replicated in the domestic sphere.

A comparable example of scenic mirroring occurs in Behn's first realistic comedy, *The Town-Fopp* (September 1676), which concerns a hero who is forced by a guardian to marry a woman he does not love, but who loves him. Shortly after his marriage, his remorse drives him to join the titular fop in a sordid brothel and court the prostitutes along with him. He is explicitly conscious that his bargains with the prostitutes are equivalent to his recent mercenary marriage ('Making a bargain to possess a Woman!', V: 4.1.428, he exclaims, talking simultaneously about both). There is, however, a more effective connection than this perfunctory signal. What gives the equivalence real richness and dramatic substance is that the scene of hollow, venal festivity in the seedy brothel is a very elaborately constructed and detailed scenic replay of the hero's wedding party in a rich, aristocratic household. In effect, we see a transformation scene, in which the lordly household becomes a brothel. So far, they have been the only two crowded indoor scenes. Both, in the same sequence, portray false merry-making; a sexually unresponsive hero (repelled firstly by his unwanted wife and secondly by the whores); masked and violent gatecrashers; a fight, and a sexual contract underwritten by law (in the second scene, the hero prepares to make a binding settlement on a prostitute). What is different in the second scene is the long dice-game in which the hero loses part of the fortune he has gained through his marriage. A gap opens in the earlier scene, and the monetary forces which had driven the marriage party are here exposed in total nakedness.

These examples of scene-mirroring from *The City-Heiress* and *The Town-Fopp* have several things in common. One is ceremony: marriage, or loyal toast-drinking. Ceremony is the façade or superstructure of a society fulfilling its own official directives. But the mirroring focuses our attention on the substructure which sustains it: violence, thuggishness, prostitution, avarice. Indeed, when Wilding and his accomplices turn up to perform the burglary, they are disguised as a lord and his retinue. 'Conduct him up with *Ceremony*' (VII: 3.1.255; italics added), says the unsuspecting Sir Timothy: ceremony and invasive crime are combined in a single complex of images. As in *The Forc'd Marriage*, the formal structures of society are both conditioned by male violence and dependent upon its permission. Ceremonies in Behn are almost always male, the very few women's ceremonies being (as in *The Forc'd Marriage*) exceptions that prove the rule.

The sequences from *The Town-Fopp* and *The City-Heiress* also feature a contrasting activity, which we have already seen to be characteristically male, and to be never convincingly enacted by women: forcible invasion, the antithesis of ceremony. The Tories in *The City-Heiress* invade Sir Timothy's and Lady Galliard's houses; in *The Town-Fopp*, there are gatecrashers in the wedding party and the brothel. As befits a burglar, for example, Wilding in *The City-Heiress* is adept at forcing his way through doors: at one point he smashes a door open. Even more revealing is the case of Sir Charles. One of the most interesting defences of Wilding is in an article by Robert Markley, whose title begins with a quotation from *The City-Heiress*: '"Be Impudent, Be Sawcy, Forward, Bold, Touzing, and Leud"'.[18] This quotes advice given to Charles by his roistering, voyeuristic uncle, Sir Anthony Meriwill (VII: 2.2.270–1). In a kind of crescendo effect, it echoes and extends some earlier avuncular advice when Charles is told that he should have 'Been very impudent and sawcy, Sir; Lewd, ruffling, mad' (VII: 1.1.438–9). It is worth, however, recalling the line which precedes this advice: 'You shou'd a hufft and bluster'd at her door' (VII: 1.1.437). Attacking women's doors is never good in Behn. Indeed, when Charles does make his conquering entrance, his first act is to brush aside the servant guarding the door. After his conquest, the most spectacular sign of Lady Galliard's collapse is that she loses authority over her servants. This is a terrible thing: one royalist charge against the puritans was that they dissolved relations between masters and servants; now a royalist is doing it himself.[19] Significantly, the particular contest of authority concerns a door: Lady Galliard commands her footman to keep the door fast shut; Charles countermands the order, and he is obeyed. When, therefore, he appears undressed on Lady Galliard's balcony, his body is again violating one of her boundaries and laying claim to it. He is like a tom-cat staking out its territory.

Conclusion

The final part of this chapter has paid deliberately little attention to the words of Behn's plays, citing them only when they help to clarify the use of stage resources. Many of the resources that Behn uses are fixed and permanent, such as the doors which pose such variable challenges for men and women, and the balconies which so poignantly frame Angellica, and so triumphantly frame Sir Charles. Other dramatists, such as Wycherley, make significant use of doors, but no other dramatist uses them so purposefully and elaborately to explore the sexual control of space; to no other Restoration dramatist is the structure of the stage so pregnant, in all its details, with the gendered iconography of the everyday world. The discovery scenes in part ensure continuity during intricately plotted plays, but the intricacy of plot in part arises from Behn's interest in conflict between spaces of differing scale, intimacy, and strangeness, and in disclosing a character on the edge of a new space and state.

Behn also uses props, such as the sword, the document, and (in *Sir Patient Fancy*) the watch, to represent and question the exercise of male control through violence, through the monopolization of language, and through bourgeois calculation and measurement. In addition she adds to the standard props some visual structures of her own, in large-scale scenic symmetries, such as those in *The Town-Fopp* and *The City-Heiress*. In her exploration of the relationship between ceremony and violence, she shows how the forms of patriarchal society may themselves be articulated through the theatrical management of space. As many critics have shown, Behn's texts are verbally rich and complex. They are visually rich and complex as well. We miss a great deal if we concentrate on the former element at the expense of the latter.

NOTES

1 She delegated artistic matters to the actors Thomas Betterton and Henry Harris, but was 'a shrewd and sensible business woman' (Philip H. Highfill, Jr, Kalman A. Burnim, and Edward A. Langhans, *A Biographical Dictionary of Actors, Actresses, Musicians . . . & Other Stage Personnel in London, 1660–1800*, 16 vols. (Carbondale and Edwardsville: Southern Illinois University Press, 1973–93).

2 *A Satyrical Epistle to the Female Author of a Poem, Call'd Sylvia's Revenge* (London, 1691), p. 5.

3 *A Satyrical Epistle*, p. 19, quoting from 'A Letter from Artemiza in the Towne to Chloe in the Countrey', lines 26–7 ('That Whore is scarce a more reproachfull name, / Then Poetesse'), John Wilmot, Earl of Rochester, *The Poems* ed. Keith Walker (Oxford and New York: Blackwell, 1984).

4 E.g. Elin Diamond, '*Gestus* and Signature in Aphra Behn's *The Rover*', ELH, 56 (1989), 520–1; Julie Nash, '"The sight on't would beget a warm desire": Visual Pleasure in Aphra Behn's *The Rover*,' *Restoration*, 18 (1994), 78; Catherine Gallagher, 'Who was that Masked Woman? The Prostitute and the Playwright in the Comedies of Aphra Behn', in *Last Laughs: Perspectives on Women and Comedy*, ed. Regina Barreca (New York, 1988), pp. 23–42. The essay also appears in *Women's Studies*, 15 (1988), 23–42, *Rereading Aphra Behn*, pp. 65–85, and in Catherine Gallagher, *Nobody's Story: The Vanishing Acts of Women Writers in the Marketplace, 1670–1820* (Oxford: Clarendon Press, 1994), pp. 1–48.

5 See Robert D. Hume, *The Development of English Drama in the Late Seventeenth Century* (Oxford: Clarendon Press, 1976), pp. 333–4.

6 *The Poetical and Dramatic Works of Sir Charles Sedley* ed. V. de Sola Pinto, 2 vols (London: Constable, 1928), II, p. 5.

7 *The Widdow Ranter* was performed after her death in 1689, and *The Younger Brother* in 1696. Both were failures.

8 See Nancy Klein Maguire, *Regicide and Restoration: English Tragicomedy, 1660–1671* (Cambridge: Cambridge University Press, 1992).

9 Corina in *The Revenge* fires a pistol at her faithless lover, but it does not discharge (VI: II. i299b–c).

10 'The probability seems to be that roles were assigned by the manager with the advice of the author', Judith Milhous and Robert D. Hume, *Producible Interpretation: Eight English Plays 1675–1707* (Carbondale and Edwardsville: Southern Illinois University Press, 1985), p. 48.

11 Recent accounts of Restoration scenery include Richard Southern, 'Theatres and Scenery,' in *The Revels History of Drama in English: Volume V, 1660–1750*, ed. John Loftis and others (London: Methuen, 1976), pp. 83–118; Colin Visser, 'Scenery and Technical Design,' in *The London Theatre World 1660–1800*, ed. Robert D. Hume (Carbondale and Edwardsville: Southern Illinois University Press, 1980), pp. 66–118; Milhous and Hume, *Producible Interpretation*, pp. 52–9; Edward A. Langhans, 'The Theatre', in *The Cambridge Companion to English Restoration Theatre*, ed. Deborah Payne Fisk (Cambridge: Cambridge University Press, 2000), pp. 1–18; and 'The Post-1660 Theatres as Performance Spaces', in *A Companion to Restoration Drama*, ed. Susan J. Owen (Oxford: Blackwell, 2001), pp. 3–18.

12 In their analysis of the production possibilities of eight Restoration plays, Judith Milhous and Robert D. Hume assume at all theatres 'the availability of six different sets of shutters (with coordinating wings and borders), divided into two distinct groups' (*Producible Interpretation*, p. 56).

13 Robert D. Hume points out that there is no hard evidence for more than one door per side at Dorset Garden, but that it is likely that there were two, 'The Dorset Garden Theatre: A Review of Facts and Problems', *Theatre Notebook*, 33 (1979), 5–7. Richard Leacroft argues for one, *The Development of the English Playhouse* (London and New York: Methuen, 1973), p. 86.

14 See Colin Visser, 'The Anatomy of the Early Restoration Stage: *The Adventures of Five Hours* and John Dryden's "Spanish" Comedies', *Theatre Notebook*, 29 (1975), 56–69, 114–19.

15 Peter Holland, *The Ornament of Action: Text and Performance in Restoration Comedy* (Cambridge: Cambridge University Press, 1979), pp. 41–2.

16 *The Roundheads* (by December 1681) portrays an affair between a young royalist and the wife of the puritan grandee John Lambert.

17 Favourable interpretations are provided in Robert Markley, '"Be Impudent, Be Saucy, Forward, Bold, Touzing, and Leud": The Politics of Masculine Sexuality and Feminine Desire in Behn's Tory Comedies', in *Cultural Readings*, pp. 114–40; and Susan J. Owen, 'Sexual Politics and Party Politics in Behn's Drama, 1678–1683', in *Aphra Behn Studies*, pp. 23–4. For a more critical reading, see Nancy Copeland, '"Who Can . . . Her Own Wish Deny?": Female Conduct and Politics in Aphra Behn's *The City-Heiress*', *Restoration and 18th Century Theatre Research*, 2nd series, 8 (1993), 27–49.

18 See above, note 14.

19 Edward Hyde, Earl of Clarendon, *The Life of Edward Earl of Clarendon*, 3 vols. (Oxford, 1759), II, 40.

4

MELINDA S. ZOOK

The political poetry of Aphra Behn

By the late 1670s, England's political culture had witnessed the defeat of consensus and the triumph of contention. The battle over the country's political and religious future pitted the old republicans, the first Whigs, and Protestant nonconformists against Tories, High Anglicans, and Catholics. No public figure, work, or spectacle was immune from the rage of party. Those who made their living by the pen felt this disputatious atmosphere keenly. Many a poet, ideologue, scribbler, and hack drew his pen 'for one Party', or both, or first for one and then for the other. Jonathan Scott may have exaggerated the fluidity of political loyalties in the era of the Popish Plot and Exclusion Crisis with his remark, that '1678's "Whigs" were 1681's "Tories"',[1] but he made an important point so often missed in recent scholarship. Politics was divided into camps in the late Stuart era, but those camps were hardly fortresses. Combatants often slipped back and forth. Writers, in particular, were attuned to the twists and turns of political fortune. Both the poet, Elkanah Settle, and the propagandist, Henry Care, after years of producing very effective Whig polemic, transferred their loyalties (Settle in 1681, Care in 1683) and put their talents to work for the court.[2]

But this was not true for Aphra Behn, one of the most prolific writers of the Restoration. Her politics throughout the 1670s and 1680s remained consistent. True, Behn had positioned herself on the winning side of the debate in the early 1680s when Whig debacle followed Whig debacle. But there she remained even as James II's policies after 1687 made his Tory and Anglican supporters ever more queasy. Behn was not 'disillusioned with James's sagacity' or any more 'tolerant' of the opposition in 1688 than she had been in 1681. Her Toryism was never 'less than wholehearted'.[3] She died in April 1689, an unreformed and unreformable Tory.

In her recent biography of Behn, Janet Todd has described her story as one of a woman 'growing into royalist politics', a 'royalism' that may be described as a brand of Toryism, but was unlike Filmerian ideology of the

Anglican pulpit. The works of Sir Robert Filmer, a staunch civil war royalist, were republished in the 1680s along with a previously unpublished
manuscript, *Patriarcha*. Filmer posited a concept of absolute and irresistible
sovereignty that was heartily embraced by monarchists, especially among
the High Anglican clergy who adhered to the Tory cause. Behn, unlike so
many other Tories, never employed the patriarchal discourse of Filmer.[4] She
was a restless intellectual, continually absorbing new ideas and experiment-
ing with them in her poetry and plays, neither of which can be analysed as
posing fixed ideological statements.[5] But her work did return time and again
to one cherished image: a liberal world of cavalier culture. Her politics, born
of aesthetics more than philosophy, congealed around an imagined world of
aristocratic ideals, pale shades of which were revived briefly with the Restoration in 1660. Not unlike her own history, about which Behn was notoriously
unreliable, she mythologized her nation's past as well. While Behn's work, as
complex and multifaceted as it was, defies any attempt to contain it within
one single determinant, it does display a marked longing for an old order
of gallantry and chivalry and abhorrence for what she saw as the new era
of popular politics and commercial values. Like Edmund Burke, who, one
hundred years later, admonished the new age of 'sophisters, economists, and
calculators', Behn too seemingly stood at a precipice, mourning the loss of
the 'age of chivalry', quarrelling with the new age of religious fanaticism,
mercantile wealth, and political opportunism.[6]

Behn lived in an age of transformative political ideology. John Locke's and
Algernon Sidney's responses to Sir Robert Filmer were written in the 1680s,
and while neither Locke's *Two Treatises of Government* (1690) nor Sidney's
Discourses concerning Government (1698) was published until after Behn's
death, they bear witness to that era's political inspiration on both great
and lesser thinkers. In the pre-Revolution era, men like James Tyrrell, Henry
Care, Robert Ferguson, Thomas Hunt, and Gilbert Burnet set forth the tropes
and idioms of Whig discourse, be it in the language of ancient constitution-
alism, republican virtue, or natural law.[7] Among the Tories, the writings of
Filmer, Roger L'Estrange and a host of Anglican clergy extolled the virtues
of passive obedience, divine right and patriarchal kingship.[8] Behn, who lived
London life to its fullest, frequenting taverns and bookshops, conversing with
young wits from the Inns of Court and collaborating with other literati, was
fully immersed in the political languages of her age. She employed numerous
discursive strategies in her prologues, epilogues, plays, and poetry. Still, her
politics stand somewhat apart from the common political currencies of her
time. While she may have toyed with some of the ideas of the philosopher
Thomas Hobbes, whose defiant materialism, atheism, and moral iconoclasm

had become fashionable at court and fed the sort of ruthless egoism and sexual aggression espoused by Restoration libertines, Behn's politics were ultimately about celebrating a 'golden age': a bygone era, epitomized by the roving cavalier, freed from the tyrannies of custom and his by elite social status to do as he pleased.

Behn's political poetry is particularly useful at illuminating her political vision. While recent scholarship has begun to pay more attention to Behn's poetry, her verse has nonetheless attracted less attention than her plays and prose works. Yet, in both Behn's lyrical and public poetry, her personal voice emerges more distinctly than in her dramatic works. Behn's plays are very good at satirizing, ridiculing, and railing against the politics of the opposition; they are less useful at establishing Behn's political aesthetics. Her poems, particularly those on state occasions, are a better indicator of Behn's true loyalties. Prior to 1685, her political verses focused primarily on the cavalier image. After 1685, the year of both the accession of James II to the throne and the death of the Duke of Monmouth, she dedicated her political poetry to the cause of the monarchy. James II himself epitomized her ideal masculine hero. While other Tories wobbled in their faith in James after 1687, and still others converted to Catholicism, Behn was steadfast, an Anglican latitudinarian, a staunch defender of the Stuart monarchy to the bitter end.

Scholars agree that the restoration of the monarchy in 1660 ushered in a new era of insecurity, uncertainty, and instability. The new realities created by years of war and factionalism could not simply be erased and forgotten by resurrecting the monarchy and its former props, the episcopal church and a loyal aristocracy, 'the fixing of old forms atop new facts', as Steven Zwicker has aptly put it.[9] But the desire was there nonetheless: to go back in time, to recreate an era of harmony between kings and nobles, a deferential and obedient people, mighty bishops and a conforming priesthood. It was in this temper that Charles II's obdurate Parliament passed a series of punitive acts (known collectively as the Clarendon Code) aimed at restricting and limiting the activities of nonconformist Protestants, whom they blamed for the Civil Wars. What the Cavalier Parliament's bitter Clarendon Code could not accomplish through the law could at least be memorialized through a colourful, hedonistic court, centred on its sardonic king and his grandees. At best, this was a parody of a harmonious past: one that never truly existed either in the days of Charles I's cool, neoplatonic court; or his father's court of beautiful and haughty magnates; or even that of Elizabeth's wooing courtiers. But it was nonetheless longed for, an imagined era of kingly magnificence and aristocratic liberality.

But, if the initial return of the Stuart monarchy in 1660 was marked by cavalier hopes, the succeeding months were marred by cavalier frustration and disappointment. The 'royal sufferers', who had lost so much in the cause of their king, found their grievances unanswered and their requests for offices and places ignored, while they watched 'old rebels' embraced and advanced in the new administration.[10] The crown's loyal elites complained bitterly throughout the 1660s that the King had shunned their claims for satisfaction and redress while his former enemies found favour. It is not surprising to find Aphra Behn memorializing the woes of the cavaliers in her song of three stanzas, 'The Complaint of the Poor Cavaliers'. Although it was not published until 1707, the song's central conceit, the lament of the poor cavaliers, speaks to the early Restoration, when it indeed was probably written. It also registers Behn's respect and admiration for the true 'sons of Gaunt', those loyal and valiant, and critiques the new king, who rewarded 'ev'ry Knave' and left 'the poor *Cavalier's* in want' (1, p. 359).

This was not atypical of Behn; her feelings for Charles II were mixed. Her desperate pleas for money during and immediately after her spying mission in Holland for His Majesty's government in 1666 had certainly gone unrequited.[11] She was royalist to be sure, but those she truly idealized were the grandees around the King, not the King, or not always *this King*. In the 1670s and early 1680s, Behn's royalist identity focused on the celebration of the 'young, gay, handsome, witty, rich' elite male.[12] Perhaps epitomized, at least initially for Behn, by John Wilmot, Earl of Rochester, whose 'continental knowledge, glamorous alcoholic style, and aristocratic insouciance', writes Janet Todd, she found irresistible.[13] The cultured male aristocrat, inhabitant of a Hobbesian world without limits, seemed to exemplify personal freedom for Behn: he was free from want (as she was not); free from customary inhibition (as women were not); and above petty nationalism and religious fanaticism. He was witty, manipulative, martial, handsome, almost always a sexual predator. But most importantly, he was a free, generous spirit, bound only by his allegiance to the traditional aristocratic code of honour and loyalty. He was also a man with presence, of a cultivated naturalness and careless nonchalance, or as Behn herself put it, of 'a careless Grandure, and a Generous Air'.[14] Her hero in the *Rover* plays, Wilmore, is probably the best example of Behn's imagined cavalier, though he reappears in various forms in her other plays and in her poetry and novels.

Charles II's natural son, the beautiful Monmouth, brought to court in 1662, may have initially exemplified the ultimate cavalier for Behn. James Scott, Duke of Monmouth and Buccleuch, was one of Behn's most 'abiding political obsessions'.[15] There are clear references to him in every literary

The Illustrious Prince IAMES
Duke of Monmouth. &c.

F.H. Van Houe. Sculp:

1. James Scott, Duke of Monmouth

genre she mastered. In her poetry alone, he is the subject of three of her songs, alluded to in her infamous epilogue to *Romulus and Hersilia* (1682), in 'A Paraphrase on Oenone to Paris' (1680), and in *A Voyage to the Isle of Love* (1685). He reappears in several of her *Aesop's Fables* (1687). More even than 'godlike' James II himself, Monmouth seized and held Behn's imagination even after his less than heroic demise in 1685. But why? Clearly, young Jemmy had the potential of being not only the darling of the people, but also the epitome of the dashing cavalier as well. Charles's favourite son was infinitely intriguing and attractive; a man with so much potential, to whom so much had been given. His mere 'being' was enough to enthral; his impolitic 'becoming' was his own ruin. For only after Monmouth played an active part in his own saga did his tragic flaw become unmistakably apparent. In the end, Behn found him, not unlike both his friends and detractors, deeply disappointing. Behn's obsession with Monmouth was that he could have been, and should have been, all that she admired and adored: the handsome, generous, daring, carefree, martial, and *utterly loyal* cavalier.

In 1662, Monmouth, who had spent his first thirteen years of life in France, was presented to his father, Charles II. The 'astonishing beauty' of the boy's 'outward form' was immediately commented upon along with his surprising lack of mental ability (see figure 1). According to Grammont, while his 'mind said not one word for him', his 'dazzling exterior was that which struck at first. All the good looks of those at court were extinguished by his'.[16] He was given apartments at Whitehall; honours and titles soon followed. In 1663 he received a dukedom (Monmouth) that gave him precedence over all dukes not of royal blood. The same year he was married to the Countess of Buccleuch and thereafter they were created the Duke and Duchess of Buccleuch.

Monmouth was graceful; he danced in court masques. He also proved, in the 1670s, that he was a consummate lover and hardy soldier. According to the Duke of Buckingham, he was 'ever engaged in some amour'.[17] By 1670, he was also captain-general of all the King's forces. Monmouth fought in the Second Dutch War, taking part in the siege of Maestright in July 1673. He was celebrated for his conduct upon his return and more honours were heaped upon him. In the words of Evelyn, 'he was master of the horse, general of the King, his father's army, gentleman of the bedchamber; knight of the garter, chancellor of Cambridge: in a word had accumulations without end'.[18] Heroic, handsome, and Protestant, Monmouth had crowd-appeal as well, a fact not lost on the growing opposition to the court by the late 1670s, nor on anyone else.

But in 1672, when Behn first began to write about young Jemmy, his political aspirations were not obvious. Her '*Song to a* Scotish *tune*' first appeared in her collaborative collection of poems *The Covent Garden Drolery* in 1672 (1, p. 9). Like all her ballads on Monmouth, it was written in a folkloric pastoral mode. As Janet Todd has pointed out, Scottish songs and ballads were popular in Restoration England.[19] Scotland was remote enough to be imagined as a kind of Arcadia, a place of quiet and simple pleasures, and the perfect setting for the pastoral idyll. Behn wrote four folk songs that were supposedly 'set' to a 'Scotch tune'. Three of these are clearly about Monmouth and imitate a Scottish dialect. Behn makes the object of her songs clear by punning on Monmouth's chosen surname, 'Scott'. He was also associated with Scotland as the Duke of Buccleuch, even more so after his defeat of the Scottish Covenanters at Bothwell Bridge in June 1679. In '*Song to a* Scottish *Tune*', Jemmy, the 'finest Swain', is cast as a shepherd, singing and dancing upon the plain; he conquers any and all 'princely Maid[s]' with sighs and looks rather than words. But this perfect pastoral scene is broken in the last stanza when Jemmy, like many a Scottish mercenary, 'to the Wars must go, / His Sheep-hook to a Sword must turn'(1, p. 9). This is probably a reference to Monmouth's fighting in the Low Countries in the early 1670s when the handsome lover and dancer, bright light of the court, became the daring soldier.

By 1681, when Behn published her second ballad on Monmouth, the political climate had radically changed. Rocked first by the Popish Plot scare starting in 1678, and second by the Whig party's campaign to bar the Catholic James, Duke of York, from the throne a year later, London experienced waves of religious hysteria and political partisanship. Monmouth had also changed, allying with the Earl of Shaftesbury and the Whigs. This, in addition to his displays of hubris and ambition, led to Monmouth's deprivation of all 'his places' in 1679 and a short exile.[20] In August and September 1680 Monmouth made his famous progress through the West Country, where he was popularly acclaimed at every stop. In Chichester, ordinary folk drank healths to the 'Protestant Duke' and sang a popular ballad with the refrain, 'Let Monmouth Reign, Let Monmouth Reign'.[21]

Although it has never been entirely clear what promises (if any) were made to Monmouth by Shaftesbury, the wily Earl, an old political veteran, has always been portrayed as Monmouth's seducer, who dangled the images of 'Scepters and Crowns', as Behn put it, in front of the naive Duke. In Dryden's famous poem, *Absalom and Achitophel*, Achitophel (Shaftesbury) tells Absalom (Monmouth) that he is 'Thy Longing Countries Darling and Desire'.[22] For Behn, it was a matter of sexual politics. Old men, no longer sexually attractive or capable, occupy themselves with corrupting the young and vigorous, whom they envy: 'But now the wisely grave, who Love despise, / (Themselves past hope) do busily advise, / Whisper Renown, and Glory in thy Ear' (1, p. 16). Regardless of what the Whigs actually intended for Monmouth, he certainly took the bait, setting himself up as the popular alternative to the Duke of York.

When Behn's 'SONG, *To a New* Scotch *Tune*' appeared as a broadside in 1681 Monmouth was already a popular topic of satire and Tory invective (1, pp. 97–8). The Yale *Poems on Affairs of State* for 1678–81 includes eight Tory poems ridiculing Monmouth.[23] But the style of Behn's 'SONG' is altogether different. Behn's Jemmy is still a delight: 'Of Royal Birth and Breeding, / With ev'ry Beauty Clad: / With ev'ry Grace Exceeding'. He is the 'Pride of all the Youths' and the 'Theam of all our Loves'. But the second stanza registers a note of discord: for on Jemmy's 'Face there lies / A Thousand Smiles betraying.' Monmouth has not simply betrayed all the pretty lasses or even simply his father, Charles II. He has betrayed the cavalier image and ethos. Young Jemmy is no longer just the beautiful swain, graceful dancer, and manly soldier; he has become tool of 'the Busie Fopps of State', who have 'ruin'd his Condition' with 'Glittering Hopes'. He has been reduced and corrupted by 'flattering Knaves and Fools'. Still, unlike his portrayal in so much of the Tory satire of the early 1680s, Behn's Monmouth is a sympathetic creature. He is passive, 'undone' by others. Nor does Behn ridicule Monmouth's intelligence, as so many did.[24] Behn's tone is neither harsh nor partisan; she maintains the pastoral imaging and the tone of a folk ditty. Her song, if anything, is a lament, mourning the ruin of the cavalier ideal.

Behn had Monmouth on her mind in 1682 as well, when she was asked to write the prologue and epilogue for the play *Romulus and Hersilia* (1, pp. 22–4). Like nearly all Behn's prologues and epilogues, these too were satiric and topical. They were also playful and provocative, meant to engage the audience by alluding to and mocking contemporary events and personalities. Thus it is unlikely that Behn thought her reference to Monmouth in the epilogue was terribly harsh, never mind seditious. But the lines, 'And of all Treasons, mine was most accurst; Rebelling 'gainst a *King* and *Father* first / A Sin, which Heav'n nor Man can e'er forgive' (1, p. 24) got her into trouble, if briefly. Both Behn and the actress who spoke the lines were taken into custody and questioned. What action if any was taken against Behn is unclear.[25] The incident seems to have been of little consequence since Behn was bold enough to publish her prologue and epilogue after the performance of the play. But it did make clear that, while Charles II was 'dissatisfied and angry with the duke of Monmouth, yet he is not willing that others should abuse him'.[26] It may also have further dampened Behn's feeling for the King.

Between 1681 and 1684, Whig efforts to obtain the exclusion of the Duke of York from the throne were vanquished; Shaftesbury died in exile; other Whig leaders were executed for their part in the Rye-House Plot, or jailed, or fled abroad. Monmouth had been in the thick of Whig plotting. On 29 June, 1683, a proclamation appeared offering a reward of £500 for his arrest and on 12 July, he was indicted for high treason.[27] Monmouth was aware of the Whig conspiracy to raise an insurrection and may well have known of the design to assassinate the royal brothers at Rye-House Mill, though he denied it. In November 1683 Monmouth met with his father and the Duke of York on several occasions. Their aim was to secure a confession from Monmouth (complete with the names of all those involved in the conspiracy) as well as to reconcile the wayward son with the court. Monmouth hoped for a pardon, though he found the process humiliating. The fact of his confession was published in the Gazette for all his former friends to see. Further, Charles II required Monmouth to rewrite in his own hand a letter drafted for him, acknowledging his role in the plot and informing against others. At first Monmouth complied but he later regretted it and asked the King to return the letter. Indignant, Charles did so but he also banished Monmouth from court and by January 1684 Monmouth found it prudent to go abroad.[28]

In Behn's third song on Monmouth, he himself regrets his fate. 'Silvio's Complaint: A SONG, To a Fine Scotch Tune', which appeared in Poems on Several Occasions in 1684, is a commentary on these events, particularly Monmouth's humiliation and fall from favour (I, pp. 82–4). Behn's Monmouth is still an 'Arcadian Swain' but now he lies 'forlorn', repeatedly sighing, ''Twere better I's were nere Born, / Ere wisht to be a King.' Once again, his problems are blamed on others: 'But Curst be yon Tall Oak / And Old Thirsis be accurst: / There I first my peace forsook, / There I learnt Ambition first.' 'Tall Oak' is almost certainly a reference to Charles II, who was identified with the oak tree after he supposedly escaped capture by hiding in one following the battle of Worcester in 1651.[29] 'Old Thirsis' is probably Shaftesbury. That Behn has Monmouth blame both the King and the Whig leader is telling. She may have felt that Charles was at least partially culpable for Monmouth's downfall by raising his ambition and seeming to prefer him to the true heir apparent, the Duke of York. Her song ends on a note of sympathy for the 'Noble Youth', whose 'Glories lye, / Like Blasted Flowers i'th' Spring.'

Behn's fixation with Monmouth is also clear in her much longer poem, A Voyage to the Isle of Love published in Poems on Several Occasions.[30] Behn is a compassionate observer of youth misled: 'But that which most my pity did imploy, / Was a young Hero, full of Smiles and Joy. / A noble Youth to whom indulgent Heaven, / Had more of Glory then of Virtue given' (I, p. 122). Monmouth is made 'vain' by the shouting rabble and faithless flatterers who stoke his ambition and call him, 'young God of War! / The Cities Champion! And his Countries Hope, / The Peoples Darling, and Religious Prop'. When the Whigs promise him the throne, he does not have sense enough to ask 'which way or how' but 'Credits all'. But with one turn of state, the 'Frenzy's heal'd' and the beautiful youth is abandoned and 'undone' (I, p. 122).

Behn was less sympathetic to Monmouth when he took matters into his own hands and launched his rebellion in June 1685.[31] It was one thing to be a misled youth, swept away by the accolades of the crowd and lies of old men; it was quite another actually to take arms against one's sovereign and lead the fanatical rabble into battle. Monmouth and his ragtag army were easily subdued and the hapless Duke was captured and beheaded. When Behn translated Aesop two years later, she made numerous allusions to late Stuart politics, often changing the moral of the stories to fit contemporary concerns. Once again, she seemed preoccupied by Monmouth, but her tone had changed. She no longer indulged Monmouth as the war hero deceived, but rather as a 'usurper' whose fate was richly deserved. So Fable xxx ends with the moral: 'A Traytor all behold with just disdaine,/ Who basely quits his cause and sovereigne' (I, p. 241).

Monmouth survived in Behn's imagination. He is the character Cesario, 'that lovely composition of Man and Angel', in her long epistolary novel, *Love-Letters between a Noble-Man and his Sister* (1684–7), and he probably inspired her portrayal of Nathaniel Bacon in the *The Widdow Ranter* (1688).[32] Had he remained loyal, 'this quondam Duke, darling of his Father, and the ladys, being extraordinarily handsome, and adroit; an excellent souldier, & dancer', as Evelyn put it, 'a favorite of the people, of an Easy nature', he would have been the exemplar of the brilliant cavalier, 'happy indeed above a Monarch'.[33] Instead he dashed all Behn's expectations. Her verses on Monmouth were not sarcastic attacks. They stand out as distinctly different from most of the Tory propaganda on Monmouth. She admired his beauty, made little of his lack of intelligence, and pitied his ruin.

Behn had a lot of reasons to admire the Duke of York, made James II upon his brother's death in February 1685. After all, he had admired her, or rather her play, *The Rover* (1677). In 1681, she dedicated *The Second Part of the Rover* to His Royal Highness, the Duke of York, during his exile in Scotland. The dedication made numerous parallels between James and Behn's cavalier hero, Wilmore, both wanderers, ever constant in their loyalty. Undoubtedly, James's accession to the throne was a momentous event for Behn, and she must have felt as if she were on the verge of a new beginning. Charles II's court may have been bright and interesting in the 1660s, but it had lost much of its glamour as factionalism and religious hysteria became ever more ardent in the late 1670s. Behn had found Charles's sacrifice of the Catholic Lord Stafford in 1680 to the 'lawless people's rage' a disgusting display.[34] And, although Charles II had done much in the last years of his life to defend his brother's inheritance and defeat the Whigs, his court and his coffers had never really been open to Behn. His sudden death could change her fortunes. Behn had certainly proclaimed her loyalty to the Duke of York throughout the years. Might he be more open, if not to her presence at court, then at least to patronizing her art?

Charles's death and James's accession afforded Behn the occasion to write public poetry, to become a panegyrist, to celebrate the monarchy in the most serious of veins. True, in her songs, prologues and epilogues, and plays she had railed against the opponents of the court and affirmed her robust royalism time and again, but her manner was playful and satiric. Now was the moment of utmost gravity, and only the most eloquent tone and awesome imaging would speak to these occasions of high political import.

Behn's pindaric on the death of Charles II begins as a rather bleak, dreamy vision that moves from Behn's own bed, from which she is awoken from 'painful sleep' by the news of the King's death, to the 'royal bed', where 'Officious Angels catch his *dying sighs*'.[35] While the poem eventually compares Charles to Caesar, Christ, Lazarus, and Moses, Behn wonders why no 'dire warnings' foretold the King's death, amazed that such a monarch could die while 'the sun and tide their constant courses keep.' Is she questioning Charles's greatness, if for a moment? The poem brightens as Behn turns to 'good JOSHUA', James, to whom Charles, like Moses, 'resigns his sway'. It ends, with 'death and midnight' hanging on every face around the King's bed. His death, like Christ's, rends the temple veil, so she imagines, thus declaring 'CHARLES a God! And JAMES a Monarch too!' (I, p. 193).

Behn throws off her elegiac tone altogether in the poem appended to her pindaric on Charles entitled, '*To His Sacred MAJESTY, KING JAMES II*'. Here Behn celebrates the young James's '*Glorious Deeds in Arms*' (I, p. 194) as well as his patient suffering during the Exclusion Crisis. The poem's last stanza makes it clear that James is the 'Sacred Promis'd Prince' that prophets foretold. Like the birth of Christ, his accession should be hailed with a star of '*that divine and gracious influence*' (I, p. 194). Apparently, Behn felt that James's elevation was of more divine interest than Charles's death.

Behn's next effort was addressed to Charles's widow, Catherine of Braganza, and, like her pindaric on the King's death, it starts with Behn herself.[36] This time she begins by apologizing to the Queen dowager for writing about Charles first, saying, '*Griefs* have self-interest too as well as *Joy*' (I, p. 196). This odd and interesting line suggests that, like play-writing, elegies earn money and that this consideration had informed her first response to the King's demise. But, having disposed of her duty, to both herself and the King, she now ponders the grief of the Queen. Naturally, Behn indulges in hyperbole, comparing Catherine's patient suffering during the Popish Plot crisis (in which she was accused of intending to poison the King) to Christ's passion. The poem ends with Catherine likened twice to the Virgin Mary, first at the foot of the cross, and secondly, holding Christ's dead body, pietà-style.

The baroque imagery of Behn's verse to the Queen was completely outdone by her ode on James's coronation.[37] At nearly a thousand lines, it is her 'longest and most ambitious pindaric poem', 'a baroque extravaganza', a monument to hyperbole.[38] Unfortunately, while Behn's true joy at the event of her hero's coronation is unfeigned, the poem itself is heavy, plodding, and stilted. Its fulsome praise and exaggerated diction have lost much of their appeal today. But Behn's hope, 'that those who read in Ages distant hence / May *feel* the very *Zeal* with which I write' (I, p. 201), is realized. Her 'zeal' for James seems to come from two sources: firstly, that the man/king/god that Behn celebrates contains and exceeds all the attributes of the ultimate cavalier; and secondly, that she thought she had a real chance of sustained patronage with this king. The James that Behn's ode acclaims is a military hero, '*the rough, stern Hero*' (I, p. 205), and a superhuman lover whose love-making is so 'fierce' that only his goddess-like Queen, Mary Beatrice of Modena, who is likened to both Venus and Juno, can withstand its intensity. James's accession makes his old opponents 'gnash their Teeth, and suffer Hell before their time', while the mighty, the brave, the long-suffering cavaliers 'are glad and gay'. A good portion of the poem describes the coronation procession, naming and praising each of the processing nobles; clearly these were the kind of men ('*generous, gay, and great*') that Behn had long celebrated and hoped to please. After all, they too might 'a noble song require'.

In a far less buoyant tone, there are several points in the poem where Behn refers to her own sad state, hinting none too subtly at her desire for princely patronage. In the eleventh stanza, she mourns the fact that she is not closer to the beautiful Mary Beatrice, but instead sits in 'silent dull obscurity' which sets her 'at *distance*, much too far' (I, p. 208). Later, after the poem describes her losing sight of the royal couple, Behn asserts that although she may 'hover' near royal magnificence, like 'hoping Lovers who at distance gaze', she is not truly part of it, but rather must 'toil for Life all day' (I, p. 212). Quite naturally, Behn, often in debt, was looking for a little steady patronage.

Unfortunately for Behn, there is little evidence that James II did anything to bridge this 'distance' between her and the court, or otherwise boost her status, wealth, or health. Behn's most famous play, *The Rover*, was performed at court twice, but the playwright herself was never there. Although an anonymous 'lady' poet suggested that Behn's coronation poem was so grand an effort that she should be rewarded with something like a house ('a sweet retreat') nothing of the sort was ever forthcoming.[39] Still, Behn was a survivor, and she moved on to other things, publishing translations and novels. She remained an undaunted royalist. When another opportunity to celebrate monarchy arose, she was there.

In January 1688, Evelyn recorded the news of the Queen's pregnancy.[40] Considering the fact that Mary, James's Queen Consort, had borne four babies since marriage (not one of whom survived infancy) and had four miscarriages, Behn's congratulatory poem on the 'universal hopes of all loyal persons for a Prince of Wales' was a bold and presumptuous act.[41] She not only presumed the live birth of a boy, she also wrote a highly political poem which, more than merely celebrating Mary's pregnancy, commented on James's increasingly difficult position. The poem begins by likening the royal child's forthcoming birth to the Second Coming, 'so long Expected, so much Wanted too' (I, p. 294). This remark – as Behn well knew – was highly ironic since the Queen's pregnancy was hardly expected and certainly unwanted. By 1688 the political nation had become both frightened and alienated by the Romanizing policies of James II. Still, it could rest peacefully knowing that James's eldest daughter, the Protestant Princess Mary of Orange, would succeed her father. The birth of a son to be raised a Catholic changed everything, and raised the possibility of an endless stream of Catholic monarchs. Behn was keenly aware of the highly charged atmosphere in which the Queen's pregnancy was announced. She played on it, pointedly, knowingly, asking why so few poets had written on 'a *Theam* so glorious and sublime?' Throughout the poem, Behn insists that the boy's 'Coming is designed'. He will 'calm the Murmurs', stifle 'factious Crouds', and overthrow 'All the Designs aspiring STATES propose' (I, pp. 294–5). This last line is a clear reference to the ambitions of Mary's husband, Prince William of Orange, who was in communication with alienated elites.[42] Behn happily warns those conspiring with Prince William that indeed the 'jig is up'. The birth of this child, she asserts, will save the monarchy of James II. He [the child] alone 'arrests the *Wheel*, in spight of *Fortunes's* Hand / And leaves the World's vast Bus'ness at a Stand' (I, p. 295). In other words, James is doomed but for this baby, who is 'A young APOLLO, rising from the Gloom, / Dress'd in his Father's brightest *Rays*' (I, p. 295). He shall disperse 'the baneful Mists of Night' and 'bless the Earth with New-*created* LIGHT' (I, p. 295). Behn also put in a plug for herself with the unborn child, on whom so much was riding, hoping that he will some day be a liberal patron of the Muses. Then 'POETS shall by *Patron* Princes live' (I, p. 296).

Fate is also a major theme in Behn's congratulatory poem on the birth of the Prince of Wales.[43] Her bold gamble (that the child would be a boy) paid off and on 10 June 1688, James Francis Edward was born, much to the dismay of all those who thought the Queen was far too weakened by her many miscarriages and bouts of illness to produce a healthy child.[44] His birth also put an end to the willingness of all those content to wait out James's reign with the knowledge that the Princess and Prince of Orange would succeed him. Gleefully, Behn claimed that she had foretold the birth of the Prince of Wales, hailing this 'Triumph over FATE' (I, p. 297). Once again, Behn implies that James's reign was heading for disaster only to be rescued by this child, who is again likened to Christ, come to save the world. But Behn was not satisfied simply to celebrate the birth of the Prince, she also used this very public moment to voice her concerns. Naturally, she mocks the dashed ambitions of William of Orange ('Methinks I hear the *Belgick LION* Roar, / And Lash his *Angry Tail* against the Shore', I, p. 298)[45], but she also has some advice for the King. When she notes that in this child's eyes one sees that he is 'Brave and the Forgiving KIND' (I, p. 298), she is probably referring to James's harsh treatment of the seven bishops whom he had imprisoned in the Tower for questioning his authority. The King, she seems to be saying, was undoubtedly brave in his soldiering days, but is now less than kind.[46] The unity of the nation requires forgiveness.

It was probably Behn's concern over the nation's growing disunity that prompted what at first reads as a troubling allusion to Catholicism. In the fifth stanza, she likens the child to Christ, who in the words of John the Baptist (Matthew 3: 12) will 'thoroughly purge the Floor or Land, / Gathering the Wheat in the Granary'. 'Then', she asserts, 'all *One FAITH*, at least *One SOUL* shall be'. Is this last line suggesting that the Prince will return England to the Catholic Church only at once to retreat from this suggestion? Sara Mendelson believes that the line merely proclaims Behn's own true Catholic sympathies.[47] But Behn probably remained an Anglican. After all, she was using an authorized Anglican Bible.[48] So is this line, as Maureen Duffy wonders, 'a clumsy slip retrieved or deliberate?' It is hard to imagine Behn being so sloppy. Janet Todd believes that the poem was meant solely to please James, not the public, who were troubled enough by the whole prospect of a Catholic heir and did not need Behn to frighten them further.[49] But Behn wrote to be published and, whereas her first objective may have been to gratify James, her second was to sell copies. Behn's desire, then, was to unify: to declare that this Prince would not necessarily demand national conversion to Catholicism, but that by his example, by his sheer magnificence and magnanimity, he would unite the English spiritually. Behn was trying to soothe fears not aggravate them.[50]

But Behn's hopeful child did not prevent his father's downfall. His birth was the very catalyst for the Revolution that brought William and Mary of

Orange to power in the winter of 1688/9. If there was to be a Protestant succession, the nation's elite had no choice but to invite the Prince of Orange and his armies to invade. Short in duration and minimal in its violence, the Revolution nevertheless overthrew a legitimate monarch and installed a new constitutionally-altered dual monarchy.[51] The accession of William and Mary was to contemporaries, as Behn put it, a 'Universal turn',[52] one greeted enthusiastically by most English, but deplored naturally by Behn. Still, her fame as public poet led to a surprise request. Some time in the first months of 1689 the Reverend Gilbert Burnet (later Bishop of Salisbury) paid a visit to Aphra Behn. His mission was probably to ask her to write in favour of the new monarchy. That he did so attests to her renown and skill as a poet on the affairs of state. It also signifies just how fluid party loyalties remained. Behn was a notorious Tory and supporter of James, and yet she was being solicited to endorse the Revolution and acclaim the usurpers. Numerous other Tories and former allies of James II had done so. Why not she? But Behn refused. Instead his visit provoked her to write what were her final and most poignant public poems.

Behn's 'A Congratulatory POEM TO HER Sacred Majesty QUEEN MARY, UPON HER ARRIVAL in ENGLAND' was published shortly after the proclamation of William III and Mary II in February 1689 (I, pp. 304–7). While the poem does celebrate Mary, as the daughter of James II, it also records Behn's deep sadness at the turn of events that swept away her beloved king and blew in the 'Belgick lion' (William), whom she abhorred. The poem begins with Behn describing her own attempt to leave London, to sail down the Thames to a 'lone retreat'. Depressed about her 'Unhappy dear Lov'd Monarch's Fate', she seeks solitude and vows never to write again 'fruitless Songs' on the affairs of this 'faithless' isle. But, as she goes down the Thames, Mary is triumphantly carried up, to 'Loud Sounds of Joy'. Behn finds herself wishing to be part of this new 'brooding spring' that Mary's arrival anticipates. Other poets have already published songs in celebration of the new monarchy; yet she has resisted, still loyal to James II. But 'now I wish'd among the Crouds to Adore, / And constant wishing did increase my Power' (I, p. 305). Thus, after asking James for his permission to honour his daughter ('Maria so Divine a part of You'), she spends the second half of the poem celebrating the new Queen. But Behn's Mary is not William's Mary, rather she is 'illustrious daughter of a King' (I, p. 305).[53]

Still, Behn's praise of Mary is muted. Unlike Mary Beatrice, she is not compared to Juno or the Virgin. Mary of Orange has conquered with her eyes, her charms and her smiles. But it is clear that Behn wishes that she had not. It is a 'face that awes and charms our hearts' only because it mirrors that of her great father. Behn admonishes Mary to remember him:

But if the Monarch in your Looks we find,
Behold him yet more glorious in your Mind;
'Tis there His God-like Attributes we see
A Gracious Sweetness, Affability,
A Tender Mercy and True Piety.

(I, p. 306)

This was certainly a minority opinion in 1689.[54] Unlike so many, including over half of the nobles Behn lauded in her depiction of James's coronation, she had not given up on James II. And in the end, she died a Jacobite. Her poem on Mary II is not a celebration of the new regime (she never mentions William). At times the tone is hardly celebratory at all. Rather it sighs with heavy resignation and takes the line that many of the 'Maryites' (supporters of Mary's claim to the throne over William's) took at the Convention Parliament of January 1689: if not the father, then at least the daughter.

In the last months of her life, as her biographers tell us, Behn was ill, probably poor, and almost assuredly depressed over the political turnabout.[55] But Behn in 1689 was not simply mourning the loss of that cavalier world that she had once so ardently celebrated or indeed the ousting of James II and all she had once thought his reign promised. In the end, as her last poem suggests, Behn was musing over the role of the writer in the recent turn of events and the power of printed persuasion. How was it that the pens of the 'Whigs' (whom she identified with merchant-class interest, lower-class fanaticism, and cultural provincialism) had persuaded, charmed, and seduced the nation into rebellion? Why had royalists like her failed? No doubt Behn's thoughts on the power of persuasion were sparked by Gilbert Burnet's invitation.

In 1689 Gilbert Burnet had already had a remarkable career, as a churchman, a scholar, a historian, and the confidant of powerful men; he was no less notorious to the reading public than Behn herself. He had mastered Latin, Greek, and Hebrew; he had studied law, chemistry, philosophy, and European history; he had travelled through Europe and lived in the United Provinces; and at various times he had gained the confidence of Charles II, the Duke of York, Louis XIV, the Duke of Monmouth, the Whig leaders (William, Lord Russell, and the Earl of Essex), and in the years immediately preceding the Revolution, the Prince and Princess of Orange. His intelligence, his moderate religious and political principles, and his able pen were valued assets in the first age of party when the printed word proved more powerful than the sword.[56] Behn may have been flattered by Burnet's request, but she did not comply. She would not hail the so-called 'Protestant Deliverer', William III, or sanction revolution. Instead, she addressed her final public poem to Burnet himself. It is he, she claims, who has conquered the nation, conquered it with his golden pen.

Behn's poem to Burnet provides an interesting contrast to another poem she wrote shortly before the Revolution. In her 'POEM TO Sir Roger L'Estrange, ON HIS THIRD PART OF THE HISTORY of the TIMES', Behn celebrated the work of the Tory polemicist (I, pp. 291–3). Like herself, L'Estrange had tirelessly defended the royalist cause and hammered that of the Whigs. The third volume of his weekly, the *Observator*, covering the period from February 1685 to March 1687, had contained a *Brief History of the Times*, in which L'Estrange claimed to have solved the mystery of the strange death of the Middlesex Justice of the Peace, Sir Edmund Berry Godfrey in 1678. L'Estrange postulated that Godfrey was not the victim of popish plotters, as the Whigs would have it, but of suicide.[57] Behn's paean to L'Estrange praises him for advancing the 'Truth' and 'rescuing the *World* from stupid ignorance' (I, p. 291). In fact, Behn uses the term 'truth' or 'true' seven times to describe L'Estrange's history, arguing that no one could possibly question the reasonableness of his argument: 'The *Picture* you have drawn is so Just, so True / We have the very *Fact* it self in view' (I, p. 293).

Burnet was an accomplished historian and propagandist as well. He had already published two volumes of his highly acclaimed *History of the Reformation of the Church of England*.[58] While in exile between 1686 and 1687, he wrote a number of pamphlets aimed at undermining James II.[59] In the summer of 1688, he had helped to 'shorten and enliven' the final draft of William's *Declaration of Reasons* which did much to 'gain the people's Affections' and win the propaganda war against James II.[60] He also published a short but persuasive defence of the Revolution that argued that James's arbitrary actions had led to the 'total subversion of the government' and that popular resistance to him was perfectly justified.[61] Burnet was clearly 'the prince's chief of propaganda' in the crucial months of the Revolution.[62]

Thus the chasm between the political visions promoted by L'Estrange and Burnet was gaping. Truth and falsehood mattered to Behn. L'Estrange was right; Burnet wrong. She realized that what had triumphed in 1688/89 was not the 'truth', but the sophistry of the writer persuasively to tell one side of the story. Lies were easily digested by the public as long as they were eloquently dressed, reasonably argued, and disguised as truth. Of course, Behn had long understood how the unthinking crowd was easily won by Whig propaganda, but Burnet and his 'Immortal Wit' could not be so quickly dismissed. Even she found his rhetoric and his fame seductive: 'The Inspiring Mind Illustrious, Rich, and Great; / A Mind that can inform your wond'rous Pen' (I, p. 307). Her poem to him alternates between eroticizing his offer, using the language of seduction; and militarizing it, using the language of siege and conquest. But Behn is not a 'Maid undone' yielding to his 'Language soft as Love' (1, p. 308). Neither is she the gullible Monmouth, flattered by dreams of fame, nor the once martial James II, frightened into retreat. She will hold sway and refuse the overtures of the most important man of the Revolution. Her 'Loyalty', unlike so many others, 'Commands with Pious Force' (1, p. 309).

The wry irony and none-too-subtle sarcasm which permeate Behn's last poem could not have been lost on Burnet. Those who knew Behn's politics knew exactly what she meant by "Tis to your Pen, Great Sir, the Nation owes / For all the Good this Mighty Change has wrought' (1, p. 309). Typically, Behn is modest about her own talents, even guilefully asserting that she had not hitherto dared to write public verse ('To Sing of Heroes and of Kings') but only dabbled in the more feminine pastoral. Now, thanks to Burnet, 'She [Behn] is allowed a more exalted thought/ She will be valu'd now as Currant Coyn' (1, p. 307). But Behn's loyalty could not be bought and sold on the streets. Though Behn makes herself sound pitiful ('The Brieze that wafts the Crowding Nation o'er, / Leaves me unpity'd far behind', 1, p. 309), she was anything but. Behn in 1689 was not weakened, or humbled, or pitied. Burnet would not be able to enact yet another miraculous deathbed conversion as he had in the case of the notorious libertine Rochester.[63] Unlike the rest of the 'giddy world' Behn was not so easily seduced, conquered, and manipulated by the 'strange effects' of Burnet's 'Seraphick Quill' (1, p. 309). In the end, her vision of the world of politics was unredeemed by the turn of 'fortune's hand'.

NOTES

1 'But he who draws his Pen for one Party, must expect to make Enemies of the other.' John Dryden, 'To the Reader', *Absalom and Achitophel* (1681); Jonathan Scott, *Algernon Sidney and the Restoration Crisis 1677–1683* (Cambridge: Cambridge University Press, 1991), p. 47.

2 As Whigs, both Settle and Care were mocked by Behn. Settle in her epilogue to *The Second Part of the Rover* (1681) and Care in her *Prologue to Romulus* (1682). About these two men, see F. C. Brown, *Elkanah Settle, His Life and Works* (Chicago: University of Chicago Press, 1910); and Lois G. Schwoerer, *The Ingenious Mr Henry Care, Restoration Publicist* (Baltimore: The Johns Hopkins University Press, 2002).

3 Sara Heller Mendelson, *The Mental World of Stuart Women* (Amherst: University of Massachusetts Press, 1987), p. 174; Janet Todd and Virginia Crompton, 'Rebellion's Antidote: A New Attribution to Aphra Behn', *Notes & Queries* n.s. 38 (June 1991), 177; Arlen Feldwick, 'Wits, Whigs, and Women: Domestic Politics as Anti-Whig Rhetoric in Aphra Behn's Town Comedies' in *Political Rhetoric, Power and Renaissance Women*, eds. Carole Levin and Patricia A. Sullivan (Albany: State University of New York Press, 1995), p. 226.

4 Todd, p. 6.

5 On this point, also see Hughes, *The Theatre of Aphra Behn* (Basingstoke: Palgrave, 2001), pp. 10–11.

6 Edmund Burke, *Reflections on the Revolution in France* (Indianapolis: The Bobbs-Merrill Co., 1985), p. 86.

7 On Whig ideology, see Janelle Greenberg, *The Radical Face of the Ancient Constitution* (Cambridge: Cambridge University Press, 2001), ch. 6; Richard Ashcraft, *Revolutionary Politics and Locke's Two Treatises of Government* (Princeton: Princeton University Press, 1986); David Wootton, ed., *Republicanism, Liberty, and Commercial Society* (Stanford: Stanford University Press, 1994); Melinda Zook, *Radical Whigs and Conspiratorial Politics in Late Stuart England* (University Park, PA: Penn State Press, 1999).

8 Tory ideology remains understudied but see Gordon Schochet, *Patriarchalism in Political Thought* (Oxford: Basil Blackwell, 1975); Phillip Harth, *Pen for a Party: Dryden's Tory Propaganda in its Context* (Princeton: Princeton University Press, 1993); Tim Harris, 'Tories and the Rule of Law in the Reign of Charles II', *Seventeenth Century*, 8 (1993), 9–27.

9 Steven N. Zwicker, 'Irony, Modernity, and Miscellany: Politics and Aesthetics in the Stuart Restoration,' in *Politics and the Political Imagination in Later Stuart Britain*, ed. Howard Nenner (Rochester: University of Rochester Press, 1997), p. 182. Also see Jessica Munns, 'Change, Skepticism, and Uncertainty,' in *The Cambridge Companion to English Restoration Theatre*, ed. Deborah Payne Fisk (Cambridge: Cambridge University Press, 2000), pp. 142–57.

10 John Evelyn, *The Diary*, ed. E. S. de Beer, 6 vols. (Oxford: Clarendon Press, 1955), III, p. 493.

11 Behn's letters are reprinted in W. J. Cameron, *New Light on Aphra Behn* (Auckland: University of Auckland Press, 1961).

12 *The False Count*, VI: 2.1.23.

13 Todd, p. 194.

14 *A Pindarick Poem ON THE HAPPY CORONATION Of His Most SACRED MAJESTY JAMES II,'* (1685), I, p. 213.

15 Janet Todd, *Gender, Art and Death* (New York: Continuum, 1993), p. 36.

16 Grammont quoted in George Roberts, *The Life, Progresses, and Rebellion of James, Duke of Monmouth*, 2 vols. (London: Longman, Brown, Green, and Longmans, 1844), I, p. 17.

17 Buckingham quoted in *DNB*, s.v., 'James Scott'.

18 Evelyn, *The Diary* IV, pp. 456–7.

19 *Works*, I, p. 375.

20 Narcissus Luttrell, *A Brief Historical Relation of State Affairs*, 6 vols. (Oxford: Oxford University Press, repr. 1974), I, p. 27.

21 *Calendar of State Papers Domestic*, 23, p. 406.

22 Dryden, *Absalom & Achitophel* (1681), line 232.

23 *Poems on Affairs of State: Augustan Satirical Verse, 1660–1714*, II, *1678–1681*, ed. Elias F. Mengel, Jr (New Haven: Yale University Press, 1965). Henceforth cited as *POAOS*.

24 For example, in 'Rochester's Farewell', (1680) possibly penned by Rochester himself, Monmouth is a 'dull unthinking thing' with a 'thick impenetrable skull'. In the anonymous, 'Satyr Unmuzzled' (1680) he is simply a 'booby', *POAOS*, II, 217, 209.

25 The incident is reported in the *Newdigate Newsletters* (29 July 1682), LC 5/191, 100; and *True Protestant Mercury* (12–16 August 1682). The charge against Behn was that she had 'committed several misdemeanors and made abusive reflections upon Persons of Quality'. The Office of Revels, PRO 5/191.

26 Charles II is referring to Dryden's satiric portrayal of Monmouth in *The Duke of Guise*. *Newgate Newsletters*, LC 5/144, p. 278.

27 Luttrell, *State Affairs*, I, pp. 263, 266–7.

28 Roberts, *Life, Progress*, I, pp. 160–71.

29 In Behn's translation of Abraham Cowley's 'Of Plants' (1689) the oak is praised for securing 'Great *Charles*' and sheltering him in its loyal branches (I, p. 311).

30 I, pp. 102–59. This a loose translation of Abbé Paul Tallemant's *Voyage de l'Isle d' Amour*.

31 Monmouth and a small band of followers landed in Lyme Regis in June 1685. While Monmouth succeeded in gathering an army of peasants and tradesmen, almost no men of quality joined his rebellion. His army was crushed at the Battle of Sedgemoor on 6 July. See Robin Clifton, *The Last Popular Rebellion: The Western Rising of 1685* (New York: St Martin's Press, 1984).

32 *Works*, II, p. 17.

33 Evelyn, *The Diary*, IV, p. 456; *Works*, II, p. 438.

34 'A POEM TO Sir Roger L'Estrange, ON THE THIRD PART OF THE HISTORY. Relating to the DEATH OF SIR EDMUND BURY-GODFREY', I, p. 292.

35 'A PINDARICK ON THE DEATH Of Our Late SOVEREIGN: *With an Ancient Prophecy on His* Present Majesty', I, p. 193.

36 'A POEM HUMBLY DEDICATED *To the Great Patern of* Piety and Virtue CATHERINE QUEEN DOWAGER. ON THE DEATH OF HER DEAR LORD and HUSBAND King CHARLES II', I, pp. 196–9.

37 'A Pindarick Poem ON THE HAPPY CORONATION Of His most SACRED MAJESTY JAMES II', I, pp. 200–21.

38 Todd, pp. 123, 346.

39 Todd, pp. 348–9; Maureen Duffy, *The Passionate Shepherdess: Aphra Behn 1640–1689* (London: Cape, 1977), pp. 246–7.

40 Evelyn, *The Diary*, IV, p. 567.

41 'A CONGRATULATORY POEM TO HER MOST Sacred Majesty, ON THE UNIVERSAL HOPES OF ALL *LOYAL PERSONS* FOR A PRINCE OF WALES' I, pp. 294–6. On Mary's pregnancies see, John Miller, *James II* (New Haven: Yale University Press, 2000), p. 180.

42 See W. A. Speck, 'The Orangist Conspiracy against James II', *Historical Journal*, 30 (1987), pp. 457–62.

43 'A CONGRATULATORY POEM TO THE King's Sacred Majesty, On the Happy BIRTH of the PRINCE of WALES,' I, pp. 297–9.

44 On the announcement of the birth, see Evelyn, *The Diary* IV, p. 587. On the Queen's health see, Gilbert Burnet, *A Supplement to Burnet's History of his Own Time*, ed. H. C. Foxcroft, 3 vols. (Oxford: Clarendon Press, 1922), III, pp. 152–3, 262.

45 The lion was the symbol of the Netherlands and used here to represent William of Orange. In 1686 Behn copied a satire on John Dryden in her commonplace book. The last two lines of the poem warn Dryden that he will only 'flourish' until he hears 'the Belgic Lion roar'. Bod. MS Firth c.16. Behn must have remembered

these lines and here mocks them and William. She, in turn, was mocked in 'A Congratulatory Poem to His Highness, the Prince of Orange upon His Arrival in London' (1688) which contained the couplet, 'Methinks I heard the Belgick Lyon roar / Landed in Triumph on the British shoar.'

46 On the trial of the Seven Bishops, see Miller, *James II*, pp. 185–8; Todd and Duffy also interpret this line as a reference to the King's treatment of the bishops, Todd, p. 403; Duffy, *The Passionate Shepherdess*, p. 274.

47 Mendelson, *The Mental World*, p. 179. On Behn's Catholic sympathies also see, Alison Shell, 'Popish Plots: *The Feign'd Curtizans* in contex' and Mary Ann O'Donnell, 'Private jottings, public utterances: Aphra Behn's published writings in her commonplace book', in *Aphra Behn Studies*, pp. 30–49, 285–309.

48 Janet Todd makes this point along with the fact that Behn was buried at Westminster Abbey in *Works*, I, p. xiv. One also has to consider Behn's rather strange 'Paraphrase of the Lord's Prayer' (1685) which certainly reads like a proclamation of her Anglican latitudinarianism.

49 Duffy, *The Passionate Shepherdess*, p. 274; Todd, p. 403.

50 That Behn was trying not to frighten her readers is also evidenced by the fact that she left off the last line of Matthew 3: 12, where John declares that He who follows him will 'burn up the chaff with unquenchable fire'. If the Catholic child is likened to Christ, then this is a very threatening image to nonconformists and Anglicans. Since the 'Smithfield fires' (the burning of Protestant martyrs under Mary I) fire had a particularly powerful and frightening association in Protestant hagiography.

51 On the Revolution see, W. A. Speck, *Reluctant Revolutionaries* (Oxford: Oxford University Press, 1988); on the Revolutionary Settlement see, Lois G. Schwoerer, *The Declaration of Rights, 1689* (Baltimore: The Johns Hopkins University Press, 1981).

52 'A PINDARIC POEM TO THE **Reverend Doctor Burnet** ON THE Honour he did me of Enquiring after me and my MUSE', I, pp. 307–10.

53 Mary was always depicted as either the wife of William III or as the daughter of James II, depending on the political stance of the writer. See Melinda Zook, 'History's Mary: The Propagation of Queen Mary II, 1689–94', in *Women and Sovereignty*, ed. Louise Fradenburg (Edinburgh: Edinburgh University Press, 1992).

54 Sentiment much more indicative of the general mood of the nation was captured in the verse collection, *The Muses Farewell to Popery and Slavery* (1688).

55 Todd, p. 425; Mendelson, *The Mental World*, p. 177.

56 On Burnet's life, see T. E. S. Clark, *A Life of Gilbert Burnet, Bishop of Salisbury* (Cambridge at the University Press, 1907).

57 The suicide theory, however, contradicted the evidence that Godfrey was strangled first and then run through with his own sword. See John Miller, *Popery and Politics in England*, pp. 158–69.

58 Both Burnet's first and second volumes (published in 1679 and 1681 respectively) of his *History of the Reformation* were received with enthusiasm. On their reception, see Clark, *Life*, p. 157. The third volume of his *History* was published in 1714.

59 Gilbert Burnet, *Some letters; containing an account of what seemed most remarkable in Switzerland, Italy, etc.* (Amsterdam, 1686); [Gilbert Burnet], *Reasons*

against the repealing the acts of parliament concerning the test (1687); [Gilbert Burnet] *An Enquiry into the reasons for abrogation of the test* (Amsterdam, 1688).

60 The full title of William's declaration is *Declaration of His Highness William Henry, Prince of Orange, of the Reasons Inducing Him to Appear in Arms in the Kingdom of England for Preserving of the Protestant Religion and for Restoring the Lawes and Liberties of England, Scotland, and Ireland* (October 1688). The words 'shorten and enliven' are Lois Schwoerer's, see her, 'Propaganda and the Revolution of 1688–89', *American Historical Review*, 82 (1977), 852. Ignatius White, Marquis d'Albeville, the English ambassador to The Hague, thought the *Declaration* would win the 'affections of the people' (Schwoerer, 'Propaganda', p. 852).

61 Gilbert Burnet, *An Enquiry into the Measures of Submission to the Supream Authority* (London, 1688). Virginia Crompton is incorrect when she argues that Burnet believed that 'the pretense of the Stuarts to produce a male heir is the *sole reason* for the dissolution of the subject's allegiance to the king', '"For when the act is done and finish't cleane, / what should the poet doe but shift the scene?":propaganda, professionalism, and Aphra Behn', *Aphra Behn Studies*, p. 141. While the *Enquiry* does further the rumour that the Prince of Wales was an impostor, the central argument of Burnet's text concerns James's dissolution of the ancient constitution and the subject's right to resist.

62 Tony Clayton, *William III and the Godly Revolution* (Cambridge: Cambridge University Press, 1996), p. 29.

63 On Burnet's famous conversion of the deist Rochester to 'a full persuasion of Christianity', as Burnet put it, see Clark, *Life*, pp. 164–5.

5

SUSAN J. OWEN

Behn's dramatic response to Restoration politics

Aphra Behn was a staunch Tory at the time when Toryism first developed. In the late 1670s and early 1680s, the country was in the grip of the Exclusion Crisis, as Whigs tried to exclude the Catholic James from succeeding to his brother Charles II's throne, and Tories defended the Stuarts. To put it crudely, Whigs (while mostly monarchists not republicans) saw Catholicism and arbitrary government as the main threats, and prioritized patriotism and parliamentary 'liberties'. Tories placed a premium on kingly authority and class hierarchy, seeing the Whig challenge as raising the spectre of renewed civil war.[1] As the political balance shifted to and fro, many dramatists shifted their allegiance with it; but Behn was a more fervent Tory than the rest. So staunch was she, indeed, that in August 1682 a warrant was issued for her arrest for effectively being too vehement in the King's support. She had written an epilogue to the anonymous play *Romulus and Hersilia* in which she criticized Charles's bastard son, the Duke of Monmouth, for being in league with the Whigs. Charles was not ready for such assiduity.[2] Even at the end of her life, when she was ill and poor and the Stuarts had been deposed by William of Orange in the so-called Glorious Revolution of 1688, Behn refused an invitation to write verse glorifying William's accession and instead wrote an ambiguous poem in which the refusal to praise William at all was the most remarkable feature.[3]

Toryism was a politics of patriarchalism. One of its key texts was Sir Robert Filmer's *Patriarcha*, written in defence of Charles I, and published in 1680 as a political intervention against the Whig opponents of Charles II's policies. This text defended royal authority by analogy with that of the father, since the king is the father of the nation. Good order rested on hierarchy in both family and state. There are occasions when Behn seems to embrace this patriarchal Toryism. For example, her play *The Roundheads* (1681) seems conventionally Tory in its sexual politics, offering the familiar association of royalism with virtue, and rebellion with women out of place.[4] Cavalier libertinism is sidelined and Behn associates lust and secret sex with canting, hypocritical puritans. Royalism is explicitly associated with chastity, as the heroine Lady Desbro refuses to be unfaithful to her parliamentarian husband:

> No, I'm true to my Allegiance still, true to my King and Honour. Suspect my
> Loyalty when I lose my Virtue.   (VI: 4.1.48–50)[5]

In her characters of Lady Lambert and Lady Cromwell, Behn makes conservative use of the figures of the shrew and the upstart woman aping the great Lady. Lady Lambert beats and bosses her husband, and interferes in political meetings. Lady Cromwell is jealous of her dignity and indignant when other women encroach on what she calls 'our Royal Family' (VI: 5.3.195). The gender transgression reinforces the social presumption, typifying a world upside-down. Lady Lambert's capacity for love – and the superior sexiness of the cavaliers – eventually restores her to the 'sanity' of political and sexual submissiveness.

Behn also uses a comic interlude of a Council of Ladies, infiltrated, and satirized 'aside', by the heroes in drag, to show the presumptuous folly and impropriety of the rebel world and to focus on a peculiarly female propensity for pettiness. She shows women in power behaving in a way which anti-suffragists were to depict two centuries later, elevating private grievances, bitchy, competitive, and silly. Thus Behn's habitual – and liberating – depiction of women who are wiser and wittier than their husbands coexists with and is overdetermined by a conventional Tory rhetoric of gender difference and female subordination.

The Roundheads, however, is an exception within Behn's *oeuvre*. Behn responded to the needs of particular historical 'moments'. *The Roundheads* was produced in the late autumn of 1681 when the political tide had turned in the King's favour. In the theatres, as in society, 'Tory Reaction' had set in with a vengeance. There was a specific context and a substantial motivation for Behn to make a vigorous effort at this time to subordinate her capacity for feminist insight to the sexually conservative tropes of Toryism in order to demonize the Whigs' attempt to 'turn the world upside-down'.

Behn was very much a writer of her own times, who had her finger on the cultural 'pulse'. She was often in the lead of new dramatic trends, the first to articulate a new mood. For example, she was the first to respond to the burgeoning political crisis of 1678/9, which led to a sharp break in the generic evolution of comedy. Sex comedy (Behn had written several) went quite suddenly into eclipse, following the astonishing failure of a series of sex comedies by major writers in the spring of 1678.[6] Then, as political crisis gripped the nation, there was a virtual cessation of comedies: only one in the 1678/9 season. That one, *The Feign'd Curtizans*, was by Aphra Behn, and was a sign of what was to come: a revival of the satire of upstarts and puritans typical of 1660s comedy, coupled with a celebration of upper-class good taste across national boundaries. Behn's play associates Whiggish anti-popery and patriotism with puritan sexual hypocrisy, folly, pretension, philistinism, and low-class money-grubbing.[7] This set the tone for a new wave of political comedies which employed methods and modes reminiscent of 1660s comedy to attack the Whigs.

At a time of acute crisis it became urgent to give ideological affirmation to Toryism, but there were other times when this was not her main priority.[8] In many of her plays, despite their Toryism, Behn dramatizes resistance to patriarchy. The authority she supported when vested in Charles and James Stuart seemed intolerable when vested in a father or husband. Even in some of her Exclusion Crisis comedies, such as *The Feign'd Curtizans* (1679) and *The Revenge* (1680), we find witty heroines who challenge their male-ordered destiny. There is a powerful resonance in the spectacle of these women evading an oppressive destiny of arranged marriage and enforced celibacy, plotting to take control of their lives, civilizing rakes and winning marriage choice and freedom of sexual manoeuvre. When necessary these heroines dress as men and fight alongside men. In both these plays Behn evokes sympathy for the victims of sexual double standards, and the double standards are subjected to explicit critique. She also extends qualified sympathy to prostitutes, women who find themselves victimized outsiders through meeting men's needs. Instead, hostility is directed at citizens, upstarts, and puritan hypocrites, in other words the middle classes and dissenters who supported the Whigs. In *The Feign'd Curtizans* Behn emphasizes that, while Whiggish middle-class patriots are to be derided, upper-class good taste is international. The play opens with hospitable exchanges between the Italian Julio and the English Fillamour. Later, English gentlemen court Italian ladies. Wit and good taste cross national boundaries, and Whiggish hostility to Catholic countries is misconceived. Class values transcend Whiggish anti-Catholic and nationalist values.

This is a different Tory ideological model from that which informs and structures *The Roundheads*. Here, women scheme for greater freedom and control within this framework of upper-class solidarity and shared values. The royalist satire of Whiggish citizens and puritans in *The Feign'd Curtizans* and *The Revenge* coexists with a kind of feminism. This is very far from being patriarchal in the Filmerian sense.[9]

The contradictions in Behn's political and sexual attitudes are nowhere more apparent than in her consistently ambivalent attitude to the libertinism associated with the Stuart brothers and the court. The Whigs made political capital out of criticizing royal libertinism and in particular out of the King's subordination to foreign and Catholic mistresses. Literary Tories such as the poet laureate John Dryden attempted to 'Extenuate, Palliate, and Indulge' the King's moral deficiencies.[10] Behn sometimes seems to share this indulgent view of libertinism. Certainly the cavalier libertines or rakes in her plays are always nicer than the lower-class buffoons, or the upstart Whig citizens and hypocritical puritans. Yet her attitude is never entirely free from reservations. She is always aware of the predatory aspects of libertinism, the sexual double standards and the social cost for women.

In *The Rover* (1677) the heroes are followers of the exiled Charles II, in exile themselves during the Interregnum. Willmore is a cavalier in political terms, as well as being cavalier in the (a)moral and sexual sense. Belville upholds the upper-class honour code and is committed to a virtuous but unattainable love, resembling the heroes of French heroic romance and English heroic drama. The play's Toryism is clear in the treatment of Blunt, a comic butt among the other men who speaks in a crude and old-fashioned country style. Blunt's wealth is intact because his estate has not been sequestered by the parliamentarians, and he may even be a supporter of the Commonwealth:

> . . . but Gentlemen, You may be free, you have been kept so poor with Parliaments and Protectors, that the little Stock you have is not worth preserving – but I thank my Stars, I had more Grace than to forfeit my Estate by Cavaliering.
>
> (v: 1.2.44–7)

For the Tory Behn this may be enough to justify the total humiliation which is his fate, as he is tricked by a whore, stripped and cast into the sewer.

Behn alters her source (Killigrew's *Thomaso*) to give more prominence to the women's desires and dilemmas, as they manoeuvre to evade their unwanted destinies of arranged marriage (Florinda) and enforced seclusion in a nunnery (Hellena).[11] Up to a point, this manoeuvring is within the framework of a Tory class perspective. For example, Florinda asserts her desire for liberty as a lady of quality:

> . . . and how near soever my Father thinks I am to marrying that hated Object, I shall let him see, I understand better, what's due to my Beauty, Birth and Fortune, and more to my Soul, than to obey those unjust Commands.
>
> (v: 1.1.19–22)

Florinda here lays claim not to liberation for women but to the privileges due to her as a woman of the upper class. Florinda may be said to espouse a form of patriarchal ideology, but modified to give her what she wants. She is extremely assertive: 'I wou'd not have a man so dear to me as my Brother, follow the ill Customes of our Countrey, and make a slave of his Sister' (v: 1.1.59–61). However, her assertiveness has often been missed by critics because it is within the parameters of her class perspective and strong moral sense

However, there are some respects in which the sexual politics of *The Rover* appear to break the bounds of Tory ideology.[12] In particular, the treatment of Willmore's predatory libertinism is ambivalent. The libertine Willmore is the 'rover' of the title in two senses, as a wandering exiled cavalier and sexually. He bears a resemblance to the libertine Earl of Rochester, to Behn's own lover John Hoyle, to Charles II and to Charles's brother James. Willmore is intensely desirable, but the presentation of his character is not entirely positive.[13] Willmore is an ambiguous figure, sexy and witty, but always in danger of becoming the mocked rather than the mocker, and the disempowered object of desire rather than the active and powerful subject. Behn gives him qualities from Killigrew's hero Thomaso, but also some characteristics from Edwardo, the fool in the source play, as well as some of Edwardo's actions, such as attempted rape of one of the heroines. This suggests at the very least some mockery of her libertine hero.

Willmore is a sex addict, averse to commitment: 'I am parlously afraid of being in Love' (v: 5.1.393–4). This sex addiction is presented as rather ridiculous. So is the fact that at times he seems as eager in pursuit of the bottle as of women. Willmore would scorn to be likened to the parliamentarian Blunt, yet Willmore shares with Blunt a preference for women of easy virtue and a predisposition to rape. Behn is often critical of mercenary motives, and Blunt, an elder brother, is resented by the dispossessed and impoverished cavaliers for his wealth. Yet, Willmore, supposedly generous, is actually quite mercenary: his first words to Hellena concern his unwillingness to part with what little money he has, and he is happy to spend Blunt's money and Angellica's. Desire for wealth (as opposed to mere bewailing of poverty) is usually associated with grasping cits like Dashit in *The Revenge* or, in Exclusion Crisis tragedies, with villains who thirst for reward, so it is surprising to find the royalist hero so mercenary.

Hellena and Willmore are very similar. But she exposes his double standards:

> WILLMORE Oh, I long to come first to the Banquet of Love! And such a swinging Appetite I bring – Oh I'm impatient. – thy Lodging sweetheart, thy Lodging! Or I'm a dead Man!
> HELLENA Why must we be either guilty of Fornication or Murder if we converse with you Men – and is there no difference between leave to love me, and leave to lye with me? (v: 1.2.183–9)

Hellena's wit makes Willmore seem ridiculous here. She mocks the familiar libertine motif that the man will die if the woman doesn't relieve his desire, and exposes the rake's discourse of love as crude sexual appetite. Later she exposes the double standard within Willmore's ideology of sexual freedom:

> . . . what shall I get? A cradle full of noise and mischief, with a pack of repentance at my back?　　　　　　　　　　　　　　　　(v: 5.1.430–1)

Willmore is at times a buffoon, at other times monstrous, as when he abandons Angellica almost casually, through boredom. Angellica almost achieves the status of a sentimentalized and tragic victim whose laments in blank verse break the bounds of comedy. Willmore is also a monster when he attempts to rape the disguised Florinda and disgusts even his friends:

> if it had not been Florinda, must you be a Beast? – a Brute? a Senseless Swine.
> 　　　　　　　　　　　　　　　　　　　　　　　　(v: 3.6.198–9)

At other times, the women are active agents in the plot, and Willmore seems comparatively passive as the women compete over him. It is far from clear at the end what Hellena has gained by manoeuvring him into marriage – and indeed, in the sequel we learn that Hellena has died and Willmore has wasted her inheritance.

The Second Part of The Rover (1681) seems clearly Tory since it was published with a Dedication to James, Duke of York, in which Behn identifies James with her hero, Willmore. Royalist politics and cavalier sexual mores are contrasted to the hypocrisy, 'ingratitude' and 'Arbitrary Tyranny' of the 'seeming sanctifi'd Faction' in the Civil Wars and their Whig descendants in the Exclusion Crisis (vi: 'Dedication', lines 12, 13, 25). In the play the verb 'Cavaliering' is used to convey both adherence to the royalist cause and sexual adventurism. James was himself a rake who (as Bishop Burnet put it) 'had always one private amour after another'.[14] So he is likely to have found the glorification of cavalier behaviour congenial.

The connection between politics and sexual politics in The Second Part of The Rover is spelt out by the play's royalist hero, Willmore. In Act 2 he contrasts his own libertinism with the sexual habits which typify a parliamentarian. He expects free sex, both in the sense that he wants to be open about it, and because he wants it without monetary or social cost: 'Let the sly States-man, who Jilts the Commonwealth with his grave Politiques, pay for the sin that he may doat in secret' (vi: 2.1.56–7). He says of his pursuit of a large woman, 'better to be Master of a Monster than Slave to a damn'd Commonwealth' (vi: 3.1.315–16). In other words, the royalist rake has a control in the sexual sphere which is denied to him in the political sphere. The play would seem to end with rakishness triumphant, there being no reformation of the rake, as in The Rover.

Yet this play offers an even more ambivalent – even negative – treatment of libertine or cavalier behaviour than *The Rover*. Despite her avowed intention of celebrating cavaliers, Behn comes close to the excoriation of libertinism which in the Exclusion Crisis was receiving explicitly Whiggish coloration, for example in the plays of Shadwell.[15] Firstly, the callousness of the rake is stressed. He speaks of his wife's death 'With a Sham sadness' (VI: 1.1.124) and seems to be as much concerned with the loss of her fortune as with the loss of her. This mercenary motivation competes with sex for priority in his mind, for 'money speaks sense in a Language all Nations understand, 'tis Beauty, Wit, Courage, Honour, and undisputable Reason' (VI: 3.1.343–5).

Secondly, it is emphasized that libertinism not only renders woman an object, but renders the identity of the object secondary: several characters, including Willmore, pursue two rich jewesses, one of whom is a dwarf and the other a giantess. The function of 'these Lady Monsters' (VI: 1.1.223–4) is to show the monstrousness of libertinism itself: its object is so irrelevant that it can even be a freak (in Restoration terms), so long as there is the spice of novelty. In Act 5 the poor giant is pushed and pulled to and fro by the various men as if she were literally an object. In the dark in 4.2 Willmore sees the maiden, Ariadne, and the courtesan, La Nuche, just as two women, and remarks, 'no matter which, so I am sure of one' (VI: 4.2.66). In 4.4 he issues instructions to another man's servants to serenade whatever lady is to be pursued, for he neither knows nor cares who it will be. The object of Willmore's pursuit changes constantly. His aim is simple: 'I must dispose of this mad fire about me' (VI: 4.2.300–1). The lack of closure at the end reinforces our sense of unregenerate cavalier predatoriness. Willmore disguises himself as a mountebank to further his love plots and the guise is symbolically appropriate.

Thirdly we are distanced from the action in a way which encourages us to reflect upon the various sex plots, rather than to engage with the characters. Thus in Act 1 we watch Ariadne and Lucia watching Willmore watching La Nuche watching her bawd, Petronella, gull Fetherfool. Similarly in Act 2 Ariadne and Lucia follow Willmore and Blunt who follow Fetherfool and La Nuche's 'bravo'. This leads to my fourth point: there is much dizzying farcical by-play and endless confusion of identity as men carry off the wrong woman and climb into bed with other men by mistake and women dress as men and (for various devious reasons) pursue each other as well as men. The effect is to engender mockery rather than royalist sympathies. Fifthly, and most disturbingly, the misogyny beneath the surface of libertinism is explicitly revealed. Willmore hates the women he desires for their beauty and wealth and for their power over himself: 'by Heaven, I will possess this gay

Insensible, to make me hate her – most extremely curse her' (VI: 1.2.392–3).
The wit which is generically supposed to excuse all often wears rather thin
and there is no strenuous effort to vindicate the rakes on political grounds.
Since Behn has explicitly coupled royalism and cavalier sexual mores, it
is anomalous from a Tory point of view that rakishness is seen to be so
obnoxious in *The Second Part of The Rover*. Most extraordinary of all is the
play's unusual ending where the courtesan emerges in triumphant possession
of the rake. For a Tory aristocrat this is a much more marked submission
than getting married as at the end of *The Rover*. After all, the man has
the power in a marriage. And it sets a completely different tone from plays
such as *The Roundheads* in which rakes seem vindicated by women's sexual
submissiveness.

However, in *The City-Heiress* (1682) condemnation of the libertines' vices
is subordinate to celebration of their political triumphs.[16] It is no accident
that the rakes are labelled by the Whig, Sir Timothy, 'Tarmagent Tories'
(VII: 1.1.33). The phrase 'Tory-rory', (VII: 1.1.259–60), applied to the Tory
knight, Sir Anthony, denotes a certain rollicking and roistering mentality.
Behn suggests that Tory libertinism is something jolly, wild and cavalier, and
preferable to whey-faced Whiggery and puritan sexual hypocrisy. Tory vices
are venial; Whig crimes the real threat to the social order.

Yet, there is a curious duality in *The City-Heiress*, for it appears that Whigs
have taken over what are usually Tory vices. Debauchery, drunkenness and
gluttony are here associated with Whiggery. The Whigs inveigh against Tory
womanizing but are lustful themselves. The Tory rake Wilding abuses the
Whig Sir Timothy:

> Very good, Sir; hark ye, I hope [your wife is] young and handsome; or if she
> be not, amongst the numerous lusty-stomacht Whigs that dayly nose your
> publick Dinners, some may be found that either for Money, Charity, or Grat-
> itude, may requite your Treats. You keep open house to all the Party, not for
> Mirth, Generosity, or good Nature, but for Roguery. You cram the Brethren,
> the pious City-Gluttons, with good Cheer, good Wine, and Rebellion in abun-
> dance, gormandizing all Comers and Goers, of all Sexes, Sorts, Opinions, and
> Religions, young half-witted Fops, hot-headed Fools, and Malcontents: You
> guttle and fawn on all, and in hopes of debauching the Kings Liege-people into
> Commonwealths-men; and rather than lose a Convert, you'll pimp for him.
> These are your nightly Debauches – Nay, rather than you shall want it, I'll
> cuckold you my self in pure Revenge.   (VII: 1.1.101–19)

Here Behn excoriates in Whigs the vices she palliates in Tories. Wilding's out-
burst suggests that self-indulgence is alright when conducted in a spirit of

good-natured generosity, but not when it is used to sugar the pill of rebellion. The difference between vice in Whigs and Tories is partly a question of perceived hypocrisy: Tories are openly self-indulgent while the Whigs are allied with the puritans (or dissenters) who profess to scorn self-indulgence. However, there is also a class issue: Wilding seems to suggest that there is something improper about 'pious City-Gluttons'. The citizens are condemned for being mean-spirited puritan kill-joys, but are only the more contemptible when they try to ape behaviour which is only excusable among well-born young rakes.[17] It is class animosity as much as political animus which makes cuckolding the Whigs a pleasant duty.

The mercenary mentality of the Whigs excuses the Tory rake. As Wilding seduces Lady Galliard in Act 4, he is rendered less culpable and predatory by her coy willingness, but also by the fact that his libertine arguments are in keeping with the attacks on the mercantile mentality which runs through the play:

> Beauty shou'd still be the Reward of Love,
> Not the vile Merchandize of Fortune,
> Or the cheap Drug of a Church-Ceremony.
> She's onely infamous, who to her Bed,
> For interest, takes some nauseous Clown she hates:
> And though a Joynture or a Vow in publick
> Be her price, that makes her but the dearer whore.
>
> (VII: 4.1.165–71)

This contrasts with the disconcertingly mercenary motives of Willmore in *The Rover*. Wilding's plan, which includes lodging his mistress with Sir Timothy in the guise of the city heiress, is based upon the mercenary character of his uncle.

As in *The Feign'd Curtizans* the Whigs are satirized for their crass patriotism and francophobia and their combination of irreligion and canting hypocrisy. They are also mocked for ridiculously bandying around accusations of 'arbitrariness' and 'tyranny', as well as for their belief that they are above the law. The Tory rakes are more refined, more sexy and more fun. Both libertinism and Toryism gain glamour and strength from their mutual association. In *The City-Heiress*, more than in any previous play by Behn, the vices of the rake are condoned or become a joke which we are invited to share, rather than to laugh at as with Willmore in *The Rover*. The need to vindicate Toryism and libertinism is paramount. Wilding's robbery of Sir Timothy (VII: 5.1) ought to be morally reprehensible, yet the robbery is presented as a comic interlude at Sir Timothy's expense, as he is exposed and savagely derided as a sexual and political hypocrite.

Behn is certainly not blind to the negative aspects of rakish treatment of women. Indeed, in this play women seem both less central than in the two parts of *The Rover* and more compromised or manipulated. Charlot, the 'City Heiress' of the title, is central to the plot but marginal to the action. She is tricked and deceived by Wilding who seduces her with lies, marries her for her money and lodges her with a City 'bawd'. Wilding's cast-off mistress Diana is married off to Sir Timothy by a trick in which she seems forced to collude, though she loves Wilding. Her fate (and the delight in Sir Timothy's come-uppance) seems at least in part due to her lower-class status. Lady Galliard is humiliated through her desire for Wilding: he sleeps with her and leaves her to be married off to her scorned suitor Sir Charles, who bullies her into submission through a forced seduction. Feminism even becomes a joke. Sir Charles tells Lady Galliard when she resists his advances, 'call up a Jury of your Female Neighbours; they'll be for me, d'ye see, bring in the Bill Ignoramus, though I am no very true blue Protestant neither' (VII: 4.2.500–2). This recalls the satirical depiction of the female parliament in *The Roundheads*. All this creates a completely different ambience from the ending of *The Second Part of The Rover*, where the courtesan La Nuche gains triumphant possession of her lover. From a modern perspective it is disturbing that women in *The City-Heiress* are treated as badly as Whigs. But since we laugh with the cavaliers at the trickery and humiliation of the Whigs, it is hard not to laugh at the women. Behn's perennial contradiction between Toryism and feminism is present in the play, but the ideological cracks are papered over. Sympathy for women is subordinated to Tory triumphalism.

The different treatment of libertinism in *The Second Part of the Rover* and *The City Heiress* is partly to be accounted for by the different time when they were produced. In *The Second Part of the Rover* Behn's commitment of dramatic energy to the anatomisation of libertinism coexists oddly with her expressed commitment to cavalier politics in the Dedication. However, the Dedication was supplied upon publication later in 1681. The play itself was produced early in 1681: references in the Epilogue suggest that it was performed before the dissolution of Parliament in January. This means that it was performed in the period before the Oxford Parliament in March 1681, during a period of apparent Whig ascendancy. As I have shown elsewhere, many dramatists at this time made concessions to Opposition sentiment.[18]

The City-Heiress, performed in the period of Tory reaction, was published with a strongly Tory Dedication, celebrating the political defeat of the Whigs in 1682 and claiming an important political role for the comic dramatist: 'seditious Fools and Knaves that have so long disturb'd the Peace and Tranquility of the World, will become the business and sport of Comedy, and at last the scorn of that Rabble that fondly and blindly worshipt 'em; and whom nothing can so well convince as plain Demonstration, which is ever more powerful and prevailent than Precept, or even Preaching it self' (VII, p. 7).

Behn exults over the defeated Whigs and mocks them – but in the City of London the Whigs were still a threat. Thanks to the continued militancy of the City, even after he has been found in possession of treasonable papers, Sir Timothy can bounce back:

> – why I'll deny it, Sir: for what Jury will believe so wise a Magistrate as I, cou'd communicate such Secrets to such as you? I'll say you forg'd 'em, and put 'em in,-or print every one of 'em, and own 'em, as long as they were writ and publisht in London, Sir. Come, come, the World is not so bad yet, but a man may speak Treason within the Walls of London, thanks be to God, and honest conscientious Jury-men. (VII: 5.1.134–9)

Coexisting with the idea of Whiggery as defeated and ridiculous, then, is a vision of it as resilient and still dangerous. This may be one reason why Behn abandons her critique of the rake: the task of demonizing the Whig is both too urgent and too demanding to permit of there being the space to sustain it.

Behn might also be engaging in direct rivalry with the Whig dramatist Shadwell. It seems significant that Shadwell's savage attack on court libertinism, The Libertine (1675), was revived around this time (May 1682) as The Libertine Destroy'd. Behn's vindication of the rake in The City-Heiress might thus have its motivation in part in the fact that she reverses Shadwellian tropes.[19] In The Libertine there is authorial sanction for an attitude of disgust at the promiscuity and venereal disease which lurks beneath the facade of nobility. In Act 2, scene 1 of The City-Heiress this attitude is satirized in Mrs Clacket, 'A City-Bawd & Puritan'. In The Libertine, rape is a serious threat and women resist it, by suicide if necessary. In The City-Heiress, Lady Galliard is a willing participant in her own seduction, putting up the expected token resistance, but willingly won over by libertine arguments. In The Libertine, libertine arguments are ruthlessly exposed. For example, the argument that the rake acts in self-defence against the woman's beauty which is a form of cruelty is satirized when Don John kills the governor of Seville: 'The jealous Coxcomb deserv'd death, he kept his Sister from me; her eyes would have kill'd me if I had not enjoy'd her, which I could not do without killing him.'[20] The libertine's claim to be 'following the Dictates of Nature, who can do otherwise?' (3, p. 55; cf. 4.3, p. 82), is ridiculed by the depiction of real pastoral virtues in the countryside (4.2). Libertine irreligion is a serious sin, punished by death and damnation. In Behn's play Tories are cheerfully irreligious. Behn predictably levels the charge of sexual hypocrisy at the godly, whereas in Shadwell's Act 3, the libertines' attempt to label a virtuous man as being a hypocrite and a 'godly whoremaster' is simply monstrous. Behn has venial and ridiculous servants; Shadwell has a serious critique of corruption in great men ramifying downwards: ''Tis true, my Master's a very Tarquin; but I ne'r attempted to ravish before' (Jacomo, 4.2, p. 78).

Other Shadwellian themes are reversed in Behn's play. Shadwell's *The Woman-Captain* begins with a satirical depiction of a young aristocrat who is preparing to waste the inheritance from his decent, puritan father, and to associate with rakes and wastrels. *The City-Heiress* opens with a satirical depiction of the Oliverian, Sir Timothy, foolishly objecting to his nephew and heir, Tom Wilding, being corrupted by fun-loving Tory rakes. Shadwell's Sir Humphrey is reproached by the good, old-fashioned steward who acts as the ignored voice of his master's conscience: 'I would have you cleanly, and serve God as my old Mr. did' (I, p. 2). Behn's Sir Timothy laments: 'Before he fell to Toryism, he was a Sober civil Youth, and had some Religion in him' (VII: 1.1.50–1). This is given further point by a regret for the passing of 'the days of old Oliver' (VII: 1.1.75). Then comes the familiar taint of puritan sexual hypocrisy: 'he [Cromwell] by a wholsome Act, made it death to boast; so that then a man might whore his heart out, and no body the wiser' (VII: 1.1.75–7).

The relationship of politics and sexual politics in Behn's drama is complex.[21] The nature and intensity of her loyalism fluctuated with the complex current of events. A further qualification is needed: though Behn was a fervent Tory all her life, she was no fanatic and should not be seen simply as a Tory ideologue. She was a consummate professional who always had an eye for what might be 'good box office'. Even satirical comedies like *The Feign'd Curtizans* are pacy and funny, full of fighting and flirting and farcical by-play to appeal to all sections of the audience. Mostly, her poems and plays celebrate wit and good nature rather than savagely exulting over her political enemies. For example, in *The Feign'd Curtizans* 'good Nature' (VI: 5.4.714) is explicitly mentioned. The play offers satire of the Protestant, legalistically minded, mercantile middle class which was the Opposition's chief base of political support. But it is not doctrinaire. There is also some criticism of the Italian customs of arranged marriage and condemning girls to nunneries: the women plot successfully to get choice and some respect in marriage. There is criticism (of a light-hearted kind) of the worst excesses of 'cavalier' behaviour, as when the libertine, Galliard, is tamed and married off. At the end everyone learns tolerance. Sir Signall speaks the last words: 'let's wink hereafter at each others frailties!' (VI: 5.4.755). Behn seems to suggest that this advice has a wide application.

The City-Heiress has a triumphant Tory conclusion. Yet even in this play of the Tory reaction period, the Whig Sir Timothy gets off lightly. The concluding note is not one of vindictiveness. Despite earlier hints about hanging, Sir Timothy will be allowed to live quietly and enjoy the use of his wealth for life, providing 'that he makes not use on't to promote any mischief to the King and Government' (VII: 5.5.579–80). Behn strikes a note of good taste, order and reason. Wilding urges Sir Timothy:

> Live peaceably, and do not trouble your decrepid Age with business of State.
> > Let all things in their own due order move,
> > Let Caesar be the Kingdoms care and love:
> > Let the Hot-headed Mutineers petition,
> > And meddle in the Rights of Just Succession;
> > But may all honest hearts as one agree
> > To bless the King, and Royal Albanie.
> > > (VII: 5.5.592–8)

Once again, good nature prevails.

And yet, it is possible that Behn wants to suggest here that vindictiveness is not necessary, since the natural (Tory) order has been tranquilly restored. We may compare the naturalness attributed to the Restoration of the monarchy in plays of the 1660s. To portray the calm triumph of Toryism – and indeed to depict Tory magnanimity – is more ideologically powerful than a note of shrill vindictiveness. Even when harmony is celebrated, Behn the staunch Tory is never far away.

NOTES

1 For an account of the Exclusion Crisis and the dramatists' response to it see my *Restoration Theatre and Crisis* (Oxford: Clarendon Press, 1996). The labels 'Tory' and 'Whig' for royalists and oppositionists acquired wide currency from about 1681, though there are examples of earlier usage: see p. xi. I have used 'Tory' for Behn's politics prior to 1681 as it is less clumsy than 'proto-Tory'.
2 Mary Ann O'Donnell suggests Behn may have left England rather than go to prison: O'Donnell, p. 6. See also Todd, p. 289.
3 Behn does praise Mary warmly, but in terms which cunningly celebrate Mary's father, the deposed King James. Todd, pp. 424–9.
4 Maybe this is because this play is an adaptation of John Tatham's *The Rump* (1660). However, Behn is perfectly capable of making alterations, as when she shifts the odium from the prostitute to the Whig citizen in her adaptation of Marston's *The Dutch Courtesan* as *The Revenge*.

5 For a fuller discussion see my '"Suspect my loyalty when I lose my virtue": Sexual Politics and Party in Aphra Behn's Plays of the Exclusion Crisis, 1678–83', *Restoration*, 18 (1994), 37–47. Elizabeth Bennett Kubek sees the play's Toryism in terms of fidelity to oaths rather than chastity: '"Night Mares of the Commonwealth": Royalist Passion and Female Ambition in Aphra Behn's *The Roundheads*,' *Restoration*, 17 (1993), 88–103.

6 See Robert D. Hume, '"The Change in Comedy": Cynical Versus Exemplary Comedy on the London Stage, 1678–83', *Essays in Theatre*, 1: 2 (May, 1983), 101–18.

7 See my *Restoration Theatre*, pp. 3, 63–5, 153–4, 172, 192.

8 See my '"Suspect my loyalty"'.

9 My argument about *The Feign'd Curtizans* differs from that of Paulette Scott, who thinks 'this play panders to and even flatters men, supporting the political and domestic *status quo*': '"There's Difference in Sexes": Masculine Sexuality and Female Desire in *The Feign'd Curtizans*', in *Aphra Behn (1640–1689): Identity, Alterity, Ambiguity*, ed. Mary Ann O'Donnell, Bernard Dhuicq, and Guyonne Leduc (Paris: L'Harmattan, 2000), p. 174. I agree with Jane Spencer that, while Behn recognizes the constraints on women, 'within them she allows the fullest possible scope to female action' and allows 'glimpses of female power': '"Deceit, Dissembling, all that's Woman": Comic Plot and Female Action in *The Feigned Courtesans*', in *Rereading Aphra Behn*, p. 100.

10 Preface to *Absalom and Achitophel*, in *The Works of John Dryden*, ed. E. Niles Hooker *et al.*, 20 vols. (Berkeley: University of California Press, 1956–2002), II, p. 4.

11 For an account of these alterations and a full analysis of the play see my *Perspectives on Restoration Drama* (Manchester: Manchester University Press, 2002), pp. 65–84.

12 For a useful discussion of tensions between Toryism and feminism in the play see Anita Pacheco, 'Aphra Behn's *The Rover, Part One*', in *A Companion to Early Modern Women's Writing*, ed. A. Pacheco (Oxford, 2002), pp. 203–15.

13 Some idea of the range of critical debate about Behn's treatment of libertinism may be gained from reactions to Willmore. Critics who see the play as (with varying degrees of qualification) a celebration of the libertine masculinity which Willmore typifies include Duffy, *The Passionate Shepherdess: Aphra Behn 1640–1689* (London: Cape, 1977), pp. 145–8; Katharine M. Rogers, *Feminism in Eighteenth-Century England* (Urbana: University of Illinois Press, 1982), p. 58; Nancy Cotton, 'Aphra Behn and the Pattern Hero', in *Curtain Calls: British and American Women and the Theater, 1660–1820*, ed. Mary Anne Schofield and Cecilia Macheski (Athens: University of Ohio Press, 1991), pp. 211–19; Laura Brown, *English Dramatic Form, 1660–1760* (New Haven: Yale University Press, 1981), pp. 60–1; and Robert Markley, '"Be impudent, be saucy, forward, bold, touzing, and leud": The Politics of Masculine Sexuality and Feminine Desire in Behn's Tory Comedies', in *Cultural Readings of Restoration and Eighteenth-Century Theater*, ed. J. Douglas Canfield and Deborah C. Payne (Athens: University of Georgia Press, 1995), pp. 114–40. For a darker view of Willmore and libertinism in the play see Jones DeRitter, 'The Gypsy, *The Rover*, and the Wanderer: Aphra Behn's Revision of Thomas Killigrew', *Restoration*, 10 (1986), 82–92; Elaine Hobby, *Virtue of Necessity: English Women's Writing 1649–88* (London:

Virago, 1988), pp. 122–7; Jacqueline Pearson, *The Prostituted Muse: Images of Women and Women Dramatists, 1642–1737* (London: Harvester, 1988) p. 153; Warren Chernaik, *Sexual Freedom in Restoration Literature* (Cambridge: Cambridge University Press, 1995), pp. 206–8; Anita Pacheco, 'Rape and the Female Subject in Aphra Behn's *The Rover*', *ELH*, 65 (1998), 323–45; Anthony Kaufman, '"The Perils of Florinda": Aphra Behn, Rape and the Subversion of Libertinism in *The Rover, Part I*,' *RECTR*, 11 (1996), 1–21. Peggy Thompson sees Willmore as ambivalently depicted but ultimately salvaged as a (problematic) hero: 'Closure and Subversion in Behn's Comedies', in *Broken Boundaries: Women and Feminism in Restoration Drama*, ed. Katherine M. Quinsey (Lexington: University Press of Kentucky, 1996); Derek Hughes sees him as intermittently 'the play's chief fool', *The Theatre of Aphra Behn* (Basingstoke: Palgrave, 2001), p. 84.

14 Gilbert Burnet, *A History of My Own Time*, ed. Osmund Airy, 2 vols. (Oxford: Clarendon Press, 1897) I, p. 405. See also Antonia Fraser, *The Weaker Vessel: Women's Lot in Seventeenth-Century England* (London: Methuen, 1984), p. 453.

15 See my *Restoration Theatre*, pp. 176–8.

16 My analysis here differs from that of Derek Hughes, who considers that 'the play constitutes Behn's greatest exploration of the ugly side of Cavalier glamour', Hughes, p. 147. For a contrasting view see Markley, '"Be impudent"', pp. 131–3.

17 We may compare James Winn's discussion of Rochester's denigration of Dryden for the obscenity he practised himself as 'likely to be a complex example of . . . class prejudice': *John Dryden and his World* (New Haven: Yale University Press, 1987), p. 226.

18 The Oxford Parliament (held in a royalist stronghold as London was a base of Whig support) was a turning point and ushered in the so-called 'Tory Reaction'. For concessions to the Whigs in plays performed in 1680/1 during the Exclusion Parliaments see my *Restoration Theatre*, pp. 82–95; and 'The Politics of John Dryden's *The Spanish Fryar; or, the Double Discovery*,' *English*, 43 (1994), 97–113.

19 I have shown that Durfey in *Sir Barnaby Whigg* reversed themes and tropes in Shadwell's *The Lancashire Witches*: *Restoration Theatre*, chapter 6.

20 *The Works of Thomas Shadwell*, ed. Montague Summers, 5 vols. (London: Fortune Press, 1927), III, Act I, p. 27.

21 Critical discussions of the politics of Behn's drama include Hughes, e.g. pp. 83–5, 133–70; Markley, '"Be impudent"'; Owen, '"Suspect my loyalty"' and *Perspectives on Restoration Drama*, ch. 3; Arlen Feldwick, 'Wits, Whigs, and Women: Domestic Politics as Anti-Whig Rhetoric in Aphra Behn's Town Comedies', in *Political Rhetoric, Power, and Renaissance Women*, ed. Carole Levin and Patricia Sullivan (Albany: State University of New York Press, 1995); Melinda Zook, 'Contextualizing Aphra Behn: Plays, Politics, and Party', in *Women Writers and the Early Modern British Political Tradition*, ed. Hilda Smith (Cambridge: Cambridge University Press, 1998); John Franceschina, 'Shadow and Substance in Aphra Behn's *The Rover*: The Semiotics of Restoration Performance', *Restoration*, 19 (1995), 29–42.

6

JANET TODD AND DEREK HUGHES

Tragedy and tragicomedy

As a dramatist, Aphra Behn is now chiefly celebrated for witty, libertine comedies which give the woman's view of the sexually predatory male and the cunning female. When she began her career, however, sex comedy had not evolved, and all three of her first plays – *The Young King* (probably first performed in 1679), *The Forc'd Marriage* (1670) and *The Amorous Prince* (1671) – were tragicomedies.[1] This was the prevailing mode in the 1660s, when she must for the first time have watched plays on the public English stage. An odd segmented form, in which melodrama was followed by romance, tragicomedy perfectly suited the obsession of early Restoration royalist dramatists with representing the recent reverses and triumphs of the British monarchy: the restored Charles II arising from the ashes of his executed father.[2] Despite the obvious moral failings of the new king and the political blunders of his first decade and despite the appearance of restrained criticism of unwise royal love in the mid-1660s, the restoration of the hero-king remained a dominant dramatic subject until 1671, though with increasing attention to its less than heroic consequence.

Amorous princes

Behn's three early tragicomedies are united in themes as well as form, depicting the heroic as quintessentially male. The first two plays trace male supremacism to its origins in warrior communities whose values are dictated by strength and soldierly prowess: a simple feudal world of aristocracy, male bonding, oaths, and romance. While portraying the glamour of this world, Behn criticizes it and its warrior cult as fierce and inimical to women, who are reduced to objects of ritual exchange. Later plays develop and refine the vision of her early attempts.

Behn herself declared that the first play she wrote was *The Young King*. Published in 1683 after its belated première in 1679, it was, according to the dedication, 'the first Essay of my Infant-Poetry'. Behn claimed its muse was '*American*', suggesting she wrote it in Surinam (VII, p. 83). Certainly the topic, the restoration of a king, belongs to the 1660s, as does its portrayal of a feudal, militaristic society. It is not known why it was not performed with her other early plays, but the delay may have been due to the failure of Edward Howard's similar *The Womens Conquest* (?Spring 1670).

The Young King portrays the temporary displacement of Orsames, heir to the throne of Dacia, by his sister Cleomena.[3] Because an oracle predicted he would be a tyrant, Orsames had been brought up in seclusion and ignorance of his birth; in compensation Cleomena has been raised on manly pursuits and prepared for rule in his place. Yet, for both, gender is powerful, and both experience problems of sexual identity. At the opening of the play, the princess feels a sexy dreaminess which makes her retreat from the hunt, while the prince, in an onrush of masculinity, rails against his passive life of musical idleness. Cleomena's first experience of love leads her to discover her feminine vulnerability: 'I have an Heart all soft as thine, all woman,' she tells her female attendant (VII: 1.2.26). By contrast, Orsames' first experience of sexual attraction leads him to attempt a rape. At the conclusion brother and sister take on their gendered 'natural' roles and throw off the disguise of nurture. Cleomena declares, 'I find I am a perfect Woman now, / And have my fears, and fits of Cowardise' (VII: 3.4.154–5).

At first sight the play seems to suggest that gender roles are innate and should be respected; yet there are some anomalies. When a male character describes the hero whom Cleomena loves (Thersander), he grows 'soft and wanton' in the description (VII: 1.1.21). 'Soft' is a frequent word in the play, especially associated with the feminine, and what is particularly odd is that the speaker is otherwise archetypally male: a gruff career soldier who abhors 'the feeble Reign of Women' (VII: 1.1.37) and finally restores the male heir to the throne. Cleomena is 'no natural *Amazon*' (VII: 1.1.74): when she admits to 'a Heart all soft', she concedes that her martial attitude comes from 'Education, / That cozening Form that veils the Face of Nature' (VII: 1.2.23–4). Yet, when she is first touched by the sight of the sleeping hero, she holds him in a highly unfeminine gaze: she even has his hair pushed back from his face to get a better look.

Although provided with an elderly tutor in his isolation, Orsames has grown up filled with aggressive male lusts. Here perhaps there is a topical reference since the play portrays a king learning to control appetite, much as the country must have hoped Charles II would do. Further topicality comes from Orsames' crude notion of kingship, which resembles the parliamentary caricature of Stuart 'divine right' doctrine. He wishes 'To have Dominion o'er the lesser World' governing 'A sort of Men with low submissive Souls, / That Barely shou'd content themselves with Life' (VII: 2.1.33–5). When his tutor argues that these humble men might 'refuse obedience to the mighty few' (VII: 2.1.43), Orsames waves the notion aside: in that case he would destroy them.

The need for monarchy is ambiguously portrayed. '[A] RABBLE OF CIT-IZENS' (VII: 4.5.128b) desire a male ruler, but their dialogue is so foolish that they can scarcely be viewed as rational. Later, when they see the king they are restoring, they are either disappointed or simply excited by novelty. The act of restoration is demythologized. Clearly from the outset of her career, Behn sees the problematic aspects of the royalist politics she approves.

The plot of Orsames' exile and restoration is based on *Life is a Dream* (*La Vida es sueño*, 1635) by the Spanish dramatist Calderón de la Barca. From this play Behn took the notion of a king imprisoned to thwart an oracle predicting his tyranny. In both works he is allowed to reign for a day, behaves tyrannically, and is returned to prison, persuaded that he has been dreaming. His day of tyranny has fulfilled the oracle, however, and he can later commence a new reign, although, even in Behn's version, the young man has little sense of kingship except as immense self-gratification and irresponsible power; he asks a neighbouring king, 'Dost see no marks of grandeur in my face? / Nothing that speaks me King?' (VII: 5.4.181–2). Yet, for all his palpable unsuitableness for rule, it remains axiomatic for Behn that a nation will never be happy till it has a legitimate prince at its head. The play ends with the aggressive Orsames giving away his more intelligent sister in a marriage she has organized for herself but which also fulfils dynastic demands.

Although *The Young King* was allegedly the first play Behn wrote, the first to be performed was *The Forc'd Marriage* (September 1670). Strikingly, it begins where *The Young King* ended, with a king rewarding a warrior with a bride. The bride is the beautiful Erminia, who is privately betrothed to the king's son, Phillander. Erminia refuses consummation with Alcippus and, maddened by jealousy, he tries to strangle her, leaving her for dead. (The influence of *Othello* was here so strong that Behn even gave the option of suffocating in the first printed edition of the play.) Still alive, Erminia disguises herself as a ghost to persuade Alcippus that he is penitent, that he will be less violent, and that he really loves the tolerant princess Galatea, who loves him and whom he rather ungraciously comes to accept. The old king is happy to agree to whatever the young people want and soon all the correct couples are joined.

The Forc'd Marriage has no single source but is influenced by several earlier plays, including *The Indian Queen* (1664) by John Dryden and Sir Robert Howard, for which Behn provided feathers from Surinam (as she claims in *Oroonoko*). In obvious allusion to the return of Charles II, *The Indian*

Queen is a play about usurpation and restoration, showing the triumph of justice through the return of the established, traditional order. In *The Forc'd Marriage*, the established order is a male conspiracy which reduces women to objects of exchange and prizes for warriors. Justice requires change: a determined female challenge to the status quo.

In the depiction of gender *The Forc'd Marriage* is curious. Male heroism can be empty and undignified – like many heroes in the serious drama of the time, Phillander is torn between the claims of sharply polarized values: vengeance, reason, and love. Yet the heroics are all in the words. In contrast to *The Young King*, the martial drama has happened before the play begins; it is in the bedroom rather than the battlefield that the heroes rage and fight. Moreover, while women are treated as simple pawns of war, they are also the main repositories of subjectivity in the play. Erminia's beauty has caused the whole family to be raised in status and she has a high opinion of her 'Quality' and a complacent sense of her power over men. This last appears particularly in a tart dialogue between her and the princess: when Galatea reminds her proud friend of what she was before Phillander's love raised her, Erminia points out that she is also loved by the man for whom the princess hopelessly pines. In other scenes, Erminia seems to relish her influence over the two powerful young men, while routinely lamenting the confusion she has caused. Yet she shares with all the women the sense that sexuality should be opposed to militarism, rather than being an extension of it. After her enforced wedding to Alcippus, she longs for the pastoral world about which Behn's female characters would so frequently fantasize. This is a realm of softness, gentleness and love, 'Free from the noise of jealousie and pride' (v: 2.3.82), and the male ideologies of honour and courage.

There may be one or two precise if coded political allusions in *The Forc'd Marriage*. To the embarrassment of her father, the Lord Chancellor Edward Hyde, the fury of Charles I's widow, Henrietta Maria, and the dismay of most of the court, Hyde's daughter Anne had persuaded Charles II that her impregnation by the Duke of York, heir to the throne, should result in marriage. Behn may have intended a *frisson* in the audience with a play that closed with two royals marrying two commoners. In *The Forc'd Marriage* such unions are desirable if the commoners are worthy or beautiful; so Behn might have been trying for a compliment to the Duke of York and his wife. There may be a further reference to Lord Arlington, the minister of state who had left her penniless when she was a spy in Antwerp. He wore a patch over his war wound and in her play the cowardly Falatius tries to persuade his doubting friends that he has been in the wars by wearing similar patches on his face.

Despite the multiple pairings common to other dramas of the time, the plot of *The Forc'd Marriage* is uncomplicated. There are mistakes and night encounters but little intrigue in the play, which is rather lacking in tension. Yet the sex struggle that would mark most of Behn's later plays is there in embryo and a shrewd spectator or reader might have discerned Behn's future preoccupation.

In his memoirs, John Downes, the Duke's Company prompter, records that *The Forc'd Marriage*, 'a good play', had a run of six days but then 'made its Exit'. It was, however, performed again on 9 January 1671. A month later, another Behn play was staged. This was *The Amorous Prince*. Like *The Forc'd Marriage* and *The Young King*, it portrayed the workings of male power within feudal military élites, but now the appetite for conquest is primarily directed against women.

Like Behn's other early works, *The Amorous Prince* relies more on costume and disguise than on staging; yet in some touches it seems clearly later than *The Forc'd Marriage*: although no sexual activity occurs onstage, it is an oddly sexy play for a woman author to own. It is hard to imagine that Behn could have opened her very first work with a post-coital scene between two unmarried lovers. *The Amorous Prince* concerns the sexual misuse of political power by Prince Frederick, who seduces Cloris, the sister of his friend Curtius and then attempts to steal Curtius' prospective bride. No longer possessing a visible military purpose, the aristocratic hierarchy has come to regard the 'Conquest' of women as its prime *raison d'être*. Only in the last couplet of the play does the reformed and now monogamous Frederick undertake to sacrifice his 'Manhood' 'to War and Love' (v: 5.3.373–4).

The subplot of *The Amorous Prince* is based on an episode from Cervantes' *Don Quixote*. Behn was fascinated by rigid misogynous Spanish or Italian society, which she tended to see as essentially comic material. The contemptuous fascination with Mediterranean culture had been inherited from the Elizabethan and Jacobean dramatists, who had used the South for revenge plays and as a cover for comment on English matters. Behn's setting allowed her to exaggerate the social distinction of the sexes and point to the absurdity of cloistering women from the world and then expecting from them morals higher than those in men.

In Cervantes, a man asks his best friend to test his wife's fidelity, but the scheme ends in adultery and tragedy. In Behn's version, Antonio, obsessed by the need to verify his wife Clarina's fidelity, persuades his friend Alberto to court her. Here there is a happy ending, since Clarina's sister Ismena, who loves Alberto, stands in for her sister throughout the trial. Yet there is a dark undertow. Alberto falls for Ismena, but until the deception is revealed he is appalled by the responsiveness of a woman he believes to be his friend's wife. All his moral conflicts are imaginary, but the situation shows the destructive potential for women of friendship between men. Male bonding was much celebrated in contemporary male-authored drama; in Behn's play it results in pain, confusion, and absurdity. Yet, while male ideals and lusts produce destructive impasses, female plotting provides a solution (for example, in the substitution of sisters). As one woman says,

> I have a thousand little stratagems
> In my head, which gives me many hopes:
> This unlucky restraint upon our Sex,
> Makes us all cunning.   (v: 2.2.180–83)

Like its predecessor, *The Amorous Prince* has divergent political messages. Prince Frederick embodies the Stuart doctrine of the divinity of kings, in which the king is responsible to God alone. But, since Frederick is also a rake who must be reformed, reverence for him is coupled with criticism of royal gallantry. In this portrayal of a sexually irresponsible ruler, *The Amorous Prince* resembles many plays written over the previous eight years, generally by dramatists who were well disposed to Charles II but disturbed at the disrepute he was courting with his promiscuity. Most tend to emphasize the ruler's neglect of his political or military duties, and sometimes to show him as the victim of scheming whores. Prince Frederick, however, is no victim: Behn portrays not the neglect of power but its abuse, and the cruel ease with which it oppresses women.

The figure of Frederick, like that of Orsames in *The Young King*, is disturbing. A prince ruled by sex is a danger to his subjects, and, whatever his initial good qualities, will become injudicious and intemperate. The amours of Frederick even provoke a normally faithful subject to plot his death. It is this sense of the arbitrariness of rank and power, even more than Antonio's trial of his wife, which gives the play its troubling seriousness. Curtius, the prince's abused friend, sounds decidedly republican as he muses on royal authority:

> – And he who injures me, has power to do so;
> – But why, where lies this power about this man?
> Is it his charms of Beauty, or of Wit?
> Or that great name he has acquir'd in War?
> Is it the Majesty, that Holy something
> That guards the Person of this Demi-god?
> (v: 4.2.151–6)

As times changed, and Behn with them, she grew more guarded.

Throughout *The Amorous Prince*, Behn uses the idea of prostitution to sum up the way in which men manipulate and oppress women. The idea is prominent both in the political and the domestic spheres: in Frederick's rakish misuse of his political power, and Antonio's misuse of his husbandly authority. Women are the objects of men's desire, men's money, and men's language. When they are not recognized as sisters, wives, mothers, or daughters, they are whores: that is their fundamental and original character, and it is one to which any woman is in danger of being returned.

Envious outsiders

The Amorous Prince appeared at a turning point in the stage portrayal of royalty. A year after its performance, England allied with France to declare war on Holland – a move which caused deep anxiety in the nation, since England was combining with an absolutist Catholic monarchy against a fellow Protestant nation. By the summer of 1672, it had become widely known that the Duke of York, who was heir to the throne in the absence of any legitimate children to Charles II, had been converted to Catholicism, and the following spring he was forced into public acknowledgment of his religion. Later in 1673, he married for the second time; his bride was the Catholic princess Mary of Modena. The succession was not yet the explosive problem it was to become in 1678–81 but James's marriage and conversion raised the possibility of a perpetual Catholic dynasty. On the stage, celebration of restoration gave way to fear about the succession; tragicomedy, apt for fêting the king's return, ceded to savage and sensational forms of tragedy, much concerned with tyranny, problematic succession, and the moral dilemmas of an oppressed subject coping with an absolute, alien or criminal ruler.

The sensational horror tragedy of the 1670s was a curious mode: audiences both admired and mocked it and also simultaneously enjoyed cynical dramas of compromised principles and political manoeuvrings. In May 1674, the young Nathaniel Lee had an interesting failure with his first play *The Tragedy of Nero*, an intense depiction of the psychology of power, in which the central character, the Roman emperor, represented motiveless evil and expanding energy within a plot of family murder. There had been power-hungry men in plenty on the Restoration stage, but they were usually reconciled or tamed at the end. This does not happen with Nero: he dies, defiantly, but his ex-subjects merely rejoice, credulously, at the emergence of another divine ruler – the Emperor Galba, who was himself to be publicly murdered after a disastrous reign of six months. Instead of the glorious restoration to which serious drama of the 1660s tended to progress, there was in these plays meaningless, cyclic repetition, in which one false god was replaced by another.

After a period of silence Behn tried her hand at a portrait similar to that of Nero; the result was her only pure tragedy, *Abdelazer*, a play which addressed and sought to neutralize problems raised by the horror plays. Based on *Lust's Dominion*, perhaps by Dekker, Day, and Haughton, *Abdelazer* was performed on 3 July 1676. The story centres on the Moor, Abdelazer, who, although originally a captive and slave in Spain, has gained royal favour and military honour, and has married a Spanish noblewoman. Like the villain of *Titus Andronicus*, he has become the lover of the Queen. He plots to revenge the ousting of his father by the Spanish and, in the process, destroys most of the royal family and its court. His instrument is the equally cruel Spanish Queen, whose infatuation with Abdelazer leads her to kill her husband, to assist in the murder of her elder son, who succeeds him, and to declare the other son, Philip, a bastard. Her beauty is declining, however, and, though she can still work magic on others (including a cardinal), she is no longer loved by the Moor. When she has served her turn, he treats her as he has persuaded her to treat so many of her family: he has her murdered. She dies wishing she had more sons to kill for Abdelazer and just as she is expecting sex with her lover, a fitting end to a career which has mixed extravagant savagery with farce. This conclusion of *Abdelazer* marks a significant change of plot from the original play: there the wicked Queen takes the unlikely step of retiring to a life of penitence.

Another crucial change Behn makes to her source is her stress on Abdelazer's alienness and destructive masculinity rather than his blackness. Unlike the original character, Eleazer, Abdelazer is never a stereotyped lustful black villain, even though he does commit the stereotypical black man's crime of attempting to rape a white woman, the Princess Leonora. The rape, although villainous, has arisen from a specific combination of circumstances and motives and is interrupted by a good Moor, Osmin: it is, then, a personal crime, rather than one characteristic of Abdelazer's entire race. Moreover, Abdelazer's aggression is in part motivated (though not, of course, justified) by the fact that, in rejecting him, Leonora expresses abhorrence of his alien body. Such abhorrence is the rule in *Lust's Dominion*, but in the different atmosphere of *Abdelazer* the moment stands out as something exceptional; when, earlier in the play, Abdelazer is banished, the objections are to the constructed features of his culture – his religion and dress – rather than to any essential racial character. Other changes also help to alleviate the unrelenting racism of *Lust's Dominion*. Behn omits the concluding expulsion of the Moors from Spain, and a royal proposal that negroes who touch Spanish women should be executed. As Jacqueline

Pearson has pointed out, she excises the moral symbolism of black and white.[4] (The word 'white', indeed, is never used in *Abdelazer*; nor is the word negro.)

Behn's subtle portrayal of Abdelazer would not have been possible had she shared the crude phobias of her source, but she is not primarily writing a play about attitudes to black people: Abdelazer's blackness makes strange that which is commonplace in any male-dominated society. In fact he is a successor to Thersander in *The Young King* and Alcippus in *The Forc'd Marriage*. Again Behn is primarily portraying conflicts within a warrior culture: the stranger who challenges that culture is also its greatest exemplar, for he is its greatest warrior.

Abdelazer's chief antagonist in the play is the younger son of the old king, Philip, the rightful heir to the throne and its possessor at the conclusion of the work. Philip is another intemperately aggressive male, and the constant pairing of him and Abdelazer emerges from Behn's rethinking of the conflicts which shape *Lust's Dominion*. The earlier play opposed absolutes: a Christian monarchy threatened by a moral and bodily alien, and by a transgressive woman. The criteria of alienness were fixed and uncomplicated. Behn, by contrast, portrays a conflict between two men who mirror each other and who are united by an imperious attitude towards women: the feature which Philip most shares with Abdelazer is contempt for the Queen Mother. Behn reveals power relationships which are fixed in structure but endlessly reversible. If, then, she persists with the theme of restoration while many others were dramatizing change, she could scarcely endorse it with less idealization.

Probably in 1679 Behn disinterred *The Young King*. She may have done so because the state of the marketplace and the nation deflected her from the kind of farcical comedy she had developed so successfully in *The Rover* and *Sir Patient Fancy*. Perhaps she found her old form inspiring again or at least appropriate for her needs since the play she staged after *The Young King* was another tragicomedy, *The Revenge*, an adaptation of John Marston's *The Dutch Courtesan* (1605). It appeared some time between January and April 1680, a year in which Tory opposition to the exclusion of James from the throne was gathering strength. It was not an appropriate moment for her usual sort of comedy.

The Revenge was published anonymously, but there is credible contemporary evidence for her authorship, and the internal evidence for Behn's hand is strong. There is, however, much near-verbatim transcription of Marston; this is presumably the reason for her unwillingness to publish it under her own name, given past charges of plagiarism, especially concerning *The Rover*. The play differs from her earlier tragedy and tragicomedies in presenting the contemporary social world; violence and aggression now inhere in a capitalist and legalistic environment rather than in a feudal one.

Marston's original is heavily laden with Christian morality, all of which Behn removes, displaying a sympathetic identification with the courtesan that is entirely absent from the source. As she lightens the character of the female transgressor, so she darkens that of the male, the entertaining city rogue Cocledemoy, whom she turns into Trickwell, a rather unpleasant gentleman who attempts to rape the courtesan. His vices are downmarket versions of those of Frederick in *The Amorous Prince*: abuse of his class and his sex.

In the main plot Wellman falls in love with a virtuous gentlewoman, Marinda, and tires of the prostitute, Corina, with whom his friend Friendly falls in love. Corina offers to gratify her new admirer if he kills her faithless lover, secretly planning to betray Friendly and have him hanged. The two friends pretend that the murder has been accomplished, but the 'victim' then teaches the 'murderer' a salutary lesson by disappearing and leaving him, apparently, in real danger of execution. In the secondary plot, Trickwell assumes a series of different disguises to perform confidence tricks and robberies upon a dishonest vintner, whom he manages to get condemned to death, though he saves his life when the victim agrees to forgive him. Both plots thus culminate in the near-hanging of an innocent man.

One significant way in which Behn alters Marston is to give the foolish vintner the vehement anti-popery which was feeding the Popish Plot scare, and with which the commercial classes based in the City were becoming increasingly associated. When the vintner is almost hanged for a crime he did not commit, he falls victim to the atmosphere which he himself has helped to create: 'Doubt not our diligence, Master, these dangerous times' (VI: 4.1.402), says the constable to Trickwell as the vintner is arrested.

The original heroine of *The Dutch Courtesan* is a malicious whore, punished with imprisonment and whipping. Behn's Corina, however, has slept only with Wellman, is victimized, and understands the power and tragedy of whoredom: 'A Whore! what tho to her that bears it 'tis a shame, an infamie that cannot be supported? to all the world besides it bears a mightie sound, petition'd, su'd to, worshipp'd as a God, presented, flatter'd, follow'd, sacrific'd to, Monarch of Monarchs, Tyrant of the world, what does that charming word not signifie!' (VI: 4.1.182–7). Corina sees herself tragically, but the play does not endorse her vision. Like Angellica in *The Rover*, she tries to kill her faithless lover but fails, and she is married off to a foolish knight who is tricked into thinking her a gentlewoman – the standard way of disposing of a fallen woman in Restoration comedy.

Rebellious subjects

Behn's interest in tragicomedy, revived by *The Revenge*, reappeared in one of her last plays, *The Widdow Ranter; or, The History of Bacon in Virginia* (1689). Like her most famous work, *Oroonoko*, this is derived from the American experiences of her youth, and is the first play to be set in British colonial America. Her earliest tragicomedies had inspected the immediate aftermath of Charles II's seemingly miraculous restoration – her subject now is almost diametrically opposed: corruption and rebellion in a distant English colony.

The historical rebellion of the English settler Nathaniel Bacon in Virginia took place in 1676.[5] Bacon had led an unauthorized campaign against the Indians, because the local government was failing to protect the settlers and was selling arms to the natives. The rebels refused the governor's orders to disband and were attacked. Their resistance collapsed when Bacon died of a fever, and – in reality though not in Behn's version – his followers were ruthlessly punished. It was a remarkable dramatic departure for Behn to give such centrality to a heroic malcontent, though she diminishes his subversiveness by removing his original opponent, the governor. Behn's Bacon therefore challenges a power vacuum and, curiously, becomes the representative of the monarchy he seems to oppose.

The play depicts three conflicting areas of male authority: the ruling council of Virginia, run partly by well-born but pragmatic gentlemen, partly by coarse, drunken, illiterate upstarts. It is menaced by the warrior native Americans, anxious to recover their ancestral territory. Bacon, an heroic dreamer who longs to equal Roman conquerors, is at odds with all groups; he is closer to the culture of the Indians than to his own, even though he has dispossessed them of their land: the play suggests that all estates and lands have to be taken from someone.

In *The Widdow Ranter* there is no supreme authority present, and the law is manifestly corrupt; hence the notion of rebellion is problematic. Even if Bacon 'fought like *Alexander*, and preserv'd the whole world from perdition', says an upstart on the governing council, 'yet if he did it against Law, 'tis Lawful to hang him' (VII: 1.2.108–10). But one heroine remarks: 'What pity 'tis there should be such false Maxims in the World, that Noble Actions how ever great, must be Criminall for want of a Law to Authorise 'em' (VII: 1.3.124–6). Behn is here addressing one of the most crucial political questions of the seventeenth century: should the power of law be absolute, or does it need to be tempered by the prerogative of a monarch not subject to it? For the opponents of James II, the king was subject to legal compulsion; for his followers, it was dangerous to bind the king in this way since the royal prerogative of mercy could mitigate the mechanical rigour of a usually corrupt law.

Further light is shed on the idea of rebellion in Bacon's insistence that, although his lands were once usurped, he has himself inherited them by right. This idea overshadows all questions of rebellion, legitimacy, and rightful authority. In 1688–9 inheritance was a topical issue, as the forces opposed to James II gathered and then overwhelmed him. *The Widdow Ranter* comes from this moment of danger and transition, when an inflexibly and foolishly idealistic king was about to become an enemy and alien to his hereditary kingdom. Bacon is not absolutely James II nor his glamorous nephew Monmouth, whose rebellion James had recently crushed, nor yet the Nathaniel Bacon of history, but the play offers some commentary on all of these men who believed rule and ownership were rightfully theirs. Beyond such topical allusions, the play delivers a sense of dissolution, in which particular history offers no guide to the present.

Bacon plays with roles from the heroic past – ineffectively since these have no place in a commercial, legalistic and unheroic time, and in a colony without authority. Characters within the play remark on his theatricality. He wants to reduce war to chivalrous duels and rhetorical confrontations, having an idealized view of language not shared by his antagonists, who use words only for deceit. Instead of inhabiting his historical moment he has the consciousness of the 1660s when the cavalier myths were fashioned; he believes in a kind of transcendental politics, true for all times and places, a belief deeply embedded in masculine classical literature like Plutarch's *Lives*, which he takes to be true history. He has faith in the integrity of language: the oath and word of honour, so important in Behn's early tragicomedies, so useless off the stage in these later years. When he has, apparently, been defeated, Bacon commits Roman suicide on the battlefield. But he commits suicide in error: the news of defeat was false.

In no earlier play had Behn shown basically good men taking opposite sides out of self-interested motives, and in no earlier play is there the murkiness of issue and injustice of outcome that characterizes the conflicts of Bacon and the Indian king and of Bacon and the Virginian authorities. The cowardly upstarts who change and rechange sides to save their own skins clearly invite condemnation, yet they also highlight the obscurity of boundaries.

The Widdow Ranter reflects and fragments royalist values. At the end of the play, class order is restored (though the rogues are pardoned) and the new governor is awaited. Despite its decadence the reconstructed order is more benign towards women than that of Behn's earlier plays, and Bacon's death shows that the increased latitude is made possible by the extinction of that machismo which Behn had always found in equal measure attractive and dangerous.

The comedy of *The Widdow Ranter* is mainly provided by the Virginian councillors, colonial versions of the city aldermen whom Behn had mocked in plays such as *The Luckey Chance*. Royalist mythology had always fastened on the low origins of anti-monarchists, as *The Roundheads* testified, both in the 1640s and the 1680s. Here Behn directs her social disdain to anyone who aspires to inappropriate place and fails to recognize that the gently born, even if card-sharpers and fortune-hunters, are natural rulers. The social chaos of Virginia has allowed a bankrupt farrier to become a preacher through forging his ordination papers, and a pickpocket to become Justice of the Peace. The response of these dignitaries to any rehearsing of the scandalous truth is not the duel of a gentleman but the law of common people: they will dishonourably sue, not honourably fight. The law is absurd in abstract and disgraceful as administered by vulgar men; it is corrupting when confused with ethics. Law becomes the opposite of loyalty, as democracy of honour.

In the hilarious drinking scene of the Committee of Safety in *The Round-heads*, written during the Popish Plot furore, Behn had reduced non-monarchical government to a farce of vulgar self-interest. In still more tense times, as James II's rule petered out, she repeated the device, portraying the Virginians setting up court aided by a great bowl of punch. Their first item before they move on to domestic bickerings is to vote themselves a new larger bowl. Such is democracy, Behn seems to say. As one onlooker remarks, 'The Country's well, were but the People so' (VII: 2.3.37). Despite all the political and social perception which her creation of Bacon implied, Behn could still not look beyond a royally sanctioned governor for any *political* resolution. Only this man will properly separate Indians and English, base- from well-born, and show who is master.

In *The Widdow Ranter*, for the last time, Behn returns to the figure of the reluctant or the vulnerable Amazon, which she had first created in *The Young King*, in the figure of Cleomena. The tragic heroine of this tragicomedy is the native American Semernia, who – like Erminia in *The Forc'd Marriage* – has been forcibly married to a warrior hero (the king, Cavernio), yet loves another man: her nation's chief antagonist, Bacon. After Bacon has killed her husband, she nevertheless feels impelled by honour to seek Bacon's death, enters battle in male disguise, and is killed by him in error. Just such an outcome had been narrowly averted in *The Young King*, where Cleomena engages her beloved Thersander in single combat, neither recognizing the other, and is nearly killed by him. These strikingly similar incidents from cither end of Behn's career show her lifelong interest in the marginality of women in a world whose systems are expressions of male strength, and her equally persistent interest in the deadly alien that lurks within the most attentive and submissive lover. Like Abdelazer, though less willingly, Bacon kills the woman who loves him.

If Semernia recalls the heroines of Behn's earliest plays, which are also set in warrior societies, the contrasting capitalist culture of the settlers in *The Widdow Ranter* produces a contrasting Amazonian figure: the Widow Ranter herself, a hard-drinking, pipe-smoking woman, bought as an indentured servant, then married and widowed by her owner, who left her rich. She gains the affections of the soldier Dareing by disguising herself as a youth and fighting a duel with him. He recognizes her, however, and lets her win. In the wider conflict of battle she cannot hold her own and she is captured. Nevertheless, if Ranter reverts to vulnerability on the battlefield, and if the capitalist economy which produced her at first relegates her to commodification and near-servitude, this economy also gives her a sequence of roles and possibilities that is denied Semernia: Ranter spends her widowhood in festive liberty; the narrower imperatives of Semernia's society force her, self-destructively, to attempt to avenge the husband she did not love upon the man she does.

Behn's reversion to the tragicomic mode in *The Widdow Ranter* accidentally provides a convenient coda to her career. In this, probably her last written play, she transmutes elements of *The Young King* and *The Forc'd Marriage* in the light of nearly twenty years' further thought about the ways in which male ambitions order society and limit women. Her first work, *The Young King*, had reconciled an Amazon with her femininity and with her enemy lover. Semernia is a more ineffectual Amazon than Cleomena, and Bacon a more dangerous enemy than Thersander; yet the martial society that had been the only possibility in *The Young King* is now restricted within narrow and sometimes exotic limits of place, time, and class. If the unsoldierly upstarts are contained, they continue to prosper, and indeed are born survivors. Shortly before Bacon dies, histrionically comparing himself to Hannibal, we see a theatrical death of another kind, when two fools from the ruling council lie down and feign death on the battlefield and then, Falstaff-like, rise to run away again another day. The end of the play is prosperous 'Repose':

> Come my brave Youths let all our Forces meet,
> To make this Country Happy, Rich, and great;
> Let scanted *Europe* see that we enjoy
> Safer Repose, and larger Worlds than they.
>
> (VII: 5.1.398–401)

For the first time outside her comedy, Behn provides a vision of the future that might be an escape from history. It is not a magical prophecy of democracy, however, and she never rejects the view of a gentleman colonist who declares, 'This Country wants nothing but to be People'd with a well-born Race to make it one of the best Collonies in the World' (VII: 1.1.105–6).

NOTES

1 *The Amorous Prince* was described on its title-page as a 'Comedy', but it is generically close to *The Forc'd Marriage*, which is described as a 'Tragi-Comedy'. Both, for example, include the apparent death of the heroine.
2 See Nancy Klein Maguire, *Regicide and Restoration: English Tragicomedy, 1660–1671* (Cambridge: Cambridge University Press, 1992).
3 Dacia was an ancient kingdom on the lower Danube.
4 Jacqueline Pearson, 'Slave Princes and Lady Monsters: Gender and Ethnic Difference in the Work of Aphra Behn,' in *Aphra Behn Studies*, pp. 227–8.
5 For a description of the Bacon Rebellion see *Strange news from Virginia* (London, 1677) and Todd, pp. 412–13.

7

ROBERT MARKLEY

Behn and the unstable traditions of social comedy

As the first professional woman dramatist in England, Aphra Behn offers rad-ically different perspectives from her male counterparts on the love intrigues, wit battles and property-mongering satire that are the stock-in-trade of Restoration social comedy. While most critics of the period now acknowl-edge that Behn was one of the most artistically and commercially successful playwrights of the 1670s and 1680s, the reasons for her success and, to some extent, the nature and significance of her achievement remain mat-ters of debate. Some commentators argue that Behn champions women's right to choose their marriage partners, and consequently identify her as a seventeenth-century feminist; other scholars maintain that she offers a much darker condemnation of the antifeminism and male libertinism of her time; and still others emphasize the ambiguities of her position as a woman writer in a misogynistic society.[1] There is, paradoxically, much to be said for all of these views: comedies such as *The Rover* (part one, 1677; part two 1681), *Sir Patient Fancy* (1678), *The Feign'd Curtizans* (1679), *The City-Heiress* (1682) and *The Luckey Chance* (1686) dramatize the allure (and difficul-ties) of women exercising their choices in love. Even as Behn criticizes the antifeminism endemic to a patrilineal society, she reminds her audiences that women have limited options and limited room to manoeuvre. In an impor-tant sense, the range of critical responses to Behn's plays reflect different perceptions of her theatrical practice and, ultimately, different conceptions of social comedy. To read her comedies within their historical, social and the-atrical contexts, then, is to confront the debates about Restoration comedy that have persisted for more than three hundred years.

The ideologies of social comedy

Restoration social comedy resists any hard and fast definitions, and the crit-ical history of the genre demonstrates that its defenders and virulent critics hold very different views about its morality, satiric purposes, aesthetic value, and historical and cultural significance.[2] Without descending to sweeping generalizations, one might define 'social comedy' heuristically by analysing, as Douglas Canfield has done, its ideological investments as well as its theatrical conventions.[3] In most comedies, upper-class, sexually attractive gentlemen (often younger sons) in need of fortunes court witty but virtuous heroines; the heroes discard old mistresses and fend off rival suitors, typically old, impotent men and conceited fops; the heroines test the depth of their lovers' attraction by refusing to have sex with them before they are married. The young lovers – with the help of sympathetic friends (often a second couple in similar circumstances) and witty servants – outwit an older generation of parents, guardians, or other killjoy authority figures. These conflicts between sons and father, or heirs and guardians, take place for – and over – the bodies of socially and sexually desirable women, those heiresses whose bodies promise the continuation of the family line and a solution to the problems of money and social status that plague the heroes. In plays by Behn's contemporaries, such as William Wycherley's *The Country-Wife* (1675) and George Etherege's *The Man of Mode* (1676), the heroes' sexual adventures offer compensatory fantasies for younger sons and debt-ridden members of the minor gentry whose attempts to live like gentlemen in a fashionable – and expensive – world threaten to overtax the networks of seventeenth-century patronage and privilege.[4] On stage, at least, young wits can triumph sexually over a doddering, impotent generation of fools, even if their incomes, lodgings, and opportunities for advancement suffer by comparison. Such comedies do not provide anything like 'realistic', extra-theatrical solutions to these dilemmas; instead, they offer comic revenge scenarios (*The Country-Wife* is a good example) in which men of business, like Sir Jasper Fidget, and upper-class fools, like Sparkish, are outwitted by the Horners of the Town.

An essential part of this fantasy of libertinism rewarded depends on playwrights' creating heroines who play the paradoxical roles demanded by a patrilineal social order: they must be alluring mistresses who are ready to become virtuous wives. The witty yet chaste heroines of Etherege's final two comedies, Gatty and Ariana in *She Wou'd if She Cou'd* (1668) and Harriet in *The Man of Mode*, for example, remain poised indefinitely for five acts between experience and innocence, between the disruptive actions of desiring women and the complaisance required of dutiful wards or daughters willing to accept marriages arranged for them. Such heroines embody the ultimate masculinist fantasy of female sexuality: their wit functions as a marker of their capacity for satisfying male sexual desire, even as their virginity guarantees the integrity of the estates that they will convey to their future husbands. They validate an ideology that both provokes and

assuages the anxieties of male spectators by justifying youth, wit, and libertine behaviour as the means by which property can be secured. Even though
Etherege and John Dryden, among other playwrights, create some memorable comic roles for the same actresses who performed in Behn's plays,
their comedies turn female wit into a mark of their heroines' complicity
in the masculine business of securing, transferring, and managing estates.
Virtuous heroines, no less than prostitutes and adulterous wives, are objectified: the estates that their bodies both represent and, quite literally, convey
are eroticized so that their personal attributes – wit, virtue, and beauty – sig-
nify less their individuality or agency than the heroes' foreordained success in
securing the dowries necessary to maintain a lifestyle of fashionable ease and
prosperity.[5]

Because beautiful, wealthy, and winnable heroines are the stuff of masculine fantasy, they are also the sites of the anxieties that inform male social
and sexual identity. Paradoxically, then, female desire becomes both the
enabling condition of comic heroines who are forever defying their parents
or guardians – and the satiric target of a masculine wit which enforces ideologies of gender, virtue, and property. Women must be chaste even though
they are always about to become whores. As Pat Gill argues, female characters on stage are portrayed as sexually rapacious beings who must be
charmed, cajoled, or browbeaten into accepting their subjection to male
socio-economic authority, even as women in the audience must be sexually-
minded enough to understand the wordplay, puns, and *double entendres*
that are the staples of rakish wit.[6] Social comedy, in effect, provides different strategies for incorporating often independently-minded women into a
system that denies or restricts their property rights in the name of an absolutist sexual morality and an overdetermined rhetoric of love: wits seduce,
fools compel, and fops have failed from the start.

Social comedy, however, also tests as well as reinforces the limits of social
and sexual decorum by exploiting the instability of a parodic, often transgressive wit. The usual targets of such satiric laughter are sexually incompetent males and unfashionable pretenders to wit, men who fail to seduce
women into the complicity demanded by a system that exploits their bodies
and denies them most legal rights. In *The Country-Wife*, for example, the
knee-jerk antifeminism that renders women either chaste vessels for transmit-
ting property among men (Alithea), hypocritical 'whores' (Lady Fidget), or
whores-in-training (Margery) is voiced by Pinchwife, a jealous cuckold, and
Sparkish, a posturing dolt. In such instances, the endemic antifeminism of
seventeenth-century society is itself riddled by tensions and contradictions –
and comic dramatists exploit, albeit often cynically, spectacles of women

violating decorum in order both to question and to justify the moral and social codes that govern a patrilineal society.

As a female playwright, Behn exploits these contradictions by shifting the experiential centre of her social comedies from masculine wit to female ingenuity. Verbal wit, the rake's weapon of choice, poses difficulties for women, who must try to avoid being seduced by a rhetoric that they find attractive but that threatens them with the potential loss of virtue, reputation, and autonomy. Because her heroines are caught in the double bind of being both desiring subjects and desirable objects, they inevitably have more at stake in questions of the heart than their suitors since, in every romantic encounter, they must hazard all they have: reputation, marriage prospects, and psychological security. To imagine something approaching happy endings for them, Behn recognizes, is to rewrite the fantasies of the rake rewarded, and to offer instead an ironic feminist alternative: the comic spectacle of heroines like Hellena in *The Rover*, Isabella in *Sir Patient Fancy*, and Lady Fulbank in *The Luckey Chance* negotiating their way between mocking or challenging masculinist 'Custom' and reassuring audiences that property and social privilege will be maintained in, through, and because of their intrigues.

In restaging the ubiquitous problems of late seventeenth-century society – the resentments of younger sons, the anguish of recalcitrant daughters, and the desperation of impoverished gentry – Behn appropriates the ironies of Restoration wit to display the effects of what recent theorists have termed 'cynical reason' – the paradoxical ways in which individuals characterize, justify, and refuse to think about their participation in social practices which are corrupt, alienating, and, for the individual, self-defeating.[7] Rather than recycling the conventions of wit comedy, Behn explores the inter-animating processes of ideological recuperation and ironic distancing that Slavoj Zizek describes as the basis of cynical reason: 'even if we do not take things seriously, even if we keep an ironical distance, *we are still doing them*'.[8] Again and again in Behn's comedies, fifth acts feature improbable conversions of comically abusive husbands or guardians, heroines who find themselves free to marry the men they love, and rakes who are won over, to some extent, by the wit and wealth of the heiresses who rescue them from genteel poverty. Rather than offering an escape from the constraints of Restoration culture, these fantasy solutions register the ironies confronting intelligent women who recognize and comment incisively on their complicity in a society that hinders or denies their rights to property, free will, and sexual pleasure. Behn's heroines are neither blinded by the ideological fantasies of patriarchy, nor intent on explicitly resisting them; they recognize what they are doing, but they are doing it anyway, and acting as though their knowledge did not matter.

Significantly the dynamics of cynical reason operate differently for women and in Restoration comedy: women bear the brunt of the compromises that men claim they have to make to thrive in a society ruled by self-seeking and double-dealing. 'Why do we daily commit disagreeable and dangerous Actions?' Congreve's Mirabell asks rhetorically in *The Way of the World* (1700). 'To save that Idol Reputation.'[9] In the play, however, Mirabell commits actions neither disagreeable nor dangerous; he is trying to reconcile his cast-off mistress, Mrs Fainall, to the marriage he arranged for her to a dishonest and conniving husband. Because Mrs Fainall has signed over control of her fortune to the hero before her marriage, she guarantees the success of Mirabell's scheme to win Millamant and, to some extent, offers him a way to present his callousness as an enlightened response to the (corrupt) ways of the world. The idol may be a false god whose worship – for women – is both disagreeable and dangerous, but Mrs Fainall continues to sacrifice (and be sacrificed) to it anyway.

In contrast to Congreve, Behn explores the psychological consequences of her characters having to negotiate a socio-economic ideology which is treated as *both* the foundation of a 'natural' order based on socio-economic inequality and royalist authority *and* as an ideological fantasy which justifies historically and culturally specific forms of female oppression. In her Pindaric ode 'On Desire', Behn's speaker asks the questions that perplex those women – Angellica Bianca and La Nuche in the two parts of *The Rover* – who surrender sexually and economically to the desire provoked by Willmore: 'What Art thou, oh! thou new-found pain? / From what infection dost thou spring?' (I, p. 281). If desire is the product of an infection, it also marks the instabilities and uncertainties that lie at the heart of individual and social identity – the irrationality which puts women in the position of acting against their better judgement. In Behn's comedies, female desire is neither travestied, as it is in figures like Congreve's Lady Wishfort, nor celebrated as the psychological cornerstone of a golden-age sexuality; instead it undermines the ideological structures of feminine identity: 'all your virtu's but a cheat / And Honour but a false disguise, / Your modesty a necessary bait' (I, p. 283). In a Pindaric addressed *to* desire, the speaker's critique is not an indictment of dissembling but an expression of the ironies of social experience: the speaker perceives herself bound by social and moral 'custom' but remains able to recognize, evade, redefine, and rationalize her violation of these strictures.

In this regard, the penchant of Behn's heroines for falling for the theatrical versions of the poem's love-object Lysander – rovers like Willmore and rakes like Gayman – dramatizes a wilful misrecognition of the inexplicable, even dangerous desire for love. Like her male contemporaries, Behn both exploits and travesties the fantasy of happy marriages, but her heroines must distance themselves from the concomitant fantasy of the rake reformed. None of Behn's women insist on the trial periods that Etherege's heroines impose on their rakish lovers: they recognize but continue to participate in the fantasies that marriage will extend indefinitely the intrigues of courtship and the timelessness of masquerade and that their royalist lovers will never turn into superannuated and jealous husbands. The heroines of Behn's comedies recognize their complicity in the social and psychological roles demanded by virtue, honour, and modesty: they know that their rovers are incapable of constancy; they know that the structure of marriage is, for women, a trap; and they know that their desire must be 'the false offspring of mistaken love' (I, p. 282), but they act – and must act – as though they do not. Behn's heroines cannot transcend, reject, or even vilify such fantasies because all of these options imply an impossible objectivity – an idealized ability to step outside of one's social and ideological roles – including those roles that human beings play for themselves in the imaginary theatre of psychic interiority. Instead, her plays explore the process – more difficult for women than for men – of ideological suturing between honour and virtue as both internalized standards of integrity and as deceptive and repressive mechanisms to constrain female desire.

Desire and cynicism

In the world of social comedy, Behn's heroines can never opt out of an existence of legal obligations, fashion, pretence, and the gendered rules of play. Declaring that 'Custom is unkind to our Sex', Isabella at the beginning of *Sir Patient Fancy* mocks the 'Obedient Daughter' who 'stands – thus – with her Hands pinn'd before her, a set look, few words, and a mein that cries – come marry me' when she is badgered by her parents into receiving the 'insupportable Addresses of an Odious Foppe' (VI: 1.1.14–19). By imitating the woman she refuses to be, Isabella distances herself from the dictates of an ideology that denies women their choice in marriage and forces them to suffer the 'numberless impertinences' (VI: 1.1.9) that attend being objects bartered by their fathers or guardians to property-seeking men. She mocks the role, in short, that many women in the audience have been forced to play in earnest.

The problem, however, with the audience's perceiving Isabella as a straightforward critic of masculinist privilege is that the lover she has chosen, Lodwick, voices the same kinds of values and assumptions about women, marriage, and money that she has mocked. The man who offers her an escape from the straitjacket of proper feminine behaviour ironically also represents the socio-economic order which demands that she ultimately reproduce the ideology of the 'Obedient Daughter'. When Isabella asks Lodwick if she can 'trust [his] honesty' if she allows him into her bedroom, he responds 'who wou'd first sully the Linnen they mean to put on?' (VI: 3.1.25) Lady Fancy's entrance prevents her response, and Behn's strategic decision to cut off the lovers' exchange points to a crucial irony in her feminist appropriation of the conventions of wit comedy: her heroines' witty lines, clever plots, and good-natured tolerance of their suitors' or husbands' infidelities cannot shield them from the consequences of living in a system that objectifies them. Isabella is a commodity like a linen shirt, and having sex with her before marriage would ruin the purchase. In brief, Isabella must play a variation of the role that she had mocked at the beginning of the play – a woman who must trust her lover's honesty. She is, ironically, both the actress and the spectator to whom her own performance must be convincing.

While male dramatists often turn bedroom farce into aggressive satires of female lust, Behn characteristically directs her audience's attention to the compromises that women are forced to make and the dynamics of cultural fantasy that encourage them to comment on their interpellation by a masculinist ideology. Later in *Sir Patient Fancy*, Lodwick ends up in Lady Fancy's bedroom, mistakenly assuming that he is visiting his chaste love Isabella. When Lady Fancy tries to seize the opportunity to have sex with the man she believes is her lover, Wittmore, he cannot respond to her advances. 'Like a bashfull Girl restrain'd by fear', Lodwick is unable to perform sexually because, as he tells Lady Fancy, 'I hate to Cuckold my own Expectations' (VI: 3.2.101–2). When he realizes his mistake, he does not reveal his identity to this 'fair dear dissembler' and seizes the opportunity to have sex with her. Later he lies to the jealous Wittmore, claiming that he and Lady Fancy were interrupted by Sir Patient – a lie that Behn underscores when she has Lady Fancy admit to her maid that 'I gave him all I had reserved for Wittmore' (VI: 4.2.8). Lady Fancy's conversion of her love into a legal and economic metaphor (the verb 'reserve' implies assets not subject to conjugal control) reveals the extent to which the language of individual desire, love, and agency is shot through with the rhetoric of calculation and marriage settlements. Isabella realizes that Lodwick has been 'false', but chooses 'to pardon him however guilty' because she credits his 'assurance to free me from this intended marriage' to Wittmore that is being forced upon her (VI: 4.1.8–9). Infidelity pales besides the coercion of a forced marriage.

Given the conventions of social comedy, it is difficult to treat Lodwick's escapade as evidence of his immorality or cruelty, in part, because his desirability depends on his rakish behaviour. Throughout Behn's comedies, the object of female desire must be a man of whom parents and guardians disapprove; defying their wishes becomes the only way for heroines to articulate the principle that women must be free to choose their husbands and reject old, ugly, foolish, and politically incorrect suitors. Almost without exception, Behn's heroines seem smarter than their lovers because, as women, they have been forced to negotiate a system that stacks the odds against them. For Isabella and Lady Fancy, young heiress and adulterous wife, the consequences of their decisions to pursue Gayman and Wittmore are potentially dire. Recognizing that men can ignore or dodge the consequences of extramarital sex, women must constantly play the dialectical roles of sexual object and faithful lover to avoid giving into their desire and falling into the comic stereotype of the fallen women. As Lady Galliard learns in *The City-Heiress*, relinquishing one's trump card leads, at best, to a consolation prize, Sir Charles Meriwill instead of Tom Wilding.

Yet at the end of *Sir Patient Fancy*, Behn complicates the stock figure of the sexually voracious woman, satirized in the plays of her male contemporaries. Lady Knowell in Act 5 blesses the match between her daughter and Leander, admitting (or claiming) that her attempts to seduce him earlier in the play were merely a test of his fidelity: 'I saw with pleasure Sir, your reclination from my addresses – I have prov'd both your Passions' (VI: 5.1.178–80). Even Lady Knowell's Latinate rhetoric and pretensions to learning cannot obscure her good nature, defined as her willingness to help the lovers circumvent the most coercive aspects of patrilineal privilege. In a final scene that parodies the conventions of comic closure, Sir Patient gives away his money, frees his wife, and tells her and the audience ''Tis well thou dost confess I am a Cuckold, for I wou'd have it be known' (VI: 5.1.704–5). Rather than a satiric target, Lady Fancy emerges by the end of the play as a pragmatist who has married a rich alderman to further her love for the penniless Wittmore. Wittmore's last lines in the play underscore the fantasy that women can somehow evade the worst aspects of arranged marriages and maintain an emotional (and financial) commitment that survives their being married off to men twice their age: 'we have long been Lovers', he tells Sir Patient, 'but want of Fortune made us contrive how to marry her to your good Worship. Many a wealthy Citizen, Sir, has contributed to the maintenance of a younger Brother's Mistress' (VI: 5.1.709–12). Wittmore acknowledges that Lady Fancy has been his co-conspirator in a self-serving scheme for his 'maintenance', but the comic frustrations he suffers throughout the play and his 'cuckolding' by Lodwick, work against our seeing Lady Fancy merely as a pawn in his cynical scheme to outwit a 'wealthy Citizen'. Sir Patient's decision to renounce his 'Conventicles', 'turn Spark', and 'keep some City

Mistress' (VI: 5.1.735–6) becomes, then, a stage-play solution to the real-world dilemmas of women forced to restrain or renounce their desires and of younger brothers forced to live by their wits – in this instance by prostituting true love to financial 'maintenance'. The love between Wittmore and Lady Fancy is rewarded to the extent that she (like La Nuche in *The Second Part of The Rover* and Leticia in *The Luckey Chance*) gets the man she wants, yet she suffers no illusions about their arrangement; in a world of cynical reason she acts as though maintaining Wittmore does not compromise her love.

Much of Behn's comedy derives from her willingness to play up the narcissism of her rakes in order to turn their preening and self-congratulatory sexuality into a mode of objectification. Even as cynical lovers like Wittmore pimp for the women they ostensibly love, they become objects of female desire precisely because they are willing to turn themselves into self-caricatures. This symmetrical objectification of male and female lovers is evident in Behn's parodic inversion of the gendered languages of merchandising and commodification. In *The Feign'd Curtizans*, Galliard describes himself to the supposed prostitute Cornelia as 'a good handsome proper fellow [who] is as staple a commodity as any's in the Nation – but I wou'd be reserved for your own use! Faith take a sample to Night, and as you like it, the whole peece.' Cornelia responds by turning his imagery back against him and asks him 'to throw in a little Love and constancy' (VI: 3.1.182–5; 189). This mercantile imagery underscores Behn's penchant for allowing her heroines to appropriate the rhetoric of wit for their own ends: Cornelia picks up the language of bargaining for sex but tries to outwit the rake at his own verbal game.[10] The speech of her kinswoman Marcella similarly negotiates the linguistic boundary between virtuous heiress and scandalous whore. While letting the audience know that Marcella is intent on maintaining her 'right down honesty . . . through all the dangers of Love and Gallantry', Behn allows the audience to enjoy the titillation of Cornelia's contingency plan: 'if all these if's and or's come to pass, we have no more to do than to advance in this same glorious Profession, of which now we only seem to be: – in which, to give it its due, there are a thousand satisfactions to be found, more than in a dull virtuous life!' (VI: 2.1.73–4; 87–90). Such imagery – the merchandizing of sexual pleasure – underscores the ironies of a symmetrical objectification: Cornelia is both a supposed consumer of Galliard's goods and a woman who ostensibly is willing to sell her sexual labour in order to preserve the fiction that women can escape having 'these if's and or's come to pass'. Behn's verbal comedy both acknowledges and forestalls the collapse of 'love and constancy' into masculine privilege and infidelity.

If rakes embody the seductive qualities of a performative masculine identity, Behn's heroines must play roles bound by the double standard of an antifeminist society. Those who remain virtuous, such as Hellena in the first part of *The Rover*, assume roles that other women – particularly her unfeigned courtesans, Angellica Bianca and La Nuche – must play in earnest: the female willing to act, and ultimately act on, her sexual desires. At the end of *The Feign'd Curtizans*, Cornelia informs Galliard that she will be 'the most Mistriss-like wife' who, by feigning to be a courtesan, has 'learnt the trade, though I had not stock to practice, and will be as expensive, Insolent, vain, Extravagant, and Inconstant, as if you only had the keeping part, and another the Amorous Assignations' (VI: 5.1.709–12). Cornelia's merchandizing metaphor renders her role as a courtesan a kind of sexual apprenticeship; marriage will allow her to enjoy her trading privileges. Rather than serving as a promissory note for her husband's sexual pleasure, however, her wit becomes a playful assertion of her political power: her 'Mistriss-like' behaviour threatens to (re)produce the marital nightmares reserved for Behn's puritanical fools. Throughout this scene, Behn exploits the gendered symmetry of cynicism. Having been dallied with by the disguised Cornelia, Galliard must recognize that her threats of insolence, extravagance, vanity, and infidelity are double-edged: they may be playful assertions of a continuing 'gallantry' after marriage but they also can be taken at face value. Like Cornelia, he knows (or suspects) what he is getting, but he acts as though he does not. The happy ending demanded by the conventions of comedy depends ironically on the fiction that Galliard and Cornelia will prove to be something other (doting husband and virtuous wife) than they have been for the previous five acts.

Characteristically, Behn emphasizes the psychological costs for women of introjecting the social norms of virtue, honour, and modesty as the bedrock values of personal identity. Behn's heroines recognize that this process of internalization is inevitable, but that recognition does not mitigate the anguish felt by, say, Angellica Bianca when she realizes that Willmore has won her heart. When Leticia in *The Luckey Chance* realizes that her beloved Belmour is alive, she struggles to explain to him her decision to marry Sir Feeble in lines that succinctly describe the divided psychology of female social existence.

> I will not justify my hated Crime.
> But Oh remember I was poor and helpless.
> And much reduc'd, and much impos'd upon.
>
> (VII: 2.2.48–50)

Her giving in to Sir Feeble's marriage proposal is, at once, a 'hated Crime' for which she accepts responsibility, a consequence of her looming poverty and her lack of a male protector, and a result of her having been 'impos'd upon' – both coerced and deceived by a wealthy and dishonest alderman. Yet, while such lines may convince the audience that her suffering is genuine, the action of the play is devoted far less to a psychological study of women trapped in loveless marriages than to comic stage business that makes the embodiments of puritanical hypocrisy, Sir Feeble Fainwoud and Sir Cautious Fulbank, the butts of ongoing jokes about impotence and cuckolding.[11] *The Luckey Chance* hinges, in part, on a series of very funny contrivances that prevent Sir Feeble from consummating his marriage, including scenes of pure farce: Belmour pretends to be his own ghost to frighten the old man into relinquishing his wife, much of his wealth, and the king's pardon for Belmour, a document that Sir Feeble had obtained fraudulently. The final comedy to be produced in Behn's lifetime apart from the farcical *Emperor of the Moon*, this play poses crucial questions about the relationship between the playwright's feminist concerns and a theatrical practice devoted more to ridiculing hypocritical alderman and self-serving misogyny than to arguing social or philosophical principles.

Staging Behn's comedies

Comparatively little attention has been devoted by critics to Behn's stage-craft, although the contemporary popularity of many of her comedies can be attributed to her superb sense of the theatre and her ability to play off serious love scenes against comic wit battles, titillating seductions, broad satire, and slapstick. Like her male counterparts, Behn relies on her audiences' desire to experience vicariously the thrill of seeing women and rakes acting on socially forbidden desires. These spectacles encourage male and female spectators both to identify with and to distance themselves from what they see onstage, bracketing for two hours the moral and social values they may hold outside the theatre. Because watching a play is a complex social experience, no performance can be reduced to monological displays of moral, religious, or political values, and interpreting three centuries of (often intermittent) revivals, adaptations, and commentary on seventeenth-century plays serves as an important means for analysing theatrical scripts which only can hint at the complexities of performance and reception.[12] In this regard, one of the problems in discussing Behn as a comic dramatist is that, particularly in the United States, critics have little theatrical experience against which to test their judgements: no multiple revivals of plays such as *The Luckey Chance* to assess which interpretations of characters work better than others, no history of different casting and design decisions to sift through, no real sense of the relationship between verbal wit and physical comedy. It is none the less necessary to consider these topics since decisions of actors, directors, and set designers have profound consequences for how spectators respond to the complexities of performance.

For this reason, scholarly questions about Behn's feminism in, say, *The Luckey Chance* cannot be divorced from the ways in which Sir Feeble and Sir Cautious appear to the audience. Although both characters speak a familiar rhetoric of misogynist complaint and condescension, their language is repeatedly undercut and their posturing morality ridiculed. In a characteristic scene, they denounce women's gossip, which they blame for instigating the ridicule and cuckolding of 'the grave and sober Part o'th Nation'. Lady Fulbank, however, undermines their pretensions to gravity and sobriety by attributing their morality to age and illness rather than conviction: 'Wise men', she asserts, 'should not expose their Infirmities by marrying us young Wenches; who, without Instruction, find how we are impos'd upon' (VII: 2.2.128; 130–2). Sir Feeble and Sir Cautious court the satiric judgements levelled against them because their unseasonable desires 'expose their Infirmities'; 'young Wenches' quickly learn for themselves that their husbands can neither perform sexually nor fill the romantic roles of dashing lover that are essential to induce women to collaborate in a system which subordinates their desires to the masculine prerogatives of virtue and property rights.

Notably, these avatars of hypocritical, antifeminist morality were played by two of the leading comic actors of the United Company, James Nokes and Tony Leigh. These actors headline the *Dramatis Personae* published in the 1687 first edition of the play, and their prominence may help explain why *The Luckey Chance* seems, to some critics, one of the less overtly feminist of Behn's comedies. While it is risky to make broad claims, three hundred years later, about how Sir Feeble and Sir Cautious may have been played and received by seventeenth-century audiences, Behn's stage directions suggest that Nokes and Leigh were given the opportunity to steal more than a few of the scenes. Sir Cautious and Sir Feeble, in this regard, are not stock figures who can be ignored or pigeonholed by critics but headlining characters who help define the hybrid nature of Behn's comic practice.

In Act 3, the elderly puritan Sir Feeble is interrupted on his wedding night by the disguised Belmour, and directed to attend an urgent meeting of 'all the Aldermen . . . at *Guild-Hall*' to deal with 'some damnable Plot' (VII: 3.1.129–30), yet another of Behn's jabs at the Whigs.[13] When he arrives at Sir Cautious's house to drag his friend to the nonexistent meeting, each man assumes that the other must have been driven mad by his young wife. The long exchange which follows allows two veteran actors to make the most of farcical misunderstandings, comic asides, and apparently a good deal of physical comedy:

SIR FEEBLE . . . – proceed to the Business good Brother, for time you know is precious.

SIR CAUTIOUS Some strange Catastrophe has happened between him and his Wife to night, that makes him disturb me thus – [*Aside*] come sit good Brother, and to the Business as you say –

They sit one at one end of the Table, the other at the other, Dick [the servant] *sets down the light and goes out – both sit gaping and staring and expecting when the other shou'd speak*

SIR FEEBLE As soon as you please Sir. Lord how wildly he stares! He's much disturb'd in's Mind [Aside] – well Sir let us be brief –

SIR CAUTIOUS As brief as you please Sir, – well Brother –

Pawsing still SIR FEEBLE: So Sir.

SIR CAUTIOUS How strangely he stares and gapes – some deep Concern! [*Aside*]

SIR FEEBLE: Hum – hum –

SIR CAUTIOUS I listen to you, advance –

SIR FEEBLE Sir?

SIR CAUTIOUS A very distracted Countenance – pray Heaven he be not mad, and a young Wife is able to make any old Fellow mad, that's the Truth on't. *Aside*

SIR FEEBLE Sure 'tis something of his Lady – he's so loath to bring it out [*Aside*] – I am sorry you are thus disturb'd Sir.

SIR CAUTIOUS No disturbance to serve a Friend –

SIR FEEBLE I think I am your Friend indeed Sir *Cautious*, or I wou'd not have been here upon my Wedding Night.

SIR CAUTIOUS His Wedding Night – there lies his Grief poor Heart! Perhaps she has cuckolded him already (VII: 3.1.289–311)

The effectiveness of this scene depends on the actors' timing and their ability to use what seem familiar mannerisms for comic effect. Thematically, each character projects his anxieties about cuckoldom onto his friend, but much of the scene's humour can be represented in print only by suggestive dashes and stage directions – 'gaping and staring' – that imply Nokes and Leigh are drawing on a familiar semiotics of physical comedy. They may well be doing a trademark routine. What seem almost meaningless verbal tics, such as the interjection 'Hum –', likely represent verbal cues for Nokes and Leigh to improvise physical comedy that exploits the frequent references to the characters' agitation. Each aside, for example, might involve the actor half-rising from his chair to face the audience, so that almost every other line in the exchange is accompanied by his popping up, sitting down, straightening his periwig, and then gaping and staring. The more farcical these physical bits become, the less likely it is that the audience sees Sir Cautious and Sir Feeble as embodiments of masculine tyranny, and the more fully they embrace their foreordained roles of cuckolds-in-the-making.

While it is difficult to reconstruct how this scene might have been played, or how it may have been integrated with other scenes, such as Sir Feeble's ugly revelations that he has spread rumours about Belmour's death in order to ensnare Leticia in marriage, the length of the exchange (over one hundred lines) suggests a hallmark routine. As a thought experiment, consider this analogy: Leigh and Nokes could be performing a Restoration analogue of Groucho and Chico Marx doing the 'Why a Duck?' scene in their 1929 film *The Cocoanuts*. If this Broadway hit had never been filmed, it would be nearly impossible to deduce from a script what makes this exchange a classic of verbal slapstick. Critics also would struggle to explain the relationship between the 'serious' plot of *The Cocoanuts* – shady land-sale schemes and forgettable young lovers trying to overcome a mother's objection to their marriage – and the comic action: Groucho, Chico, Harpo, and Zeppo playing roles which are primarily excuses for the physical and verbal routines that they had honed through years in Vaudeville and on stage.[14]

My point is not to argue that there is one 'correct' way to play Behn onstage but that the hybrid forms of many of her comedies – *The Widdow Ranter* (1689), for example – suggest that their performances may have been as complex as their thematic structure. Consider the options for the actors playing Sir Cautious and Sir Feeble on the first day of rehearsal for a contemporary production of *The Luckey Chance*. A director who wanted to play up the dark aspects of Behn's critique of masculinist privilege might encourage her actors to play the aldermen as more-or-less serious, if often thick-headed, villains, who must appear enough of a threat to highlight the grim situations in which the heroines find themselves. In this scenario, the audience is presented with the spectacle, at once entertaining and horrifying, of aldermen, identified with the repressive forces of Whig hypocrisy, conniving to force Leticia and Lady Fulbank into the roles of dutiful wives. The director, however, finds that, despite her efforts to emphasize Behn's satire of masculinist tyranny, her two actors keep reverting to type: they play Sir Cautious and Sir Feeble as comic dupes, or satiric butts, who farcically undercut the seriousness of their roles by resorting to verbal mannerisms and sight gags designed to get as many laughs as possible. While the actors keep reassuring the director that they recognize the violence and aggression against women represented by these comic villains, in rehearsal they mug shamelessly to their imagined audience. The scene between Sir Cautious and Sir Feeble threatens to turn into pure slapstick.

As opening night approaches, the director and her actors reach a complex compromise that derives, in large measure, from how they perceive Sir Cautious and Sir Feeble interacting with other characters, particularly the actresses playing Leticia and Lady Fulbank. Although in the table scene they continue to play to the audience, much of the comedy comes from their acting as straight men in scene after scene in which they are outwitted by their wives, Gayman and Belmour. Their inspiration comes from an unusual source: both actors are intrigued by the performance of Louis Calhern in the Marx Brothers' *Duck Soup* (1933), playing the comic villain, Ambassador Trentino, against Groucho's Rufus T. Firefly and Chico and Harpo's inept spies, Chicolini and Pinky. Calhern went on to a successful career playing serious dramatic roles in dozens of films, but in *Duck Soup* he is the perfect foil: he acts as though he is in a white-knuckle espionage movie and is forever angry, aghast, and frustrated each time one or more of the Marx Brothers abuses him.[15] His Ambassador Trentino, then, parodies the kind of role that, in a different genre, could be taken seriously; he remains incapable of learning from experience that Chicolini and Pinky are never going to start behaving like 'real' spies. The actors playing Sir Cautious and Sir Feeble are drawn to the Marx Brothers as a heuristic means to solve the problems of coming up with a 'producible interpretation' of *The Luckey Chance*.[16] They have no way except such an analogy to deal with the gaping and staring that Behn indicates are crucial to a key scene's visual comedy.

My analogy to the Marx Brothers is intended to suggest the need for a critical vocabulary to explore how different registers of performance might overlap in Restoration comedy. While the plot of *The Luckey Chance* asks that the audience take seriously the threat that Sir Feeble and Sir Cautious pose to the young lovers, the long scenes that Behn gives to Nokes and Leigh suggest that audiences appreciated a hybrid form that celebrated different acting styles. In the theatre, plays such as *The Luckey Chance* and the posthumously produced *Widdow Ranter* may have looked more like a Bollywood extravaganza than a decorous drawing-room comedy. Drawing on their generic knowledge that old, impotent husbands never win in social comedy, spectators might well respond to Sir Cautious and Sir Feeble as figures no more (or less) threatening than Ambassador Trentino. The irony, of course, is that the self-serving politician of the 1930s ready to go to war over Groucho's insults caricatures threats much darker than can be contained in an antiwar comedy. As a hybrid, social comedy too represents, mocks, and seeks to defuse the forces that threaten to disrupt its generic commitment to marriages and happy endings.

If literary critics relinquish the default assumption that Restoration comedy was a static, drawing-room genre, then they have a wider range of critical tools with which to explore the ironies of late seventeenth-century theatrical performance. In her comedies, Behn repeatedly exploits the abilities of her actors to parody the roles that, on other nights, they play seriously. In Act 4, Gayman, played by Thomas Betterton, declares once again his love for Lady Fulbank, played by Elizabeth Barry, not realizing that she was the supposed old hag with whom he agreed to have sex in exchange for money. Using the same ring that the disguised heroine had given him the night before, Gayman presents this shop-worn token of his love in the hyperbolic language of Restoration tragedy:

> By this dear Hand,
> And by this Ring, which on this Hand I place,
> On which I've sworn Fidelity to Love;
> I never had a Wish or soft Desire
> To any other Woman,
> Since *Julia* sway'd the Empire of my Soul!
>
> (VII: 4.1.23–8)

Because the audience, as well as Lady Fulbank, knows that Gayman's fidelity did not prevent him from, as he believes, prostituting himself, his protestations make him the butt of the joke, and the speech may well elicit laughter at his expense. Betterton the comic actor, in effect, is parodying Betterton the tragedian; he is playing himself playing the role of a serious lover in a situation in which his character is both sincere (he really loves Lady Fulbank) and double-dealing (he will do anything for money, including having sex with a she-devil). Lady Fulbank controls the scene, yet she too is discomfited comically when Gayman describes the woman he embraced as 'a Carcase . . . so rivell'd, lean, and rough – a Canvas Bag of wooden Ladles' (VII: 4.1.83–4). At the end of the play, when she reveals that she was the mysterious woman, she throws this description back in his face; again, the Etheregean hero becomes the butt of the theatrical joke. Libertinism is simultaneously rewarded and mocked.

Comedy and its consequences

Since the Collier controversy at the end of the seventeenth century, Restoration comedy has been attacked by critics for its immorality.[17] Admirers of Etherege, Wycherley, Congreve, and other Restoration playwrights mounted two paradoxical defences: their comedies offer what the nineteenth-century critic Charles Lamb called a 'Utopia of gallantry', an aesthetics of wit, and, consequently, comic spectacles of immorality and impropriety have no consequences outside the theatre; or these comedies provide serious, even profound satires of universal human follies and vices.[18] In an important sense, Behn's social comedies – perhaps more than any other works of the period – suggest some of the ways in which the interpretations may overlap. In effect, Behn's plays superimpose amoral and moral criteria of judgement that ask the audience to respond to the plays as both fantasy and as 'realistic' comedy commenting incisively on social, moral, and political issues. They portray, often brutally, the predicaments, even the stark realities, facing women in the seventeenth century, but they also reprogramme masculinist fantasies of complaisant women to focus on the comic significance of female desire.

It is significant, in this context, that Behn defends her dramatic practice in the Preface to *The Luckey Chance* by identifying her works with broadly accepted comic traditions, represented by friends such as the playwrights John Crowne and Edward Ravenscroft as well as the Jacobean playwrights Beaumont, Fletcher, and Shakespeare. She accuses her critics of employing a prudish double standard to single out her plays as somehow more bawdy than those of her male contemporaries – and therefore more likely to embarrass female spectators. While it would be a mistake to ignore her charges of gender bias, her comments, as Laurie Finke and Marcie Frank astutely suggest, need to be read in the context of Restoration critical prefaces; typically, playwrights respond to criticism or indifferent third-night receipts by castigating inattentive or biased audiences.[19] In defending her comedies, Behn does not have to excuse any theatrical failures and therefore she is able to attribute the charges levelled against her to jealousy: 'unbyast Judges of Sense', she claims, would have to acknowledge that she 'had made as many good Comedies, as any one Man that has writ in our Age' (VII, p. 217). Given the success of many of her plays, Behn is neither bragging nor exaggerating: even if 'the Woman damns the Poet' for critics who find her plays bawdy, their critique can be dismissed as a knee-jerk reaction to her success. Their attempts to tar *The Luckey Chance* 'with the old never failing Scandal – That 'tis not fit for the Ladys' (VII, p. 215) is as much an attack on those female audience members who get her jokes as it is on the dramatist. Behn's comedies are 'not fit for the Ladys' *not* because they traffic in 'bawdy' – what Restoration comedy doesn't? – but because the dramatist demystifies the spectacle of female complicity in the misogynist value systems of her time: heroines who seem to be ideal marriage partners – young, rich, and beautiful – do not buy into the fantasy of the rake reformed and regard their own objectification with cynicism. They may ultimately have to act as though they are unaware of the consequences of their complicity, but they recognize those costs all the same. In depicting the dilemmas and ironies of women forced to test the limits of social and sexual propriety, Behn insists that the women in the audience get the joke: female desire and self-interest can be reconciled only in the fantasy solutions of old men unaccountably giving up the very trappings of success – women and wealth – to disenfranchised gallants.

Behn's insistence on writing comedies that mock 'the old never failing Scandal' of masculine authority ironically comes at the expense of the rake-hero. Rather treating her heroes as embodiments of a heartless libertinism, Behn turns Willmore, Wilding, and her other rakes into idealized and objectified figures, who are nonetheless crucial to the fantasies that feminine desire can be freed from masculinist compulsion, masculine good nature distinguished from careless cruelty, and female sexuality enjoyed without its material consequences – shame, suffering, and pregnancy. It is not that Behn lacks psychological insight into the male mind or, even less, that she lacks the talent to mimic the theatrical language of psychological depth. Rather her heroes must always be less than the apparent sum of their parts: although they all are physically attractive, witty, loyal to the royalist cause, and always on the verge of coming into their rightful inheritances, they exist only in dialectical opposition to their foils: the old men, foolish husbands, and overprotective guardians who embody the ideological machinery of repression. Willmore and his compatriots have, in effect, no interiority because the very psychology of masculine identity can find its expression only in the puritanical logic of repression and self-denial and in the concomitant antifeminist attacks on women for their 'failures' to stabilize masculine identity irrevocably in crisis. In her comedies, to paraphrase Pope, most men have no characters at all: character and good nature are incompatible because the psychology of male insecurity demands that female desire be restricted to endless validations of masculine self-worth. What Behn's heroines can expect from their lovers, then, are only the parodic performances – rakes playing the roles of faithful lovers. In a comic universe dominated by cynical reason, however, playing along with such fantasies provides perhaps 'the Ladys' with their best and only revenge.

NOTES

1 For representative views, see Catherine Gallagher, 'Who Was That Masked Woman? The Prostitute and the Playwright in the Comedies of Aphra Behn', in *Rereading Aphra Behn*, pp. 65–85; Derek Hughes, *The Theatre of Aphra Behn* (Basingstoke: Palgrave, 2001); Susan J. Wiseman, *Aphra Behn* (Plymouth: Northcote House, 1996); Todd; Sue Owen, 'Sexual Politics and Party Politics in Behn's Drama, 1678–83', in *Aphra Behn Studies*, pp. 15–29; Ros Ballaster, 'Fiction Feigning Femininity: False Counts and Pageant Kings in Aphra Behn's Popish Plot

Writings', in *Aphra Behn Studies*, pp. 50–64; Heidi Hutner, 'Revisioning the Female Body: Aphra Behn's *The Rover*, Part I and II', in *Rereading Aphra Behn*, pp. 102–20; and Robert Markley, '"Be impudent, be saucy, forward, bold, touzing, and leud": The Politics of Masculine Sexuality and Feminine Desire in Behn's Tory Comedies' in *Cultural Readings of Restoration and Eighteenth-Century English Theatre*, ed. J. Douglas Canfield and Deborah Payne (Athens: University of Georgia Press, 1995), pp. 114–40.

2 See John Harwood, *Critics, Values, and Restoration Comedy* (Carbondale: Southern Illinois University Press, 1981), and Robert Markley, 'The Canon and its Critics', *Cambridge Companion to English Restoration Theatre*, ed. Deborah C. Payne (Cambridge: Cambridge University Press, 2000), pp. 226–42.

3 J. Douglas Canfield, *Tricksters and Estates: On the Ideology of Restoration Comedy* (Lexington: University of Kentucky Press, 1997).

4 See Robert Markley, '"Still on the Criminal's Side, against the Innocent": Libertines and Legacies in the Plays of Etherege and Wycherley', in *Blackwell Companion to Restoration Drama*, ed. Sue Owen (Oxford: Blackwell, 2001), pp. 326–39.

5 On social comedy, see Harriett Hawkins, *Likenesses of Truth in Elizabethan and Restoration Drama* (Oxford: Clarendon, 1972); Michael Neill, 'Heroic Heads and Humble Tails: Sex, Politics, and the Restoration Comic Rake', *The Eighteenth Century: Theory and Interpretation*, 24 (1983), 115–39; Jacqueline Pearson, *The Prostituted Muse: Images of Women and Women Dramatists, 1642–1737* (London: Harvester, 1988); Robert Markley, *Two-Edg'd Weapons: Style and Ideology in the Comedies of Etherege, Wycherley, and Congreve* (Oxford: Clarendon Press, 1988); Brian Corman, *Genre and Generic Change in English Comedy 1660–1710* (Toronto: University of Toronto Press, 1993); and Derek Hughes, *English Drama, 1660–1700* (Oxford: Clarendon, 1996), pp. 113–61, 185–239.

6 Pat Gill, *Interpreting Ladies: Women, Wit, and Morality in the Restoration Comedy of Manners* (Athens: University of Georgia Press, 1994), p. 73.

7 On cynical reason, see Peter Sloterdijk, *Critique of Cynical Reason*, trans. M. Eldred (Minneapolis: University of Minnesota Press, 1987), and Slavoj Zizek, *The Sublime Object of Ideology* (London: Verso, 1989), pp. 32–3, 42–5.

8 Zizek, *Sublime Object of Ideology*, p. 33.

9 *The Complete Plays of William Congreve*, ed. Herbert Davis (Chicago: University of Chicago Press, 1967), 2.1.265–6.

10 See Paulette Scott, '"There's Difference in Sexes": Masculine Sexuality and Female Desire in Behn's *The Feign'd Courtesans*', in *Aphra Behn (1640–1689): Identity, Alterity, Ambiguity*, ed. Mary Ann O'Donnell, Bernard Dhuicq, and Guyonne Leduc (Paris: L'Harmattan, 2000), pp. 167–76; Todd, pp. 242–4; Alison Shell, 'Popish Plots: *The Feign'd Curtizans* in Context', in *Aphra Behn Studies*, pp. 30–49; and Jane Spencer, '"Deceit, Dissembling, all that's Woman": Comic Plot and Female Action in *The Feigned Courtesans*', in *Rereading Aphra Behn*, pp. 86–101.

11 See Anita Pacheco, 'Consent and Female Honor in *The Luckey Chance*,' in *Aphra Behn (1640–1689)*, pp. 145–54; Hughes, *The Theatre of Aphra Behn* (Basingstoke: Palgrave, 2001), pp. 158–70; and Todd, pp. 356–63.

12 See Janet Todd, *The Critical Fortunes of Aphra Behn* (Columbia, SC: Camden House, 1998).

13 On Behn's satire of the Whigs, see Owen, 'Sexual Politics and Party Politics in Behn's Drama', pp. 15–29; Ballaster, 'Fiction Feigning Femininity', pp. 102–20; and Markley, '"Be impudent, be saucy, forward, bold, touzing, and leud"', pp. 114–40.

14 See Joe Adamson, *Groucho, Chico, Harpo, and Sometimes Zeppo: A History of the Marx Brothers and a Satire on the Rest of the World* (New York: Simon and Schuster, 1973).

15 Calhern appeared as a third- or fourth-billed star in movies such as *Julius Caesar* (1953), *The Prisoner of Zenda* (1952); *Notorious* (1956), and *Blackboard Jungle* (1955); and he starred in John Sturges' biopic of Oliver Wendell Holmes, *The Magnificent Yankee* (1950).

16 See Robert D. Hume and Judith Milhous, *Producible Interpretation: Eight English Plays 1675–1707* (Carbondale: Southern Illinois University Press, 1985).

17 See Michael Cordner, 'Playwright versus Priest: Profanity and the Wit of Restoration Comedy', in *Cambridge Companion to English Restoration Theatre*, pp. 209–25.

18 Charles Lamb, 'On the Artificial Comedy of the Last Century', in *The Life and Works of Charles Lamb*, ed. Alfred Ainger, 12 vols. (London: Macmillan, 1899), II, p. 281. See pp. 277–89.

19 On Behn's criticism see Laurie Finke, 'Aphra Behn and the Ideological Construction of Restoration Literary Theory', in *Rereading Aphra Behn*, pp. 17–43, and Marcie Frank, *Gender, Theatre, and the Origins of Criticism: From Dryden to Manley* (Cambridge: Cambridge University Press, 2003), pp. 91–100.

8

HELEN M. BURKE

The Cavalier myth in *The Rover*

The Rover. Or, The Banish't Cavaliers is the most frequently performed and read of Aphra Behn's plays, yet, when it was first staged by the Duke's Company at the Dorset Garden Theatre in London in March 1677, Behn went to some lengths to conceal her authorship of this play.[1] The 'Person of Quality' who wrote the prologue (most likely Behn herself) used masculine pronouns to refer to the author, and this 'Person' further diverted attention away from the playwright by suggesting that this author was *'unknown'* (v: Prologue, 5). As the acknowledged author of six plays, Behn was hardly an unknown in London's theatre-going circles at this time. In 1675, indeed, she had been listed in a theatrical compendium as *'Astrea Behn*, a Dramatic writer, so much the more considerable as being a Woman, to the present English stage'.[2]

Why, then, did this 'considerable' woman dramatist employ these strategies of concealment? The reason most frequently advanced is that Behn was trying to avoid a plagiarism charge relating to her use of material from *Thomaso, Or The Wanderer*, a play written by Thomas Killigrew, the recently retired Master of the Revels and manager of the rival King's Players at Drury Lane.[3] The playwright's own words in the third issue of her play are also often invoked to support this reading. In this issue, Behn finally acknowledged her authorship of *The Rover* and, in a postscript, she revealed that initially she had trouble getting her play printed because of the rumour that it was *Thomaso* 'alter'd'. *'The Play had been sooner in Print,'* she wrote, *'but for a Report about the Town (made by some either very Malitious or very Ignorant) that 'twas* Thomaso *alter'd; which made the Book-sellers fear some trouble from the Proprietor of that Admirable Play'* (v: Postscript, 1–3). In this chapter, however, I will suggest that Behn's desire for anonymity, as well as her continued insistence that her play was not '*Thomaso alter'd*', had more to do with her parodic use of this borrowed material and her complex, feminist-inflected brand of royalism than the simple fact of borrowing itself (Killigrew, after all, had also borrowed much of *his* play from older sources).[4] A parody always exists in a fraught relationship with its original; while it flatters its source by imitating it, it also offers an indirect criticism through its comic reworking of the source material. *The Rover* stands in just such critical relationship to Killigrew's play and, as we will see, there were political implications to her critical 'altering' that Behn wished to disavow.

Thomaso was written in the 1650s while Killigrew was in exile with Charles I and his court, and it takes its meaning, at one level, from the life of the author. The principal character in this baggy, ten-act play is an exiled cavalier who shares the same first name as the author (Thomaso) and by showing the heroic as well as the rakish side of this character, Killigrew undoubtedly hoped to dispel the persistent and damaging rumours about his own dissipation and 'Letcherie' (he was lampooned for 'Letcherie' in 1642, and charges that he had disgraced the King by his licentious behaviour surfaced while he was an ambassador for the court in Italy in 1649).[5] But this play, when it first appeared in print in a richly bound volume in 1664, also acquired meaning from the royalist propaganda that circulated in print and on the stage during the early Restoration – propaganda that anxiously sought to impose a romantic and providential framework on the deeply disturbing events of the Interregnum.[6] As Harold Weber has pointed out, such propaganda frequently focused on Charles's strange adventures and miraculous escapes during his period of banishment. To cite Weber: 'The role reversal forced on Charles during the escape dramatize[d] the license and disorder of those years when England betrayed its monarchical traditions; his return as king signal[ed] an end to the upside-down carnival world that the nation had so long endured.'[7] Killigrew's *Thomaso* can be regarded as a variant of this royalist 'wonderful travels' genre. Much of this play is devoted to following Thomaso's adventures as he pursues the famous courtesan, Angellica Bianca, and two lesser-known courtesans, Saretta and Paulina and, during this period of disorder, the cavalier colonel dons disguises, gets into fights, and rubs shoulders with mountebanks, clowns, con-men, and monsters. But this carnivalesque world is ultimately contained within a romantic and religious narrative that asserts aristocratic values by revealing the cavalier to be the saviour of the imperilled maiden and, by extension, of the imperilled nation.[8]

Before the play began, we are told, Thomaso has rescued the virtuous and noble virgin, Serulina, from 'the licenc'd Lust of common Souldiers',[9] and this heroic past, together with his devotion to sacred music and St. Cecilia (T1: 3.4; T2: 1.1), already mark Thomaso out as the disguised warrior-knight, the guardian of the political and religious order in the traditional romance. When he rescues the disguised Serulina from a rape attack by his own subordinates, Edwardo and Ferdinando, this traditional order also begins to reassert itself, and it triumphs definitively at the end of the play when Thomaso foils a plot on his life by the courtesans and rescues Serulina from a forced marriage engineered by her tyrannical brother. In what could be read as a royalist allegorization of the Restoration, the figures of misrule, Angellica, Edwardo, Ferdinando, and Paulina, depart for the carnival in Venice, while the 'Wanderer' assumes his long deferred leadership role as the husband of the 'bright Serulina' (T2: 5.10), the virgin who stands for the captive nation. The frontispiece of the collection in which this play appeared also explicitly encouraged this kind of political reading. This illustration shows Killigrew at his writing with a stack of his plays, one of which is *Thomaso*, by his side. But, hanging directly over these plays is a portrait of Charles I, and underneath the frontispiece is an inscription reminding the reader of Killigrew's service to both Charles I and Charles II; it reads 'Thomas Killigrew, Page of Honour to King Charles the First Groome of the Bedchamber to King Charles the Second and his Majesties Resident with the Republique of Venice in the year 1650'.[10]

By the late 1670s, however, the political failures and libertine excesses of the King and the court had put stress on the myth of the noble cavalier,[11] and the theatre was registering this change. Plays had become more bawdy and more cynical, and the rakish cavalier was the focus of intense scrutiny in royalist, as well as anti-royalist, drama. There was still a discernible difference, however, between how the two political camps represented this controversial figure. The anti-royalist, Thomas Shadwell, for example, drew the rake in his comedy, *The Libertine* (1675), as a vicious and ruthless seducer who lacked any redeeming features, while the court 'wit' and former exiled cavalier, Sir George Etherege, gave his rake complexity and glamour (albeit of a devilish kind) in *The Man of Mode* (1676). Despite his flaws, the aristocratic rake is still a transcendent figure in Etherege's drama; if he finally triumphs, it is because of his superior intelligence, breeding, and gallantry.

By taking up Thomaso's story, then, Behn was entering the political fray, and because of her loyalist background – like so many of the cavaliers, she had done foreign political service for the King, and she was friends with many of the court 'wits', including Killigrew – it might have been expected that she would produce another transcendent rake of the Etherege variety. To a certain extent, too, she does. The plot of *The Rover* revolves around the sexual adventures of a group of penniless exiled cavaliers – most notably, Willmore (the 'Rover') and Belvile, his colonel – during carnival time in Naples, and, like the rake hero in pro-royalist comedies, these cavaliers finally emerge victorious from all their love skirmishes. By the end of the play, Willmore and Belvile have won the hands of two noble and rich sisters (Hellena and Florinda), and those characters who served as obstacles to this restoration of English aristocratic power – the courtesan, Angellica, who temporarily distracted Willmore with her love, and the girls' brother, Don Pedro, who tried to force Florinda into an arranged marriage and Hellena into a convent – are defeated and marginalized. But a feminist difference also complicated Behn's royalism, leading her to formulate a less than flattering view of her triumphant cavalier hero – and, from the play-within-the play in Act 4, scene 2 of *The Rover*, it is clear that Behn thought that this feminist critique was best delivered anonymously and in the guise of an 'unknown' young man.

The drama that the cross-dressed Hellena stages for Willmore and Angellica in this fourth act, indeed, could be regarded as a metacommentary on Behn's political and dramatic art in *The Rover* and, as such, it provides a good point of entry into this complex work. This play-within-the play is set in motion when Hellena, '*drest in Man's Cloths*' (v: 4.1.278b), spies Willmore talking to Angellica on the street, shortly after he has sworn to give the courtesan up and, as is clear from her asides, the heroine feels a complex mix of desire and resentment at this spectacle of cavalier infidelity. She first states that Willmore's 'unconstant humour' makes her love him all the more (v: 4.1.281), but a moment later she reconsiders and swears that she will do something 'to vex him for this' (v: 4.1.285). As we see from the ensuing scene, this 'vexing' has a dramatic component; it consists of putting on a show that effectively topples the cavalier from his heroic pedestal. Pretending to be a young man from a wealthy and noble family, she tells 'a Tale' (v: 4.1.304) about a 'young *English* Gentleman' who first seduced and then callously abandoned a young woman from that family (v: 4.1.311–39), and by telling her story with 'Art'– her statement that she is 'too young to tell [her] Tale with Art' (v: 4.1.304) is clearly disingenuous – she succeeds in transforming the cavalier from an object of admiration into an object of derision and scorn. Angellica, who is the immediate audience for this performance, becomes convinced that Willmore is the 'cunning flatterer' (v: 4.1.333) in question, and she turns on him in fury. And the theatre spectators, who are the larger audience, get to laugh at the cavalier as he moves around the stage pursued by the two angry women. 'So, so, the storm comes finely on', Willmore mutters in an aside, as the women hurl abuse at him (v: 4.1.375).

The mocking dramatic 'art' in *The Rover*, I suggest, emanated from a similar complex mix of emotions on the author's part, though the object of Behn's desire and resentment was not an individual cavalier but the system of male aristocratic privilege that the cavalier hero represented. As she openly stated in many of her writings, Behn desired the same liberties as her male cavalier counterparts but as a woman she was also frequently frustrated in these desires.[12] She thus occupied the same kind of liminal position as Hellena in the above scene and, like her cross-dressed heroine, she takes revenge by putting on a show that turns one embodiment of this male aristocratic privilege – Thomaso – into a comic butt. As noted above, Behn uses the same basic triangular configuration of virgin/whore/cavalier as Killigrew but, as Jones DeRitter first pointed out, she also reconfigures this triangle so as to engineer the collapse of the male hero and to invent an alternate more elevated role for women.[13] In her carnivalesque inversion of the cavalier myth, as we will see, it is the woman – virgin and whore alike – who are the agents of correction and restoration.[14]

Behn first signals the centrality of the woman by multiplying the number of virgins in her play – she has not one but three – and by foregrounding the views of two of these virgins. In the discussion between the sisters, Florinda and Hellena, in the opening scene of the play, we get the female perspective, as it were, on the traditional romance plot and, as this discussion reveals, this perspective is highly critical of the male dominance of this plot. Both sisters reject the roles assigned them by their father (an arranged marriage for Florinda and a nunnery for Hellena), and both express their determination to disobey these paternal commands and follow their own desires. Behn also begins her assault on traditional distinctions within and across gender lines in this first scene by giving these young women the bawdy, witty lines that were reserved for the courtesans or for the male cavalier characters in Killigrew's play. When Hellena announces that she is going to escape the fate of the nunnery and 'provide' herself with a man during the carnival (v: 1.1.34), she echoes a statement made at the beginning of *Thomaso* by Killigrew's Angellica who, in hanging out her sign, announces that she is seeking her 'pleasure' after the 'Nunner[y]' of her jealous old lover's bed (T1: 2.1). And when Hellena paints a sexually graphic and disgusting picture of what marriage to an old man would be like (v: 1.1.107–11), she echoes lines used by Thomaso's male friend, Harrigo, in the earlier play (T2: 2.1).

In devising their own plan to get out the patriarchal prison, all three of Behn's virgins also show the initiative and daring reserved for cavaliers and courtesans in Killigrew's play. As the one who came up with the carnival plan and as the one who explicitly expresses the desire to 'Ramble' (v: 1.1.168), Hellena most closely resembles the cavalier hero, and it is she who is undoubtedly the leader of this band of feisty virgins; 'We'll out-wit Twenty Brothers, if you'll be rul'd by me', she tells her sister (v: 1.1.165–6). But her kinswoman, Valeria, as well as Hellena herself, provide the costumes necessary for the escape, and even Florinda, who most resembles Killigrew's romantic heroine, plays an active role. Like Serulina, Florinda has been rescued in the past by a noble cavalier colonel (Belvile, in this play) and like her too, she voices a conventional concern for her 'Soul' (v: 1.1. 21; 3.1.51) and her 'Honour' (v: 1.1.69). But this conventional side does not prevent her from devising her own rescue plan or from enclosing this plan in a letter to Belvile (v: 1.1.177–9). In each of the three significant male/female encounters that occur in the next scene – Hellena / Willmore, Florinda / Belvile, Lucetta / Blunt – it is also the woman, whether virgin or courtesan, who initiates, controls, and advances the action. As soon as Hellena sees Willmore, she says, 'I'le to him' (v: 1.2.121), and, through her witty word-play and gypsy role-playing, she gets him to agree to a future meeting without assuaging his 'swinging Appetite' (v: 1.2.184). At the same time, Florinda uses her gypsy wiles long enough to slip the reluctant Belvile the letter detailing her escape plan, and the courtesan, Lucetta, uses her seductive arts and 'Wit' (v: 1. 2.197) to flatter and lure away Blunt.

The cavaliers, for their part, are implicitly 'feminized' by being on the receiving end of these exchanges, and Behn further suggests their ineptitude as heroes by other subtle alterations of the *Thomaso* plot. As the colonel and the one who has rescued Florinda from 'the Licenc'd Lust of common Souldiers' (v: 1.1.67), Belvile *should* be the main focus of interest if this was a 'proper' (that is, male-centred) romance. But it is his subordinate, Willmore, who dominates the action in this scene and, as is demonstrated in his encounter with the first group of masquerading women, this 'mad' sol-dier, as Frederick calls him (v: 1.2.60), embodies the very licence and lust that endangered the heroine in the first place. Belvile has to order Willmore not to use 'violence' as these women depart with other men (v: 1.2.93). The par-allelism between Willmore and the country booby squire, Blunt, throughout this scene also suggests that this central cavalier character should be viewed as a comic butt. Like Blunt, Willmore is a naive outsider who has to be instructed about the courtesans and the mores of the country and like Blunt, who *struts and Cocks* in front of Lucetta (v: 1.2.197b), he also makes him-self ridiculous in front of these masquerading women with his extravagant courtly conceits. When he tries to impress one of these women with these flowery conceits, Belvile pointedly reminds him that he 'stink'st of Tar and Ropes Ends, like a Dock or Pest-house' (v: 1.2.90–1). In asserting to Belvile that he is 'no tame sigher, but a rampant Lion of the Forrest' (v: 1.2.100), Willmore also demonstrates the classic boastfulness of the mock-chivalric or false knight, and the fact that Hellena and other characters in the play address him as 'Captain' (v: 1.2.168) further encourages this identification. As a 'Captain', Willmore is aligned with a whole series of swashbuckling, dis-orderly braggart soldiers in theatrical history, ranging from Plautus' *miles gloriosus* to Jonson's Captain Bobadil and 'Il Capitano in the *commedia dell'arte*.

The unorthodox gender oppositions that are set up in this first act are then played out in the rescue plot that occupies most of the rest of the play and, as this plot unfolds, the cavalier myth takes a further beating. If we follow Willmore's progress, we see that for most of the play, Behn's principal cavalier character fails miserably in the role of heroic saviour, the role that ultimately serves to legitimate the cavalier's final ascendancy in Killigrew's drama. In response to Hellena's question about his ability to 'storm' a nunnery wall during their first encounter, Willmore certainly promises that he can storm 'most furiously' (v: 1.2.162), and in response to Belvile's request for aid in storming Florinda's wall, he is equally emphatic. 'Kind heart', he says, 'if we Three cannot weave a String to let her down a Garden-Wall, 'twere pity but the Hang-man wove one for us all' (v: 1.2.254–5). His last ringing words to Belvile at the end of Act 1, too, are 'I will not fail you' (v: 1.2. 311). These words, however, are soon exposed as empty braggadocio. The only 'storming' that Willmore does in Act 2 is in the house of the courtesan, Angellica (she asks him, at one point, if he could not 'storm on still', v: 2.1.403) and, to get into her bed, he overrides his colonel's wishes and breaks his promise to meet Hellena. Because of his drunken celebration in the wake of his sexual conquest of Angellica, then, he is unable to fulfil his promise to aid his colonel in rescuing Florinda. Instead, in further violation of his duties as a hero, he draws on his commanding officer and threatens rape on the heroine himself. The drunken sot who chases Florinda around the garden is the very antithesis of the hero, as the distressed damsel herself suggests when she describes him as 'a filthy Beast' (v: 3.2.139).

In thus reducing her cavalier hero to a rapacious beast, Behn also makes her most politically daring revision of Killigrew's plot. In *Thomaso*, there is a similar rape attempt on the romantic heroine Serulina but it is Edwardo, the character who most resembles Blunt, who is the perpetrator. Since this character is vaguely identified with the parliamentarians and the country gentry who supported the uprising against the King, this rape attempt would have worked to discredit the anti-royalists: indeed, as Susan Owen points out, the usage of rape as a 'trope of monstrosity' for the Civil War rebellion was common in royalist writing at this time.[15] In giving the rape attempt to Willmore, however, Behn implicitly suggests that the cavalier and the aristocratic system he represents pose as great a threat to the safety of the nation as the rebellious country gentry, and this point is further driven home by the parallelism created between Willmore and Blunt (Edwardo's replacement) in this scene. As DeRitter points out, Florinda's 'filthy Beast' comment creates an imaginative link between the cavalier hero and the '*Essex*-Calf' (Blunt) (v: 3.2.94) who has just crawled out of the 'Common Shore' after his failed sexual escapade with Lucetta.[16]

Willmore's pattern of not delivering on his boasts is repeated in the next rescue attempt and, as he fails to meet his obligations as a lover and soldier, he is shown to be an ever-increasing greater danger to the play's most noble characters. Immediately after the fiasco in the garden, an apologetic Willmore tells the furious Belvile that he will 'set . . . all right again', and he promises to 'do his Business' in relation to any rival for Florinda (V: 3.2. 223; 233). But a moment later, he is engaged in a brawl with Don Antonio, a rival for Angellica, and when Belvile returns to help him in this fight, he, not Willmore, is arrested. With the classic insouciance of the *miles gloriosus*, the still-inebriated Willmore reels home to sleep, leaving his commanding officer to be locked up by foreign soldiers (V: 3.2.265–6). In Act 4, just as the disguised Belvile is about to whisk Florinda off to the church to marry her, Willmore also unwittingly 'outs' him in front of Don Pedro and, in so doing, he causes the heroine to be locked up. And shortly after this, he unwittingly puts this heroine in new and more terrible jeopardy by again mistaking her for a courtesan. As he begins to pursue her on the street, so does her brother, Don Pedro, and this pursuit drives Florinda into the cavaliers' lodging where she is subjected to the threat of gang rape and incest. Blunt, who has been abused by the courtesan, Lucetta, is the first to express his intention of raping her but Willmore, Frederick, and Don Pedro join him in his plan and, in what is arguably the lowest moment in the play's depiction of the cavalier character, Willmore quarrels with the other men over who should have her first (V: 5.1.87–9).

In contradistinction to Killigrew's play, too, Behn refuses to allow Angellica to be the scapegoat for this kind of male degeneracy. In *Thomaso*, the virgin / courtesan distinction is overlaid by a set of broader moral and ethical distinctions, corresponding approximately to a soul / body, sacred / profane dichotomy. Even while Thomaso is still pursuing his rakish lifestyle, for instance, he forbids Harrigo to name Serulina and Angellica together, saying the 'one is my religion, the other my sport and diversion' (T1: 4.2). And at the end of the play when he does name the two women together, it is to point to the differences between 'a vertuous passion and a lustful flame', between 'her [Serulina's] noble mind' and 'others, [that are] malicious and bloody' (T2: 4.9). The women themselves also accept their place within this moral, as well as sexual, economy. Angellica reiterates the adage 'once a whore and ever' and agrees that she is 'not a good woman' (T1: 2.4), and Serulina echoes this view when she states that 'a Virgin once blown upon by the world . . . is for ever stain'd' (T1: 4.2). In finally opting for Serulina over Angellica, then, Killigrew's hero can be seen to have done the right thing on all fronts, and his political and financial reward – he is restored to power and riches by his marriage – can be seen as an appropriate reward for his moral rectitude.

In Behn's play, however, the line between virgins and courtesans is blurred from the beginning and the meaninglessness of this distinction becomes even more pronounced when her Angellica begins to talk and act like the play's romantic heroine. Critics have sometimes suggested that Hellena is Angellica's alter ego in this play and there is certainly evidence to support this view.[17] Angellica competes directly with Hellena for Willmore's love in Behn's play and, in her first scene with the cavalier, the courtesan takes up the critique of mercenary marriages that Hellena began in the first act. At one point too, Willmore confuses the two women; when the masked Angellica arrives to shoot him in the last act, he runs up and begins to flirt with her, under the mistaken impression that she is his 'pretty Gipsie' (v: 5.1.189). In the high seriousness with which she pursues her lover throughout this play, however, Angellica is even closer to the romantic Florinda and her prototype, Serulina, and Behn reinforces this connection by giving the courtesan the language and actions of a heroine in a heroic drama or tragedy.

In the first love scene between Angellica and Willmore, the courtesan speaks in blank verse, a form that is generally reserved for serious drama, and after she falls in love in this scene, her allusions to her 'Soul' (v: 2.1.342; 4.1.473), her 'Virgin heart' (v: 4.1.234), and her 'Vows' (v: 4.1.274; 5.1.243) further link her to the heroines of this kind of drama and to the traditional economy that these heroines uphold. Her decision to give up all for love after this conversion – the only pay she asks of Willmore is 'thy Love for mine' (v: 2.1.418) – and her subsequent decision to kill Willmore after he has failed to keep his promise make her, in effect, the play's best spokeswoman for traditional, self-sacrificing femininity. To shoot Willmore would bring certain death to herself but, having recognized that she has lost his love and her own 'Honour' (v: 5.1.270), she is prepared to kill and be killed in keeping with the demands of romantic femininity's self-annihilating code. Far from vindicating the cavalier, then, Willmore's final rejection of Angellica further damns him (at least in the terms of a traditional moral and sexual economy) and his last action of trying to buy her 'credit' with a purse of gold (v: 5.1.288–9) completes his condemnation. The cavalier rake, this action suggests, is the real whore since he is incapable of thinking outside a cash economy.

How, then, did Behn get away with such criticism? Why (despite her fears) was her play a success even with the very aristocratic spectators she ridiculed? To answer this question, it is again useful, I suggest, to look at Hellena's 'art' in the play-within-the play scene discussed above. In this scene, Hellena mixes her condemnation of the 'young *English* Gentleman' with flattering comments on his 'Charms' and 'Beauties' (v: 4.1.316, 330) and, after the moment of discomfort mentioned above, Willmore chooses to concentrate on the latter. He reads female adulation not condemnation into her story and is ultimately buoyed rather than dismayed by her performance. The ending of *The Rover* is available for a similar double reading by any aristocratic male spectator at this play. At one level, this ending serves to complete the travesty that Behn began in Act 1 when she gave the initiative to the women in the rescue plot. It is not a man but the quick-thinking Valeria who finally saves the heroine from the risk of rape and incest, and this gender difference in the romantic plot is foregrounded by the reaction of both the cavalier colonel and the romantic heroine herself. Before Valeria intervenes, Belvile stands around in dismay, not knowing what to do to deliver Florinda from her plight – 'now I fear there is no way to bring her off,' he says (v: 5.1.104–5) – and after her delivery, Florinda recognizes Valeria, not Belvile as her 'dear Preserver' (v: 5.1.133). Her embrace of Valeria at this point, it could be argued, points obliquely to an alternate kind of political order, one in which women, not men, would have the leading role.

At another level, however, this last scene provides a cover for the comic butt when it gives Willmore the opportunity to intimidate Don Pedro into accepting the marriage of Florinda and Belvile and his own marriage. This action, of course, stretches credibility (we are asked to believe that a noble Spaniard, who can draw on the military aid of the viceroy's son, is so intimidated by the very idea of a 'surly Crew' (v: 5.1.365), of penniless English sailors that he instantly drops his opposition to the marriage of his two sisters). Nevertheless, through this action, the cavalier hero can be said to have made good on his original promises to deliver both virginal heroines, and the artful Hellena herself suggests this reading just prior to this action. When she says to Willmore, 'now Captain, shew your Love and Courage; stand to your Arms, and defend me bravely, or I am lost for Ever' (v: 5.1.464–6), she directs the audience to forget her cavalier's demonstrated history of heroic failure and see him only as the traditional knight in shining armour – a type of Thomaso.

If Behn began to restore the cavalier hero in a more earnest manner in the two plays that could be read as sequels to *The Rover* – *The Feign'd Curtizans, or, a Nights Intrigue* (1679) and *The Second Part of the Rover* (1681) – it was also because the conditions for her earlier kind of mockery no longer existed. At the end of *The Rover*, when Willmore complains about how 'severely' Hellena has used him in the past, his intended bride replies: 'That's all one, such usage you must still look for, to find out all your Haunts, to raile at you to all that Love you, till I have made you love only me in your own defence, because no body else will love [you]' (v: 5.1.396–8).[18] This promise can be read as a veiled statement on Behn's part about her own future intentions as a dramatic writer, a warning that she was going to continue her satiric attacks on the cavaliers until they reformed – at least in their relation to women.

But the promise that she would 'raile' at the cavalier to 'all that Love you' also suggests that Behn's mockery is a kind of 'intramural' one, one that takes for granted the very aristocratic hegemony which it lampoons. During the height of the Popish Plot scare and the Exclusion crisis (1678–81), it was no longer possible to have that sense of certainty. To 'raile' at the cavaliers in the theatre then was no longer 'to raile at [them] to all that Love [them]' since the Whig Opposition was now in the ascendancy and, faced with this different political and social reality, Behn began, as it were, to restore Thomaso, making the cavalier rake once again the centre of the drama and giving him back much of the status that he had in earlier Restoration comedies.[19] As she does so, her whores and virgins lose much of their previous psychological and sociological depth; in these more explicitly royalist plays, the women once again become largely symbolic signifiers that serve as guarantors of aristocratic male *virtu*.

This shift is already apparent in *The Feign'd Curtizans*. In this play, as in *The Rover*, the action of this play takes place in Italy, and again the central male character is a rakish English gentleman (Galliard) who is bent on pursuing courtesans over the advice of his more serious-minded companion (Sir Harry Fillamour). Here, however, Galliard does not get drunk or attempt any rapes and the blame for his womanizing is lessened by the fact that the courtesan whom he pursues, La Silvianetta, proves to be a total fiction constructed by two of the play's scheming virgins; both Cornelia, a character who has Hellena's wit and energy, and Laura Lucretia, a character who has Angellica's serious-mindedness, pretend to be the courtesan, La Silvianetta. Ostensibly this 'feigned courtesan' pretext fulfils the same function as the masquerade costumes in *The Rover*; it is the means by which the virgins free themselves from the convent, a forced marriage, and an oppressive patriarchy. But it is also a means by which Behn delivers her cavalier hero from having to deal with the sticky ethical problems created by his exploitation and abandonment of the Angellicas of the world – her means of getting him out, as it were, from under the feminist gun. This strategy of restoring the cavalier's innocence by reducing the courtesan to an empty signifier is also repeated in the other plot strand that involves Fillamour and Marcella, Cornelia's older sister and the Florinda of this play. Fillamour is momentarily distracted from his devotion to Marcella by another imagined courtesan who goes by the name of Euphemia. But, like Belvile in *The Rover*, he does not succumb to this temptation and, when Euphemia turns out to be Marcella in disguise (like Florinda, she too adopts a courtesan name to escape a forced marriage), even this momentary errancy is put under erasure.

As the image of the 'feigned courtesan' works to debunk the stereotype of the degenerate cavalier, it also works to reinforce the stereotype of Whig/Puritan credulity and hypocrisy and, in so doing, it takes aim at the Whig opposition that had fanned the Popish Plot scare of the previous year. As Alison Shell points out, Behn was making an implicit comment on the Popish Plot when she transformed the whore into a wholly illusionary threat since, for puritan and Whig propagandists, it was that great 'Whore of Babylon', the Catholic Church, which was reputedly behind the plot to kill the King and enthrone his brother, James, Duke of York.[20] Through the characters of Tickletext and Squire Buffoon, too, Behn more directly targeted these propagandists. Tickletext is a puritan divine who travels with the young country squire, Buffoon, to protect him against the 'eminent danger . . . of being perverted to Popery' (VI: 1.1.183–4) and, at the beginning of the play, he warns his pupil against everything associated with 'Popery' including the 'Romish Curtizan' (VI: 1.2.101). Secretly, however, Tickletext pursues the very courtesans he condemns and, as he competes with Galliard for the 'La Silvianetta' through ever more grotesque antics, his anti-courtesan and anti-'Romish' rhetoric is exposed as so much hypocritical cant. The anti-Catholic posturing of the Whig faction, this subplot suggests, is of a similar nature; it is a mere pious mask for self-interest and appetite.[21]

The Second Part of The Rover, which was performed at the darkest moment (from the royalist perspective) of the Exclusion Crisis, is even more partisan and, consequently, much closer in tone and style to its Killigrew source than the first *Rover*. As noted above, in the frontispiece of his collection, Killigrew created an imaginative link between his 'Wanderer' and the Stuart princes, and he tacitly instructed his readers to interpret his fictional cavalier's trials and tribulations as an allegory of their recent history. In the dedication to *The Second Part of The Rover*, Behn provided a similar kind of political framing for her hero. Addressing herself to the Duke of York, who had gone into voluntary exile in an attempt to diffuse the Exclusion crisis, she links James's sufferings to the past sufferings of the 'Royal Martyr', Charles I, and also to the 'Storms of Fate' suffered by her fictitious cavalier (VI, pp. 15, 47). Her 'faithful Soldier', she writes to James, was '. . . driven from his Native Country with You, forc'd as You were to fight for his Bread in a strange Land, and suffer'd with You all the Ills of Poverty, War and Banishment, and still pursues Your Fortunes' (VI, pp. 46–50).

These framing remarks, and the biting remarks in the same preface about the Whig leaders who have stirred up the people against James – a 'Politick self-interested and malicitious few,' Behn suggests, 'betray the unconsidering Rest' with their 'lucky Cant' (VI, pp. 19–21) – instruct us how to read the romantic plot and the comic subplot of this play, and also how to understand the changes in the Willmore of this play. In this sequel, Willmore is still in exile (this time in Madrid), and once again he is a penniless cavalier. As befits his royal prototype, however, he is now a 'Noble Captain' (vi: 1.1.19), a soldier who is admired by all the other noble characters in the play; even his principal rival in love, the English ambassador's son, Beaumond, for instance, admits that he is 'brave, handsom, gay, and all that Women doat on' (vi: 2.1.326–7).[22] If this Willmore rails 'roughly' at women when we first meet him (vi: 1.1.34), excuses are also provided for his cynicism and bitterness. His 'Saint' Hellena (vi: 1.1.72–3) is dead, we soon learn and his most recent lover, the whore, La Nuche, has jilted him in favour of a rich old man, Don Carlo. We are also encouraged to read these romantic losses and betrayals allegorically when Willmore moves from railing against La Nuche to railing against 'Fortune':

> *Carlo* the happy man! a Dog! a Rascal, gain the bright *La Nuche*! Oh Fortune! Cursed blind mistaken Fortune: eternal friend to fools! Fortune! that takes the noble rate from man, to place it on her Idol interest.   (vi: 1.1.28–30)

La Nuche, these lines suggests, is a figure for those historic changes and forces that had driven out the noble James and set up the 'Politick self-interested and malitious few' – the mercantile Whig faction – in his place. In making this connection between 'Fortune' and La Nuche, Behn is also drawing on a well-established literary convention. *Fortuna* was often represented as a whore, as evidenced, for example, by the player's speech in Shakespeare's *Hamlet* in which Priam's fall is blamed on the 'Strumpet Fortune' (*Hamlet*, 2.2.504).

Willmore's pursuit of La Nuche and his attempt to win her back from her mercenary suitors, then, dramatizes the royalist political struggle during the Exclusion Crisis, and because the romantic quest is infused with this abstract, allegorical meaning, this play takes on some of the artificial, stylized quality of a royalist masque. Willmore again underscores the larger abstract stakes in this quest when he states that La Nuche is 'the promis'd good, the Philosophick treasure' for which he toils (vi: 3.1.240–1), and the rich Beaumond (who soon displaces Don Carlo as Willmore's chief rival) also draws attention to the connection between La Nuche and 'Fortune' when he describes her as a 'Beauty . . . whose charms have power to fix inconstant Nature or Fortune were she tottering on her Wheel' (vi: 1.1.150–1). When La Nuche vacillates between Beaumond and Willmore, as she does throughout the play, she behaves like 'Fortune . . . tottering on her Wheel', and she makes explicit the philosophical and political alternatives represented by these lovers in a masque-like tableau in Act 5. 'What shall I do?' she asks, pointing first to Beaumond and then to Willmore: 'here's powerful Interest prostrate at my feet, Glory, and all that vanity can boast; – But there – Love unadorn'd, no covering but his Wings, No Wealth, but a full Quiver to do mischiefs' (VI: 5.1.92–5). At the end, when La Nuche decides to throw her lot in with Willmore and follow him 'as fortune pleases' (VI: 5.1. 504), there is also very little psychological preparation for her change of mind. Her decision to trust in his 'word' rather than in the 'formal foppery of Marriage' (VI: 5.1.508–10) is rather dictated by the ideological need to show the restoration of a political and social economy based on the bond of honour rather than on contract – to dramatize 'Fortune' turning her wheel back to the side of the noble wanderer.

Even as Behn sacrifices the complexity of her female characters to the needs of royalist propaganda during this crucial period for the monarchy, however, it should also be noted that she does not entirely abandon her earlier 'vexing' feminist habits. In this last play, for instance, there is also a rich virgin (Ariadne) who pursues Willmore, and by the logic of *Thomaso* and the traditional aristocratic romance, Willmore should have finally chosen this virgin for his bride. When instead Behn makes the whore the transcendental signifier – the fantasy that guarantees her royal hero's triumph at the end of this play – she once again suggests the arbitrariness of this virgin/whore division and, by linking this whore to the unstable *Fortuna*, she also gestures, however obliquely, at the instability of all such female signifiers.

The mountebank drama that is central to this play's comic subplot creates a similar disturbance at the interior of this royalist allegory. This mountebank drama (which is again drawn from Killigrew's play) is staged by Willmore as part of his counterplot against the two country squires, Fetherfool and Blunt, who are scheming to 'domineer' over Willmore and the other 'Renegado Officers' (VI: 1.1.222–3) by marrying a pair of rich Jewish women 'Monsters' (VI: 1.1.169). The squires first intend to transform the 'Monsters' – a giant and a dwarf – into average-size women with the aid of the magical baths of a visiting Mountebank but, by impersonating the Mountebank and, with the assistance of two of his loyal officers, Willmore foils their plot and exposes these squires as treacherous fools. Because these country squires have many of the same Whig/puritan associations as Blunt in *The Rover* or Squire Buffoon in *The Feign'd Curtizans*, this victory also seems, at first glance, to reinforce the aristocratic triumph of the main romantic plot. The scene in which these two 'politick Asses' (as Willmore calls them) (VI: 1.1.242) anxiously purchase fake potions from the fake Mountebank in the hope that these potions will make them 'vigorous and brave' and transform them into 'the Heroes of the Age' (VI: 2.1.199, 201–2), for example, can be read as a not-so-subtle satire on those Whig pretenders to power – many of them of the 'country' party – who supported the Duke of Monmouth in the current crisis. And the Mountebank's whole spiel about transformation and 'Reformation' – the 'Divine Baths of Reformation' are his most famous ware (VI: 2.1.273) – can be read as a metaphor for that reformist Whig 'Cant' that Behn denounces in her preface. The Mountebank's allusion to 'the old Oracle of the box, which resolves all Questions' (VI: 2.1.274–5) also establishes the satirical political subtext of this scene. Many of those who supported the Duke of Monmouth during the Exclusion Crisis claimed that there existed a box that contained proof of his legitimacy.[23] But by putting this 'box' among the Mountebank's fake wares, Behn suggests that such claims are totally fraudulent

But in suggesting that there is no 'Oracle' that can transform flawed mortals into the 'Heroes of the Age', Behn also comes dangerously close to suggesting that her own royalist dramatic art – the art she is now using to transform a brutish cavalier into a 'noble' one – is also fraudulent. The 'renowned Man of Arts and Science' (VI: 3.1.243–4) who stands on his stage and attempts to seduce the watching 'Rabble' with his promises of magical 'Reformation' is also suggestive of the renowned playwright herself in her new role as royal propagandist – a connection that is reinforced by the theatrical elements which surround the Mountebank's show. His drama, like the playwright's own, is also accompanied by singing, dancing, and harlequin acts. In the prologue to this play, too, Behn explicitly represents herself as a kind of con artist and her present work as a kind of 'cheat':

> Poets, like States-men, with a little change,
> Pass off old Politicks for new and strange;
> Tho the few men of sense decry't aloud,
> The cheat will pass with the unthinking Crowd:
> The Rabble 'tis we Court, those powerful things,
> Whose voices can impose even Laws on Kings.
>
> (VI: 231)

While these lines could be read as Behn's ironic commentary on the state of the drama in the current, Whig-dominated theatre, they could also be read as her implicit admission that her 'restored' Rover is a bit of a fiction – one necessitated by the politics of the moment. Hellena's carnivalesque laughter, it could be concluded, was never far from the surface when Behn dealt with the cavalier myth and, indeed, this disruptive laughter would break out again after 1681, when the wheel of fortune really began to turn in favour of the royalists. The celebratory yet also critical treatment of Tom Wilding, the Tory rake hero of The City-Heiress; or, Sir Timothy Treat-all (1682)[24] is proof, for instance, that Behn had not forgotten Hellena's promise to 'raile' at her royalist rake hero and treat him 'severely' whenever she encountered him.

NOTES

1 See Jane Spencer, *Aphra Behn's Afterlife* (Oxford: Oxford University Press, 2000), pp. 187–222.
2 Edward Phillips, *Theatrum Poetarum, or a Compleat Collection of the Poets, Especially the most Eminent, of all Ages* (London: Charles Smith, 1675), p. 255.
3 See, for example, Spencer, *Aphra Behn's Afterlife*, p. 23.
4 See the introduction to *The Rover* in *The Works of Aphra Behn*, ed. Montague Summers, 6 vols. (London, 1915), I, p. 4.
5 For the autobiographical elements in *Thomaso* see Alfred Harbage, *Thomas Killigrew, Cavalier Dramatist, 1612–83* (1930; New York: Benjamin Blom, 1967), pp. 226–8, 73, 88.
6 Paula R. Backscheider, *Spectacular Politics* (Baltimore and London: Johns Hopkins University Press, 1993), pp. 3–31.
7 Harold Weber, *Paper Bullets: Print and Kingship under Charles II* (Lexington, Kentucky: University Press of Kentucky, 1996), pp. 26, 28.
8 For the frequency of this kind of political allegory in the love plot of Restoration serious drama, see J. Douglas Canfield, *Heroes and States: On the Ideology of Restoration Tragedy* (Lexington, Kentucky: University Press of Kentucky, 2000).
9 Thomas Killigrew, *Thomaso, Or The Wanderer*, in *Comedies and Tragedies* (London, 1664), Part 1: 350. Subsequent citations from *Thomaso* will refer to this edition, and Part 1 and Part 2 of this play will be cited, respectively, as T1 and T2. References will also include act and scene number.
10 Killigrew, *Comedies and Tragedies*, Part 1, Frontispiece.
11 See Derek Hughes, *The Theatre of Aphra Behn* (Basingstoke: Palgrave, 2001), p. 83.
12 See Jessica Munns, '"I by a Double Right Thy Bounties Claim": Aphra Behn and Sexual Space', in *Curtain Calls: British and American Women and the Theater, 1660–1820* (Athens: Ohio University Press, 1991), pp. 193–210.
13 See Jones DeRitter, 'The Gypsy, *The Rover*, and the Wanderer: Aphra Behn's Revision of Thomas Killigrew', *Restoration*, 10 (1986), 82–92.
14 For a similar argument about Behn's revision of the female role in this play, see Heidi Hutner, 'Revisioning the Female Body: Aphra Behn's *The Rover*, Parts 1 and 11', in *Rereading Aphra Behn*, pp. 102–20.
15 Susan J. Owen, 'Sexual Politics and Party Politics in Behn's Drama, 1678–83' in *Aphra Behn Studies*, p. 16.
16 DeRitter, 'The Gypsy, *The Rover*, and the Wanderer', p. 87.
17 See Nancy Copeland, '"Once a whore and ever"? Whore and Virgin in *The Rover* and Its Antecedents', *Restoration*, 16 (1992), 20–7.
18 'You' is inserted in the third quarto.
19 For the view that Behn gradually grew into royalist politics, see Todd.
20 Alison Shell, 'Popish Plots: *The Feign'd Curtizans* in context', in *Aphra Behn Studies*, p. 39.
21 For a similar reading, see also Owen, 'Sexual Politics', pp. 16–18.

22 For a similar reading of Willmore, see also Robert Markley, '"Be impudent, be saucy, forward, bold touzing, and leud": The Politics of Masculine Sexuality and Feminine Desire in Behn's Tory Comedies', in *Cultural Readings of Restoration and Eighteenth-Century English Theater* eds. J. Douglas Canfield and Deborah C. Payne (Athens, Georgia: University of Georgia Press, 1995), pp. 114–40.

23 See note to line 274 in Todd, *The Second Part of the Rover*, VI, p. 458.

24 For a persuasive account of Behn's ambivalent treatment of the royalist rakes in *The City Heiress*, see Hughes, *Theatre*, pp. 147–57.

9

ROS BALLASTER

'The story of the heart': *Love-Letters between a Noble-Man and his Sister*

In the final stanza of Aphra Behn's pastoral poem, 'The Golden Age', the authenticity, integrity, and moral credit of the poem's nostalgic idealism is radically undermined by revealing the interest of its speaker:

> But *Sylvia* when your Beauties fade,
> When the fresh Roses on your Cheeks shall die,
>   Like Flowers that wither in the Shade,
> Eternally they will forgotten lye,
> And no kind Spring their sweetness will supply.
> When Snow shall on those lovely Tresses lye
> And your fair Eyes no more shall give us pain,
>   But shoot their pointless Darts in vain.
> What will your duller honour signifie?
> Go boast it then! and see what numerous Store
> Of Lovers, will your Ruin'd Shrine Adore.
>   Then let us *Sylvia* yet be wise,
>   And the Gay hasty minutes prize:
> The Sun and Spring receive but one short Light,
> Once sett, a sleep brings an Eternal Night.
>
> (I, p. 35)

The ideal of the economy of the 'gift', the language of pastoral 'liberty', is a ploy to get something for nothing. And the name Sylvia encourages us to connect this beloved with the beleaguered heroine Behn was writing about at the same time ('The Golden Age' was published in her *Poems Upon Several Occasions* of 1684), the recipient of the urgent love letters from her sister's husband, who uses the precedent of the 'golden age' to seduce her into giving him the final favour as a gift to cement their love. In *Love-Letters between a Noble-Man and his Sister*, Philander tells his Silvia that he has left cabals at court to come to her father's country seat and await her summons from a cottage in the grounds; all around him he sees the pleasures of 'natural' love unhindered by taboo (against incest especially since theirs is counted by law an incestuous desire), rule and regulation:

> every Sound that meets the sense, is thy proper Musick, oh Love! and every thing inspires thy dictates; the Winds a round me blow soft, and mixing with the wanton Boughs, continually play and Kiss; while those like a coy Maid in Love resist and comply by turns; they like a ravisht vigorous Lover, rush on with a transported violence; rudely imbracing its Spring drest Mistress, ruffling her Native order, while the pretty Birds on the dancing Branches incessantly make Love; . . . no Parents checking their dear delights, no slavish Matrimonial tyes to restrain their Nobler flame. No spyes to interrupt their blest appointments, but every little Nest is free and open to receive the young fletch't Lover; every bough is conscious of their Passion, nor do the generous pair languish in tedious Ceremony, but meeting look, and like, and Love, imbrace with their wingy Arms, and salute with their little opening Bills. (II, p. 35)

Both the poem and the prose narrative deploy pastoral personae to explore the nature of love in a 'fallen' environment. The latter also carries with it a series of analogies to contemporary political and social scandals which give this exploration additional depth and resonance. *Love-Letters* refers to two linked public events of the period. First, the elopement of Ford, Lord Grey of Werke, with Lady Henrietta Berkeley, his wife's younger sister, which resulted in Grey's trial (along with five supposed accomplices) for 'Unlawful Tempting and Inticing' of Henrietta to 'Unlawful Love' and carrying her away from her father's house with 'an intent to cause her to live in a Scandalous manner' with him; the trial took place on 23 November 1682 and all the defendants (bar one supposed accomplice) were found guilty, only for the matter to be compromised and no judgement recorded after Henrietta Berkeley's marriage to Grey's factotum, Mr Turner, was proved. Shortly afterwards a transcript of the trial proceedings was published but the affair had already been made notorious by Lord Berkeley's placing of an advertisement in the *London Gazette* in late September 1682 offering a £200 reward for information leading to the return of his errant daughter. Second came the discovery among a group of Whig Protestants, including Grey, of a plot to murder Charles II and his brother and expected successor, the Catholic James Duke of York, on their return from Newmarket in the Spring of 1683. James Scott, Duke of Monmouth, Charles II's illegitimate son by Lucy Walter, around whom leading Protestants had begun to rally in an attempt to promote him as an alternative successor to the Catholic James, went into hiding at the home of his mistress, Henrietta Wentworth in Bedfordshire; he returned to be reconciled to his father the following

November. Other conspirators were less fortunate; William Lord Russell, Thomas Armstrong, and Algernon Sidney were executed, and the Earl of Essex slit his own throat in the Tower. Grey was arrested on 25 June 1683 but succeeded in escaping abroad with Henrietta Berkeley in tow.

The first volume of the *Love-Letters*, dedicated to Thomas Condon, a young captain and ardent supporter of the Duke of York, was licensed in October 1683 and published by Randal Taylor in 1684. A tightly written series of letters, largely between the two lovers, it charted the intrigue between them and eventual flight. Behn presented the epistolary exchange as one between a supporter of the sixteenth-century Duke of Condé, leader of the Huguenot faction in France and his mistress from a loyal Catholic family, conflating this earlier Duke to some extent with the leader of the mid-seventeenth century 'Fronde' against Louis XIV's Regency. The second volume of 1685 was dedicated to Lemuel Kingdon, paymaster-general to the forces in Ireland and one of the prime movers against Monmouth, whose invasion in July 1685 after the death of his father and accession of his Catholic uncle had been rapidly quashed. Although Behn must have turned it round very rapidly following the defeat at the battle of Sedgemoor, she did not deal with the collapse of the Monmouth faction but rather invented a series of intrigues, infidelities and new sexual pursuits for Silvia and Philander in continental Europe. It was not until the third part of 1687, two years after Monmouth's execution and Grey's accommodation with James II at a cost of £40,000 and a full confession brokered by the Earl of Sunderland, that she turned to a close account of the weakness at the heart of Monmouth's support. In this concluding part she also recounted Silvia's development as a full-blown female libertine. The dedication on this occasion went to Sunderland's wild son, Robert Spencer, a convert to Catholicism; Janet Todd speculates that Sunderland himself may have commissioned the third part from Behn with a 'spin' in accordance with Grey's portrayal of Monmouth as a weak and divided leader which could serve as a monitory example to his son.[1] Todd also notes that part 3, despite its disavowals in its closing sections, was much more historically accurate than the first two, following 'in the actual rebel footsteps of Grey and Henrietta as they trundled around the Low Countries and Germany',[2] possibly with the assistance of access to Grey's confession extracted on paper from him by Sunderland but not published until 1754 with the title *The Secret History of the Rye-House Plot*.

Although the relation between historical events and Behn's plots in the *Love-Letters* can be easily tracked as above, the ideological intent of the story's 'parable' has proved more opaque for critics, who appear to be divided between those who view Silvia and Monmouth/Cesario as contrasting characters – Silvia's narrative one of courtesan ascendance and imitation of masculine libertinism and Monmouth/Cesario's one of emasculation and domestic decline from potential heroism[3] – and those who view Silvia and Monmouth/Cesario as analogues of each other, virtuous figures seduced into rebellion and departure from traditional loyalties and values.[4] This same division is apparent between the same critics in their evaluation of Silvia: she is cast either as a positive model, a figure of monarchy, authority and fictional power who comes to eclipse the compromised figures of the Stuart kings themselves, or she is viewed as a negative example of decline from innocence into politico-sexual chicanery. But the experience of conflicting interpretation, ambiguous reference, and slippage of meaning is one that is inscribed into the novel itself and is, in fact, structural to its understanding of the necessarily 'fallen' nature of political and sexual life.

In the fallen world, the relationship between sign and referent is always unstable, always open to slippage depending on the desire of the addressee to produce a meaning which suits his or her own interest. In the second part of the *Love-Letters*, Silvia suspects that Philander's affections have been alienated during their separation, a feeling reinforced when she receives a cold letter from him accusing her of jealousy and suspicion. She mourns the loss of a simple correspondence between word and body, when both mutually reinforced a message of unequivocal love in their early courtship:

> Oh *I* have known a time – but let me never think about it more! it cannot be remembered without madness! What think thee fallen from love! to think that I must never hear thee more pouring thy Soul out in soft sighs of love? A thousand dear expressions by which I knew the Story of thy heart, and while you tell it, bid me feel it panting . . .   (II, p. 189)

Stories of the heart, it appears, are less easy to decipher and easier to impersonate than the naive or idealist reader supposes. Silvia's readers know, or at least suspect, that even this early 'paradise' of love housed 'inauthenticity' in the shape of a lover who can only 'feel' love when he turns it into a verbal (as opposed to corporeal) narrative and casts himself as central protagonist. His cold letters to Silvia are accompanied by feverish narrative accounts to his friend, the Dutch prince Octavio of his pursuit of the lovely married Calista, unaware that his new love-object is Octavio's sister. At the end of his second letter to Octavio which details his full possession of Calista's charms, he comments 'I have sent you a Novel, instead of a Letter of my first most happy adventure' (II, p. 272).

Narrative proves to be just one among a number of forms of exchange that develop as surrogates for and instigators of 'feeling' in persons estranged from the primary pleasures of a 'golden age'. Indeed, the deeper 'allegory' of this novel may chart the development of the novel in general in the period: from naive reading of the letter as self-expression in part one, to an understanding of the role of 'reading' in constructing narrative meaning in part two, to a fully performative understanding of the activities of both reading and writing in the novel in the third part. William B. Warner concludes that 'Silvia appears less as a single character than as a sort of personification of the novel on the market'.[5]

In Behn's narrative universe, fallen nature brings with it the instigation of elaborate rituals and structures which serve as forms of exchange, to establish social relationship between parties who can no longer deal directly or honestly with each other and for whom desire has become perversity. New pleasures tied to the pursuit of domination over others, political or sexual, develop to take the place of innocent dyadic union. And as Silvia's comments on Philander's letter demonstrate, the spoken word is replaced by the written text, a form which impersonates the physical presence and is open to more abuse than the 'signs' of the body. In the fallen world, forms of written 'credit' are volatile rather than authentic. Throughout the novel, Behn plays with the idea of instability of paper credit in three fields of social interaction in which it takes a prominent role: courtship (the love letter), spying (the informant letter sometimes deploying cipher) and gaming (the gambler's bond, chit, or paper money). As these forms of paper credit take precedence over authentic physical 'expression', the body itself becomes a form of malleable text. Lovers can impersonate each other's bodies: both Silvia and Calista adopt male disguise, Silvia's maid Antonett can impersonate her mistress in the bedchamber and Brilljard, Philander's servant, can substitute for Octavio in the same encounter. Even Silvia's pregnancy, first noted shortly after Philander's departure for Cologne in part two but not completed until after Calista's (presumably premature) delivery in part three, appears to be something that can be forgotten or recalled at will according to the character's own narrative convenience.

In each part of the *Love-Letters* one trope of exchange – courtship, spying, gaming – comes to govern our reading of Silvia's narrative's 'progress', if progress it can be called, from naive reading to cynical performance. These are tropes to which Behn returned repeatedly, especially in her own epistolary performances, her letters and reports written while on her spying mission to the Netherlands on the part of the English government,[6] and purported letters reproduced in 'The History of the Life and Memoirs of Mrs Behn' of 1698, as well as the 'Love-Letters to a Gentleman' reproduced in the same publication and probably composed during her romance with John Hoyle in the late 1670s and early 1680s.

Letters: courtship

you . . . have prescrib'd me Laws and Rules, how I shall behave my self to
please and gain you
    ('Astrea to Lycidas', *Love-Letters to a Gentleman* in *Works*, III, p. 266)

The first part of the *Love-Letters* draws on the tradition of the *Lettres Portugaises*, first translated into English in 1678 by Sir Roger L'Estrange which in turn exploited the voice of female complaint associated with Ovid's seduced and abandoned correspondents in the *Heroides*.[7] Here, and in the *Love-Letters to a Gentleman*, Behn impersonates the Portuguese style, a studied artlessness in writing which invokes the thrills and sensations of the body as a testimony of sincere passion by contrast with the elaborate rhetorical figuration associated with the dominant prose medium for amatory narrative of the seventeenth century, the romance. This tradition privileges the pleasure of sight; the abandoned heroine bemoans the loss of the vision of her beloved, his physical presence is a guarantor of his affection and his absence the grounding premise of her own (hysterical) writing. Moreover the Ovidian/Portuguese heroine struggles to assert her mastery of both the relationship and her writing, having learnt the rules and customs of love from her seducer who has now abandoned her. Behn, however, is concerned in the first part only with the period of courtship itself – the period of instruction and exchange – rather than its aftermath. Nevertheless, the reader is constantly aware of the lack of equivalence between male and female correspondent (and the vast majority of the letters are from Silvia and Philander alone); while Philander imitates a familiar style, he teaches it to Silvia who reproduces his language believing it to be an authentic and transparent medium for the conveyance of 'true love'. She 'credits' his vows and assurances, investing them with her own desire for their authenticity. Silvia, unlike her reader, fails to see the inequality of rhetorical experience in their relationship and asserts triumphantly at the close of part one:

when a true view is taken of the Soul, when no base interest makes the hasty bargain, when no conveniency or design of drudge, or slave, shall find it necessary, when equal judgments meet that can esteem the blessings they possess, and distinguish the good of eithers love, and set a value on each others merits, and where both understand to take and pay; who find the beauty of each others minds, and rate 'em as they ought, whom not a formal ceremony binds (with which I've nought to do; but dully give a cold consenting affirmative) but well considered vows from soft inclining hearts, utter'd with love, with joy, with dear delight when Heaven is call'd to witness; She is thy Wife, *Philander*, He is my Husband, this is the match, this Heaven designs and means . . .

    (II, p. 112)

Silvia has learnt the language of Philander here, the claim that 'free' love is an exchange between equals; it is 'free' of the 'formal ceremony' of marriage which conveys familial (especially paternal) consent. Silvia abandons one form of constraint and structure – the role of dutiful daughter in her father's house – only to fall victim to another: the role of acquiescent mistress.

The Portuguese and libertine rhetoric Silvia is learning from her more experienced lover is a language that consistently denies its own rhetorical status. The premise of the love-letter is the physical absence of the beloved; the letter is a substitute for that body, but it also insistently privileges the bodily sign over the word, spoken or written. Silvia asserts that 'The Rhetorick of Love is half-breath'd, interrupted words, languishing Eyes, flattering Speeches, broken Sighs, pressing the hand, and falling Tears' (II, p. 33). In her next letter she complains 'the story of the heart cannot be so well told by this way as by presence and conversation' (II, p. 38). However, when the lovers do finally successfully meet in a midnight tryst, the body fails them both: Silvia faints in an excess of excitement and Philander finds himself unable to complete her ravishment, whether through premature ejaculation or impotence (his account leaves this ambiguous). The love-letter itself is also prone to fail to meet its ideal, to act as a straightforward and unambiguous conduit for the desire between two correspondents. Behn makes full use of the physical machinery of the letter novel; one letter is hidden under strawberries brought to Silvia in a basket and almost discovered by her mother when she calls for a dish to place them in (II, p. 32): Philander instructs Silvia in another to burn the letter as he has not had time to counterfeit his hand (II, p. 47): the romance is nearly discovered when a visiting noblewoman seizes the letter Silvia is writing in jest but Silvia's quick thinking passes it off as a letter she is writing on behalf of her less literate servant Melinda.

The body, the letter, the family, courtship itself, are all exposed to be determining structures that the writer only imagines him or herself able to control or transcend. The dismissal of such structures as mere 'formality' on the part of the lovers is in itself a convention which is learned. Admittedly, at this stage in the narrative these conclusions are left for the reader to deduce and the main 'reader'/recipient of the text, Silvia herself, remains locked in the pleasurable delusion of a primary intimacy with her lover, which is entirely original and free of pre-scription.

The first part of the *Love-Letters between a Noble-Man and His Sister* also operates on a fairly simple level of political allegory by comparison with the two later parts. Silvia is a Tory heiress, her lover a Whig conspirator, and his rhetoric exposes the self-interest and potential anarchy behind the Whig Protestant critique of the Stuart monarchy. In a rare political exchange between the lovers, Philander reveals that he supports Cesario, the rebel son and also the man who seduced Philander's own wife, not out of conviction of Cesario's rightful claim to the throne but rather because Philander sees it as an opportunity to further his own ambition. If the principle of hereditary monarchy is done away with, who is to say that Philander himself might not come to have a claim? 'I may rise' comments Philander 'but I cannot fail' (II, p. 47).

Without the formal convention of hereditary monarchy, even if it is a legal fiction, all that remains is the competition of individual wills. However, there is no evidence that Silvia changes her political loyalties even if she abandons her filial ones. This, in itself, suggests that the correspondence between amatory and political plots is not absolute in the narrative. Sexual and political loyalty are not simple analogues to each other, as the continuing parts will reveal. As the novel continues, sexual and political plots come to follow increasingly separate paths.

Adventures: spying

As successful and popular as the amatory epistolary novel in the late seventeenth century was the epistolary account purported to be by a spy. Almost exactly contemporary with the first two volumes of the *Love-Letters between a Noble-Man and his Sister* was the French text by a Genoese journalist called Paolo Marana entitled *L'Espion Turc* which appeared in four slim volumes in Paris (and the last in Amsterdam) between 1684 and 1686 and was translated into English as one volume in 1687. Seven more volumes of letters appeared first in English and then translated back into French from 1691 onwards: all six hundred letters are ostensibly written by a spy for the Ottoman court named Mahmut living in Paris disguised as a Moldavian translator between 1637 and 1682. Behn would probably, given her appetite for French fiction, have read the text as it appeared in French; it offered a form of popular history and satire making parallels between French and Ottoman absolutism, but much of its appeal lay also in conveying the paranoia and isolation of the foreign correspondent living abroad in constant fear of discovery. Grey's account of his exile after 1683 in the Low Countries shares Mahmut's ever-present fear about suspicion falling on him from within his own camp as well as from his enemies. And the constant financial difficulties. Grey complains that, when his attempts to secure some protection from the Elector of Brandenburg[8] were frustrated by the intervention of James II, 'I had before me the prospect of being always a vagabond, and that a poor one too.'[9] Behn in her letters from the Low Countries of the 1660s complains repeatedly of lack of funds to support her spying venture: she was detailed to report on the plans of exiled regicides including her old acquaintance and possibly lover, William Scot, whom she had befriended when she travelled to Surinam several years earlier.

The conventions of the epistolary 'spy' account overlap in Behn's novel with those of the popular 'courtesan' narrative of the late seventeenth century. Like the Duchess of Mazarin, whose story was told by César Vichard de St-Réal in his 1675 *Memoires de Mm. La Duchesse de Mazarin*, Silvia elopes abroad in male disguise and proves doubly attractive to both the male and female sex in this guise. As Alison Conway notes, 'Curiosity governs the courtesan narrative's logic',[10] a characteristic which also marks out the prospective spy and associates the heroine Silvia with her creator, Aphra Behn, the woman writer who discovered she could make more profit and win more credit through writing narratives of love than by secret correspondence as a spy.[11] Behn herself learnt a (fairly simple) cipher to produce written reports for her employers about her activities among rebels in the Low Countries, and Margaret Ferguson suggests we can extend the notion of the spy's cipher to her understanding of the exchange between readers and writers: 'a type of code or secret writing that invites (but may also resist) full deciphering by reader and spectators with varying amounts of information about the authorial subject(s)'.[12]

In the second part, Behn complicates the interpretative exchange by opening out the cast of characters and discussing the contradictory impulses behind both reading and writing as forms of social/sexual interaction. We encounter a new suitor for Silvia, a Dutch nobleman called Octavio, who pursues her with the honourable aim of marriage. Philander's enforced separation from Silvia when he is banished from Holland under pressure from his political enemies results in his infidelity in Cologne with the lovely Calista, the convent-bred wife of an old Spanish count; Philander, ignorant that Calista is Octavio's sister, discloses the affair by letter to his new Dutch friend. Octavio's attempts to win Silvia are undermined by the plotting of Brilljard, Philander's man-servant and Silvia's 'husband' himself enamoured of her, and Antonett, Silvia's French maid, who is pursuing an affair with Brilljard. There is then a symmetry between the plots of the first and second part in that at their centre is the account of the seduction of an innocent young woman subject to the control of a lascivious old man (Count Beralti in part 1, Count Clarinau in part 2), but the second part also marks significant departures establishing a virtuous brother-sister pairing in the shape of Octavio and Calista to act as a contrast to the incestuous brother-sister pair encountered in the first part, and seeing the servants actively scheme to undermine rather than support the activities of their employers (in part one Brilljard and Melinda, Silvia's maid, are go-betweens and co-conspirators for the lovers).

The plots of part 2 introduce the reader and characters to new pleasures, those of manipulating the feelings and responses of others for personal gain. They also repeatedly expose how readers and writers project their own desires into the texts they consume and produce. Thus, when Silvia 'stages' herself for Octavio as a prospective mistress by lying in dishabille with a book of amours in her hand on a sofa hung inside with images of classical heroes being tempted from manly glory by prospects of sexual pleasure, Octavio responds by casting himself at her feet and requesting that she recompense his lost honour only with her love; her narrative dictates his own unwitting response. Meanwhile, Silvia herself gains pleasure from this encounter; the narrator reports that 'I have heard she said she verily believ'd that acting and feigning the Lover possest her with a tenderness against her knowledge and Will' (II, p. 202).

If the hidden springs of plot become more opaque to the characters in part two, the introduction of an omniscient narrative voice provides more interpretative guidance for the reader. While Silvia experiments with fairly crude forms of dissimulation in order to try and persuade Octavio to reveal what he knows about Philander's behaviour in Cologne, the narrator gives us an insight into the different motives behind all the characters' actions; s/he acts as a 'spy' for the novel's reader. Pleasure in looking now becomes the prerogative of the reader who watches events unfold through the narrator's eyes with voyeuristic interest but also a certain measure of critical distance. In one critical scene Silvia and Octavio discover Brilljard's deceit; he posed as Octavio in order to blackmail Silvia into offering him a night of passion in exchange for information about Philander's infidelity. His plot was foiled by Silvia's deploying Antonett in her place and his own over-enthusiasm in the consumption of an aphrodisiac which caused a stomach disorder on the night of their tryst; part 2 comically replays the events of part 1 in that the servants reproduce the scene of failed coition between their mistress and master of the first part. This discovery leads Silvia to tell Octavio her whole story:

She recounts to him at large the story of her undoing, her quality, her Fortune, her nice education, the care and tenderness of her Noble Parents, and charges all her Fate to the evil Conduct of her heedless youth: Sometimes the reflection on her ruin, forces the Tears to flow from her fair Eyes, and makes *Octavio* sigh and weep by simpathy: Sometimes (arriv'd at the Amorous part of her relation, she wou'd sigh and languish with the remembrance of past Joys, in their beginning love;) and sometimes smile at the little unlucky adventures they met with, and their escapes; so that different passions seiz'd her Soul while she spoke, while that of all love fill'd *Octavio*'s: He doats, he burns, and every word she utters inflames him still more; he fixes his very Soul upon her Tongue, and darts his very Eyes into her face, and every thing she says raises his vast esteem and passion higher: In fine, having with the Eloquence of sacred Wit, and all the Charms of every differing Passion finisht her moving tale, they both declin'd their Eyes, whose falling showers kept equal time and pace, and for a little time were still as thought. (II, p. 247–8)

Silvia's effective and affective narration results in a proposal of marriage from Octavio which she accepts, conveniently forgetting her previous union with Brilljard; Octavio accordingly hands over to her his last letter from Philander which exposes the latter's perfidy in full. The 'story of the heart' in the second part has become a conscious performance on the part of narrators whose 'secret' motives are exposed to the reader through knowing commentary.

However, the activities of the 'spy' are directed by another, superior power elsewhere, just as Silvia's performances continue to be dictated by those of Philander (even his silence is a form of agency in her life). The third part of the novel begins to explore a more reckless, indeed unscripted, insertion of the self into narrative where protagonists 'gamble' their entire futures in pursuit of short-term, often perverse, moments of control. Here, Behn begins to turn to a full-blown critique of the notion of the 'freedom' of the individual will, of a self untrammelled by 'formal' structure, at the same time as she recognizes that effective performance, indeed survival, in an unstable and exploitative political world, requires a leaven of cynicism, an awareness of forms and their determining power.

Amours: gaming

'I do but (by this soft Entertainment) rook in my Heart, like a young Gamester, to make it venture its last Stake'
('Astrea to Lycidas', 'Love-Letters to a Gentleman', III, p. 264)

Each part of the *Love-Letters* reworks similar narrative elements through an increasingly complicated and also comic model of interpretative exchange. The third part is dominated by the trope of gambling, the idea of a form of engagement with the world that involves risk equivalent to the prospect of gain. Characters come to risk all in the hope of gaining or regaining control and domination of others. This part works with a familiar set of narrative components but increase the stakes. In this third part a third ageing male authority figure is introduced after Count Beralti (Silvia's father in part 1), and Count Clarinau (Calista's husband in part 2) in the shape of

Sebastian, Octavio's uncle, who takes his place in an even longer line of 'commonwealth' ageing lechers in Behn's writing. Octavio now occupies the position of Philander in the first and second parts, installed in a 'private' lodging proximate to the country house and pursuing access to his mistress, Silvia, who encourages the old man, as her maidservant Melinda did in the first part, to think he has a prospect of winning her. Sebastian is accidentally killed with one of his own pistols in a bedside tussle with Octavio and the lovers elope. Meanwhile Philander is also found in bed with his mistress by her elderly husband who dies from a pistol shot mistakenly fired by Philander. Philander comes to Brussels where Silvia and Octavio are now installed and Silvia unexpectedly and perversely chooses to elope with Philander after the two men have been involved in a sword-fight. Delivered of her child, she succumbs to Brilljard's attentions in order to gain his assistance in fleeing the neglectful care of the now sated Philander. With Brilljard's connivance Silvia makes a secret journey to Brussels, where she finds Octavio ready, as his sister has done, to retire disillusioned to a monastery; she, along with the narrator, attends the magnificent ceremony which sees him take these holy orders.

With the assistance of her page, who obtains male clothing for her, Silvia leaves her country retirement once more to take up residence in Brussels; on her way she encounters a lovely rakish young Spaniard named Alonzo, who confides his amorous history to the attractive boy whose bedchamber he is sharing. In Brussels, Sylvia puts herself in Alonzo's way so that he is fascinated by her charms. She now embarks on an affair with Alonzo and, along with Brilljard, who has become her pimp, fleeces him of his considerable wealth.

Silvia's history is interrupted by an account of Cesario's failed attempt to gain the throne of 'France', a scandalous account of Monmouth's invasion of England in 1685. If Cesario has an analogue, however, within the text it is Octavio rather than Silvia. Like Octavio, Cesario is divested of his heroic potential as a result of an unfortunate passion. Like Octavio, he is given a 'vision' of his emasculation which he finds himself either unable or incompetent to interpret. The magician Fergusano (Robert Ferguson, a Scots Independent preacher and secretary to Shaftesbury) shows him his future in an adamantine book 'where all the Destinies of Princes are Hieroglifick'd' (II, p. 404). The rock divides to show a young hero kneeling at the feet of a fair woman while little cupids dress him up effeminately (the same pictorial allegory as was inscribed upon the pictures inside Silvia's sofa in part 2). He is shown on a sea shore presented with a robe and crown before the scene is obscured by clouds. Cesario's counsellors persuade him to take the vision as a sign that with the aid of the mistress on whom he dotes, Hermione

(Monmouth's mistress, Henrietta Wentworth), he will enjoy military success if he lands on England's coast to take the throne.

Philander joins Cesario in his invasion but retreats from the field of battle and Cesario, despite fighting boldly, is finally found, alone except for his page boy, and weeping in the deserted forest that has been the scene of his defeat. He goes to his death ignominiously, writing submissive letters to the king and justifying his passion for his mistress on the scaffold. The parallel between Cesario and Octavio is maintained throughout the third part. Both 'gamble' their prospects for earthly happiness away. It is Octavio who explicitly represents his history as that of a gamester in his final letter to Silvia:

> *There is a Chance in Love as well as Life, and oft the most unworthy are preferred; and from a Lottery I might win the Prize from all the venturing Throng with as much Reason, as think my Chance should favour me with Silvia; it might perhaps have been, but 'twas a wonderous Odds against me. Beauty is more uncertain than the Dice; and tho' I ventured like a forward Gamester, I was not yet so vain to hope to win, nor had I once complain'd upon my Fate, if I had never hop'd but when I had fairly won, to have it basely snatch'd from my Possession, and like a bafled Cully, see it seiz'd by a false Gamester, and look tamely on, has show'd me such a Picture of myself; has given me such Idea's of the Fool, I scorn to look into my easy Heart, and loath the Figure you have made me there.* (II, p. 370).

Yet even after this exchange, Octavio allows himself to be gulled by Silvia and releases funds to support her in her, he thinks, newly penitent condition. Like Cesario, he remains a 'fool' throughout, unable to read critically or to abandon his addiction to his mistress.

Silvia is also a gambler, but she scrutinizes the odds with more care. When Philander first starts to pursue Silvia again, we are told that 'She found *Philander* now in a Condition to be ever taking from her, while *Octavio*'s was still to be giving; which was a great Weight in the scale of Love, when a fair vain Woman guides the Balance' (II, p. 346). However, Silvia unaccountably decides to elope with Philander and give up her 'credit' with Octavio, a decision which is left unexplained by the narrator. The reader is left to conclude that the desire for mastery over an other has now become the sole motivator behind the 'fallen' woman's behaviour. Like her tutor, Philander, Silvia is in love with her own narrative authority and, like him, she considers the unfaithful partner a loose end who must be drawn back into her narrative ambit. Like Philander, too, she is quickly bored and indifferent once her narrative supremacy has been proved. After the elopement and delivery of her child by Philander shortly thereafter 'she considers herself a new Woman, and began, or rather continued, to consider the Advantage she had lost in

Octavio' (II, p. 365). Philander's thoughts stray back to Calista at the same time.

Philander's own career as a gambler continues, with his decision to abandon Cesario at the scene of battle. Strangely, the narrator defends this choice arguing that it proves, not lack of courage, but rather that 'he disliked the Cause, disapproved of all their Pretensions, and look'd upon the whole Affair and Proceeding to be most unjust and ungenerous' (II, p. 433). A far cry indeed from the opportunistic Philander of the first part who hoped possibly for a crown for himself as a result of his involvement in conspiracy against the crown.

In the third part, the narrator becomes both more individualized and loosens her grip on the interpretation of narrative event and character, in keeping with the more 'cynical and anarchic' trajectory the tale had taken from its opening which had implied a straightforward parable of libertinism coming to a bad end.[13] Motive and behaviour become blacker, more opaque, and more self-destructive – in keeping with the metaphor of gaming – and the narrator proves herself unable to control either narrative event or its reading. She, and it is only in this volume that the narrator's sex is identified, becomes rather an affective commentator, responding with feeling, and indulging acts of identification and objectification rather than directing the reader in acts of critical reading. Thus, the narrator makes herself most visible at the scene of Octavio's induction into the Order of St Bernard, presenting herself as a sentimental female reader sighing with her fellows at the sight of the lovely young man donning his white robes and bending his lovely head to have his locks shorn. 'For my part, I swear I was never so affected in my Life, with any thing, as I was at this Ceremony, nor ever found my Heart so oppressed with Tenderness' (II, p. 383). So too, despite her condemnation of Cesario in the concluding passages, the narrator is moved to sympathy and tenderness at the image of the lonely hero weeping in a forest after his defeat: 'I say, who that beheld this, would not have scorn'd the World, and all its fickle Worshipers? have curst the Flatteries of vain Ambition, and priz'd a Cottage far above a Throne? a Garland wreath'd by some fair innocent hand, before the restless Glories of a Crown?' (II, p. 433).

Like her perverse characters of the final part, the narrator now appears to be driven by hidden passions and feelings, unable or unwilling to explore or question the desires that move her. Critical judgement is almost entirely abandoned. The novel concludes with a purely descriptive account of the lovers' fortunes: Silvia, banished from Brussels by the governor for her notorious behaviour, moves on 'and daily makes considerable Conquests where e'er she shows the Charmer' (II, p. 439), while Philander is ultimately pardoned and restored to favour at court 'being very well understood by all good Men' (II, p. 439).

In the cynical fallen world of the concluding part of the *Love-Letters*, desire becomes equivalent to perversity and even the narrator is unable to pass a moral judgement on her characters or her tale, their behaviour the necessary result of political and sexual circumstance for which they cannot, apparently, be blamed. Honest or open dealing is the act of a 'fool', self-delusion an act of survival, and the outcome of any event or act is beyond prediction. Behn's narrative takes a direction which may have been a surprise even to its author in that it moves beyond a representation of the determining power of language and outward form with which it opened, to imply the chaotic, haphazard, and contingent nature of desire, political, social and economic. Ultimately, life is a gamble and its winners and losers are the product of opportunity and circumstance rather than value.

NOTES

1 Todd, p. 387.
2 Todd, p. 388.
3 See Alison Margaret Conway, 'The Protestant Cause and a Protestant Whore: Aphra Behn's *Love-Letters*', *Eighteenth-Century Life*, 25 (2001), 1–19; Ellen Pollak, 'Beyond Incest: Gender and the Politics of Transgression in Aphra Behn's *Love-Letters between a Noble-Man and his Sister*', in *Rereading Aphra Behn*, pp. 151–86; Francis F. Steen, 'The Politics of Love: Propaganda and Structural Learning in Aphra Behn's *Love-Letters between a Noble-Man and his Sister*', *Poetics Today*, 23 (2002), 91–122.
4 See Mona Narain, 'Body and Politics in Aphra Behn's *Love-Letters between a Noble-Man and his Sister*', in *Women Writing, 1550–1750*, ed. Jo Wallwork and Paul Salzman (Bundoora: Meridian, 2001), pp. 151–62; Donald R. Wehrs, 'Eros, Ethics, Identity: Royalist Feminism and the Politics of Desire in Aphra Behn's *Love-Letters*', *Studies in English Literature, 1500–1900*, 32 (1992), 461–78.
5 William B. Warner, *Licensing Entertainment. The Elevation of Novel Reading in Britain, 1684–1750* (London and Berkeley: University of California Press, 1998), p. 86.
6 In *Calendar of State Papers (Domestic) 1665–6*, transcribed in W. J. Cameron, *New Light on Aphra Behn* (Auckland: University of Auckland Press, 1961).
7 See Ros Ballaster, *Seductive Forms: Women's Amatory Fiction from 1684 to 1740* (Oxford: Clarendon Press, 1992), ch. 3.
8 Ruler of the Protestant principality of Cleve which bordered on Holland and features in the novel as 'Luke-land'. Grey and his companions fled here and the ambassador, Fuchs, sought, unsuccessfully since pressure was brought by James II, to aid them in settling there.
9 Ford, Lord Grey, *The Secret History of the Rye-House Plot* (London 1754), p. 90.

10 Conway, 'The Protestant Cause', p. 2.
11 Ballaster, *Seductive Forms*, pp. 79–80.
12 Margaret Ferguson, 'The Authorial Ciphers of Aphra Behn', in *The Cambridge Companion to English Literature 1650–1740*, ed. Steven N. Zwicker (Cambridge: Cambridge University Press, 1998), p. 227.
13 Todd, p. 386.

10

LAURA J. ROSENTHAL

Oroonoko: reception, ideology, and narrative strategy

Oroonoko and its critical reception

Recent criticism of Aphra Behn's *Oroonoko* has attempted to untangle its complex web of political and ideological investments, an approach encouraged by the novel's representation of the seventeenth-century English colonial project that in many significant ways has shaped the modern world. Set in Coramantien on the coast of Africa and in an English colony in Surinam, *Oroonoko* tells the story of an African prince captured into slavery by an unscrupulous English slave-ship captain. Prince Oroonoko had befriended the captain when selling slaves to him; the prince thought he was a guest on the ship, but the captain saw him as a potential commodity. When they arrive in the Caribbean, Oroonoko becomes a paradoxical 'royal slave': the other slaves bow down before him as their king (even though he may have traded some of them into their current slavery); the English, who also recognize his nobility, keep him in an elegant plantation house, guarded and entertained by the novel's narrator. The English promise, but never deliver, freedom for Oroonoko and his wife Imoinda. Oroonoko's royalty means that he does not suffer the usual hardships of slavery; still, he longs for release. Imoinda's pregnancy brings the narrative to a crisis over the fate of their child: Oroonoko leads a rebellion to secure their liberty, but it fails due to the lack of resolve among the other slaves. (The wives beg their husbands to stop fighting; as in Oroonoko's story, domestic interests compete with the defence of honour.) The English promise clemency, but instead torture the African hero. Desperate and furious, the prince kills his pregnant wife to protect her from rape (and presumably from producing more slaves as well), but in his grief over Imoinda's death he becomes helpless to wreak the revenge he had planned. Oroonoko dies through a process of slow, horrific dismemberment at the hands of the colonial authorities; his enemies divide his body into pieces and send each one to a different part of the colony.

Behn infuses the novel's two locations with different meanings and distinct political and economic systems. In Coramantien, the ageing king lives in luxury surrounded by the beautiful women of his harem; he leads a nation of noble warriors and possesses absolute authority over his subjects. This authority even extends to his ability to demand that any woman he chooses join his harem. His grandson Oroonoko offers hope for the future: he has proven himself in battle; he possesses extraordinary beauty; he has been educated in a range of subjects (including European history) by a French tutor. In *Oroonoko*, Coramantiens place a high value on honour, defined as martial courage for the men, chastity and obedience to husbands for the women, and fulfillment of one's natal destiny for both. While Behn's depiction of Coramantien has recently been shown to be less of a fantasy version of an exotic 'other' than had been previously believed,[1] it nevertheless also suggests an idealized version (with some complications, to which I will return) of a traditional monarchical society, and in particular the Stuart dynasty to which she remained loyal throughout her life.

Consistent with her use of geographical difference to represent political difference, Behn distinguished the slavery in her fictional Africa from the slavery in the New World. In Behn's Coramantien, we mainly see slaves circulating as part of a gift economy rather than as commodities: most memorably, Oroonoko meets Imoinda by bringing her slaves as a consolation for her father's death on the battlefield (a death that saved Oroonoko's life). Coramantines practise slavery as an expression of their rigid hierarchy and warrior culture rather than as a commercial transaction: when the Coramantines fight a war, the defeated combatants become slaves. But even this practice honours differences in rank, for Oroonoko at one point befriends rather than enslaves the noble general he has defeated. The cosmopolitan Oroonoko himself, however, has already been influenced by European practices: he sells his slaves to the English, an activity that seems to underwrite the luxury that the Coramantine aristocracy clearly enjoys. The prince thus stands on the border between the traditional, hierarchical culture of Coramantine and European mercantilism, a position that leaves him vulnerable to capture.

While Coramantien evokes a traditional absolutist society with some signs of outside influence, Surinam represents the hazards, violence and complexities of the seventeenth-century's emergent system of mercantile capitalism. Behn describes the lush beauty and abundant natural resources that Surinam possesses, but also the harrowing violence that profiting from them seems to demand. Here three groups live in an uneasy relationship with each other: the native Surinamese, the African slaves, and the English colonists. The English tenuously dominate: they have sailed to the Caribbean and claimed property from natives in order to profit from plantations cultivated by enslaved Africans. While ostensibly still under the authority of their king, in this remote location a group of ambitious, dishonourable, and violent men run the colony. The colonists appear at first to have established peace with the natives, trading with them and depending on them for local knowledge, but even this proves explosive. Ambitious men with little respect for rank run the colony's economic production through brutal force. The English colonists live in Surinam to make money; they treat African slaves as commodities in order to produce other commodities for an increasingly global marketplace.

The conflicts in both locations take place over the liminal bodies of Oroonoko and Imoinda. In Coramantien, Imoinda's body becomes a point of contention between Oroonoko and his royal grandfather: the grandfather possesses her but cannot make love to her; Oroonoko makes love to her but cannot possess her. To expel the threat of incest that Imoinda's contested possession raises, the grandfather transforms her from her proper role as gift between men to the humiliating position of a commodified slave, now presumably vulnerable to far worse forms of sexual violation. (Although interestingly and in spite of Oroonoko's great anxieties about this matter, it seems that in both locations Imoinda cannot be raped. In her possession of an internal virtue that defies male desire, she anticipates Richardson's *Pamela*.) In Surinam, the colonists deceptively lead Oroonoko to believe (for a while at least) that his aristocratic status will preserve his body from commodification. When he recognizes their duplicity and rebels, tortuous punishment and ultimately death by dismemberment become his fate, literally fragmenting a royal slave already fragmented within. In Coramantien Oroonoko struggles unsuccessfully to posses Imoinda's body; in Surinam he struggles unsuccessfully to possess his own.

Oroonoko, then, touches on the most pressing political, economic, and ideological issues of its time; there has been wide disagreement, however, about the way it represents them. While some readers have taken the sympathetically depicted slave rebellion to suggest the author's opposition to slavery, others have noticed complications to this view: Oroonoko trades slaves himself, non-royal slaves betray their leader and thus appear to deserve slavery. The narrator clearly admires the African prince, but critics have also identified elements of condescension, prejudice, stereotyping, and objectification. Few have ignored Behn's physical description of her hero, which suggests that his beauty lies in his similarity to whites (with the notable exception of his skin colour). Evidence that the author supports and condemns colonialism has been found as well: on the one hand, the entire narrative explicitly constitutes a complaint that the English have let this rich and beautiful land slip out of their hands; on the other hand, most of the colonists themselves appear inferior to the noble Oroonoko. Behn depicts the system of colonial slave labour as dangerously unstable and constantly hovering on the edge of unspeakable violence. Yet implied comparisons between the sophisticated Oroonoko and the barbaric colonists also reveal another agenda, for *Oroonoko* divides its characters quite starkly by class. Within both the English and African settings, the novel suggests a tight correspondence between birth and worth. Finally, while Behn has been honoured as the first woman professional writer, readers have disagreed as to whether or not she advances feminist possibilities in this novel. The narrator herself is forced to lead a relatively independent life as the result of her father's death and at times she objects to the ways in which gender limits her authority. The Coramantine heroine Imoinda possesses not just beauty, but military prowess. Nevertheless, Imoinda also fulfils stereotypes of idealized femininity: she strictly upholds sexual virtue, she obeys Oroonoko's grandfather without question, she allows Oroonoko to 'ravish' her and later to kill her. One critic has even argued that through this novel Behn competes with Imoinda for the privilege of bearing Oroonoko's legacy, although in the form of a book rather than a baby.[2] Behn might advance the cause of women participating in the public intellectual sphere, but, at the same time and in spite of her condescension toward the colonists, she too makes a profit from colonialism by circulating Oroonoko's story in a capitalist marketplace.

These disagreements, however, also demonstrate the great importance that *Oroonoko* has acquired in literary studies. Most of these arguments about race, class, and gender in the novel have appeared recently as part of an upsurge in interest in Behn in general and *Oroonoko* in particular. Admired in the early eighteenth century and even more so in its dramatic adaptations by Thomas Southerne and others, *Oroonoko*, along with most of Behn's writing, dropped out of the literary canon by the century's end. At that time women writers had to maintain a reputation for propriety that Behn's life and work defied. But even when such demands faded in the twentieth century, Behn still at first received relatively limited attention. Sandra Gilbert and Susan Gubar's groundbreaking *Madwoman in the Attic* (1979), which considered the challenges facing early women novelists, nevertheless gave the impression that nineteenth-century women novelists had no female precursors. Scholars had certainly known about Behn, but had generally dismissed her as a commercial hack instead of a serious literary artist. As feminist criticism became a more powerful force in the academy and broadened the range of acceptable writing to include women who might not fit traditional ideals of greatness, however, Behn's astonishing output demanded a second look.

Author of plays, poems, translations, and novels, Behn had more of her plays produced in the Restoration than any other writer except John Dryden. While writing for the marketplace marked her as a 'hack' to earlier generations, feminists found Behn's professionalism and her apparent libertinism part of her fascination. In this context, *Oroonoko* emerged as a particular object of interest because it appeared to be autobiographical, telling the story of a young woman who travels to Surinam without the limiting presence of a husband or father. Interest in Behn was thus justified by the potential to help build an alternative canon of women writers with alternative perspectives – and especially alternative political views. At first, Behn's plays seemed to defy this hope, her libertinism marking her as 'one of the boys'. (More recent criticism, however, has revealed Behn as a remarkably astute reader of gender politics in her plays.) *Oroonoko*, however, tells the story, at least in part, of a complicated friendship between an independent white woman colonist and an enslaved African prince. The potential parallels have proven irresistible: in the novel, both Oroonoko and the narrator live in some form of exile, both feel themselves to be superior to the brutal colonists, both engage in intellectual pursuits, both have either lost or become estranged from fathers or father figures, both have time on their hands, both love stories, both display curiosity about their natural surroundings and the Surinam natives, both express themselves eloquently.

These parallels initially suggested the potential for some kind of political analogy: that is, that Behn might have had particular sympathy for Oroonoko because as a woman she too had experienced injustice. The text, however, supports neither abolitionist ideas nor explicitly protests gender inequality: *Oroonoko* has therefore demanded subtler reading strategies. In a landmark essay, Laura Brown argued that the limits of Behn's vision (her 'racism', in modern terms) should not prevent us from seeking the possibilities of the novel's social critique. Brown argued that the death of the royal slave functioned as an allegory for the end of Stuart power: not only does Oroonoko embody the heroic qualities that Behn admired in Charles I, but both the Stuart king and the royal slave were destroyed by the same emerging forces of mercantile capitalism. Others followed this general strategy, finding links between Oroonoko's and the narrator's exclusion from Lockean conceptions of property ownership, a form of resistance in Oroonoko's and Imoinda's refusal to produce another slave for their captors, and a form of critique in the author's unwillingness to sanitize the violence of colonialism and slavery, especially in contrast to those who adapted the novel for the stage.[3] Critics, however, continue to disagree over the extent to which Behn naturalizes or holds up for scrutiny the colonial slave system.

This brief summary of the novel's reception[4] suggests that critics have been drawn to ideological readings because of the novel's subject, but also because the novel itself initially entered the modern canon for reasons other than aesthetic ones. *Oroonoko* has thus been scrutinized for its representation of slavery, colonialism, race, class, gender, political philosophy and economic history as perhaps no other work from the long eighteenth century has been. Clearly the story demands this kind of reading. Understanding the ideological investments of any literary work, however, also depends on an understanding of exactly how the text itself is working; the novel's form and complex artistry have attracted less attention.[5] In spite of considerable serious and productive attention to the complex web of ideological engagements in the novel, we have yet fully to appreciate the narrative's intriguing artistry. In the rest of this essay, then, I will try to suggest the ways in which *Oroonoko*'s form – something regularly analysed in the study of other novels but often overlooked in *Oroonoko* – not only might help us read the novel's ideological representations with greater precision, but might also suggest Behn's unappreciated significance in literary history.

Narrative strategies in *Oroonoko*

Most interpretations of *Oroonoko* look to the narrator for the author's perspective. The first-person style and truth claims of *Oroonoko* certainly encourage the conflation of author and narrator, and indeed critics in the early twentieth century delighted in dismissing Behn as a liar and a plagiarist on this basis, suggesting that she never travelled to Surinam and instead copied her details from genuine travel narratives. But what would happen if we treated *Oroonoko* as a more self-conscious literary production, whether the author intended it to be one or not? True, Behn probably travelled to Surinam in her youth and may have met a royal slave: several instances of African royalty captured into slavery attracted attention in the eighteenth century. Yet other elements suggest artistic invention rather than strict autobiography. Compelling evidence identifies Behn as the legitimate daughter of a barber and a wetnurse;[6] thus the narrator's claim to be waiting for her father, the appointed lieutenant-general of thirty-six islands as well as Surinam, clearly differs from any possible experience of the historical Aphra Behn. That the author belonged by birth to the class of the men in the story whom the narrator holds in contempt is surely a meaningful discrepancy.

Behn claimed that she threw *Oroonoko* together in a few hours. Whether we take this at face value or not, she nevertheless organized the narrative with sophisticated techniques that critics would later associate with the novel. Her most prominent technical accomplishment is the subtle shift in narrative perspective indirectly through different characters. After a brief discussion insisting on her own experience as eyewitness to the events about to unfold, the narrator identifies the hero as the source for anything reported that she did not see. Thus Behn introduces a narrator within a narrator, a relationship between Oroonoko and the primary narrator that involves stories, within the novel's fiction, that he tells to her, that she will in turn tell to us. Sometimes we even have a narrator within a narrator within a narrator. In Coramantien, the king has several scenes alone with Imoinda that we learn about: he tries to seduce her, he demands to know the name of her husband, he sells her into slavery whereupon she begs for death instead. We must imagine that Imoinda related these scenes to Oroonoko upon their reunion, who related them to the narrator, who relates them to us. Yet Behn also includes a synthesizing, semi-omniscient authorial voice that differs from that of the narrator, for certain events take place that none of the three story-telling characters witness. We have an account, for example, of Aboan's seduction of Onahal (Oroonoko's friend Aboan, we recall, seduces the harem's matronly but still attractive guardian to distract her while Oroonoko consummates his secret marriage to Imoinda). While Aboan might have had the opportunity to describe this to Oroonoko, other scenes become more difficult to explain without this semi-omniscient source who knows more than the two main sources of information (the narrator's eye-witnessing and the story-telling of Oroonoko – and to a less extent, Imoinda). For example, the novel describes Oroonoko's efforts to rouse the other slaves to rebellion when he *escapes* the watchful eyes of the young narrator. We also read about scenes of torture from which the narrator flees. While Oroonoko could possibly have told her about these, it is difficult to imagine that in his madness and rage he took the opportunity to relate in such precise details his killing of Imoinda (for which there were no other witnesses), nor could he possibly have related his own grotesque death scene, which the narrator declines to 'eye-witness'. All of these gaps point to a distinction, albeit a subtle and unstable one, between the young narrator and the author who tells her story.

The section of the novel that Oroonoko tells, which does not come to us directly but rather filtered through the young narrator, has a distinctly different style from the second half, which is reported directly by her. The difference between the Coramantien section and the Surinam sections has been attributed to Behn's use of romantic conventions to describe a place she has never visited (Africa) and a newspaper-style report of a place she actually visited, a slave colony in the Caribbean.[7] This observation alone, however, does not sufficiently recognize Behn's sophisticated artistry and her incorporation of techniques she learned in the theatre. The high romantic style of the Coramantien story becomes appropriate because within the novel's fiction it originates in the voice of Oroonoko, and this is how his character, which benefits from the conventions of Restoration tragedy, would describe the personal history that led up to his enslavement. Like the (often exoticized) heroes of Restoration tragedies, Oroonoko initially faces a classic conflict between love and honour when his grandfather demands that Imoinda, who has already secretly married Oroonoko, join his seraglio. In a combination of heroic passion and emergent bourgeois affective individualism, Oroonoko loves Imoinda against the norms of his culture, which practises polygamy. Through this love, he even experiences a new eloquence that he did not, he insists, previously possess. But this instinctive love clashes with his royalist and familial loyalty, which demands that he obey this selfish king.

The narrator's passionate admiration for Oroonoko has been read as an expression of Behn's own royalist ideology, and yet the sequence of events in the novel in some ways works against the grain of the young narrator's enthusiasm by demonstrating the vulnerability of this system. The old king has become impotent both sexually and militarily. Since he cannot defend his nation without his grandson, he desperately needs Oroonoko, and yet he will not give up Imoinda. While absolutist ideology demands Oroonoko's obedience to his king and grandfather, a different, more individualistic, more modern sense of honour suggests that he should rebel. Here Behn confronts the contradiction between her own royalism and her simultaneous sympathy for marriages based on bourgeois affective individualism. Oroonoko tries (unsuccessfully) to separate these elements: he tries to rebel against the grandfather's personal affront without disturbing the political hierarchy in a sort of 'surgical strike' to deflower Imoinda without confronting the old man as either his king or his grandfather. Oroonoko has no long-term strategy; instead, he acts with the single-minded goal of consummating his marriage. Trying to save her own life when caught, Imoinda falsely claims that Oroonoko raped her. This lie has the opposite effect of making the grandfather angrier; he thus sells Imoinda into slavery where she will become vulnerable to more rape. Yet the grandfather comes to regret his harshness and, fearing his weakness without Oroonoko's military assistance, tells his grandson that he has put Imoinda to death.

The conflict between Oroonoko and his king leaves the Coramantien state in limbo. Oroonoko at first refuses to fight and later throws himself into battle hoping to embrace death; nevertheless, he has become alienated from the court. While a stage tragedy might at this point have Oroonoko finally challenge the grandfather for the throne in memory of Imoinda, *Oroonoko* offers nothing so clear. The grandfather is not a terrible king who deserves to be toppled, just a selfish, indulgent, and impotent one. His offence to Oroonoko has been private, rather than public. Here we have no tragic climax, but rather an anticlimactic stasis that foreshadows Oroonoko's Surinam experience. Oroonoko languishes in his tent long after the battle has been won; the officers 'invented all sorts of Diversions and Sports, to entertain their Prince' (III, p. 81). When he finally, with great reluctance, begins to socialize again, his old friend the English captain and slave trader betrays him. This capture tears Oroonoko away from a situation that seems to have no solution: Coramantien life has become dismal, static, and oppressive. Without a queen (he has interest in no other woman), Oroonoko would end his 'noble race'. It becomes difficult, then, to read his story as an uncomplicated endorsement of absolutism. Oroonoko later wants to go back to Africa, but what would he go back to? In Coramantien terms, Imoinda is polluted and his marriage incestuous; further, the impotent grandfather hangs on to power. While Oroonoko longs to escape the relentlessly ignoble Surinam colony, Coramantien maintains the (impotent) patriarchal structures that Behn mercilessly mocked in her comedies.

The second part of the novel, set in the colony of Surinam, introduces the narrator as eyewitness. With a subtle shift in perspective, we no longer have Oroonoko's (mediated) heroic vision, but instead the more worldly perspective of a young woman living in a distant land over which her father was supposed to officiate. Here we find, as I will later explore, even more disconcerting contradictions between the narrator's vision and the implications of narrative events. In the second half, the style shifts noticeably. For example, Oroonoko (through the narrator) describes his initial meeting with Imoinda in abstract terms: 'he was infinitely surpriz'd at the Beauty of this fair Queen of Night, whose Face and Person was so exceeding all he had ever beheld; that lovely Modesty with which she receiv'd him, that Softness in her look' (III, p. 64). By contrast, the narrator's journalistic style of close, 'realistic' observation reveals details missing in the first half that would be more likely to stand out as exotic to an English observer: Imoinda, she notes, has intricate birds and flowers carved all over her body. In his heroic style focused on love and honour, Oroonoko relates no specific details about the environment in his part of the story. In the voice of the 'eye-witness' narrator in a foreign land, however, Surinam itself almost becomes a character. In fact, the narrator postpones the promised story of the royal slave in the opening first to describe the animals – marmosets, parakeets, macaws, snakes, flies 'of amazing Forms and Colours' – and the native people of Surinam, who produce 'Baskets, Weapons, Aprons, etc.' (III, p. 58). Oroonoko fights many battles in Africa, but his story never offers the kind of gory detail that the narrator describes, for example, when Oroonoko fights a tiger, a 'monstrous Beast of might, size, and vast limbs', who came:

with open Jaws upon him; and fixing his Awful stern Eyes full upon those of
the Beast, and putting himself into a very steddy and good aiming posture of
Defence, ran his Sword quite through his Breast down to his very Heart, home
to the Hilt of the Sword.   (III, p. 97)

Surely battle-scenes in Africa would have lent themselves to the possibility
of this kind of detail, but Oroonoko does not express his experience this
way. The narrator's voice, by contrast, gathers its force through details that
convey both the beauty and the horror of her colonial sojourn. She notices
the local climate (so humid that it renders most weapons useless), the number
of bullets in the tiger's heart, the gold dust in the hands of the natives, but
also the mutilated bodies of the native Surinamese warriors, the body of the
footman who was nailed to a tree, the stench of Imoinda's decaying corpse,
and the torture wounds in Oroonoko's flesh.

The two parts thus differ significantly in tone and style, but at the same
time their conflicts parallel each other, almost like heroic and fallen versions
of the same kind of story. In both locations, love and liberty conflict with
inept local authority. Behn includes similar details as well: the narrator's
father, who would presumably bring a more decent order to the colony,
never arrives; like Oroonoko's father, he too is dead.[8] As in Coramantien,
in Surinam no one very reliable seems to be in charge, but in both places
Oroonoko (at first) lives in physical comfort: Trefry, who buys him, soon
recognizes the slave's quality, promises him his freedom, and treats him with
respect. No one expects him to work. In both locations, Imoinda's falls
at key moments reveal their love for each other: just as she fatefully fell
into Oroonoko's arms in the Coramantine court, so Clemene (Imoinda) in
Surinam now similarly falls in a faint into the arms of Caesar (Oroonoko)
when she recognizes him as her husband; in full heroic style 'Caesar swore he
disdain'd the Empire of the World, while he cou'd behold his Imoinda, and
she despised Grandure and Pomp, those Vanities of her Sex, when she cou'd
Gaze on Oroonoko' (III, p. 92). Like the grandfather, the English believe
that Caesar will not tolerate the truth, so, like the grandfather, they lie to
him. The English keep Oroonoko under close watch, a job that falls mainly
to the narrator.

While rank in both halves allows Oroonoko privileges, as a prince his
future clearly rests on his ability to save his 'noble race' – an ambition
destroyed by the slavery of colonial mercantile capitalism, but also blocked
by the traditional royalist society of Coramantien. No doubt, the disappoint-
ments of the colonial world are more deeply, permanently, and violently
devastating. Yet the ambitions of his own royal family in Coramantien leave
Oroonoko vulnerable to being swept away into these mercantile horrors. The

novel represents military honour as a constitutive aspect of Coramantien culture, but we never learn what the wars are being fought over. Could the prospect of greater profits from the slave trade to support his luxurious palace have played a part in the grandfather's policy decisions, which doomed all thirteen of his sons to death on the battlefield? The grandfather creates a crisis of succession by refusing to return Imoinda; Coramantien's royal absolutism has no way to solve the problem of a monarch who alienates the only remaining heir. So, while Behn associates Coramantien with Stuart monarchy, heroic drama, and romance, she does so in ways that do not simply idealize either this disrupted line of power or these increasingly satirized literary genres.

Oroonoko tells stories of lost things in both sections: a lost hero, most of all, but also a lost colony, a lost youth, a lost love, a lost baby, lost fathers, a lost dynasty, lost trust, lost literary genres, and perhaps lost faith. While *Oroonoko* creates its innovative literary form by combining realism and romance – although perhaps more self-consciously than has been previously thought – we might thus want to add another genre from which Behn draws: the elegy. We know from the first page that Oroonoko will die in Surinam, for the narrator promises to show us 'the scene of the last part of his Adventures' (III, p. 57). Behn elegizes without a simple or unified political agenda: while Oroonoko's final dismemberment graphically suggests the horrific possibilities of a capitalist culture that has no respect for traditional status, he doesn't have a promising life to which to return in the royalist Coramantien. As many have observed, *Oroonoko* provides a scathing critique of certain aspects of modernity with a full acceptance of others. But the representation of the paradoxical royal slave constitutes not a call to action, but an elegy for the last son of a noble race. Behn maintained her loyalty to the Stuarts throughout her life; nevertheless, in *Oroonoko* we find an admission that an historical era has ended.

If *Oroonoko* is an elegy, then Surinam is the grave. On the one hand, the narrator explicitly propagandizes her readers to support English colonization: she tempts readers with the prospect of delicate fruits, curious little animals, perfumed air, golden dust, and innocent natives. Yet the novel, on the other hand, constantly undermines the young narrator's optimism: the intriguing little monkeys and brilliantly feathered birds give way to the ferocious tiger with bullets in its heart and the eel with the power to paralyse. The representation of Surinam's natives more forcefully conveys this contradiction. The natives at first resemble 'our first Parents before the Fall' (III, p. 59); when provoked by the Dutch, however, they hang mothers with their children and nail dismembered footmen to the trees. The most vivid illustration of this tension comes when the narrator and Oroonoko visit the natives out of their shared curiosity. At first the two groups cheerfully exchange hospitalities: the English taste spicy Surinamese meat; the Surinamese finger the clothing of their visitors. The narrator's brother teaches the natives to kiss, and they try this new technique on the narrator and on each other. Interrupting this kissing party, Oroonoko asks to see their warriors, but 'for my part I took 'em for Hobgoblins, or Fiends, rather than Men' (III, p. 102). The shocking appearance of the warriors comes from their grotesque competitions, consisting of contemptuous self-mutilation until one party gives up or dies. This spectacle horrifies Oroonoko, although his own self-mutilation when later captured by the English echoes it. Surinam seems to be infectious: weapons rust and become useless; Imoinda's dead body rots quickly among the leaves, her stench replacing the sweet smells the narrator describes in the opening; Oroonoko 'goes native' in the worst way.[9] A romantic lover in Coramantien, Oroonoko murders his wife and unborn child in Surinam; a noble warrior in Coramantien, in Surinam he tears his own bowels out of his body.

When she wrote *Oroonoko*, Behn could not have known that she would die soon after; mortality, however, clearly permeates the narrative.[10] Behn closes by suggesting that her own literary immortality and the immortal greatness of the royal couple are bound together: while Oroonoko merited a better fate and a better poet 'to write his praise', she hopes that her own wit has sufficient force for this task. Yet this lack of confidence suggests that she is not sure that Oroonoko's story will be told forever or that she has sufficiently mastered sublimity; she is not so sure about immortality itself. Oroonoko doesn't seem convinced of immortality either, at least in its Christian form. While entertaining him and Imoinda, the narrator tried 'to bring her to the knowledge of the true God'. Discussion of God only meets with extreme scepticism by the royal slave:

> But of all Discourses *Caesar* lik'd that the worst, and wou'd never be reconcil'd to our Notions of the Trinity, of which he ever made a Jest; it was a Riddle, he said, wou'd turn his Brain to conceive, and one cou'd not make him understand what Faith was. (III, p. 93)

Indeed, faith seems a more and more distant possibility as 'Christian' comes to mean the same thing as 'liar'. In fact, the narrator herself, who keeps insisting on faith, here lies most egregiously to Oroonoko: their conversations about God and Christianity take place in the larger context of her greatest betrayal. Caesar comes to believe that the colonists are deliberately delaying their promised freedom in order to claim his child as their slave:

> This thought made him very uneasy, and his Sullenness gave them some Jealousies of him; so that I was oblig'd, by some Persons, who fear'd a Mutiny (which is very Fatal sometimes in those Colonies that abound so with Slaves that they exceed the Whites in vast Numbers), to discourse with *Caesar*, and to give him all the Satisfaction I possibly cou'd. (III, p. 93)

The narrator tries to distract Caesar and Clemene from thinking about their earthly child by introducing them to the Holy child. Yet the transcendent father/son/holy ghost strikes Caesar as absurd. Thus the author starkly exposes the duplicity of the young narrator who attempts to control the royal slaves through Christianity and 'faith'. The narrator seems to believe in God and earthly male authorities, even if they never arrive. Her faith in honourable leaders who rule by divine right becomes clear through her contempt for the low-class, profoundly inadequate men who govern through horrific violence. The narrator does all she can to gain Caesar's trust: she tells stories, she leads him to adventures in the forests, she distracts him with the natives. But Oroonoko nevertheless comes to see through her; she blatantly fails at her assigned task of containing his dissatisfaction. Critics have read Caesar's address of the narrator as his '*Great Mistress*' (III, p. 93) as either erotic or as an expression of Behn's own class snobbery. But both of these readings, while not implausible, elide the identities of the author and the narrator. The author's unstable distance from this narrator, however, allows us to see Oroonoko's obsequiousness toward the narrator as canny. The prince has the narrator believing that, as she insists, 'my Word wou'd go a great way with him' (III, p. 93), but the events of the novel starkly reveal her utter misreading of their relationship. Caesar's quiet retirement at one point raises the narrator's suspicions and a confrontation indeed suggests, to her great offence, that he was harbouring doubts that the colonists planned to free him. The narrator knows these doubts are justified, but instead she again demands his faith: what advantage, she asks

> wou'd it be to doubt? it would but give us a Fear of him, and possibly compel us to treat him so as I shou'd be very loath to behold: that is, it might occasion his Confinement. (III, p. 94)

Believe blindly against your better judgement, the narrator insists, or face imprisonment. The narrator immediately recognizes her strategic error; she strives to soften his resentment, but in vain. She has revealed herself to Caesar as no different from the rest of the Christians. When Caesar at the end names Banister as the 'only Man, of all the Whites' (III, p. 118) able to speak the truth because Banister has promised that Caesar will die like a dog, does he include the narrator?

Just because *Oroonoko* suggests differences of perspective between the author and the young narrator, of course, does not mean that we should see no connection between them. Clearly the narrator, while not exactly identical with the author, functions in some ways as a younger version of herself – a version with perhaps greater faith in royal authority, patriarchal security, and English power. The author also exposes the importance of intellectual labour in the emergent mercantile economy, although she suggests its failures as well. Yet to read the narrator as identical with the author misses *Oroonoko's* subtle ironies: the blatant advocacy of the colonial project while detailing its horrors; the explicit admiration for royal authority while describing the vulnerability of such a society; the admiration for the native inability to comprehend lying by a woman who betrays the hero; the idealization of the sexual innocence of the natives while teaching them to kiss; the use of God as part of the young narrator's strategy for turning the African hero into a slave. These ironies point to *Oroonoko* as innovative in its narrative technique, differing from both heroic romance and literal-minded journalism. Behn, I have suggested above, manipulates the narrative's point of view to offer the perspectives of distinct narrative voices. One of these belongs to Oroonoko, who tells his story to the narrator in the style of heroic romance befitting his character. The other narrative voice belongs to an elite young woman who admires Oroonoko for providing the grandeur missing from the violent, corrupt, and exploitative colony of slave plantations, but who also betrays him when he appears to threaten it. Oroonoko, Imoinda, and their unborn child violently lose their lives in Surinam. Perhaps it was in Surinam too that the author began to lose her faith.

NOTES

1 Joanna Lipking, 'Confusing Matters: Searching the Backgrounds of *Oroonoko*', in *Aphra Behn Studies*, pp. 259–81.
2 Margaret Ferguson, 'News from the New World', in *The Production of English Renaissance Culture*, ed. David Lee Miller, Sharon O'Dair, and Harold Weber (Ithaca and London: Cornell University Press, 1994), pp. 151–89.
3 Laura J. Rosenthal, 'Owning Oroonoko: Behn, Southerne, and the Contingencies of Property', *Renaissance Drama*, n.s. 23 (1992), 25–58; Charlotte Sussman, 'The Other Problem with Women: Reproduction and Slave Culture in Aphra Behn's *Oroonoko*', in *Rereading Aphra Behn*, pp. 212–33; Suvir Kaul, 'Reading Literary Symptoms: Colonial Pathologies and the *Oroonoko* Fictions of Behn, Southerne, and Hawkesworth', *Eighteenth-Century Life*, 18 (1994), 80–96.
4 For more detailed reception histories, see Jane Spencer, *Aphra Behn's Afterlife* (Oxford: Oxford University Press, 2000) and Janet Todd, *The Critical Fortunes of Aphra Behn* (Columbia, SC: Camden House 1998).

5 See Derek Hughes, 'Race, Gender and Scholarly Practice in Aphra Behn's *Oroonoko*', *Essays in Criticism*, 52 (2002), 1–22.
6 See Todd, ch. 1.
7 William C. Spengemann, 'The Earliest American Novel: Aphra Behn's *Oroonoko*', *Nineteenth-Century Fiction*, 38 (1984), 384–414.
8 Imoinda's father is dead too; his death in battle brings Oroonoko to her.
9 Spengemann, 'Aphra Behn's *Oroonoko*', p. 403.
10 See also Shirley Tatum, 'Aphra Behn's *Oroonoko* and the Anxiety of Decay', in *Aphra Behn (1640–1689): Identity, Alterity, Ambiguity*, ed. Mary Ann O'Donnell, Bernard Dhuicq, and Guyone Leduc (Paris: L'Harmattan, 2000), pp. 131–8.

11

JOANNA LIPKING

'Others', slaves, and colonists in *Oroonoko*

Oroonoko continues to strike new readers with its sheer historical surprise: the first English woman author to have had a full professional career, nearing the end of her life, set down an unexampled tale of a black African prince betrayed into slavery in a New World English colony. Though writing in evident haste – '*I never rested my Pen a Moment for Thought*' (III, p. 56) – Behn produced a story so original and so powerful that it started a procession of Oroonoko-like figures in stories, plays, poems, and popular news reports. When her name and writings sank into disrepute, *Oroonoko* remained the work for which she was most steadily remembered. After interest in her writing revived, beginning around 1900, it gradually gained notice as a literary novelty, even a small classic in its own right. Current attention to women's writing and to matters of race have now combined to make it, for all its pell-mell sentences, perhaps the most widely reprinted and studied prose tale to come from early modern England. Yet for a comparatively short tale, *Oroonoko* has had a distracting variety of readings. Over three centuries, the exceptional woman author and her singular black hero seem to have stood on radically shifting grounds.

These shifts reflect, of course, what readers of different periods have looked for in literary works and have singled out in writings by women; but they also reflect a broadening comprehension of the vast global changes that lie behind Behn's tale, enriching some peoples, dispossessing or destroying others, and transforming beyond recognition the world of the Atlantic basin. Early readers spoke of *Oroonoko* as the 'True History' announced in its subtitle, about an exotic prince Behn had known on her travels and was moved to memorialize. Her biographers now agree that she was in the short-lived colony of Surinam at least briefly around the start of 1664, although the detailed colonial records do not confirm her claim of her father's appointment to the military post of lieutenant general (not lieutenant governor, as many studies have said). Nor are there any models for such captive figures as Oroonoko and Imoinda, or for that matter any slaves at all who were so familiarly known. In its next phase, fitted to the progressive ordering schemes of early literary historians, *Oroonoko* was not first-hand testimony but a new contribution to realistic fiction, if stamped by the ruling codes of heroic drama and romance. It pointed forward to the rise of the novel, the advance of women's writing, and, most surprisingly, the earliest stirrings of humane protest against plantation slavery. Recently, to a new generation of readers less concerned with the era of slavery than with extended colonial domination, such a chronicle of progress seems only a schoolbook triumphalism. The more widely *Oroonoko* has been read, the more deeply it has been searched for Behn's entanglements, as both actor and storyteller, in structures and discourses of power. These are usually understood through the common coordinates summed up in a 1992 essay title, 'The Politics of Gender, Race, and Class',[1] or else traced in configurings of non-obvious details that might appear in the field study of an ingenious contemporary anthropologist.

Each of these approaches has been accepted and overstated, energetically disputed and set aside, only to come back, moderated but not superseded. All point, after all, to essential qualities of the story. Unlike its various adaptations and imitations, Behn's original is vividly circumstantial, with a sometimes brutal factuality. Her truth claims still exert their fascination; even the wild life of long-forgotten Surinam has undergone much scholarly inspection, and some details of colonial life that might seem symbolic touches – colonists dressed in taffeta, slaves smoking tobacco – prove to be everyday custom. Fully argued anti-slavery sentiment lay a century in the future, but pity for Behn's slave hero, who casts off his slave name and finally everything that belongs to his life, stands in high relief against the scattered dry notations to be read in the contemporary records: 'some 60, very thin ordinary slaves', 'a stout man slave leaped overboard and drowned himself', 'for Negro man 36 Copper Barrs', 'pretty good Slaves but many small ones amongst them'.[2] Modern sensitivity to forms of oppression can seem to miss entirely the effects of an author who believes in privilege, reveals interesting double motives in her best characters, and so often loves her schemers. Yet in her tale, as in the records, nothing comes to us unmediated; of the three populations Behn juxtaposes – native Americans, West Africans, and white colonists – only the Europeans recorded themselves or read her story. Open and exploratory in so many ways, *Oroonoko* seems to live in its own conceptual loop. Moreover, as an unstable text full of shifts and near-contradictions, it proves singularly well adapted to the examination of power as something that is continually remade in ever-reconstituted forms.

But to enter its loop is difficult. Behn calls her colonial setting an '*other*' or an 'obscure World' (III, pp. 56, 88), and it has receded far from us.

Rarely does a literary work become canonical without a historical field of related works, some small subgenre of two or three stories from Barbados or Jamaica, say, against which *Oroonoko* might be measured. The meanings and associations of our familiar terms – 'race' or 'ethnicity', 'slavery', 'colonialism', along with 'commerce', 'government', and others – seem to lie behind a screen. (That slaves were property, for example, does not catch the sense of many writers that slaves were money.) Those were not Behn's guiding terms; their meanings were developing, and they would change more the next year with the new reign of William III. Background documentation is full and carefully kept, but it is about complex dealings among white men. As Janet Todd has noted, *Oroonoko* has been made an 'iconic' text, like *The Tempest* and *Othello*.[3] But it is precisely not *The Tempest* or *Othello* in its imaginative rendering of places, peoples, and developments existing off the stage or the page, in a brief, unmythified time somewhere between the wonders of the discovery era and the solidities of empire.

Relations with 'Others'

Early readers' acceptance of *Oroonoko* as 'true history' is a testament to a quick, communicative style that looks very much like reportage, to their own avidity for remarkable stories, and to the wholly uncertain boundaries between fact and fiction in the late seventeenth century. Many New World travel accounts included such common fictions as Behn's non-tropical perpetual springtime and rumoured 'Mountains of Gold' (III, p. 104), or sometimes even marvels out of Pliny's *Natural History* and other ancient sources; romances offered themselves as continuations of classical history. Clever London writers, Behn among them, swore to the authenticity of every strange or lurid detail. But where Behn repeatedly invokes the greatness of her great man, the high task fallen to her 'Female Pen' (III, p. 88), her first commentators focused instead on her personal attachment to her hero. The young playwright Thomas Southerne, when he recast her tale as a hugely successful London play, wondered why as an established and prolific playwright she had not staged Oroonoko's story herself. Perhaps, he conjectured, 'she could not bear him represented', since he had 'heard from a friend of hers, that she always told his story more feelingly than she writ it'.[4] Thus Southerne validated the real existence of his hero while suggesting his own fuller expression of feeling. A few decades later, a young actor from Behn's theatre world was said to attest that she 'always spoke so tenderly of Oroonoko, that it was impossible for him to have been a fictitious person'.[5] Meanwhile, in a 1696 'Memoir' prefacing Behn's posthumous *Histories and Novels*, a gabby 'Gentlewoman of her Acquaintance' claimed to defend Behn from 'unjust

Aspersions' about a concealed love intrigue between the young author – described as a girl prodigy, all innocent allure – and her attractive hero. 'Gentlewoman's' memoir, padded out with various far-fetched adventures, circulated in all six editions over the next half century.

Apart from the appeal of inside gossip and a habitual quasi-jovial personalizing of what women wrote, these first comments show a striking obliviousness to the kind of racial barriers now embedded in our sense of Western history. Oroonoko is Behn's intimate, as he is within the story with all the main male characters – taken as 'his dearest Brother' (III, p. 87) by Trefry, the overseer at Parham plantation where he is sold, and taking as a parent the local planter Colonel Martin, with support from 'all the Gentlemen of the Country' (III, p. 95). Trefry and a susceptible 'hundred *White* Men' yearn in vain for Oroonoko's African beloved, Imoinda, though she is 'too great' (III, p. 63) for them. 'No Man, of any Nation' could resist, Trefry says (III, p. 90). The colour bar so strictly marked in colonial societies under the British Empire is not in place here. Indeed, for all Behn's designating and describing of skin colours, 'race' in its modern sense is a word she almost never uses. Oroonoko vehemently denounces whites – he becomes a sort of racist in reverse – and once calls the white slave managers '*a degenerate Race*' (III, p. 105), but both he and the narrator are more biting when they talk about 'Christians'. The three population groups of characters come equally from different 'countries' or 'nations', and a few – Oroonoko's exiled French tutor, his African enemy Jamoan, and the sun-browned fisherman trader – move laterally into other groups. It is 'race' as Behn commonly uses the term, to mean lineage – most clearly when lineage is royal or noble – that is put forward as visible and intrinsic.

The model friendly 'others' in nearly two centuries of travel literature, as in the opening of Behn's tale, had been the New World Indians. Doubly misnamed, but of the West Indies and wholly unknown in Europe, they were idealized in many accounts as attractive, innocent, and sociable. Almost as if discovering heroes and heroines, Sir Walter Raleigh reported of one people of Guiana, encompassing Surinam, 'in all my life either in the Indies or in Europe did I never behold a more goodly or better favoured people, or a more manly', and he recalls seeing hundreds of scenes of native modesty among the women, 'and of those very young, and excellently favoured which came among us without deceit, stark naked'.[6] Texts provided with illustrations – narratives by Hans Staden and Jean de Léry, for example – show handsome, dignified, classically modelled figures, although they may be performing human sacrifice or preparing to eat a roasted foot. Montaigne pressed the point in his provocative essay 'Of Cannibals', drawing on reports from Brazil. Constructing an anti-Europe of prelapsarian noble savages who did not know how to lie but ate their enemies, he suggested, first, that what was natural and uncorrupted was of higher value, and then that nothing but cultural partiality made cannibal practices seem more barbarous than those of Christian Europe. Behn's generic guileless natives seem more entertaining and piquant than challenging; little about them is genuinely alien, although the practice of ritual self-mutilation by Indian war captains seems to be her invented detail. The challenges to European values, the inversions of what is civilized or savage, are played out in the main story of her African hero with 'nothing of Barbarity in his Nature' (III, p. 62), caught in a European world of compromise and duplicity, who meets his end at the hands of a 'wild' Irishman, 'a Fellow of absolute Barbarity', amid a 'rude and wild' rabble (III, p. 118).

Published travel reports on sub-Saharan Africa were both less frequent and more derivative.[7] Seventeenth-century Europeans did not know the West African interior beyond the string of fortified coastal stations where they traded. For Behn, that was an opportunity, a convenient blank space on the contemporary map into which she could inject her romance tale of honour and love, a form that 'had traipsed all over the world', in J. Paul Hunter's summmation, 'without any significant effect on how people thought, acted, or felt'.[8] Only a few details seem identifiably West African: the canopy and carpets, the strict sequestration of the king's women, the frequent wars and sale of war captives – but these are set amid vaguely 'oriental' ceremonies and dancing, a vaguely classical military camp, intrigue and gossip that might belong to a European court, and (for a satiric anti-Europe touch found also among Behn's Indians) careful provision for the security of older women. To many present-day scholars, Africa as a single continent – 'Africa', in quotation marks – is a Western construct, an invented or appropriated place. 'Narrative about Africa', Achille Mbembe remarks, 'is always pretext for a comment about something else, some other place, some other people'.[9] Behn's 'Coramantien' – not in reality 'a Country' (III, p. 60) but only a main English trading station on the Gold Coast, in modern Ghana – seems to hold out the nostalgic possibility that somewhere, in some ordered kingdom, an ideal of heroic male valour might survive in pure form and an ideal faithful love be reinvented.

The hero of this blank space is an improbable figure, as heroes are. Clearly writing against what she knew as common ethnocentric stereotyping, Behn describes him as a marvellous exception, meeting European standards of beauty, courtly refinement, and wit, 'more civiliz'd, according to the *European* Mode, than any other had been' (III, p. 82). Michael Craton characterizes him as 'a European *philosophe* in blackface', and Laura Brown notes how smoothly he fits 'the trope of sentimental identification by which the native "other" is naturalized as a European aristocrat'.[10] Yet Behn's early readers, so quick to accept Oroonoko as a real African, were not simply romance-minded. If they were also readers of the travel literature that made up so large a part of popular printed matter, they might have come upon similar figures. Early European traders knew no 'Africa', only different peoples in separate nations and ports. However indifferent to their black slave cargoes, they did not project the sweeping racial clichés that grew up with the slave trade back upon the Africans they traded with. Whether Othello or other black characters ever figured in anyone's thought would be worth knowing.

Early reporters seem to hold no settled view. Many are derogatory and all are thoroughly Eurocentric, especially about African customs. But some writers describe with surprise and admiration selected individuals or groups they find to meet European standards of looks and civility. A Sierra Leone prince – with the same caveat Behn uses (III, p. 63), 'bating his complexion' – is found 'a very handsome man; his aire was courteous and majestick'.[11] A French reporter, generally impressed by the superior Gold Coast inhabitants, describes reciprocal visits with a local governor he finds more engaging than all the rest combined. 'Nothing barbarous' but 'much humanity', is his verdict, without the flat nose or 'that large mouth that the other blacks have', his features showing 'pride and much gentleness'.[12] In 1665 Behn's Gold Coast 'Coramantien' was taken by the Dutch and renamed, but all through the eighteenth century the British favoured fort workers and slaves called 'Coramantines' as exceptionally noble and intelligent, if also proud and rebellious.[13] Meanwhile pre-slavery reports still in circulation in the great travel compilations of Hakluyt and Purchas recounted meetings with Europeanized rulers, especially in the Portuguese Congo: one king is 'magnificall, and wittie . . . wise in counsell . . . besides very liberal and courteous'; another, likewise 'liberall', is 'verie favourable to all Travellers, and doth delight verie much to heare of forreigne Countries', 'amazed' when told of Queen Elizabeth.[14] What seems unprecedented is not Oroonoko's wit or even his European education, but his open trustfulness. From the beginning, the experienced West African traders were found only too shrewd, 'very wary people in their bargaining, and will not lose one sparke of golde of any value'.[15] The ease with which a prince is kidnapped, along with 'about an hundred' court youths (III, p. 83), and the ruthlessness he meets, suggest some influence of widely circulated atrocity stories in Bartolemé de Las Casas, Montaigne, and other sources about Spanish treachery and cruelty to gentle and magnanimous New World kings.

Oroonoko's sudden abduction carries him to Behn's 'obscure' colony, long since lost to the Dutch in 1667, remote from her readers. But Surinam lay at the heart of the growing slave trade. At the time of her visit, Behn could have seen there only about three thousand black slaves, though, as she says, exceeding the whites 'in vast Numbers' (III, p. 93).[16] By the time she wrote, however, slaving was 'a booming business', if not yet fully organized; the English colonists would soon acquire about a quarter of a million Africans and always clamoured for more.[17] That number would grow tenfold.[18] In all, of the estimated eleven million slaves ultimately shipped to destinations in the Americas, fully ninety per cent would be sent to the South Atlantic, not to the North American colonies; among British transports, the figure was nearly eighty per cent. Neither Behn nor her readers, of course, could foresee the scale of the slave shipments into the South Atlantic slave system, the rigour of the labour it extracted, or the death trap it would be. That has been fully explored as a historical subject only in recent decades. But after slave trading and then slave holding ended, by successive parliamentary acts in the first third of the nineteenth century, readers of *Oroonoko* knew very vivid accounts of wrongs and the entire domination of white over black.

Early slavery

From the nineteenth century, Oroonoko was seen as Behn's imagined character, perhaps inspired by a glimpse of 'some Indian Othello' during her travels or possibly by news of a captive Guinea king on display in England.[19] Now her woman's sensibility was found to take a different turn. Swinburne, in some very rich prose, lauded 'the noble impulse of womanly compassion and womanly horror' that made her tale 'one ardent and continuous appeal for sympathy and pity, one fervent and impassioned protest against cruelty and tyranny'.[20] Ernest Baker, in the first twentieth-century edition, summed up the work as 'the first emancipation novel'.[21] But the widespread claim that *Oroonoko* was a protest raised protest. After all, Oroonoko himself deals in slaves on quite a lavish scale, presenting 'an hundred and fifty' war trophies to Imoinda, selling 'abundance' to the captain, promising 'a vast quantity' as ransom (III, pp. 64, 82, 93). At the end of the story, the system stands as it was. It was only rank, critics argued, that made for the sense of injustice, the sentimental appeal of his story and those it inspired throughout the eighteenth century, just when the mounting slave millions were in transit. 'Your free-born Briton could feel for a prince, particularly a prince in distress', scoffed Wylie Sypher.[22] Still, a male author had not produced this innovative story. Women scholars of the later twentieth century saw a natural, even irresistible parallel between the struggling independent-minded woman author, particularly outspoken on women's subjection in forced marriages, and her cultivated African, owned and controlled whatever his finer feelings. Like Swinburne, feminist biographer Angeline Goreau in 1980 saw 'impassioned attack', and with Baker classed the work as 'perhaps the first important abolitionist statement' in English literature.[23] What was slavery to Behn? Can she be said to have a view of it?

Although slavery had long since vanished from Northern Europe and the English took pride in their ancient Saxon heritage of liberty – liberty, they chiefly meant, from Europe's tyrants and popes – slavery was a long-familiar institution, in the Bible, the Greek city states, imperial Rome, many places over the world. It was still practised in Christian and Muslim countries of the Eastern and Western Mediterranean, including parts of Southern Europe. Some West African trading districts had always exported (and sometimes imported) slaves, sending them north over the trans-Saharan caravan routes and, from the mid-fifteenth century, supplying them to Portuguese ships for new plantations in the Atlantic islands and the American colonies. In addition, the Spanish and Portuguese had at first enslaved large numbers of native Americans. Reflecting this variety, the early adventures of Robinson Crusoe, set in the 1650s, include his two years as a captive slave in Morocco, an effort at planting in Brazil with a black slave and two white servants, and an attempted voyage to Africa for an illicit contract cargo. Though without any legal title, Crusoe also sells his Moroccan boy assistant and accepts with pleased aplomb the Carib Friday's vows of permanent subjection. Behn too employs the term 'slave' rather loosely to refer to the European indentured servants, the 'Attendants' (III, p. 59) taken by local Indians in wars, and 'our *Indian Slaves*, that Row'd us' (III, p. 103), who apparently come from the small population of four hundred Indian slaves recorded in Surinam in the 1660s but may possibly be only servants.[24] Yet she is clear about the central labour system, drawing what would come to seem an immutable linkage of blacks, slavery, and sugar: 'Those then whom we make use of to work in our Plantations of Sugar, are *Negro's*, *Black*-Slaves altogether' (III, p. 60).

The importation of Africans spreading across the Caribbean was a response to a highly profitable product combined with a shortage of workers. In effect, when the colonies found themselves faced with the same conditions as those of the Roman Empire – 'expanding markets and limited labor supplies'[25] – they took what Braudel has called 'that huge and traumatic step backwards'[26] and reinstituted the vast and inflexible agricultural production system of the Romans. Already more strict than other forms of slavery, this system now had a 'starkly racial character' that proved 'more profoundly oppressive and more socially divisive',[27] generating 'race', generating 'Africa'. Moreover, in Surinam and the English islands, slave trafficking, previously left to various European merchants, had become the business of the Stuart crown. Just before the time of Behn's visit, Charles II had chartered a company, The Royal Adventurers into Africa – replaced in the next decade by the more efficient Royal African Company – headed by his brother (later James II), for the purpose of controlling and profiting from the sale of slaves to English colonies. The colonists disliked the system and quite regularly evaded it, but how could Behn oppose it? The unnamed Lord Governor in her tale, Lord Willoughby of Parham, was under instruction to disseminate the Company's plan to provide 'a competent and a constant supply of Negro-servants' so 'necessary' to the planters.[28] The long lists of important courtiers and merchants who made up the subscribers included Lord Arlington and Thomas Killigrew, Behn's employers on her spying mission to the Low Countries in 1666–7, and Lord Lauderdale, the prominent uncle of the Scottish lord to whom she dedicated *Oroonoko*.[29] When Oroonoko is associated with the Romans of history, when he feels an allegiance to the Stuart royal line, he is not only showing a refined affinity with two prestigious European cultures but deepening the paradox of his status as 'Royal Slave'. Chief trader in his own kingdom, someone flung from the apex of a pyramid to its base, he is also associated with those who ruled major slaveholding societies in the West and were in their persons all that a slave was not.

With her cool explanation of 'the most advantageous Trading' for slaves to 'make use of' (III, p. 60), Behn was up to date. But it is a measure of the distance of the colonies from Europe and the unexamined way in which slave labour was adopted that, even in 1688, she apparently could not take for granted that her readers would know what it was. As she fills in the background of Oroonoko's story, Behn provides what amounts to an introductory primer on its practical workings: slaves' prices and their contract sale in lots, their separation and renaming, their customary clothing, plots of ground, holiday music and communal festivities, the precautionary surveillance and, at intervals, the escalating cycles of fear and violence. The men who wrote from the colonies were occupied with administration and religion, history and natural history, and the unending policy and factional disputes that stuff out the colonial state papers. It was left to the woman storyteller to sketch a general outline of this new kind of mixed society. While Behn scholars argued for decades about whether *Oroonoko* was based on first-hand experience, historians drew on its passages as a valuable collateral source.

Oroonoko's story, however, does not treat ordinary slave life. Instead it dramatizes what observers understood to be wrongs or special harshnesses, portrayed as they are suffered personally, always in an exacerbated form. There were both official and anecdotal reports about kidnappings of small groups lured aboard ships and sold, a recognized outrage and against

Company policy, since it stopped trade.[30] Here a prince and heir is betrayed with his hundred noble companions. (When Behn numbers people in hundreds, she inflates population groups in the records.) Gentlemanly trust and hospitality prove elaborate pretences that abruptly give way to open force and calculation about the men as physical specimens. On the ships, many anonymous slaves committed suicide or refused to eat and mounted attacks if they could. Slave traders record their use of shackles, force-feeding, and other measures. Oroonoko's shock and desperation are seen at close hand. Slavery has earlier been defined as worse than death for well-born Africans, and Oroonoko furiously refuses the 'Indignity', 'Disgrace', and 'shameful Fetters' (III, pp. 83–4), only to be restrained by promises instead of fetters. This is not the translatlantic slave journey known as the Middle Passage, with its foulness and mortality, but only, he thinks, 'a tedious Voyage' (III, p. 86). At its end, the common slaves simply emerge from the hold – presumably not a place where Oroonoko 'decently might descend' (III, p. 83) when he had toured the ship as a royal guest – and with the courtiers vanish into slavery. Behn focuses on the contrast between Christian deceit and Oroonoko's 'Heathen' honour (III, p. 84), and she does not explain here or later how the many women and children came to be enslaved.

If *Oroonoko* is not about the Middle Passage, it is also not about the cane fields or sugar machinery. The uncomplaining slave workers provide a friendly chorus confirming Oroonoko's greatness. Joyfully reunited with Imoinda, he lives among the white colonists in a storybook slavery of polite visits, hunting, and exploration. The politeness is strained, however, by the non-appearance of the absent governor who can grant Oroonoko's promised freedom, and his growing suspicions and fear that the child Imoinda is carrying will be born a slave. This was a feature of slavery that received much comment, occasionally pitying but mainly matter of fact. Like the parents, slave children were classified as chattel or real property, essentially as they would be if they were crops or livestock; in Behn's coarse phrasing, 'all the Breed is theirs to whom the Parents belong' (III, p. 93). This case is aggravated not only by the lovers' long-delayed, virtuous, tender, and fully sexual union, but because Oroonoko, like Imoinda, is the last of his 'Race' (III, p. 93) and their child promises to be a royal heir. But while Oroonoko often speaks about virtue, he is always reticent about rank. What immediately moves him are Imoinda's 'Griefs' (III, p. 104).

Now Oroonoko turns leader, as he did with his army in Africa, addressing the male slaves not about his circumstances but theirs. It is a stirring 'Harangue . . . of the Miseries, and Ignominies of Slavery' (III, p. 105). Others in Behn's time freely characterized slavery as an unhappy state and also noted its cruel abuses, but the common refrain was that it was 'necessary'. Other invented slave orations or dialogues, which were just beginning to appear, are eloquent on slave miseries, but they typically collapse into assurances of glad service to kind masters. Oroonoko's speech does no such thing. It presents a serious, uncompromising (and also clearly gendered) plea for the dignity of all men. But it also introduces new elements that recharacterize the colonial scene, point to conditions that Oroonoko has not seemed to see, and sometimes sit oddly in the tale.

First, Oroonoko dwells on the slaves' overwork and mistreatment, unending 'Drudgeries . . . fitter for Beasts than Men' and the special cruelty of indiscriminate punishments, bloody whippings that should be revenged, he says, 'with a Life of some of those Tyrants' for 'every drop' (III, p. 105). Yet these are the slaves at Parham, ruled by the mild Trefry, among plantation inhabitants against whom Oroonoko has previously sworn he would 'sooner forfeit his eternal Liberty . . . than lift his Hand' (III, p. 94). Next he challenges the right of ownership of '*an unknown People*' who have not '*Vanquish'd us Nobly in Fight*' but only '*Bought and Sold*' commercially; here he apparently draws a distinction between the domestic slaves ('*the Sport of Women, Fools and Cowards*') and field labourers ('*the Support of Rogues, Runagades*') (III, p. 105). But his argument is 'curious', as Anita Pacheco has pointed out, characterizing the speech as 'military rhetoric' affirming 'a regard for human dignity that is rooted not in compassion, but in pride'.[31] As Oroonoko should surely know, most of these slaves have been vanquished in war, not, to be sure, by the English, but by Oroonoko himself. It was he who sold them, with 'all the profit' (III, p. 61). He seems now to approve only of the first stage of the one form of enslavement in which he participated in Africa, because it alone can count as manly. He has also always cultivated these 'unknown' English, and has chosen to spend his time with women, at 'Sports' (III, p. 96), or with gentlemen planters who bear no resemblance to the '*degenerate Race*' with '*no one Humane Vertue*' (III, p. 105) he now excoriates. Finally, after some discussion of women's role, Oroonoko concludes with a sweeping appeal to the abstract ideal of liberty. Liberty has been the central subject in the earlier negotiations about his case. Now he calls on the slaves to embrace liberty rather than slavery 'if they Dy'd in the attempt' (III, p. 106). In Roman history this had been both an ideal and a practical legal distinction; in English history it was a familiar trope that Behn's readers would have recognised, invoked in political speech by royalists as well as republicans.[32]

We do not learn if a slave population more bravely bent on liberty might be able to gain it, as Oroonoko thinks, or, more probably, could be talked back into slavery by the 'fair means' (III, p. 108) Trefry advises. The low types Oroonoko has described now appear. Led by Behn's second villain, the deputy governor Byam, they mount a precipitous disorderly attack. The main body of slaves, demoralized by their fearful women and children, give up and abandon Oroonoko. It is the start of his gradual isolation, until he stands as a single hero in some remarkable pictorial scenes. Now, abandoned, Oroonoko comes up with a theory of natural slavery that dates back to Aristotle. While contemptuous of all Christians as unprincipled hypocrites, he also furiously scorns the slaves as made 'by Nature' only to be slaves, 'Dogs, treacherous and cowardly, fit for such Masters' (III, p. 109). Readers, if they liked, could settle back in their chairs; slaves were not Romans or Englishmen but a dependent, naturally servile people led this way and that. Oroonoko's descriptions of cruel whippings stand, however, and are borne out by what happens to him.

If this uprising followed the pattern of slave plots reported from the colonies – such as one in Barbados that was described in a 1676 pamphlet, one of many led by slaves identified as Coromantines[33] – we might expect many of the features here: the planning under cover of holiday feasting; the rumours and panic among the women colonists; public punishment of ringleaders by such elaborate, prolonged, purposefully intimidating means as whipping and hot pepper, gelding and dismemberment, slow burning alive, and the mutilation of corpses; also, here and in many reports, stoic defiance like Oroonoko's on the part of tortured slaves. A contemporary observer in Surinam noted with interest but no shred of sympathy that 'the most exquisite tortures . . . for a terrour and example to others' were endured by retaken runaway slaves 'without shrinking'.[34] It seems probable that Behn had glimpsed not 'some Indian Othello', but rather possibilities for the heroic in slave resistance and intransigence.

But Behn has rearranged these elements, interrupting the simple sequence of offence and punishment and stretching out events through the rest of her tale. Oroonoko has led an escape, potentially threatening, as Behn notes, but not outright rebellion. White colonists and black slaves do not face each other across a colour bar but divide along class lines around Oroonoko. Oroonoko's friends, planters 'of the better sort' (III, p. 107), not only sympathize with him but, implausibly, may have colluded in the mass escape. When the slaves turn to face their attackers, the killing or wounding of whites, even of the deputy governor, are not viewed as punishable acts but are reported with satisfaction. (In fact, Behn and Martin openly wish for Byam's death.) Later, when the recaptured slaves are supplied with whips and turn on Oroonoko, they are nearly ordered to whip the overseer, Trefry, for defending him. At every point, Oroonoko's white friends strongly object to Byam's use of force. And indeed, Byam does not use the machinery of colonial justice to restore and preserve security. When his flattery, assurances, and even a written contract persuade Oroonoko to surrender, Byam has him bound and cruelly whipped only – it is said three times – to gratify his 'revenge'. When Oroonoko vows his own 'dire Revenge' (III, p. 111) – now the word occurs nine times – Byam for self-protection calls on his disreputable Council, which sentences Oroonoko to be hanged as 'an Example' (III, p. 112). When Oroonoko's friends eject Byam and the Council and protect him at Parham, Byam plays a trick and has it invaded. Oroonoko is taken and publicly executed, not by hanging but by slow dismemberment. It is a two-man revenge plot, played out within the framework of colonial slave discipline, ending in judicial murder.

Unjustified torture of a noble victim told in gruesome physical detail: no wonder later readers were left feeling that they had read an exposé. Oroonoko himself is often filled with outrage, and in Behn's assurances that Council members and the Justices met later retribution there seems a thread of unsatisfied anger. Behn's contemporaries, however, do not seem to have taken such a view. Capital punishments in England then were cruel, and those who reported on slave punishments in the colonies seem interested but quite unmoved. 'Very exquisite Torments', commented Hans Sloane, a cultivated physician and scholar, who details the various tortures and mutilations and then roundly defends them.[35] Behn's literary followers, in pursuit of more decorous sentimental effects, largely left such violence out. So far as we can judge, Behn's early audience was impressed not by the injustice and violence, but by Oroonoko and his heroism. But in the last part of the tale, the promising, bountiful colony is revealed as a place of division and misrule. Many individual observers and much new legislation characterized the slaves as 'brutish'. In Behn's story, the colonial managers are the brutes.

Colonial society

Recent critical interpretations of Oroonoko show complex new methods and sympathies: 'The injunction is to read in reverse, against the grain, between the lines, from below. The wretched of the earth are talking, and we are all trying to listen.'[36] As a woman, Behn is expected to hold a different or dissident view of power, yet as a white European, she is inevitably in service to power, colluding with it and constructing it in her writing. She portrays 'others' who rise above European moral laxity, but read from below and against the grain, she is seen to be subordinating and even betraying the 'others' she warmly praises. Her friendships and enmities prove illusory; she may demean Europeans, but foreseeably shares a superiority over the wretched. Where she can be observed shaping available materials, Behn shows a strong taste for dramatic polarities, but read between the lines, her text is full of tensions and contradictions. Even her authorial control can seem a form of 'colonial mastery'.[37]

Undoubtedly Behn writes as a frank and ardent colonialist, pausing twice to mourn Charles II's loss of so rich a land. In an ode the year before *Oroonoko*, she had lauded the 'Brave' settlers of Jamaica who 'have by Conquest made it all your own' and paid 'such Useful Tribute' to James II.[38] In *Oroonoko*, her native American scenes with their attractive primitivism and new encounters are readily seen to express colonialist ideology. 'Very useful' Indians whom the colonists 'caress' provide necessary services for 'unvaluable Trifles' (III, p. 60) and are likened to swift animals; the trade for an overflowing catalogue of exotic natural specimens and artefacts is defined by Laura Brown as a 'discourse of imperialist acquisition' that points to 'imperialist exploitation';[39] quite charming contact scenes in a town of distant Indians might seem 'an exemplary drama of reciprocity', as Suvir Kaul notes, but quickly establish a comfortable cultural and technological superiority.[40] For Behn the colony is a place of leisure, witty company, and adventures; no one struggles for a livelihood. But at its edges it holds danger, and friendship motivated by fear. Behn seems to view relations with native Americans as a test of courage and civility. Oroonoko, who supremely has those virtues, establishes 'perfect, open, and free Trade' (III, p. 103) with the Indians, but later when the Dutch treat them 'not so civilly' (III, p. 100), they rush in and commit butchery. Behn herself is among the brave few who 'venture' (III, p. 100) when most others fall behind. Her closer test, however, is with Oroonoko himself.

The most striking weather change in critical opinion is found in Behn's relation to her hero, which no longer springs from admiration and attachment, or compassion for his sufferings, but from complicity and exploitation. While readers usually trace her participation in culture or discourse, not her intentions, some charges against her are startling: that she is racist, for example, or personally responsible for Oroonoko's death. But to a wide range of readers, the narrator's self-descriptions are deeply suspect. Despite her claims for influence in the colony, as many critics have noted, she distrusts Oroonoko, flees with the other women, and fails to save him from being whipped, then absents herself when he is taken and murdered. Long ago Martine Watson Brownley sensibly pointed out how useful it is that Behn's high hyperbolic style and extreme characters are grounded by an ordinary narrator of uncertain convictions and presence of mind.[41] Jane Spencer has traced Behn's helplessness to her femininity – her mother and sister are likewise helpless bystanders – which she escapes only as a writer.[42] Later readings are more severe. Behn's narrator is not only placed – or places herself – in a pivotal role as agent for the colony, fearing, placating, watching, and also protecting a hero of fiery moods. She is not only a worldly observer who frankly assumes some admixture of calculation and likes the art of the stratagem, and also represents herself in some very slippery language, as Robert Chibka has shown.[43] Much worse, she knowingly deceives Oroonoko with false promises to keep him in slavery, as if writing in the first person to discredit herself, casting herself with the two smoothly lying villains she does much to make us hate.

Behn's scene-building has its rough edges.[44] The right of the narrator or Oroonoko's other friends to promise that freedom will be granted by the absent governor remains unclear. Here Behn had little to guide or obstruct her. Slavery in the English colonies was left undefined, so Oroonoko's case could only be a matter of custom and common opinion, although Imoinda's slave status seems unambiguous. Behn may only claim to know what that opinion would be. What might have happened if Oroonoko had been patient – all he promises is 'to rest, yet a little longer' (III, p. 94) – is foreclosed by Imoinda's approaching childbirth. What the narrator might have done to act more forcefully is foreclosed once Oroonoko is bound and whipped 'like a common Slave' (III, p. 111). After this violation, Oroonoko stays alive solely to take revenge and then, he says, 'scorns to live with' and is 'resolv'd not to survive his Whipping' (III, pp. 112, 113), referring to it bitterly through the rest of the story. The humane ministrations – most unusual colonial scenes – relieve his pain; otherwise, the narrator and the others can only try to talk a hero out of being heroic. His physical decline and frantic moods make him increasingly a spectacle of 'otherness', but he speaks with still greater poise.

Imoinda, the hero's retiring feminine counterpart, is a less appealing character than she must once have been, but she has come into the spotlight. Here the critique is of Behn as author. First, she creates a female love object far more limited than herself, naturally submissive, wholly subordinated, sometimes mentioned almost as an afterthought. Moreover, as consideration of race displaces gender, Imoinda also disrupts the earlier feminist identification of woman author with her slave hero by showing the failed solidarity of the white woman with the black one. A much-repeated argument by Margaret Ferguson, calling attention to Imoinda as 'other other', casts Behn as other woman in latent 'competition . . . for Oroonoko's body' – a return to the suggestive subtext of 'Gentlewoman' in 1696 – that produces Behn's book and obliterates Imoinda's child.[45] Others have found 'conflictual relationship' in the ways Imoinda is made alien by her extensively carved and mutely sacrificed body,[46] or emphasize her association with rape and bodily decay.[47]

While African reports described male patricians and warriors, polygynous West African societies produced no Imoindas. Behn seems to have constructed her from an amalgam of earlier romance and epic characters – and perhaps also the modest Indian maidens and Amazons who were reported to live near the Amazon River – and then called her in or out to support Oroonoko's scenes. Imoinda is present to fight beside her husband, for example, but not present after his whipping when the colonists nurse him back to health. Sometimes she seems like a decorous European heroine, sometimes quite foreign; an author stands to be criticized either way. But Imoinda always seems to be in the service of some planned symmetry.

Like Montaigne's cannibals, non-Europeans in Surinam illustrate strict and simple virtue in love. In contrast to Deputy Governor Byam, who has an Indian mistress, the African male slaves show a strong attachment to family, *'more dear to us than Life'*, and their wives 'pay an intire Obedience' (III, p. 107). But these virtues are domestic, not heroic; the wives quickly impede the men's honour. Only Imoinda fights on bravely with poisoned arrows although heavily pregnant, with a non-European physical hardiness, and only she supports her husband's honour. Oroonoko's oration here seems central. Both lovers observe the two linked principles he had urged on the male slaves: for the men, *'Honour was the First Principle in Nature'* (III, p. 106), which the wives should accept and follow even at the cost of their lives, but the wives in turn require men's *'equal Care'* (III, p. 106). Imoinda must be killed not simply so Oroonoko can assert ownership of her body or their child,[48] but because when Oroonoko pursues his 'first principle' and seeks revenge, Imoinda faces rape and killing. By his code, he must protect her. Once Behn understands it, she approves his deed: 'we thought it Brave and Just' (III, p. 113).

Again Behn has tightened the noose, with Oroonoko's desperate moods about Imoinda's ravishing or death in the African scenes, his later protectiveness, and Imoinda's extreme modesty. Yet the demands made on both characters are very extreme. Behn wants pathos as well as heroic principle and its logic. To create a mood of tender agreement, joyful on Imoinda's side, she introduces an African belief about the afterlife (one found in many reports about slaves) and an accepted African custom of wife-killing, carried out personally if husbands love the wives. For the moment, both characters seem primitive, almost childlike, virtuous in the remote style of Montaigne's cannibals. It almost seems a relief when Oroonoko succumbs to a more understandable grief and rage.

Meanwhile, the ignoble colonists are shown ready to violate female as well as male honour, or simply to attack a woman. The documents often mention whipping and torture of male slaves, entirely legal and in fact increasingly mandated. But early English colonial reports leave unmentioned the threats to slave women of forced liaisons or sexual violence from the predominantly male white populations. Perhaps Southerne in his play made Imoinda into a white woman partly because her key scenes with his predatory governor would have brought this non-subject only too visibly before the London audience. Oroonoko's vision of Imoinda 'Ravished by every Brute' and put to 'a shameful Death' (III, p. 113) reinforces the unrestrained mob rule of the seamy colonists who overrun Behn's Edenic landscape in the last part of the tale.

What led Behn in her last year to look back to vanished colonial scenes as laboratories of misgovernment, as she did also in her late play *The Widdow Ranter*? Perhaps she saw strong material in her memories or had old scores to settle, but many critics have heard a Tory warning voice about England: a reminder of the martyrdom of Charles I or the dangers immediately threatening James II and the looming power of the Dutch; at least, a broadly sketched parable about the void left by a missing Lord and incursions by low upstarts. But *Oroonoko* does not seem to have a simple political key. The colonists do not fall into line in political parties, as real colonists, facing new circumstances and making new alliances, often did not. Both villains, the captain and deputy governor, are clearly agents of the king in control of many men, and Oroonoko recognizes their authority. If *Oroonoko* offers a critique of commerce, it does not seem complete. The cunning slave captain, for whom any African is saleable, might be seen to show an incipiently Whiggish ruthless greed, and Byam's group plans to hold Imoinda and her child as slaves. However, Byam – in real life a staunch Royalist official with Surinam estates and also a well-born wife – is demoted here to an unpropertied intruder. According to Behn, he 'had nothing, and so need fear nothing' (III, p. 107), and is privately not only a bully but a sponger who wants to live 'at other Peoples Expence' (III, p. 113). What Byam effectively controls is a caricature government: a Falstaffian 'comical' militia (III, p. 107), a lawless and brawling Council given legal authority, the 'wild' Irish assassin Banister, 'inhumane' Justices (III, p. 118), and an executioner. Class and respectability are prominent, but so is administrative power.

Behn's Surinam might be viewed not as a mirror of England, but as a developing colony at a very early stage. Many early observers contrasted the admirable landscapes with the uncontrolled inhabitants, given to drinking, swearing, fighting, and 'lascivious Abominations',[49] with rusty arms and absurd social pretensions. That many colonists came as transported criminals and vagrants or as indentured servants led to broad stereotyping. An early visitor called Jamaica 'the dunghill whereon England doth cast forth its rubbidge: rogues and whores and such like people'.[50] A later popular author repeated 'dunghill' and unloosed his eloquence, including 'The Receptacle of Vagabonds, the Sanctuary of Bankrupts, and a Close-stool for the Purges of our Prisons'.[51] Behn draws on such planter stereotypes, especially in her portrait of the Council. But she has made a distinction: the low characters in her story are the government, are the law. The upper-class planters who discern natural differences and are drawn to Oroonoko also resist being governed. They are not fond of the Lord Governor, whose job was to regulate from above, implementing unwelcome home policy. In the colony, they do not join with the militia, and they expel Byam and his Council, posting guards against them. Trefry calls Byam's use of his colony-wide authority a 'Tyrany' and argues that Parham, as the private land of a royal appointee, is 'a Sanctuary' like a royal palace, 'exempt from the Law' (III, pp. 112–13). Thus the colonists are divided, an aggressive new civil administration in conflict with recalcitrant gentleman landholders.

This has at least some status as 'true history'. Planters who had exercised unlimited control over their lands and their slaves as private property did not always cooperate with the centralized administration that was needed for safety as the colonies grew and slave majorities increased. A multiplying network of new colonial laws designed to punish or prevent every form of slave misbehaviour also had to be accompanied by laws against owners who protected their slaves from punishment or shielded runaways.[52] *Oroonoko* closes on two disparate versions of slave management: overbearing or fearful men aggressively bent on exerting force against Oroonoko and others whom they do not own, and the men of quality who quietly manage their own estates. Colonel Martin, given the last word among the characters, refuses Oroonoko's remains on his land and 'swore . . . he cou'd govern his *Negroes* without Terrifying and Grieving them with frightful Spectacles of a mangl'd King' (III, p. 118). A coherent older set of rights is being broken too.

A postcolonial reader might point out, as Richard Frohock has, that Behn has cordoned off the cruelties. She attributes 'violence and the less palpable acts of imperialism to the "other" immoral and lower-class whites', even though Martin's supposedly benign counter-vision of subjection without violence is mere 'storytelling'.[53] Yet this is not quite true. Oroonoko's account of promiscuous bloody whippings and the machinery mobilized against him leave some impression of institutional violence. And while the English colonial system proved 'impossible to maintain' without 'police regulations',[54] that issue was not yet settled. Some people argued for humane arrangements. In 1701, Christopher Codrington, a wealthy colonial governor and literary patron with a link to Behn,[55] received a frightened report that Coromantine slaves had decapitated an important planter. His reaction was that Coromantines were a nation of 'born Heroes', so the planter must have been 'guilty of some unusual act of severity, or rather some indignity'.[56] He and the London Council wanted to see all slaves protected from inhumanity. Instead the colony passed an entirely typical law that imposed death or mutilation on any slave who hurt any white. It gave protection not to slaves or the rights of owners but to white skin.

Behn is not greatly interested in law, although she shows its place in her three different societies. Her interest is in human agreements, not without firm subordination but, as she portrays them, freely recognized, unforced, reciprocal. There is a very wide range: reverence toward monarchs and leaders, oaths among men, vows between lovers, trade relations, marital relations, confidences and help among friends, and not a little strategizing and cajoling. Opposed to these are the snare of false vows or outright force. Oroonoko reacts strongly to both broken faith and any physical compulsion, sensitive even to Behn's passing mention of his possible confinement, 'not so Luckily spoke' (III, p. 94). Both violate his honour, as Behn emphasizes. When writing of lesser occasions, she also often uses forms of the word 'oblige', referring to what is obligatory, what obligates oneself or others, or simply what obliges and pleases. All are proper social ties or ligatures. This running theme is made visible in her final scene. With a compliment to Banister because his crude words of menace are true, Oroonoko chooses to stand untied. Thus he alters and in a fashion civilizes his barbaric killing. Struggling in the English colony, nearly lost to memory, he is in his own country.

NOTES

1 Heidi Hutner, 'Aphra Behn's *Oroonoko*: The Politics of Gender, Race, and Class', in *Living by the Pen: Early British Writers*, ed. Dale Spender (New York: Teachers College Press, 1992), pp. 39–51.
2 *Documents Illustrative of the History of the Slave Trade to America*, ed. Elizabeth Donnan, 5 vols. (Washington, DC: Carnegie Institution, 1930–5), I, pp. 202, 204, 226, 240.
3 Janet Todd, *The Critical Fortunes of Aphra Behn* (Columbia, SC: Camden House, 1998), p. 124.
4 Thomas Southerne, Preface to *Oroonoko*, ed. Maximillian E. Novak and David Stuart Rodes (Lincoln: University of Nebraska Press, 1976), p. 4.
5 *A General Dictionary, Historical and Critical*, III, p. 149 (1735), quoted in Jeslyn Medoff, '"Very Like a Fiction": Some Early Biographies of Aphra Behn', in *Write or Be Written*, ed. Barbara Smith and Ursula Appelt (Aldershot, and Burlington, VT: Ashgate, 2001), p. 265 n. 19. Medoff also studies the biographical readings and speculations in 'Amalgamating an Author: Aphra Behn in Two Biographies of the Long Eighteenth Century', in *Aphra Behn (1640–1689): Identity, Alterity, Ambiguity*, ed. Mary Ann O'Donnell, Bernard Dhuicq, Guyonne Leduc (Paris: L'Harmattan, 2000).

6 *The Discovery of the Large, Rich and Beautiful Empire of Guiana* (1596), in *Selected Writings*, ed. Gerald Hammond (Harmondsworth: Penguin, 1986), pp. 95, 100.
7 The heavy reliance of West African travel books on print sources from an earlier period is laid out by Adam Jones, 'Semper Aliquid Veteris: Printed Sources for the History of the Ivory and Gold Coasts, 1500–1750', *Journal of African History*, 27 (1986), pp. 215–35.
8 J. Paul Hunter, *Before Novels* (New York and London: W. W. Norton, 1990), p. 353.
9 Achille Mbembe, *On the Postcolony* (Berkeley: University of California Press, 2001), p. 3.
10 Michael Craton, *Sinews of Empire: A Short History of British Slavery* (Garden City, NY: Anchor Press, 1974), p. 252; Laura Brown, 'The Romance of Empire: *Oroonoko* and the Trade in Slaves', in *Ends of Empire: Women and Ideology in Early Eighteenth-Century English Literature* (Ithaca: Cornell University Press, 1993), p. 35.
11 Nicolas Villault de Bellefond, *A Relation of the Coasts of Africk called Guinee* (London, 1670), p. 133.
12 'Relation du voyage fait sur les costes d'Afrique', in *Recueil de divers voyages*, ed. Henri Justel (Paris, 1674), p. 16 (translation mine).
13 Examples were gathered by Wylie Sypher, 'A Note on the Realism of Mrs Behn's *Oroonoko*', *Modern Language Notes*, 3 (1942), 401–5. On their role in earlier slave revolts, see my 'Confusing Matters: Searching the Backgrounds of *Oroonoko*', in *Aphra Behn Studies*, pp. 269–70. For an argument that they may have been named in circular fashion for their qualities, rather than place or ethnicity, see Craton, *Sinews of Empire*, pp. 74–5.
14 Samuel Purchas, *Hakluytus Posthumus or Purchas His Pilgrimes*, 20 vols. (Glasgow: J. MacLehose and Sons, 1905–7), VI, p. 485; XVI, p. 270.
15 Richard Hakluyt, ed., *The Principal Navigations Voyages Traffiques & Discoveries of the English Nation*, 12 vols. (Glasgow: J. MacLehose and Sons, 1903–5), VI, p. 173. In Behn's lifetime the main export from the Gold Coast still was gold.
16 Richard Price, *The Guiana Maroons: A Historical and Bibliographical Introduction* (Baltimore: Johns Hopkins University Press, 1976), p. 7.
17 Richard S. Dunn, *Sugar and Slaves: The Rise of the Planter Class in the English West Indies, 1624–1713* (New York and London: W. W. Norton, 1973), pp. 230–1, 234.
18 James A. Rawley, *The Transatlantic Slave Trade: A History* (New York: W. W. Norton, 1981), p. 428. Rawley also distinguishes slave destinations.
19 George Saintsbury, *The English Novel* (London: J. M. Dent, 1913), p. 51; W. J. Cameron, *New Light on Aphra Behn* (Auckland: University of Auckland Press, 1961), p. 7. Both of these suggestions incidentally point to the frequent blurring of the distinction between Africans and Indians.
20 Algernon Charles Swinburne, 'Social Verse', in *Studies in Prose and Poetry* (London: Chatto & Windus, 1894), p. 95.
21 Ernest A. Baker, *The Novels of Mrs Aphra Behn* (London, 1905; reprinted Westport, Ct: Greenwood Press, 1969), p. xxiii.
22 Wylie Sypher, 'The African Prince in London', *Journal of the History of Ideas*, 2 (1941), 237.

23 Angeline Goreau, *Reconstructing Aphra: A Social Biography of Aphra Behn* (New York: Dial Press, 1980), p. 289.

24 Price, *The Guiana Maroons*, p. 7.

25 Herbert S. Klein, 'Slavery in Western Development', in *The Atlantic Slave Trade* (Cambridge: Cambridge University Press, 1999), p. 3. Klein includes a useful bibliographical essay.

26 Fernand Braudel, *The Mediterranean and the Mediterranean World in the Age of Phillip II*, trans. Siân Reynolds, 2 vols. (New York: Harper & Row, 1972–3), II, p. 734.

27 Dunn, *Sugar and Slaves*, p. 225.

28 From *The Several Declarations of the Company of Royal Adventurers* (London, 1667), repr. in Elizabeth Donnan, ed., *Documents*, I, p. 156.

29 Donnan, *Documents*, I, pp. 169–72.

30 For examples see Donnan, *Documents*, I, pp. 124, 269–70, 419, and my 'Confusing Matters' in *Aphra Behn Studies*, pp. 268–9. Even more dramatic examples by the Spanish in South America were circulating in English translations of Las Casas.

31 Anita Pacheco, 'Royalism and Honor in Aphra Behn's *Oroonoko*', *SEL*, 34 (1994), 498.

32 For example, Edward Chamberlayne in his regularly republished survey guide to England cites on the principle of 'the Subjects just Liberties' the authority of 'the best of Kings', Charles I. *Angliae Notitia: or the Present State of England, 20th Edition* (London, 1702), p. 83.

33 *Great Newes from the Barbadoes* (London, 1676). Patterns in reported slave plots are traced by Jerome S. Handler, 'Slave Revolts and Conspiracies in Seventeenth-Century Barbados', *New West Indian Guide*, 56 (1982), 5–37. Handler makes clear the deep uncertainties about what slaves planned and how far colonists understood it.

34 George Warren, *An Impartial Description of Surinam* (London, 1667), p. 19.

35 Hans Sloane, *A Voyage to the Islands . . . with the Natural History of [Jamaica]*, I (London, 1707), p. lvii.

36 Philip D. Morgan, 'Encounters between British and "Indigenous" Peoples, c. 1500–c. 1800', in *Empire and Others: British Encounters with Indigenous Peoples, 1600–1850*, ed. Martin Daunton and Rick Halpern (Philadelphia: University of Pennsylvania Press, 1999), p. 43.

37 Stephanie Athey and Daniel Cooper Alarcón, '*Oroonoko*'s Gendered Economies of Honor/Horror: Reframing Colonial Discourse Studies in the Americas', *American Literature*, 65 (1993), 429.

38 'To Christopher Duke of Albemarle, on his Voyage to his Government of Jamaica, A Pindarick', in *Works*, I, p. 224. Ironically, Albemarle was among the colonial governors who, like Behn's version of Byam, joined with the Irish and lesser holders to undermine the established planters; see Dunn, *Sugar and Slaves*, pp. 160–1. The original 'Conquest' was over Spain.

39 Brown, 'The Romance of Empire', p. 43.

40 Suvir Kaul, 'Reading Literary Symptoms: Colonial Pathologies and the *Oroonoko* Fictions of Behn, Southerne, and Hawkesworth', *Eighteenth-Century Life*, 18 (November, 1994), 82–3.

41 Martine Watson Brownley, 'The Narrator in *Oroonoko*', *Essays in Literature*, 4 (1977), 174–81.

42 Jane Spencer, *The Rise of the Woman Novelist: From Aphra Behn to Jane Austen* (Oxford: Oxford University Press, 1986), pp. 50–2.

43 Robert L. Chibka, '"Oh! Do Not Fear a Woman's Invention": Truth, Falsehood, and Fiction in Aphra Behn's *Oroonoko*', *Texas Studies in Literature and Language*, 30 (1988), 522–4.

44 For example, when Oroonoko is kidnapped he has 'drunk hard of Punch' and wines (III, p. 83), but later Behn often has his company because 'he cou'd not Drink' (III, p. 93).

45 Margaret W. Ferguson, 'Juggling the Categories of Race, Class and Gender: Aphra Behn's *Oroonoko*', *Women's Studies*, 19 (1991), 170–1. This essay has been twice reprinted and is echoed in other essays by Ferguson.

46 Ros Ballaster, 'New Hystericism: Aphra Behn's *Oroonoko*: The Body, the Text and the Feminist Critic', in *New Feminist Discourses: Critical Essays on Theories and Texts*, ed. Isobel Armstrong (New York: Routledge, 1992), pp. 290–4.

47 Athey and Alarcón, '*Oroonoko*'s Gendered Economies', pp. 426–37.

48 Charlotte Sussman points to ways in which their scenes seem to touch on resistance to childbearing, a topic in Caribbean slave history, in 'The Other Problem with Women: Reproduction and Slave Culture in Aphra Behn's *Oroonoko*', *Rereading Aphra Behn*, pp. 212–33.

49 Henry Adis, *A Letter Sent from Syrranam, to his Excellency, the Lord Willoughby* (London, 1664), quoted in Janet Todd, p. 37. Todd's chapters 3 and 4 provide a sense of the political and personal quarrels in the colony.

50 Henry Whistler, 'A journall of a voardge', BL Sloane MS 3926, in C. H. Firth, ed., *The Narrative of General Venables* (London: Longmans, Green, 1900), p. 146. The quotation has been modernized.

51 Edward Ward, *A Trip to Jamaica: With a True Character of the People and Island* (London, 1698), p. 13.

52 On slave law see Dunn, *Sugar and Slaves*, pp. 238–46.

53 Richard Frohock, 'Violence and Awe: The Foundations of Government in Aphra Behn's New World Settings', in *Women at Sea: Travel Writing and the Margins of Caribbean Discourse*, ed. Lizabeth Paravisini-Gebert and Ivette Romero-Cesareo (New York: Palgrave, 2001), pp. 44, 54–5.

54 Elsa V. Goveia, 'The West Indian Slave Laws of the Eighteenth Century', *Revista de Ciencias Sociales*, 4 (1960), 82.

55 In *Oroonoko*, Behn says that she has put Colonel Martin into her 'New Comedy' (III, p. 111). When that play, *The Younger Brother*, was posthumously published in 1696, its editor, Charles Gildon, dedicated it to Codrington. Todd, p. 39, speculates that Codrington and Behn may have been known to one another.

56 *Calendar of State Papers, Colonial Series* (Great Britain: Public Record Office), *America and West Indies*, 1701, no. 1132. The colony was Antigua.

12

JACQUELINE PEARSON

The short fiction (excluding *Oroonoko*)

With the exception of *Oroonoko*, Behn's short fiction has had relatively little critical attention.[1] There are fourteen attributed tales, of which five, including *Oroonoko*, were published separately, under Behn's name and presumably by her: *The Fair Jilt: or, the History of Prince Tarquin and Miranda*, and (probably) *Agnes de Castro: or, the Force of Generous Love* in 1688, *The Lucky Mistake*, and *The History of the Nun: or, the Fair Vow-Breaker* in 1689. The others, 'Love-Letters', 'Memoirs of the Court of the King of Bantam', 'The Nun: or, the Perjur'd Beauty', 'The Adventure of the Black Lady', 'The Unfortunate Bride: or, the Blind Lady a Beauty', 'The Dumb Virgin: or, the Force of Imagination', 'The Unfortunate Happy Lady', 'The Wandring Beauty' and 'The Unhappy Mistake: or, the Impious Vow Punish'd', were published posthumously, between 1698 and 1700.[2]

Criticism has been relatively sparse, especially of the posthumous texts, because they raise difficult issues about generic terminology, and their shortness may make them seem like a dead end in the rise of the novel: Ian Watt's classic *The Rise of the Novel* (1957), for instance, relegates Behn to a couple of footnotes, seeing the 'rise' of the novel as a wholly male-dominated phenomenon identified with new concepts of realism and the individual, and the associated rise of the middle-classes. This is surely not the case, however, since Behn's short fiction seems to meet all the criteria for the status of novel adduced by J. Paul Hunter: contemporaneity; credibility and probability; familiarity; rejection of traditional plots; tradition-free language; individualism, subjectivity; empathy and vicariousness; coherence and unity of design; inclusivity, digressiveness, fragmentation; self-consciousness about innovation and novelty.[3] That some of the fictions are translations or adaptations of other authors has also tended to deter critics. Moreover, the authorship of the posthumous works has been vigorously questioned.[4] What unites the fiction definitely by Behn is 'psychological realism and an interest in the influence of education',[5] though such a description fits at least some of the posthumous fiction, like 'The Dumb Virgin'. It was certainly in the interests of Samuel

Briscoe, the publisher, to insist that the texts he was selling were by the commercially attractive 'Wonder of her Sex', the 'late celebrated Mrs Behn' who intriguingly joined a 'Masculine Vigor and Spirit' to a feminine 'softness' (III, pp. 332, 338). But even her publishers had to acknowledge that the posthumous tales may be very different from the undoubted works. The Advertisement to 'Memoirs of the Court of the King of Bantam' admits that its 'Stile . . . [is] so very different from Mrs. *Behn's* usual way of Writing', but turns this to an advantage by offering the reader the cultural capital of an apparently intimate insight into the life of a literary celebrity – 'it was a Trial of Skill, upon a Wager, to shew that she was able to write in the Style of the celebrated *Scarron* . . .' (III, p. 272).[6] Behn's work is allusive, and a full-scale attempt to emulate a popular French writer is not inconceivable. Moreover, recent studies of the Spanish sources of Behn's fiction suggest that the posthumous works use similar sources, and in similar ways, to the fiction that Behn published.[7] However the 'case is not proven', and a 'shift in style' from complex narratives to 'simpler patterns'[8] may imply not a change in authorship, but a movement from romance to 'novelistic principles' of 'topical, domestic, bourgeois frames of reference',[9] which might simply show Behn at the forefront of cultural innovation. To my ear – admittedly not a scientific test – 'The Unfortunate Bride' and 'The Dumb Virgin' seem most likely to have a Behnian core, or to ventriloquize Behn most effectively; 'The Nun' and 'The Wandring Beauty' show least signs of her trademark characteristics (though both nonetheless use motifs that were attractive to her, like the nun in the former and the lady errant in the latter).

Behn is consistent in her choice of dedicatees for her published fiction – young men, sometimes fellow writers, who shared her Tory politics, and were sometimes Catholics or even Jacobites, like Richard Maitland and Henry Nevil Payne, dedicatees of *Oroonoko* and *The Fair Jilt*. Payne had been implicated in the Catholic Meal-Tub Plot along with Thomas Dangerfield, whose name Behn provocatively appropriates for the doomed hero of 'The Dumb Virgin'.[10] Sir Roger Puleston, dedicatee of *Agnes de Castro*, was a convert to royalism, and George Granville, later Lord Lansdowne, dedicatee of *The Lucky Mistake*, was a royalist member of a distinguished royalist dynasty. Samuel Briscoe, on the other hand, directed the posthumous work to a much more disparate range of dedicatees. Baron Cutts of Gowran, to whom Briscoe dedicated 'The Dumb Virgin', is a most unlikely Behn dedicatee, a follower of Monmouth and William III,[11] perhaps chosen in a conscious strategy to distract attention from the possibly subversive political subtext of the tale, whose hero is given the name of a Catholic plotter. Arthur Mainwaring, dedicatee of 'The Unhappy Mistake', was an ex-Jacobite who became one of the Whigs' strongest apologists, and again it is possible that Briscoe's choice of dedicatee was meant to create a readership that was politically more broadly-based than this tale, set in the Interregnum and with a cavalier hero, would seem naturally to suggest.[12]

This raises the question of how far Behn's fictional narratives represent her royalist Tory politics in a coded form. Briscoe's dedications suggest that they were appropriable and readable even by political opponents. A number of critics have found such codes in Behn's drama, and I have argued elsewhere[13] that some of Susanna Centlivre's plays, while apparently operating within the conventions of intrigue comedy, actually allegorize and serve as propaganda for Whig principles of liberty and property and of social contracts of various kinds; could a similar case be made for Behn's narratives as coded Tory propaganda?

I think this case can be made, though only in general terms. However, where there is explicit social criticism of Whig politics or personalities, as in 'The Unfortunate Happy Lady', where the widowed Philadelphia has as many suitors as 'our dear King *Charles*' is besieged by factions of 'canting Whiggish Brethren',[14] we can be least confident that the voice is Behn's. In 'Memoirs of the Court of the King of Bantam', Wou'd-be King probably satirizes the Whig Shaftesbury, whose enemies believed he coveted the elective monarchy of Poland: that internal evidence allows the events of the novel to be dated to 1683,[15] the year of Shaftesbury's death, makes this particularly plausible.

Behn's dedications certainly assign literature a political role. *The Lucky Mistake*, dedicated to Granville at 'this Critical Juncture' – the flight of James II and accession of William III – explicitly identifies 'Authors' with the state of the 'Nation' (III, p. 165). Elsewhere, we are invited to suspect the presence of Tory codes, without being able to grasp these with full clarity; and I suspect this is a conscious authorial ploy, designed to gratify Tory readers without decisively alienating others. *The Fair Jilt* draws connections between its plot and its plotter dedicatee Payne, who is invited to extend his protection to Tarquin, 'a Prince unfortunate', since Payne's loyalty to the Stuart monarchy demonstrates there is no 'better Man, or more certain Friend' (III, p. 4). However, Tory allegory rapidly breaks down in the narrative itself. Tarquin is identified with 'our King *Charles* of blessed Memory' (III, p. 27), but a prince with a debatable title, honourable but easily manipulated by the woman he loves, a failed murderer, victim of an abortive execution, is an uneasy model of the Stuart monarchy. Or perhaps, as the dedication suggests, Behn demonstrates her characteristic contradictory royalism, well aware that James II has shown 'less Fortitude and Vertue' than his followers (III, p. 27). The tale where I most strongly suspect political allegory is 'The Dumb Virgin', whose hero is given the name of the plotter Dangerfield. Dying, having unknowingly seduced his own sister and murdered his father, he reveals that his true name is 'Cla–' (III, p. 359). This fragmentary name, if it could be interpreted, might offer a key. Possibly Behn, though, simply emphasizes the cost of disguise – a masquerade provides a symbolically evocative scene for the first meeting of Dangerfield and his sisters – and the dangers plotting can bring to the English 'family', whose factions share a national identity despite political differences.

Elsewhere, Behn certainly praises Stuart kings – Charles II is a *'wonderful Good-natured and a Well-bred Gentleman'* whose 'long . . . Reign' is hoped for.[16] But her divine-right royalism is in strong tension with her vigorous questioning of the rights of domestic patriarchs. In *The Lucky Mistake* M. de Pays is thwarted in his plans for the future of his daughters, and eventually acquiesces in accepting their choices (though his name identifies him explicitly with the French nation, and therefore she adroitly avoids questioning the authority or wisdom of the English monarchy). The wicked brother in 'The Unfortunate Happy Lady' and the *'Passionate'* (III, p. 415) father in 'The Unhappy Mistake' could likewise be taken to imply a critique of divine-right rule. In the posthumous work, political contextualisation sometimes appears as little more than local colour, or an attempt to simulate Behn's narrative voice, as in 'The Unhappy Mistake', where Miles Hardyman, whose rashness almost causes tragedy when he believes his beloved's brother is a rival, is explicitly made a cavalier, 'a Great Loyalist' who carries a tobacco box with a portrait of Charles I, and the tale is set during Cromwell's rule, its long-postponed happy ending significantly placed at a point when the 'Royal Family had not . . . been restor'd much above a Twelve Month' (III, pp. 422, 432). The love-theme is persistently couched in the language of politics – title, prerogative, subjection (e.g. III, p. 423) – though this seems more reminiscent of the coming strategies of Whig writers like Centlivre than of Behn's undoubted prose fiction.

Although Behn felt no difficulty about the terminology 'Novel' for even the shortest of the short fiction, title pages stage a typological battle between 'Novel' and 'History' or 'True History', as Behn or her publishers choose to label *Oroonoko*, *The History of the Nun*, 'The Nun', 'The Unfortunate Happy Lady' and, in one version, *The Fair Jilt* and *Agnes de Castro*.[17] This is clearly connected to the author-narrator's desire to insist on the truth of the narrative and the eye-witness authority of the narrator. Thus the dedication to *The Fair Jilt* insists that it is not a novel but *'Truth . . . Reality, and Matter of Fact'* of which the author was partly *'an Eye-Witness'*, partly the recipient of confidences from the hero himself (III, p. 4). The involved female narrator[18] is a key feature in much of Behn's fiction: she is a confidante of the heroes of *Oroonoko* and *The Fair Jilt*, helps unearth the truth and discredit the villainess Moorea in 'The Unfortunate Bride', and is a hidden other self for Isabella in *The History of the Nun*, tempted by the 'Innocence and Quiet of a Cloyster' but ultimately, like the heroine, choosing 'the false ungrateful World' with its 'Nonsense, Noise, false Notions and Contradiction' (III, p. 213). This narrator has special authority not only as an eye-witness but as a woman, who is used especially in the posthumous fiction to comment with an insider's acuity on the weaknesses of womankind.[19]

However, the distinction between novel and history was as unstable for Behn as for us, for this involved narrator can be found not only in the histories but also in the 'novels', as in 'The Dumb Virgin', where the narrator knows the family, is an eye-witness, and speaks English to Dangerfield. To take an extreme case, in 'Love Letters', it is provocatively unclear whether this constitutes a fictional fragment or an autobiographical revelation. This might be a positive advantage in the games with cultural capital played by Behn's posthumous literary executors, but would not be alien to Behn herself with her self-conscious narratives which alternatively approach and withdraw from romance forms and claims to literal veracity.

Behn, it seems, aims for a 'breezy colloquial quality and Defoe-like "I was there" technique',[20] which includes a plausible casualness about details and a relaxed willingness to concede when details are forgotten – 'The Rest I have forgot . . .', 'as near as I can remember . . .'[21] But why is the claim not only to verisimilitude but to literal historicity (intermittently) so important? Theorists of the novel have accounted for the genre's rise through ideas of a 'democratization of empiricism', even an 'epistemological crisis', which produced a 'destabilization of generic categories', so that the novel defined itself through connections with history, memoirs, travel-writing, journalism.[22] Her claims to historical truth dogged early criticism of Behn, so that she was appraised not on her aesthetic abilities but on her truth-telling.[23]

There is clearly a gendered element in this hostile early criticism, since Behn was subjected to moral criteria different from those assumed for her male contemporaries. However, her insistence on truth may also have been related to issues of gender. A self-confessed female writer needed as a matter of urgency to locate a basis for her claims to authority, and the special status of an eye-witness was one solution to this problem. Moreover, in seventeenth-century ideologies of gender, women were supposedly less rational than men, and since irrational imagination was gendered feminine – as in 'The Dumb Virgin' where the mother's 'Force of Imagination' imprints itself on the bodies of her daughters as physical deformity and dumbness – Behn may have seen the claim to truth-telling a useful way of claiming both feminine imagination and masculine reason.

Except for *Oroonoko* Behn's fiction takes female central characters, often facing them with impossible or paradoxical moral dilemmas which test them to the utmost. So *The History of the Nun* demonstrates, with great psychological insight and moral complexity, how a woman celebrated for holiness can become both a bigamist and 'the Murderess of two Husbands (both belov'd) in one Night' (p. 257).

The characterization of these heroines may emphasize passive suffering – Constantia and Agnes in *Agnes de Castro*, or Bellamora in 'The Adventure of the Black Lady' – or active resolution – Arabella in 'The Wandring Beauty' or Philadelphia in 'The Unfortunate Happy Lady', though her most complex heroines, like Miranda in *The Fair Jilt* and Isabella in *The History of the Nun*, transcend these categories. Their careers tend to be related by female narrators who are involved observers or even participants, and who are crucial in the complex strategies with frames which the fiction adopts. Both *The History of the Nun* and *The Fair Jilt*, for instance, begin with lengthy introductions which complicate the moral structures we might expect. In *The Fair Jilt*, the long opening section, to which we might reasonably turn for moral guidance on how to read the story, oddly attacks male pretenders in love, and so seems to begin not by moral criticism of Miranda – as an attempted rapist and murderess an easy object for moralizing comment – but by implicit defence of her as one whose actions are motivated by the irresistible power of love. Later in this story, too, the contrast between what the narrator tells us with its rich eye-witness detail, and other available voices, becomes pressing. When the narrator, ventriloquizing public opinion, writes of Miranda as a harlot 'possess'd by so many great Men and Strangers before . . . all the Lewdness of her Practices with several Princes and great Men' (III, pp. 29, 42), she invokes a part of the story we have not been told and may not, therefore, find convincing. When we are told 'They say' that Miranda has repented (III, p. 48), the contrast between this bald statement and the rich detail and psychological insight of the rest of the tale allows it to end on an ironic note where the narrator might be questioning rather than confirming traditional morality and closure.

Behn's narrative voices seem sometimes to accept, sometimes to critique, received ideologies of gender. 'The Unfortunate Happy Lady' accepts stereotypes of female talkativeness – 'our sex seldom wants matter of tattle' (III, p. 369) – and 'The Unfortunate Bride' repeats the phrase ''tis the Humour of our Sex' to refer to women's alleged tendencies to deny something we truly want, or to want to see something forbidden (III, pp. 327, 332). Such phrases, though, tend to occur in the doubtful posthumous fiction, and in any case one suspects lip service only is being paid to such stereotypes: the author herself offers a model for female linguistic empowerment quite different from the 'tattle' confessed by her narrator.

Moreover, it is striking how often her heroes challenge received gender ideologies, since they are often explicitly described as atypical men, like Rinaldo in 'The Lucky Mistake', who ultimately succeeds in winning his love Atlante:

> Though it is now too much the nature of that inconstant Sex to cease to Love as soon as they are sure of the Conquest. But it was far different with our *Cavalier*. (III, p. 181)

Here fidelity in love and royalism in politics are identified, and Rinaldo is seen as 'different' from stereotypes of the emotionally illiterate male. Frankwit, the ill-fated hero of 'The Unfortunate Bride', is a similar unmanly man, 'softer', 'humble' (p. 325).

Behn, celebrated in her own day as 'Loves great *Sultana*', has also been read more recently as primarily a writer of 'amatory' or 'erotic' fiction, a 'great writer of romantic fiction', whose narratives focus on desire.[24] William Congreve defines romance fiction as dealing with 'the constant Loves and invincible Courages of Hero's, Heroins, Kings and queens, Mortals of the first Rank', where 'lofty Language' and 'impossible Performances' work to 'elevate and surprise' the reader.[25] Behn's shorter fiction certainly assumes the forms of romance, with love between hero and heroine finally vindicated even when impeded by a hostile father or other authority-figure (as in 'The Lucky Mistake', 'The Unfortunate Happy Lady' and 'The Unhappy Mistake'), and with the repeated use of classic love triangles, resolved sometimes tragically (as in *The History of the Nun*, where Isabella unknowingly contracts a bigamous second marriage, and 'The Nun', where love for Elvira causes the friends Sebastian and Enrique to kill each other), sometimes happily (as in 'The Lucky Mistake', where Rinaldo and Atlante succeed in marrying).

Behn's fiction, however, simulates the forms of romance rather than buying into the romance world of love and honour. Part of Behn is always anchored in the practical realities of the real world even as she creates the '*Phantastique*' world where love triumphs.[26] In a description which is still one of the best general comments on Behn's fiction, Robert Adams Day argues that what is new is its 'clashing levels of diction, setting, plot, description, narrative voice – the reader's expectations are constantly being aroused and defeated in the most surprising ways'.[27] This may take the form of oscillation between romance and 'novelistic' or even 'journalistic'[28] elements which contradict romance's tendency to universalizing and idealizing by rooting these events in a practical world of day-to-day reality.

The large romantic affirmations of the text are constantly undercut by financial realities, for the tales are anchored in economic as much as erotic desire. 'The Unfortunate Happy Lady', as Helen Hackett points out, 'is a romance in its plot', but 'differs from romance not only in its terse brevity and its contemporary London setting, but also in its obsessive interest in its characters' bank balances'.[29] In 'The Adventure of the Black Lady' or 'Memoirs of the Court of the King of Bantam', economic consumption is the only thing that makes possible or sustainable amatory consummation. In 'The Unhappy Mistake', the characters' sufferings are caused by the patriarch Sir Henry Hardiman's embargo on a marriage between his son Miles and the 'most beautiful' Diana Constance, because she has only 'an indifferent Fortune' (p. 415). Sir Henry insists that '*Money is Beauty, Virtue, Good Humour, Education, Reputation, and High Birth*' (p. 417), and, although the rhythm of the romantic plot discredits this, money is lovingly and in detail written into the reconciliations which conclude the tale, where, as in Jane Austen's novels, love can thrive only when rooted in material prosperity.

Behn is often brutally direct and specific about sums of money: 'he promised him Ten Thousand Pounds in ready Money besides; whereas the young Ladies were to have but Five Thousand apeece'; 'Isabella's dead mother had left Jewels, of the value of *2000l* . . . as also some 3 or *400l* in Gold'.[30] Behn's consciousness of her own place in the marketplace[31] perhaps leads her to draw attention to that marketplace by insisting on the economic basis of beauty, grandeur, and love; and the fact that writing itself forms so crucial a motif in this novel and elsewhere likewise cements this connection.

In *The Fair Jilt*, Miranda is a larger-than-life romantic figure fresh from the heroic play and conceived in terms of exaggeration and overstatement – 'all the Charms that ever Nature gave . . . something divine . . . universally adored . . . thousands of people were dying by her Eyes . . . the most wond'rous Object of Beauty he had ever seen' (III, pp. 10–11) – except that she is anchored in a world of economic exigencies that never troubled Lyndaraxa. Her heroic status depends not on inner reality but on constant outer display, which in the real world necessitates lavish resources. In order to retain her status, she needs to persuade her heroic-romantic husband Tarquin to make a squalid attempt to murder her sister and conceal the fact that Miranda has embezzled her money. Heroism, including 'female Heroism',[32] is radically problematized.

As the tale progresses, the discrepancy between Miranda's and Tarquin's lavish accoutrements – 'twelve Footmen, and four Pages . . . all in green Velvet Coats, lac'd with Gold, and white Velvet Trunks . . . She was dress'd in a black Velvet Gown, with a rich Row of Diamonds all down the fore-part of the Breast, and a great Knot of Diamonds at the Peak behind; and a Petty-coat of flower'd Gold, very rich, and lac'd . . . A Gentleman carried her great Velvet Cushion before her, on which her Prayer-Book, embroider'd, was laid' (III, pp. 27, 35) – and the moral substance behind this widens to a gaping 'ironic gap' which challenges the romantic narrative we are apparently being offered.[33] This becomes especially clear when we note that part of this lavish description is of Miranda's attending the execution of Van Brune, where she is herself punished for procuring his attempt to murder her sister. Given the importance of clothes in this novel's ironic vision, it is altogether appropriate that what saves Alcidiana from murder is that Tarquin's bullet 'missed her Body, and shot through her Cloaths' (III, p. 39); conspicuous consumption endangers but also saves. The relationship between clothes and bodies in Behn often calls attention to this ironic gap, as the problematic relationship between inner self and the outer signs of that individual's status as a social being becomes explicit.[34] The 'quality' of great men and women – to use a recurrent word in Behn's text (e.g. III, pp. 10, 12, 26) – as often seems ironically as straightforwardly presented.

The setting up and undercutting of romance is crucial to the text, a process performed through images of clothes and through the constant contrast between outward appearance and inner reality. It is also brought about by the novel's recurrent emphasis on public opinion. It is this rather than any romance concept of truth which moves the plot, and this highlights the degree to which Behn's plots turn on ideas of 'status inconsistency' as well as money.[35] *The Fair Jilt* is on one level a drama of public opinion, with the careers of the protagonists being played out within a fully public sphere. We learn, for instance, that in the legal dispute between Miranda and the Friar the 'Gown-Men . . . Churchmen' support him, the 'Men of Quality' her (III, p. 26); the trial of Van Brune is likewise a public spectacle, with 'all the Ladies' supporting him, and 'the whole City . . . with one accord' (III, pp. 33, 34, 35) against Miranda. Finally, 'People' (III, p. 38) turn against Alcidiana, who pursues the page to his death although she has recovered from his murder attempt. In this and other tales, perhaps especially *The History of the Nun*, we are given insight into a world where the separate spheres of a male public world and a private female world have not yet crystallized. Private female lives are lived in public and have public consequences. The drama of public opinion in *The Fair Jilt* makes, in the first instance, this point. It also highlights the moral complexity of the action, where boundaries between right and wrong become in every way hazier than we might expect, and gives the reader a decisive role in this drama, as a member of the 'People' whose opinions will decisively sway the action, as they rescue Prince Tarquin from execution.

The 'ironic gap' in *The Fair Jilt* is, however, not confined to the revelation of the unheroic roots of heroic love. The tale moves provocatively between heroic romance and a kind of epic satire, through alternative overstatement and undercutting, on romance and heroism, where sex and shopping challenge the romantic absolutes of love and honour. One key element in the management of this 'ironic gap' is the novel's engagement with narrative and dramatic stereotypes and particularly Behn's use of gender inversions. Her depiction of Miranda's obsessive love for Friar Francisco (né Henrick) depends on a reversal of the male gaze and an appropriation of the language of male desire and female objectification so that Miranda becomes the desiring subject and the Friar the passive object: 'he appear'd all that is adorable to the fair Sex, nor cou'd the mis-shapen Habit hide from her the lovely Shape it endeavour'd to cover . . . She gaz'd upon him . . . till she perceiv'd the lovely Friar to blush' (III, p. 12). The scene in the confessional where Miranda attempts to rape him is partly a gleeful empowerment through gender reversal of her bad heroine, but perhaps also invites us, through defamiliarization, to consider the moral issues raised by the popularity of rape and attempted rape as a motif in Restoration drama and fiction.

Although Behn certainly deals with love and desire, it is not always understood how ironic her narrative voice can be. The tales rarely, indeed, celebrate desire. Although the introduction to *The Fair Jilt* unambiguously praises love, the 'most noble and divine Passion of the Soul', as that which makes us civilized and indeed human – 'and without it, Man is unfinish'd, and unhappy' (III, p. 7) – desire is essentially problematic in Behn's fiction. The introduction to *The Fair Jilt*, with its praise of love and long satirical exposé of the male fop, forces us to read the story of Miranda in different moral and conceptual frames simultaneously.

Ruth Salvaggio argues that in Behn's world women's desire was unspeakable, and that Behn struggles 'to write the script of feminine desire' but is constantly doomed to failure because of social and philosophical pressures which define women as passive objects of male desire.[36] In 'The Adventure of the Black Lady', Salvaggio argues, what has been read as a story of mutual love overcoming obstacles is actually concerned only with the gratification of male desire, for female desire is unwritable.

> The reunion of Bellamora and Fondlove, far from proceeding from feelings of mutual love, proceeds instead from the desire of Fondlove . . . Bellamora's own desire has no place in this story . . . It constitutes the romance plot without the woman's passion for the simple reason that woman's passion had no way to direct its energies down the path of women's desire.[37]

I am not convinced by this reading of Behn's fiction in general and this very short novel in particular, partly because the conventions of Restoration narrative tend to imply rather than state motive, and partly because in Behn desire – whether male or female – is by definition forever thwarted, forever shifting and mutable. What motivates Bellamora to sleep with Fondlove is not, it seems, primarily her own sexual desire but her dislike for the man her parents are trying to force her to marry, and also her 'Inclinations to *pity him*', as a result of which she '*ruin'd [her] self*' (III, p. 318). Nonetheless, it is possible that the italicized 'pity' serves as a euphemism for sexual desire, and it is also true that Bellamora herself accepts responsibility for her actions. She may not explicitly confess her desire for Fondlove, but, like Millamant's for Mirabel in *The Way of the World*, it is spoken by its very silence. Women's sexual desire may be unconfessable, even in the libertine world of Restoration London, but this is not to say it is unexperienceable or unscriptable. A later novel, Sarah Scott's *Millenium Hall* (1762), will lay down a blueprint for noble behaviour for a woman in Bellamora's condition: like Miss Selvyn's mother, she should despise herself for her weakness and resolutely refuse to marry the father of her child because he must despise her too.[38] Bellamora likewise fears that Fondlove 'can never love me after' (III, p. 318), but Behn's tale is more practical and believable than Scott's as Bellamora settles for a moderate happiness. It is, moreover, significant that the love affair arrives at a happy ending because of two women, his sister and her landlady. It may be that female desire must be displaced, to use Salvaggio's word, but that it is displaced on to other women suggests that, although self-protection renders it prudent for Bellamora not to speak of her own desire, that desire exists and is powerful. Ultimately 'The Adventure of the Black Lady' is a slight comic tale with a satirical edge rather than a tragic story of the exclusion of women from the script of desire.

In Behn's fiction, however, desire is problematic, and the reasons for this are more internal than external. It 'is not in our power' to keep resolutions, however sincere our intentions, for 'nothing is so deceitful as human Hearts' (III, pp. 211–12). Our desires constantly shift, like Isabella's in *The History of the Nun*. At first happy to be a nun, she falls in love with Henault and elopes with him, but when he is believed dead she marries Villenoys. When Henault returns, she murders him to conceal her bigamy, and because 'the Dead are soon forgotten, and she now lov'd only *Villenoys*' (III, p. 249). The paradoxical nature of desire is sometimes gendered; *The History of the Nun*, although the action queries this, generalizes that male hearts are especially deceitful, for 'Women are by Nature, more Constant, and Just, than Men' (III, pp. 211–12). However, 'The Unfortunate Bride' assumes that these paradoxes are specifically female, 'for 'tis the humour of our Sex, to deny most eagerly those grants to Lovers, for which most tenderly we sigh; so contradictory are we to our selves' (III, p. 327).

However, the general conclusion seems to be that the paradoxes of desire are human rather than gender-specific. 'The Unfortunate Bride' in particular writes the paradoxes of desire into the very fabric of the plot. In this tale male and female voices are quite evenly balanced, as they share literacy and the ability to write social verse, and as, typically for Behn, terms gendered female in contemporary love-rhetoric – '*Charmer*', for instance – are applied to male characters (III, p. 330). In this tale there is an argument going on about desire which, although it takes place between Belvira and her lover Frankwit, does not seem to imply that attitudes to desire will be naturally programmed along the lines of biological sex. Belvira fears that desire by definition exists only when unfulfilled, and is destroyed rather than completed by 'the last Enjoyment' (III, p. 327). 'Pleasure is but a Dream . . . Women enjoy'd, are like Romances read . . . which, when found out, you only wonder at your selves for wondering so before at them. 'Tis expectation endears the blessing' (III, p. 328). Frankwit instead argues 'that expectation were indeed a Monster which enjoyment could not satisfy' (III, p. 329). It may be that here Behn offers a reversal of gendered voices since Belvira is putting forward a traditionally masculine view, Frankwit a traditionally feminine one, at least in the terms that will be understood by Behn's successors like Delarivier Manley and Eliza Haywood.[39] In this particular tale, however, these irreconcilable differences in ways of understanding desire can only end tragically.

Because of the paradoxes of desire, the heroic gestures of the high romantic main plots may be cut across by characters who philosophically accept second best and an ordinary level of happiness. So Alcidiana in *The Fair Jilt* loses her aristocrat suitor when her money is lost and makes do with a merchant, 'perhaps the best of the two' (III, p. 47), Lady Friendly in 'Memoirs of the Court of the King of Bantam' seems to accept her husband's infidelities philosophically, and in *The Lucky Mistake* Charlot cedes Rinaldo to her sister and marries Vernole, who originally courted Atlante, for 'I was not so much in love with *Rinaldo*, as out of love with a Nunnery' (III, p. 201).

There are motifs that recur in Behn's fiction – nuns; broken vows; incest; disability – and in addition each of the most successful tales gains an organic unity through prioritizing a recurrent theme or metaphor. In 'The Nun' repeated questions of meaning (III, pp. 299, 303, 306) slightly complicate what is otherwise the most stereotypical tale in the Behn oeuvre. 'The Dumb Virgin' uses one of Behn's most frequent metaphors for femininity, disability, in the dumbness of Maria and the deformity of Belvideera; but representation itself is simultaneously thematized, as Maria is not only herself a '*wondrous piece of Art'* but also 'a great proficient in Painting' (III, pp. 354, 345), who appropriates and perfects the male gaze by successfully completing a portrait which is abandoned by a painter who is dazzled by her beauty. In 'Memoirs of the Court of the King of Bantam', metaphors of theatricality support an exuberant comic plot of deception and self-deception. As Wou'd-be King believes he is asserting his kingly potency over Valentine Goodland, he and his supporters are actually gulling King, who is exposed as a *'Pageant'*, a *'Property King'* (III, pp. 280–1). The plays visited, *A King and No King* and *The London Cuckolds* (III, pp. 286, 288) offer a comically over-exact commentary on this action.

In the most complicated manipulation of metaphor, 'The Unfortunate Bride; or, the Blind Lady a Beauty', blindness in a range of senses becomes a leading metaphor. Like the twin images of physical deformity and muteness in 'The Dumb Virgin', Behn uses blindness here as a metaphor for the 'lack of social power accorded to women', and there is a 'complex . . . play with images of sight',[40] with words like 'sight', 'eyes', 'view', 'gazed', 'blind' and 'blindness' echoing through the text.[41] The tale uses these metaphors in a fable about 'masculine specularity and narcissism', using 'tropes of vision and economic exchange',[42] but they also connect with the argument between Frankwit and Belvira about desire, discussed previously. Cupid's blindness connects the literal state of the blind Celesia and the paradoxical nature of desire.

Finally, it is worth noting how motifs of writing and reading are thematized in Behn's fiction, as she offers implicit comments on her own craft which can be highly ambivalent. In *Agnes de Castro*, 'The Lucky Mistake', and 'The Unfortunate Bride', for instance, forged or appropriated letters risk catastrophic results. In 'The Unfortunate Bride' the appropriation of letters by the 'Blackamoor Lady' Moorea – 'black in her mind, and dark, as well as in her body' (III, pp. 331–2) – causes Belvira to believe that Frankwit has betrayed her and precipitates the tragic conclusion. Moorea's blackness defines her action as evil: but perhaps, as Catherine Gallagher suggests, it also, like that of Oroonoko, should be identified with the blackness of ink and so with the act of writing itself, whose ambivalence, especially in the case of a female agent and consumer, is highlighted.[43]

In *The Fair Jilt*, the introduction defines writing as the preserve of the 'Fop in Fashion', who spends his mornings reading and writing *'Billets-doux'* (III, pp. 7–8): the Fop therefore becomes a comic version of the author herself. Miranda's power springs partly from her superior control over literacy, for she is its master rather than its servant: in one of the novel's characteristic deflations, we are told she 'had read much, and retained all that serv'd her purpose' (III, p. 11). Henrick like the Fop is a victim of literacy, for 'all the Letters he writ were intercepted' (III, p. 14). Later Miranda suffers 'the Shame of Writing' (III, p. 20) when she sends letters to the Friar which he reads, and her 'soft Billets' to Van Brune are 'produc'd in open Court' against her (III, p. 19–20). However, if women's writing is shame, it is also power, as Miranda 'caused Letters to be written from *Germany*, as from the Relations of *Van Brune*' (III, p. 38) to obfuscate the case against Tarquin.

Behn's heroines tend to be very literate, like Atlante and her sister Charlot in 'The Lucky Mistake', who walk followed by a footman carrying their books (III, p. 173). Women's reading is often implicitly associated by Behn with sexual danger but also with sexual pleasure: Vernole makes his romantic assault on Atlante by offering her 'a very fine Book, newly come out, of *Delicate Philosophy*, fit for the Study of Ladies' (III, p. 177). Atlante later provides an alibi for time spent with Rinaldo by claiming that she was 'got into a Book, which had many moving Stories very well writ, and that she found herself so well entertained, she had forgot how the Night passed' (III, p. 190). Likewise in 'The Dumb Virgin', the disastrous incestuous encounter between Maria and Dangerfield takes place in the 'Library', to which she has retired 'to ease her melancholy by reading' (III, p. 352).

Behn's short fiction, then, explores themes of politics, of desire, and of gender through a dense tissue of metaphors – of nuns, disability, theatricality, literacy itself – and through a series of complex narrative frames and narrative voices which produce alternations between romance and irony, idealistic affirmation and critical questioning. Her work constantly surprises the reader, producing 'bold prose experiments', 'astonishing innovations'.[44]

NOTES

1 But see Ros Ballaster, '"Pretences of State": Aphra Behn and the Female Plot', in *Rereading Aphra Behn*, pp. 187–211; Jacqueline Pearson, 'Gender and Narrative in the Fiction of Aphra Behn', *Review of English Studies*, n.s. XLII (1991), pp. 40–56, 179–90 and 'The History of *The History of the Nun*', in *Rereading Aphra Behn*, pp. 234–52; Ruth Salvaggio, 'Aphra Behn's Love: Fiction, Letters and Desire', in *Rereading Aphra Behn*, pp. 253–72.
2 For the bibliographical history of Behn's fiction, see O'Donnell and also *Works of Aphra Behn*, vol. III.
3 J. Paul Hunter, *Before Novels: the Cultural Contexts of Eighteenth-Century English Fiction* (New York: Norton, 1990), pp. 23–5.
4 See Jane Spencer, *Aphra Behn's Afterlife* (Oxford: Oxford University Press, 2000), pp. 125–6; Todd, p. 317.
5 Spencer, *Aphra Behn's Afterlife*, p. 125.
6 That Thomas Brown was translating Scarron for Briscoe at this time may call in question Behn's authorship or simply suggest that she had early tapped into a cultural preoccupation. See Spencer, *Aphra Behn's Afterlife*, pp. 125–6; also Germaine Greer, 'Honest Sam. Briscoe', in *A Genius for Letters: Booksellers and Bookselling*

from the 16th to the 20th Century, ed. Robin Myers and Michael Harris (Winchester: St Paul's Bibliographies, 1995), pp. 33–47.

7 See Dolors Altaba-Artal, *Aphra Behn's English Feminism: Wit and Satire* (Selensgrove PA: Susquehanna University Press, 1999).

8 Spencer, *Aphra Behn's Afterlife*, p. 126.

9 Helen Hackett, *Women and Romance in the English Renaissance* (Cambridge: Cambridge University Press, 2000), p. 188.

10 The exception is *The History of the Nun*, which carries a – perhaps – ironic dedication to another vow-breaker and adulteress, Hortense Mancini, Duchess of Mazarin.

11 *Works*, III, p. 336.

12 *Works*, III, p. 422.

13 See e.g. *Aphra Behn Studies*, especially Susan J. Owen, 'Sexual Politics and Party Politics in Behn's Drama, 1678–1683', pp. 15–29; Alison Shell, 'Popish Plots: *The Feign'd Curtizans* in Context', pp. 30–49; and Ros Ballaster, 'Fiction Feigning Femininity; False Counts and Pageant Kings in Aphra Behn's Popish Plot Writings', pp. 50–65; *Susanna Centlivre*, ed. Jacqueline Pearson, in *Eighteenth-Century Women Playwrights*, ed. Derek Hughes (London: Pickering and Chatto, 2001), III, pp. xviii–xx.

14 *Works*, III, pp. 320, 382.

15 *Works*, III, p. 459.

16 'Memoirs of the Court of the King of Bantam', 'The Unfortunate Happy Lady' (III, pp. 285, 382).

17 *Works*, III, pp. 51, 205, 293, 361, 1, 127.

18 See Martine Watson Brownley, 'The Narrator in *Oroonoko*', *Essays in Literature*, 4 (1977), 174–81; Jane Spencer, *The Rise of the Woman Novelist: From Aphra Behn to Jane Austen* (Oxford: Blackwell, 1986), and Pearson, 'Gender and Narrative'. The lack of this involved narrator in 'The Nun' and 'The Unfortunate Happy Lady' may argue against Behn's authorship.

19 E.g. in 'The Unfortunate Happy Lady' and 'The Unfortunate Bride' (III, pp. 369, 327, 332).

20 Robert Adams Day, 'Aphra Behn and the Works of Intellect', in *Fetter'd or Free? British Women Novelists. 1670–1815*, eds. Mary Anne Schofield and Cecilia Macheski (Ohio, Athens: Ohio University Press, 1986), p. 382.

21 'Memoirs of the Court of the King of Bantam'; 'The Adventure of the Black Lady' (III, pp. 291, 315).

22 Hunter, *Before Novels*, p. 198; Michael McKeon, *The Origins of the English Novel* (London: Radius, 1998), pp. 65, 25.

23 See Ernest Bernbaum, 'Mrs Behn's Biography a Fiction', *PMLA*, 28 (1913), pp. 432–53.

24 See e.g. Ros Ballaster, '"Pretences of State"' and *Seductive Forms: Women's Amatory Fiction from 1684 to 1740* (Oxford: Clarendon Press, 1992); John Richetti, *The English Novel in History 1700–1780* (London: Routledge, 1999), p. 18; Ruth Salvaggio, 'Aphra Behn's Love', p. 253.

25 William Congreve, Preface to the Reader of *Incognita* (1692); quoted by Brean S. Hammond, *Professional Imaginative Writing in England 1670–1740* (Clarendon Press, Oxford, 1997), p. 110.

26 I quote the song which opens Behn's *Abdelazer* (1676; V, p. 248).

27 Day, 'Aphra Behn and the Works of Intellect', p. 382.
28 Hackett, *Women and Romance*, pp. 188, 189.
29 Ibid., p. 192.
30 'The Wandring Beauty'; *The History of the Nun* (III, pp. 408, 238–9).
31 See Catherine Gallagher, *Nobody's Story: the Vanishing Act of Women Writers in the Marketplace 1670–1834* (Oxford: Clarendon Press, 1994).
32 Hackett, *Women and Romance*, p. 27.
33 Jessica Munns, '"With nosegays and gloves . . . / So trim and gay": Clothing and Public Execution in the Eighteenth Century', in *The Clothes that Wear Us: Essays on Dressing and Transgressing in the Eighteenth Century*, ed. Jessica Munns and Penny Richards (Newark: University of Delaware Press, 1999), p. 272.
34 Behn often symbolizes culture by clothes, sometimes in ambivalent ways, as in the episode in *Oroonoko* where the narrator and her brother visit the village of the naked natives of Surinam dressed 'with Silver Loops and Buttons, and abundance of Green Ribon' (III, p. 101).
35 McKeon, *Origins of the English Novel*, p. 258.
36 Salvaggio, 'Aphra Behn's Love', p. 253, 258.
37 Ibid., p. 262.
38 Sarah Scott, *Millenium Hall* (London: Virago, 1986), p. 168.
39 Haywood's *Fantomina* (1725) elaborates the conceit that, while women are naturally faithful, men are not 'able to prolong Desire . . . after Possession', Paula R. Backscheider and John J. Richetti, eds., *Popular Fiction by Women 1660–1730: An Anthology* (Oxford: Clarendon Press, 1996, p. 233). It is a repeated point in Manley's *The New Atalantis* (1709), ed. Ros Ballaster (Harmondsworth: Penguin, 1992) that men 'cool and neglect [women] after possession' (p. 80).
40 Ballaster, 'Aphra Behn and the Female Plot', pp. 203, 201.
41 See e.g. III, pp. 327–8.
42 Ballaster, 'Aphra Behn and the Female Plot', pp. 199–200.
43 Gallagher, *Nobody's Story*, p. 61.
44 Hammond, *Professional Imaginative Writing*, p. 110; Day, 'Aphra Behn and the Works of Intellect', p. 382.

13

JESSICA MUNNS

Pastoral and lyric: Astrea in Arcadia

The pastoral tradition

Pastoral lyrics express the town persons' view of an alternative life that has never existed. From the lyrics of Theocritus (*c.* 310–250 BCE), Moschus (fl. *c.* 150 BCE) and Bion (fl. *c.* 100 BCE) to the Restoration, the pastoral lyric offered an urbane and often wittily erotic representation of country life. The shepherd's life was depicted as an idyllic existence, barely at all laborious, and much occupied with love and composing verse. Virgil (70–19 BCE) set an indelible mark on the form with his ten eclogues (composed probably around 37 BCE) which extended the range of the pastoral lyric to include politics, prophecy, and patronage. Since classical antiquity, the *Eclogues* have been understood in terms of the civil wars that followed the assassination of Julius Caesar and Augustus Caesar's assumption of power. Virgil's shepherds, despite their pastoral location amidst fields and herds, and their concerns with love, do not exist in an entirely serene environment. The famous opening lines of Eclogue 1 set the contentment of Tityrus, who has his farm, against the anguish of Meliboeus, who has lost his – perhaps due to the redistribution of land following the civil wars:

> Beneath the Shade which Beechen Boughs diffuse,
> You, *Tity'rus*, entertain your Sylvan Muse.
> Round the wide World in Banishment we rome,
> Forc'd from our pleasing Fields and Native Home:
> While stretch'd at Ease, you sing your happy loves,
> And *Amaryllis* fills the shady Groves.[1]

Tityrus' happy 'ease' can seem callous compared to Meliboeus' destitution; certainly, the pastoral from now on can have a backdrop of politics and violence. Virgil's 4th Eclogue predicts the return of the Golden Age with the birth of a marvellous boy, and for centuries afterwards this was taken as an indication that God had granted Virgil, as a virtuous pagan, a vision of

Christ's birth. This belief endowed the pastoral tradition with the possibility of a serious and Christian mood, further enhanced by the concept of Christ both as a lamb and as a shepherd. Eclogues 1 and 9 both refer to the power of patrons at court, bringing politics of faction into the mode and also raising issues with regard to the conditions necessary for writing poetry. There is an inbuilt irony in the idea that, in order to 'escape' the busy world of factional politics and warfare, the poet of pastoral contemplation must also be very aware of that world – and support the 'right' faction as well as find the 'right' patron. The Renaissance revival of interest in Virgil ensured that these topics, along with evocations of rural simplicity, and the homoeroticism of Eclogue 2 (borrowed from the Greek prototypes), continued to be an element in many pastoral lyrics and dramas.[2]

This rich mixture created a very flexible form which, while it idealized an imagined past could also criticize the present. Pastoral forms could depict varieties of lifestyles and sexualities: they could provide occasions for courtly entertainment, and also for the expression of opposition politics inside and outside the court. The pastoral was always a form – a mode of expression – not a genre, and examples of the pastoral can be found in dramas, and novellas, as well as in lyrics during the Elizabethan and Jacobean eras. The court of Charles I, and in particular the groups around his French wife Henrietta Maria, encouraged the production of pastoral verse dramas. Pastoral verse, however, was not only written by courtiers, or by the poets in their pay. Pastoral, again in this following the model of Virgil, was seen as a form appropriate to lighter verse and as a kind of training ground for poets before launching into greater forms such as the epic. The puritan John Milton, who highly disapproved of Charles's court, religion, and politics, wrote a number of pastoral poems, and most notably in *Lycidas* (1633) used the form – among other topics – to express his criticisms of contemporary political and religious life. Andrew Marvell, like Milton no friend to the Stuart court, was also a skilled practitioner of the pastoral lyric. Women wrote pastoral verse too – Amelia Lanyer's *Description of Cookham* (1611), for instance, contains many of the idealizing elements associated with the form. During the Interregnum and early Restoration, Katherine Philips, 'the Matchless Orinda' (1631–64), and later on Anne Finch, Countess of Winchilsea (1661–1720) used pastoral verse to celebrate female friendship and rural retirement.

If one of the primary topics of the pastoral was love, what sort of love was being celebrated or sought varied. The love celebrated in a pastoral poem could take many forms. The work might celebrate constant matrimonial love, a homoerotic love for a beautiful boy; a sexless neo-Platonic relationship; the close friendship of women; or a libertine expression of the delights of sexual variety to be found in a nature untrammelled by man-made laws and the customs of society. This last type of pastoral verse flourished during the Restoration, often written by courtiers, giving expression to the sexual laxity for which the court was famous. With light dusting of Hobbesian philosophy, the state of nature was celebrated in pastoral terms, as a state of free love for all.

In the late seventeenth century the pastoral remained a popular form, offering writers a very rich and varied series of styles and moods. Apart from the commitment to depictions of pastoral ease and plenty, the mode was remarkably open. Marked equally as a male and female mode, found in poems, dramas, and novellas, and capable of sentiment and satire, eroticism and neo-platonic chastity, the form could be light-hearted or philosophic, courtly or critical.

Aphra Behn

Such an open mode was clearly attractive to Aphra Behn who used the pastoral form in a variety of ways, taking the pastoral name Astrea as her *nom de plume*, and addressing male friends with such Arcadian names as Strephon, Celadon, Daphnis, or Lycidas. Throughout her writing life, Behn wrote in the pastoral mode: her short stories and novellas frequently have pastoral settings and incidents, and certainly have recourse to the language and tropes of pastoral, and her plays frequently include pastoral lyrics. Behn wrote a large body of pastoral verse, published in her collection *Poems on Several Occasions: with A Voyage to the Island of Love* (1684); further verse, some of it pastoral, was published in the *Miscellany Poems* of 1685, and in her final collection, *Lycidus, or, The Lover in Fashion* (1688). Her pastoral verses were also published as contributions to other collections of verse, as well as in her own plays. Her range was wide and included translations and paraphrases of Latin, French, and Italian literature. She also wrote regular and pindaric odes, and pastoral elegies, such as 'On the Death of the Late Earl of Rochester' (*Miscellany*, 1685), mourned as 'The Young, the Noble Strephon'. Some of her finest pastoral verses are short songs such as 'Cease, cease, Aminta to complain', very much in the style and mood of the Earl of Rochester's 'All my past life is mine no more'. However, she also wrote lengthy works, such as the psychological analysis of love in *Voyage to the Isle of Love*. The moods of her pastoral lyrics are as varied as her verse forms, from the light-heartedly erotic to the poignant and tragic, or the visionary and satiric as in 'The Golden Age'.

Heidi Laudien has suggested that Behn rewrote 'constructions of gender and sexuality by using a subversive form of the pastoral . . . "pastorelle" for its femocentrism'. Laudien argues this was necessary since 'pastoral is at its core a heterosexual system'.[3] However, as we have seen, pastoral was never simply heterosexual, and Behn did not need to feminize the pastoral, since it was already a strongly feminized form. Indeed, for Behn as for other practitioners of the mode, its charm and utility lay in its traditions of gender ambiguity. Behn did not need to subvert the form or change its topics to include homoerotic themes, but certainly she could and did play changes upon its moods. Behn's pastoral verse, for instance, differed from that of the period's other female practitioners of the mode. She did not follow the modest pastoral tradition of a Katherine Philips. Arlene Stiebel has, indeed, argued that Philips' neo-platonic poems of pastoral retirement and friendship addressed to Lucasia are erotic same-sex poems; but as she also notes the 'literary and cultural conventions of friendship' help to 'mask' the poems' eroticism and sexual orientation and preserved Philips' 'respectability'.[4] Behn certainly used neo-platonic tropes of souls blending into each other, along with the furniture of retirement – groves, shades, and thickets – but eroticism is not masked in her poetry, and the style and mood she followed was that of the male libertine poets. Her muse was amorous, not chaste, and frequently gave expression to her characteristic concerns over the unequal play of power in love relations. Behn charted new territory for a woman writing love poetry, just as she did as a woman writing drama.

Behn is famous for claiming the 'Priviledge for my Masculine Part the Poet in me' (VII: 'Preface', lines 119–20) in her preface to her play *The Luckey Chance* (1686). When she wrote pastoral lyrics in the classical mode, and published translations and paraphrases in collections alongside male poets, she asserted that privilege as much as in her plays. In her pastoral lyrics her voice is not necessarily androgynous, but it is certainly not always clearly marked as either female or male. And, when writing clearly as a woman, her very lack of, or rejection of a mask of modesty and respectability is in itself a factor that reverses and destabilizes the conventions and expectations of gender. Behn frequently confuses and conflates issues of gender: sometimes she writes as a male lover addressing a woman, and sometimes, as in 'To the fair Clarinda, who made Love to me, imagin'd more than Woman' (appended to *Lycidus*, 1688) as a woman to a woman. Frequently she writes as a woman to a man, and sometimes the gender of the addressee is not clear, as in her poem 'On the death of Mr Grinhil, the famous painter' where she notes, approvingly, that he had 'all that cou'd adorn a Face, / All that cou'd either Sex subdue' (I, p. 43). In 'Our Cabal' (*PSO*, 1684), Behn also depicts male lovers, describing a Mr J. H. (usually taken to be her lover John Hoyle), as '*Lycidus*, that haughty Swain' who scorns the female beauties that throng around him and concentrates his attention on Philander. They are 'Too Amorous for a Swain to a Swain' (I, p. 51), yet there is no disapproval in the description of Philander's bisexual attractions: 'A softer Youth was never seen, / His Beauty Maid; but Man, his Mein' (I, p. 52). Bisexuality interested and perhaps amused Behn and surely destabilized a normative heterosexuality in which gender roles were predetermined and limited to female subordination, male domination. Indeed, in Behn's writing gender categories are never simple or stable.

Shifting and destabilizing the categories of gender is one way of negotiating that conundrum and it is worth remembering that male poets of the period also 'cross dressed' in their writings, as in Rochester's 'Artemiza to Chloe' (1680). In writing amorous pastoral verse, and even in confusing socially marked gender characteristics, Behn was a major participant in one of the period's dominant modes of literary expression, and in her pastoral poetry, as in her dramas, she wrote in similar styles and tones to those of her male peers. Behn was acutely aware of the extent to which women writers were disadvantaged both in terms of their gender and education. Her poem to Thomas Creech, addressed in suitable pastoral terms 'To the Unknown DAPHNIS on his Excellent Translation of *Lucretius*' (1683), thanks him lavishly for having given her access to classical poetry:

> Till now I curst my *Sex* and *Education*,
> And more the scanted Customs of the Nation,
> Permitting not the Female Sex to tread
> The Mighty Paths of Learned *Heroes* Dead.
> The Godlike *Virgil* and Great *Homers* Muse
> Like the Divine Mysteries are conceal'd from us
> (I, p. 25)

Now, however,

> . . . Thou by this *Translation* dost advance
> Our Knowledge from the State of Ignorance,
> And Equallest Us to Man! (I, p. 26)

Translations and paraphrases of classical literature extended and validated Behn's poetic range. Indeed, Carol Barash notes that '[F]or Behn, translation and paraphrase were sites for revisionary poetics, places where she could expose the cultural codes at work in poetry and the world that produces and consumes it'.[5] Moreover, Ovid's *Heroides* had provided a model, admittedly a male model, for writing as a desiring woman. Behn's poem 'A Paraphrase on Oenone to Paris', based on one of Ovid's *Heroides*, was published in Jacob Tonson's *Ovid's Epistles, Translated by Several Hands* (1680), alongside poems by Dryden and Thomas Otway. Inclusion in this collection enabled Behn to take her place in a volume of classical verse and Ovid's epistle gave her the 'right' to write in a female voice.

The speaker in this poem is Oenone, who was loved by Paris before he met Helen. Oenone writes to Paris reminding him of their love and pleasures to expresses her grief at her desertion. Behn's Oenone repeatedly stresses that she brought Paris her youth and virginity, 'A spotless Maid into thy Arms I brought' (251) unlike his new love Helen, who 'with Love has treated many a Guest' (252). Oenone's love is characterized by a kind of innocent eroticism, as when she reminisces in a dramatic present tense about their earlier happiness:

> Now uncontroul'd we meet, uncheck't improve
> Each happier minute in new joys of Love!
> Soft were our hours! And lavishly the Day
> We gave intirely up to Love and Play.
>
> (I, p. 14)

As in Ovid's poem, Behn makes a play with tenses to increase the sense of pathos. Oenone's memories of her past happy guiltless sexual encounters with Paris are expressed in the present tense, while she laments her abandonment in the past tense. The apparently illogical tense sequence provides an effective emotional index to how much Oenone lives in the happy past, and her unhappy present is relegated to the past. The tense changes enact Oenone's own personal fall from a grace of happiness that knew no guilt into history, filled with the destructive knowledge of betrayal and shame.

Oenone's pastoral simplicity assumes that sex is natural, loving, pleasurable, and, until betrayal, without shame:

> 'Twas thou wert Honour, Glory, all to me:
> Till Swains had learn't the Vice of Perjury
> No yielding Maids were charg'd with Infamy.
> 'Tis false and broken Vows make Love a Sin,
> Hads't thou been true, We innocent had been.
>
> (I, p. 19)

In paraphrasing Ovid, Behn alters many of its materials, much of its mood, and Oenone's character. Ovid's Oenone has a rather nagging tone as she reminds Paris that she was a rather well-known and popular water nymph when he was a mere servant. Behn reverses the relative status of Ovid's characters, as her Oenone claims she is proud to be 'humbly born, / Even tho; it renders me my *Paris* scorn' (I, p. 18). A strong contrast is thus built up between the humble, pure, loving Oenone and her royal rival, and between

Oenone's habitat of 'cooling Groves' (1, p. 14), the 'Flow'ry Green' (1, p. 19) and Helen, seen on her sea-borne arrival in Troy, seated under a canopy of 'Antique work in Gold and Silver made' (1, p. 17). Behn's Oenone locates Paris's desertion in his entry into a court world of deception, all unknown to his 'rural' mistress:

> How much more happy are we Rural Maids,
> Who know no other Palaces than Shades?
> Who want no Titles to enslave the Croud,
> Least they shou'd babble all our Crimes aloud.
> No Arts our good to show, our Ills to hide,
> Nor know to cover faults of Love with Pride.
>
> (1, p. 18)

Barash suggests that 'Behn further complicates the sources and consequences of Oenone's story by making Oenone attracted to Helen as well as to Paris' (1, p. 15). This seems a large extrapolation from the references to Helen's beauty, which, as in the lines cited above, associate her with art and artifice in a poem in which nature is constantly privileged as moral, amorous, passionate, and true. Certainly, however, Helen is the rival, and as in so many Restoration tragedies, there is a strong contrast between the beautiful but dangerous Cleopatra/Roxana figure of Helen, and the loyal and rather wifely Oenone.

Along with the court, art, and hence deception, Helen is also tainted by her phoney claims to be a rape victim. Oenone recalls that she eloped with Theseus, claiming that she was raped, and that now her new elopement with Paris is called 'Rape' to hide the 'Adult'rous Deed'. 'Is it thus', Oenone asks, that 'Great Ladies keep intire / That Vertue they so boast and you admire?' In fact, very much in line with the more cynical Restoration assessments of rape, Oenone wonders if this is 'a Trick of Courts, can Ravishment/ Serve for a poor Evasion of Consent?' (1, p. 18). Such tricks and evasions are not necessary in Oenone's pastoral world, where sexual desire is followed by acknowledgement, consent is given without shame, and leads to fulfilment and contentment.

For Behn, as for other writers of her age, the pastoral provided an appropriate setting for love, and its tropes functioned as an accessible shorthand for definitions and discussions about love. Key terms in Behn's pastoral verse are words such as 'uncontroul'd', 'uncheckt', 'wanton' 'play' and 'generous', as well as 'shame', 'honour' and 'infamy'. Unless and until some event intrudes to mar the bliss of love in the pastoral setting, the element that Behn constantly stresses is its innocence and lack of any of the normal social consequences. Pastoral love is pure and pleasurable because it is freely given and accepted and precisely because none of the constraints of wealth, birth, parents, religion, or the fetishization of chastity take place – at least not at first. However, the pastoral is a permeable world, and, at times, an illusory one.

For instance, in her novella, *The History of the Nun: or, The Fair Vow-Breaker* (1689), Isabella's lover Henault fears that if he abducts her from her convent he will be disinherited and they will live in poverty. Isabella responds with a speech that brings the rhetorical figures of the pastoral into play:

> *I never thought of living, but by Love; and if I considered it at all, it was, that Grandure and Magnificence were useless Trifles to Lovers, wholly needless and troublesome, I thought of living in some loanly Cottage, far from the noise of crowded busie Cities, to walk with thee in Groves, and silent Shades, where I might hear no Voice but thine; and when we had been tir'd, to sit down by some cool murmuring Rivulet, and be to each a World, my Monarch thou, and I thy sovereign Queen, while Wreaths of Flowers shall crown our happy Heads.* (III, p. 237)

Isabella's sentiments are entirely proper, not to say clichéd: love rather than wealth, the country rather than the city, solitude rather than crowds, and flowers rather than jewels. They are also shown to be entirely mistaken: once they have eloped and settled in a farm their crops fail and their animals sicken. Henault has to join the army, where he is presumed killed in battle, Isabella remarries and when her husband reappears she murders him. The idyll of pastoral simplicity fails and is replaced by a narrative of murder and execution.

Indeed, an ironic perspective on the pastoral was not unique to Behn, its arch simplicity and artfully artless prettiness could always lend itself to mockery. In *As You like It*, Jaques and Touchstone are always there to deflate the charming illusions of those gathered in the Forest of Arden. More crudely and iconoclastically, Rochester, a poet Behn warmly admired, in 'Fair Cloris in a piggsty lay', gives us the image of a peasant girl who sleeping amidst her 'tender herd' – of pigs not sheep – dreams happily of being deflowerd by 'one of her Love Convicted Swaines' and 'wakeing Friggs / . . . and her own Thumb between her leggs, / She's Innocent and pleas'd'.[6] Behn, however, does not so much mock the pastoral as display her awareness that the pastoral fantasy is one thing for men and another for women. Male poets may write happily of toying with Amaryllis in the shade and vanquishing her modesty, but for Amaryllis pregnancy, abandonment, and shame are the likely outcomes. Oenone's lament or Helena's tart rejoinder to Willmore in *The Rover* when he offers her free and uncommitted love – 'what shall I get? A cradle full of noise and mischief, with a pack of repentance at my back?' (v: 5.1.503–4) inscribes a double standard in love that sexual libertinism could never resolve – or, indeed, often cared to resolve.

In both plays and poems, Behn does, however, frequently probe these inequalities. Her poem 'A Voyage to the Isle of Love' (*PSO*, 1684) based on the Abbé Paul Tallemant's *Voyage de l'Isle d'Amour* (1663) is written in the persona of a man, Lisander, who describes to his friend Lycidus, his fatal pursuit of the lovely Aminta. The poem is written in a series of sections that describe the emotional *carte d'amour* through which the lovers journey on their stay in the Isle of Love – and which include 'The River of Pretension' as well as the 'Bower of Bliss'. Many of these sections refer to allegorical personifications. The section on Honour, for instance, addresses it as a *'mighty Phantom!'* and goes on to characterize honour's *'chiefest Attributes'* as *'Pride and Spight'* (I, p. 148). Honour's *'Votaries'*, and victims *'most consist of Womankind'* who even when filled with love dare not 'confess the change' and therefore flee *'the Bower of Bliss'* (I, pp. 149–50). If only the loved female entered the Bower of Bliss, she would find a carefree world: 'Love *has nothing here to do*, / *But to be wanton, soft and gay*' (I, p. 154), and she would dare to express desire and *'yielding owns her* Love *above her Reasonings'* (I, p. 155). When however, Aminta does eventually respond, Lisander is stricken with that most Restoration of male misfortunes, a sudden impotence:

> A while all Dead between her Arms I lay,
> Unable to possess the conquer'd Joys;
> But by degrees my Soul its sense retriev'd;
> Shame and Confusion let me know I liv'd.
> I saw the trembling, dis-appointed Maid,
> With charming angry Eyes my fault up-braid.
>
> (I, p. 156)

Not long after this embarrassing non-conclusion, Aminta suddenly, mysteriously, dies (I, p. 157). Entry into the Bower of Bliss, so dangerous to men in Edmund Spenser's allegorical epic, *The Fairie Queene*, is lethal to a woman in Behn's poem. As S. J. Wiseman remarks, '[W]here premature orgasm temporarily castrates Lisander, sexual pleasure kills Aminta.' Wiseman suggests that Aminta's death resolves the narrative of desire and conquest, followed by an attenuation of the old desire and 'a moving-on of desire to a new object'. Instead of a tale of abandonment and betrayal – as in 'Oenone to Paris' – Aminta's death provides a 'forceful stopping of the story of desire'.[7] Even with the tale thus curtailed to avoid Aminta's abandonment, her sudden demise registers a recognition of the inequality of free love. The problems a woman may encounter in the pastoral world of love and sexuality may, however, be not so much lethal as disappointing. Behn treated the topic of male impotence and pastoral desire in a more light-hearted vein in 'The Disappointment' (*PSO*, 1684).

'The Disappointment' is a version of the 'imperfect enjoyment' poem, that is a poem that describes an unsuccessful sexual encounter in which the male lover fails to satisfy his partner. This was a pre-eminently male genre, of which the best-known example is Rochester's poem, 'The Imperfect Enjoyment' (1680), in which following a sexual failure the male addresses his penis with a mixture of chagrin and wry amusement. The sexual 'fault' in these poems, however, is located not just in the malfunctioning male member, but in the woman: she is too modest or too eager, too demanding, or too beautiful. Behn's poem is a paraphrase of a French poem 'Sur une impuissance' by de Cantenac (1661) in which the lover, unsuccessful one day, returns to triumph the next.[8] De Cantenac's poem has an urban setting, but Behn places her encounter deep in the pastoral world where

> One day the Amorous *Lysander*,
> By an impatient Passion sway'd,
> Surpriz'd fair *Cloris*, that lov'd Maid,
> Who could defend her self no longer.
>
> (1, p. 65)

At first all goes well for the lovers; they find a 'lone Thicket made for Love' and Cloris 'with a Charming Languishment, / Permits his Force', and, although she cries '*My Dearer Honour ev'n to You / I cannot, must not give*' (1, pp. 65–6), she is also embracing him. The lovers' growing passion is explicitly described in terms of the usual tropes of erotic love poetry that conflate sexuality, religion, and nature. Lysander caresses her vagina, the 'Altar', that 'Awful Throne, that Paradice', 'That Fountain where Delight still flows', and their 'Bodies, as their Souls, are joyn'd' (1, p. 66). But even as they seem about to climax, 'Ready to taste a thousand Joys', Lysander becomes impotent, 'Excess of Love his Love betray'd', and despite all his attempts at manipulation 'The Insensible fell weeping in his Hand' (1, p. 67). The climax of the poem's sexual narrative is, in fact, the absence of climax. Cloris, aroused by failure from her trance of delight, reaches for 'that Fabulous *Priapus*, / That Potent God, as Poet's feign' but finds that the poets do indeed 'feign' and exaggerate the power of the phallus – and what she finds 'beneath the verdant Leaves' is a 'snake' (1, p. 68). The snake in this instance is the penis/phallus/priapus, and perhaps also the biblical snake that stole into paradise and led to the fall of man. That snake encouraged lustful love; however, this snake signals the waning of lust in a wittily heterodox conceit that turns the fall from grace into a fall from pleasure.

The poem's most remarkable variation on its specific model and the other 'imperfect enjoyment' poems lies in the way it is centred less on Lysander than on Cloris, less on his pleasure than on hers, and less on his misery than her 'disappointment'. Cloris filled with 'Disdain' and 'Shame' runs away, leaving her would-be lover 'fainting on the Gloomy bed' (1, p. 68). As Barash notes, in stanza XIII Behn conflates two Ovidian myths of metamorphoses, that of Daphne pursued by Apollo and that of Venus mourning Adonis. Barash notes that, 'taken together, these two myths shift the story to the point of view of a disappointed and fearful – but nevertheless desiring woman'.[9] One might wonder also if the conjunction of Daphne, who became a laurel tree, emblem of poetry, and Venus, who in the Adonis myth transforms him into a flower, does not also indicate the entry of the disappointed yet desiring woman into creativity – into verse. In the final stanza the poem is even more firmly female-centred. The narrative voice enters to state 'The *Nymph's* Resentments none but I / Can well Imagine or Condole'. Lysander's misery, on the other hand, 'none can guess . . . / But those who sway'd his Destiny' (1, p. 69).

'The Disappointment' is an exercise in the erotic pastoral popular with male writers and presumably readers of the time. However, as Behn handles the topic, the centre of attention shifts from male to female, and from penis to vagina. The pastoral realm where swains consummate their desires with willing nymphs is refigured as a deceptive landscape: thickets may invite, but swains cannot always perform: leaves may be 'verdant' but what they hide is the snake of impotence. If the genders constructed in this poem are clearly biologically male and female, they are less clearly culturally marked. Lysander and Cloris are not androgynous, but conventionally marked gender characteristics cross over in this narrative of desire and frustration. There is a witty reversal of conventional gender expectations in the image of the active girl running 'Like Lightening through the Grove' leaving the wilting male behind in the thicket (1, p. 69). Lysander cannot perform the male sexual function: Cloris is angry not sweetly understanding, and she is active while he is passive.

In marked contrast to the failed sexuality of 'The Disappointment' or the tragic sexual encounters of 'Oenone to Paris' and *A Voyage to the Isle of Love*, Behn creates a world of sexual fulfilment and plenty in 'The Golden Age. A Paraphrase on a Translation out of French' (*PSO*, 1684). This poem is loosely based on the prologue to Torquato Tasso's pastoral drama *Aminta* (1573), and both have a common source in Ovid's *Metamorphoses*, Book 1, 89–112, describing the felicity of the first age of man when agriculture, law, seafaring, and warfare were unknown. Behn presents the reader with a sumptuously erotic and fertile nature that enacts and incites the acts of love:

> The Groves appear'd all drest with Wreaths of Flowers,
> And from their Leaves dropt Aromatick Showers,
> Whose fragrant Heads in Mystick Twines above,
> Exchang'd their Sweets, and mix'd with thousand Kisses,
>   As if the willing Branches strove
>   To beautifie and shade the Grove
> Where the young Wanton Gods of Love
> Offer their Noblest Sacrifice of Blisses.   (I, p. 30)

Throughout the poem Behn stresses that in the golden age, sex was guiltless, harmless, and entirely without any of the usual social consequences. In the world created in this poem, women can freely enjoy sexual love:

> The Nymphs were free, no nice, no coy disdain,
> Deny'd their Joyes, or gave the Lover pain;
> The yielding Maid but kind Resistance makes;
> Trembling and blushing are not marks of shame,
>   But the Effect of kindling Flame:
> Which from the sighing burning Swain she takes,
> While she with tears all soft, and down-cast eyes,
> Permits the Charming Conqueror to win the Prize.
>   (I, pp. 32–3)

The traditional language of sex as warfare is retained but softened, the 'Conqueror' is 'Charming', the 'Prize' is freely given, and, most significantly, 'Trembling and blushing are not marks of shame' but of arousal and pleasure. As Achsah Guibbory remarks of these lines, 'the maids "yield" not to men but to their own desires, and do so for *their* pleasure. This is a world of reciprocity.'[10] Central to the visionary sexuality Behn depicts is the absence not only of shame and guilt, but also of male violence.

Stanza III opens declaring that in the golden age 'The stubborn Plough had then, / Made no rude Rapes upon the Virgin Earth' and in stanza v the age is characterized as being without 'Rapes, Invasions, Tyrannies' (I, p. 32). The emphasis on the absence of rape in the golden age is notable, and Ann Marie Stewart has contrasted the repeated descriptions of love without violence in this poem with Behn's play *The Rover* (1677) where Florinda is repeatedly threatened with rape.[11] Rape, however, is impossible in the golden age of Behn's poem, as are the pain and shame of male impotence suffered by her Lisander and Lysander since male sexuality is described as gentle, even with implications that it is non-penetrative. The third stanza declares that the earth produced 'without the Aids of Men: / As if within her Teeming

Womb, / All Nature and all Sexes lay' (I, p. 31). The penis, once again a snake, is benevolent in this Eden where 'Snakes securely dwelt / Not doing harm, nor harm from others felt'. They are 'Innocently' played with by the 'Nymphs' since 'No spightful Venom in the wantons lay; / But to the touch were Soft, and to the sight were Gay' (I, p. 31).

The 'modern' social world that is antithetical to free and happy sexual intercourse frames the descriptions of the golden age of sexual reciprocity. Stanzas III to V function as anti-strophes as Behn defines her golden age through negation. Stanza III describes a time before agriculture, and stanza IV asserts that this was also an age before war, when 'Monarchs were uncreated', when law was unknown, before religion 'set the World at Odds', and when ambition was unknown (I, p. 31). Stanza V declares that the words and concepts of 'Right and Property' were unknown since 'Power' which 'taught Mankind to invade' and 'Pride and Avarice' were also unknown and had not yet unleashed upon the world 'Rapes, Invasions, Tyrannies' (I, p. 32). In many ways this is the traditional golden age of Ovid; however, Behn's depiction of the 'Blest Age' (I, p. 30) is more passionately expressed and very directly linked to sexuality as she replaces the entire social and political system of her world with one where 'Lovers . . . uncontroul'd did meet' (I, p. 33). In this world, 'every Vow' was 'inviolably true' and without any 'fear of Gods', religion, or law, which are mere 'Politick Curbs to keep man in' through the creation of the idea of sin. Stanzas VIII and IX move from the basic structures of political control to the social formations they sustain, concentrating on 'Honour! Thou who first didst damn, / A Woman to the Sin of shame' (I, p. 33). As Guibbory points out, Behn 'shows how private sexuality is bound up with a whole range of practices in the public sphere'.[12]

Honour means that women must guard and commodify their beauty to 'Tempt, not gratify the World' (I, p. 33). The absence of economic anxiety in 'The Golden Age' is as notable as is the absence of rape, and this can also be compared to the sexual encounters in *The Rover*. In that play, as in many Restoration sex and courtship comedies, economic concerns underwrite nearly all the relationships. From the courtesan Angellica Bianca's advertisement of herself for a 'Thousand crowns a month' (V: 2.1.116), to the whore Lucetta's thefts, and the virtuous Hellena's sizable dowry, desire and economic gain are interwoven. 'The Golden Age' examines and reverses the limitations, inhibitions and humiliations that women experience in love and which many of Behn's other poems and plays depict. The ethos and traditions of pastoral mythology enable Behn to combine eroticism with a social and political vision of an impossible and improbable world where women and men meet without inequality, fear or guilt.

In the final stanza the poem energetically but rather abruptly moves away from evocations of the golden past and denunciations of the corrupted present. Stanza x opens urging that the 'Golden age again / Assume its Glorious Reign'. The 'young wishing Maid' is told to confess her wishes and give over all her 'Arts' of concealment:

> The Mystery will be reveal'd,
> And she in vain denies, whilst we can guess,
> She only shows the Jilt to teach man how,
> To turn the false Artillery on the Cunning Foe.
>
> (I, p. 34)

The return to the present, where desire is 'conceal'd' and where women must 'Jilt' as part of the warfare between the sexes, is then dismissed: 'Thou empty Vision, hence, be gone, / And let the peaceful, *Swain* love on' (I, p. 34); and the poem moves into the *carpe diem theme* mode. As the poetic genre alters, so also does the poetic voice, which had been general, widely observational, and genderless (even if the joys of the golden age are largely centred on female sexual pleasure). The voice now becomes more particular, and takes on a masculine tone, appropriate to the *carpe diem* theme, as '*Sylvia*' is warned that 'Beauties fade' and that when she is old and white haired her honour will be of little comfort to her (I, p. 35). Given the care that has gone into describing precisely why the 'modern' age is inimical to the free expression of desire, the rather conventional last lines, 'The Sun and Spring receive but our short Light, / Once sett, a sleep brings an Eternal Night', are rather anti-climactic. The swerve into *carpe diem* certainly provides an upbeat and apparently optimistic ending, but unlike, for instance, Marvell's energetic conclusion to 'His Coy Mistress' the invitation to seize the day does not flow from the previous stanzas. The conclusion can, perhaps, follow if we read the earlier verses as part of the 'Artillery' of love, and as an erotic titillation leading to a seduction. However, from stanzas III to IX the analyses of the social and political conditions creating sexual inhibition work against reading the poem simply as a libertine invitation to present love. Behn surely wished to unite the sexual ease of libertinism with the happy innocence of the pastoral, re-envisioned as distinctly female-friendly, and moved from the never-never land of pastoral to the present. However, the moment that vision is historicized it becomes problematic. Behn was a friend of libertine wits and dependent also on a *status quo* that supported her profession and sustained her imagination. The tropes of freedom in 'The Golden Age' are those we find elsewhere in her work, as are the condemnations of hypocritical and destructive inhibitions. However, as a Tory and loyal royalist, she could hardly conclude with an unmediated image of the present as a cruel and corrupt world where monarchs are tyrannical rapists. Rather, through a strenuous but imperfect conclusion she attempts to *will* a more perfect past onto the imperfect present.

In 'The Golden Age', Behn depicts an ideal world where female desire can be acknowledged and enjoyed, and is empowering. However, in 'On Desire. A Pindarick' (appended to *Lycidus*, 1688), we are very much in *this* world, where desire must be concealed. Desire is greeted in the invocation at the start of the verse as a 'new found pain' and an 'infection' that has gained 'vast Dominion' over the speaker's heart. The uneven lines and stanzas of the pindaric form are well suited to the expression of ecstasy and confusion, regret and excitement. The poem moves from invocations to and evocations of desire, via its various attributes, to direct address to philosophers – do they know how to quench desire – and finally speaks to the 'fair ones' who lie about desire (I, p. 283).

The first half of the poem describes the speaker's previous imperviousness to attempts to arouse her desire:

> Not Beauty could invite thee then
> Nor all the Arts of lavish Men!
> Not all the powerful Rhetorick of the Tongue
> Not sacred Wit cou'd charm thee on;
> Not the soft play that lovers make.
>
> (I, p. 282)

Indeed, the speaker wished to experience desire and took herself to the appropriate pastoral locations, searching 'In silent Groves, in lonely bowrs: / On Flowry beds where lovers wishing lye' (I, p. 282). Lysander's 'Eyes' have, however, at last penetrated and when the 'dear Shepherd' appears, 'I faint, I dye with pleasing pain' and when she touches him she loses the ability to speak, 'My words intruding sighing break' (I, pp. 282–3). S. J. Wiseman notes the paradox, typical of Behn's verse and prose narratives, that, even as desire removes control from the speaker, it also enables her to narrate her feelings in a 'partially compensatory' manner.[13] This, as Wiseman indicates, is Oenone's situation. However, the trajectories traced in 'On Desire' take a rather different direction. The speaker has wanted to experience desire and has actively sought it, and, although it now overwhelms her with 'burning feaverish fits' and fractures her speech, it also educates her. In her address to the 'fair ones' she reveals that when women are chaste it is not 'real virtue makes you nice' but a 'want of dear desire'. To experience desire is to realize that 'virtu's but a cheat / And Honour but a false disguise' (I, p. 283). The speaker, as the impetuous rushing form of the verse conveys, is exhilarated by the experience of desire that not only excites her physically but also gives her a new understanding of her world. The combination of desire and knowledge leads her to a rather remarkable conclusion – 'tho with virtue I the World perplex' she will give way to Lysander and to her desire. The verse concludes with a self-justificatory reference to the classics: 'So *Helen* while from *Theseus* arms she fled, / To charming *Paris* yields her heart and bed.' The reference is not of the most elevated variety – as Oenone had remarked, Helen was a byword for her numerous lovers – but it is defiant. Lysander has found the 'weekness of my sex' (I, p. 284), but there is also strength in the speaker's willingness to experience her desires to the full. Having sought to experience 'the nimble fire, that dost dilate / Thy mighty force thrô every part' (I, p. 282), she now welcomes it. In the light of 'On Desire', one can read the last stanza of 'The Golden Age', with its invitation to Sylvia, per-haps, as just such a challenge – imprudent and rash though it may be – to deceive the world with the show of virtue but let the lover into 'heart and bed'. In all, 'On Desire' is a poem remarkable for its frank avowal not merely of female weakness and loss in the face of desire, but of female desire for desire, and willingness, once it is found, to risk all for it – and to burst into racing language. 'On Desire' is not a modest poem: it is harsh, scornful, and courageous.

The pastoral in the form which Behn and her contemporaries used for erotic fantasies of desire, and as a locus for irony and wit with regard both to love and society, was not continued into the next age. The concept of nature altered, and a post-Newtonian age traced vast movements in nature and admired the awesome design of the Creator. There was little room in this concept of nature for the conventions of sighing shepherds and coy nymphs. Behn's was the last great age of courtly pastoral verse, when thickets, groves, and bowers invited and provided a locus for examinations of the complexity of human sexuality. New configurations of human biology altered ideas of gender and affected the extent to which women could be depicted as sensual and desiring, or men as weakly sighing. When Anne Finch reviewed the poets of her age in 'The Circuit of Apollo' (1712) she had her god consider but reject Behn's claims to the laurels:

> He said amongst Femens was not on the earth
> Her superior in fancy, in language, or wit,
> Yet owned that a little too loosely she writ;
> Since the art of the Muse is to stir up soft thoughts,
> Yet to make all hearts beat without blushes or faults.[14]

Behn's pastoral muse, however, was not merely loose, but was also political; not only in the overt politics of state but in her sexual politics. Like her male contemporaries, she wrote of a highly sexualized pastoral world, but, unlike the majority of their verse, her verses did not merely enact the drama of female sexual submission. When her females yielded and suffered, they complained: frequently she reversed the tropes and expectations to present women in the ascendant. Moreover, she reinterpreted the tropes of sexual conquest so that precisely 'blushes' need not be 'faults', rather 'Trembling and blushing are not marks of shame' but the signs of mutual pleasure.

NOTES

1 John Dryden's translation, *The Works of Virgil. Pastoral I.; or, Tityrus and Meliboeus* (1697), in *The Poems of John Dryden* ed. James Kinsley (Oxford: Clarendon Press, 1958), vol. II.
2 Richard Barnfield's pastoral sonnet cycle, *The Affectionate Shepherd* (1595) is merely one of the more overtly homoerotic uses of the 'classic' pastoral tradition. A collection of essays on Barnfield's verse, *The Affectionate Shepherd, Celebrating Richard Barnfield*, ed. Kenneth Borris and George Klawitter (Selinsgrove: Susquehanna University Press, 2001) usefully places Barnfield in a context of late Elizabethan pastoral poetry exploring unconventional sexual liaisons.
3 Heidi Laudien, 'From Pastoral to "Pastorelle": A New Context for Reading Aphra Behn', in *Aphra Behn (1640–1689): Identity, Alterity, Ambiguity*, ed. Mary Anne O'Donnell, Bernard Dhuicq, and Guyonne Leduc (Paris: L'Harmattan, 2000), pp. 91–9.
4 Arlene Stiebel, 'Subversive Sexuality: Masking the Erotic in Poems by Katherine Philips and Aphra Behn', in *Renaissance Discourses of Desire*, ed. Claude J. Summers and Ted-Larry Pebworth (Columbia: University of Missouri Press, 1993), p. 231.
5 Carol Barash, *English Women's Poetry, 1649–1714: Politics, Community, and Linguistic Authority* (Oxford: Clarendon Press, 1996), p. 108.
6 *The Poems of John Wilmot, Earl of Rochester*, ed. Keith Walker (Oxford: Blackwell, 1984).
7 S. J. Wiseman, *Aphra Behn* (Plymouth: Northcote House, 1996), pp. 19–20.
8 Behn's poem 'The Disappointment' was first published in the 1680 edition of Rochester's works and was long thought to be by Rochester.
9 Barash, *English Women's Poetry*, p. 124.
10 Achsah Guibbory, 'Sexual Politics/Political Sex: Seventeenth-Century Love Poetry', in *Renaissance Discourses of Desire*, p. 218.
11 Ann Marie Stewart, 'Rape, Patriarchy, and the Libertine Ethos: The Function of Sexual Violence in Aphra Behn's 'The Golden Age' and *The Rover*, Part I', *Restoration and Eighteenth-Century Theatre Research*, 12:2 (Winter 1997), 26–39.
12 Guibbory, 'Sexual Politics / Political Sex', p. 220.
13 Wiseman, *Aphra Behn*, pp. 21–2.
14 Lines 11–15 from Anne Finch's 'The Circuit of Apollo', *The Meridian Anthology of Early Women Writers, from Aphra Behn to Maria Edgeworth*, ed. Katherine M. Rogers and William McCarthy (New York: Meridan/Penguin, 1987).

14

LINE COTTEGNIES

Aphra Behn's French translations

In the mid 1680s, Aphra Behn started translating from French into English at speed. She had been to France early in 1683 on a trip which, although undocumented, appears to have allowed her to perfect her knowledge of French.[1] In the seventeenth century, the translation of the classics was recognized as a prestigious activity, but this was not the case with the translation of contemporary authors. Almost all theoretical texts about translation were specifically concerned with Latin and Greek, as for instance Cowley's short preface to his *Pindarique Odes* (1656), where he gave a particularly felicitous expression to the seventeenth-century paradigm contrasting literal, or 'servile', translation, and free (or 'libertine' as he has it) translation. In his influential preface to *Ovid's Epistles* (1680), Dryden replaced this dichotomy with a ternary model, famously setting forth the three ways open to a translator as 'metaphrase' or word-for-word translation, 'paraphrase', or translation 'with a latitude', and finally 'imitation', in which the translator 'assumes the liberty not only to vary from the words and sense, but to forsake them both as he sees occasion'.[2] It is most likely Behn was familiar with this text, as she herself, while claiming she could not read Latin,[3] contributed an Ovidian translation to the collective volume. However, as Elizabeth Spearing writes, 'consideration of late seventeenth-century theories of translation in relation to the works of Aphra Behn is of limited usefulness',[4] as she dealt with mostly unchartered territory by translating very contemporary authors from the vernacular. This allowed her to make the original texts her own in a variety of ways, and, as will be apparent, she utilizes the whole range of strategies Dryden had outlined – which calls into question his neat categories and forces us to revise the status of translation in the seventeenth century.

For Behn seems to have quickly perceived the commercial potential of the contemporary curiosity for recent French best-sellers: she thus translated in quick succession Tallemant's allegorical narrative, *Le Voyage de l'Isle d'amour* and its sequel, in 1684 and 1688 respectively, La Rochefoucauld's maxims, in 1685, and Bonnecorse's prose narrative, *La Montre*, in 1686. This rhythm even accelerates with her translations of Fontenelle's *Entretiens sur la Pluralité des mondes* and *Histoire des Oracles* both appearing in 1688.[5] It is a measure of her commercial sense, and that of her booksellers, that two of these texts were the objects of fierce competition among English translators, Fontenelle's *Entretiens* and La Rochefoucauld's *Reflexions morales*.[6] The list of her translations attests to her incredible productivity; but it also poses the question of her motivations, other than commercial, in translating such a variety of texts. As will become apparent, her French translations fully deserve to feature in the canon of her original works, and allow a fascinating insight into her mind and politics.

It is easy to understand why she turned to the glib, allegorical poetry and prose of the *précieux* writers Tallemant and Bonnecorse – these were works greatly in favour among *précieuses* and their aristocratic milieus in France, and, as such, of great interest to Behn's own aristocratic readership. In fact, she freely rewrites the originals to reflect the politics and foppish court life of Restoration England. For instance, as Spearing has shown, she familiarizes Tallemant's amorous texts for an English ear by changing the names of the heroes to make them relate to her own poetry, and includes specific references to the sexual politics of her times. As a result, her version has an even stronger emphasis on love as a sophisticated game requiring skill and control. By doing so, she turns three rather superficial, *précieux* allegories into documents about Restoration tastes.[7] But while the amorous texts show a playful Behn conversant with the witty, cynical idiom of Restoration poetry, her translations of La Rochefoucauld and Fontenelle draw attention to another facet of her talent: her interest in difficult philosophical texts. With these translations, on which the rest of this essay will more particularly focus, not only does she prove a first-class translator, in command of an astonishingly wide range of strategies and techniques, fully aware of her practice, but she also follows an ambitious intellectual and political agenda. With the Fontenelle translations in particular, she offers a serious contribution to the contemporary intellectual debates, encompassing topics ranging from astronomy to biblical criticism, while claiming a space for women in the philosophy and science of her day.

Textual elements

It is impossible to ascertain whether Behn chose the works she translated or followed the prompting of her booksellers.[8] However, the selected authors all had one thing in common: they wrote for similar, polite circles of gentlemen and ladies – the kind of audience for which Behn had already been writing and translating poetry. Both François, duc de la Rochefoucauld and Bernard

Le Bovier de Fontenelle attended the elegant 'salons' of the *précieuses* and the court circles. The former's immensely popular *Réflexions morales*[9] were a collection of epigrammatic maxims in which he attempted to demystify idealized notions of morality and reveal the unsavoury motives of self-love or self-interest at the root of all actions. The latter's *Entretiens sur la pluralité des mondes*, a work of scientific vulgarisation, caused quite an uproar because of its sceptical inferences; it featured a nobleman teaching a 'marquise' lessons in astronomy, their conversations frequently adopting the gallant, bantering tone that would have suited the salon or the drawing-room. As such, their worlds chimed in with the Tory, aristocratic bias of Behn's oeuvre. In fact, she even occasionally uses the works as vehicles for topical political references: in her preface to *Reflections*, for instance, she mocks the obduracy of the 'hardened Whig' (IV, p. 2); and in the final reflection, she introduces a covert reference to the Duke of Monmouth. La Rochefoucauld intended the maxim as an attack on aristocratic heroism, which he saw as a product of the pursuit of glory, claiming that common people could be just as heroic through ignorance. Behn politicized the maxim by changing the opposition to heroes and traitors – a possible allusion to Monmouth who had just been executed.[10] But Behn's interest in modern science went beyond the restricted social, worldly interactions both works staged. This is shown by her more serious translation of *Histoire des Oracles*, itself an adaptation by Fontenelle of a controversial Dutch work first published in Latin by Van Dale. It was a historical account of oracles in classical antiquity, and could not qualify as drawing-room literature. Contrary to the translation of La Rochefoucauld, published as an appendix to a poetry miscellany (and as such, to be read in the same sitting as a continuation of the social games the collection both staged and participated in), the Fontenelle texts were issued separately in 1688. The *History of Oracles* was ostentatiously published as an anonymous piece, with no names of author, translator, or bookseller on the title-page, as if the treatise was highly contentious. Its dedication to the Lord Chancellor, and Behn's initials at the end of the epistle indicate however that this must have been a ploy to titillate the readers' imagination. These various editorial apparatuses suggest that for Behn and her bookseller, each translation was a commercial event to be staged in a different way to arouse the public's interest. But these strategies also reveal that Behn's attitude towards translation changed over the years.

Her translation of La Rochefoucauld's *Reflections on Morality or Seneca Unmasqued,* published in *Miscellany*, was announced on the general title-page, which might indicate that the publisher thought he could capitalize on the translation as a selling point. But, although Behn refers to 'the Duke of Rushfaucave' in her preface (signed Astrea,[11] which was one of her pennames), the names of the author or translator are not mentioned on the title-page – only the table of contents gives 'Mrs A. B.' as the author's name. It is as if the editorial apparatus tried to present the text surreptitiously, and deceptively, as an after-thought, a bonus in the miscellany. The structural coherence of the volume was enforced through several devices, such as including the amorous couple Lysander and Aminta who featured repeatedly in her poetry and also echoed that of *The Voyage to the Isle of Love*. The preface itself was presented as an epistle from Astrea to Lysander, making the translation part of an amorous strategy of seduction of a reluctant lover by the female translator – thereby encouraging the kind of semi-autobiographical reading with which Behn liked to titillate her reader, seemingly referring him or her to the Lysander of her own poetry.[12] She changed the order of the maxims to group all those concerned with love at the end, and applied some of the general ones about the passions to love in particular. The collection is thus appropriated as a free imitation rather than a faithful translation, joining the game of partly-fictional social interactions the miscellany exemplifies. Behn playfully presents herself as a co-writer of the maxims, on a par with 'Monsieur the Duke': the reflections, she claims, 'will spoil neither of our Reputations: since we both of us pretend to some other Pieces, that have indured the Test' (IV, p. 3).

This is not the case, however, with *A Discovery of New Worlds*, the title-page of which, in contrast, proudly highlights the role of the translator with Behn's full name in large capital letters, while Fontenelle's is not mentioned. It also advertises the preface ('wholly new', *Works*, IV, p. 69) as an 'ESSAY on translated PROSE' and as a new, exciting philosophical contribution to the debate about Copernicanism, refuting 'Father Tacquet, and others'. This title-page, for which however Behn was not necessarily responsible, suggests a new attitude towards translation, but is also emblematic of her astonishing literary ambition and commercial instinct, as of her bookseller's. First, the 'ESSAY on translated PROSE' – obviously meant as a counterpart to the Earl of Roscommon's *Essay on Translated Poetry* (1684) – symbolically marks the emergence of prose translation as a fully respectable literary activity. It is now considered the earliest theoretical text on prose translation in English, an important landmark in the history of the recognition of the modern translator. Yet only a fourth of the essay is concerned with translation (less than four pages in *Works*). Many of Behn's remarks as a practitioner of translation make good sense, as when she positions herself in the debate between literalism and imitation by opting for a middle ground between the two; yet her historical remarks and those pertaining to language are a little hazy. She placed English closer than French to Latin, so explaining why it was easier to translate from Latin or Italian into English than it was from French.

The essay consists of a series of desultory, often satirical, remarks about the French nation and language (and English francophilia), and the conclusion is that it is much easier to translate from Italian into English, because the 'Genius and Humour' of England and Italy agree: this is not the case, she claims, with France. Although the essay reveals that Behn knew about contemporary debates, and had acquired some valuable experience in the field of translation, one cannot help feeling that the self-proclaimed 'ESSAY on translated PROSE' (elsewhere referred to as 'The Translator's Preface') was an alluring yet partly deceptive subtitle. The second section of the preface, which deals with the contemporary debate about Copernicanism and biblical criticism, is well-informed and topical. Behn claims it will be of interest to all the curious, especially ladies. But her contribution to this debate is by no means original: some of her arguments come indeed straight from Father Tacquet (whose treatise had been published back in 1669) and even from a 1640 treatise by John Wilkins.[13] That each publication was intended as a commercial venture, complete with a marketing strategy, does not mean, however, that her work was totally derivative. Her incredible creativity proceeds from acts of ventriloquism and this is probably why she found translation so congenial a task.

Behn's translation of La Rochefoucauld

In her lively translation of La Rochefoucauld, Behn ranges between literalism and free re-creation, and she even includes two maxims of her own: although she omits a few of the Duke's original reflections and changes the order of the sequence, about two-thirds of those she does translate are quite faithful. A third consists of 'imitations' which differ from the original in a significant way. One of the main aspects of Behn's *Reflections* is the feminization of the speaking voice. As Elizabeth Spearing puts it in her study of *The Voyage to the Isle of Love*, Behn practised 'transvestite ventriloquism' by slipping into a male persona; for her, 'the politics of translation' was tantamount to 'a form of sexual politics'.[14] In *Reflections*, Behn often appropriates the French, male, aristocratic persona of La Rochefoucauld by feminizing the speaker's voice and applying a female perspective. Yet something of the male speaker's status and voice is retained in the process. In a few cases, the speaker's misogyny is simply played down, as when Behn turns satirical anti-feminist comments into rules about human beings in general. This feminist agenda sometimes leads her to adopt a provocative stance. In his male-oriented perspective, La Rochefoucauld writes: 'When we are tired of loving someone, we are quite content to find this person has been unfaithful to us.' Behn adapts this maxim to women in general, and her persona becomes a counterpart of the

Restoration rake. She gaily asserts: 'When we are weary of a Lover, we are very well pleased to find him unfaithful, that we may be disingaged from our Fidelity.'[15] Feminizing the maxims, although often done playfully, thus proves a meaningful experiment that interrogates gender politics.

In fact, La Rochefoucauld was perceived in England as a cynic and an exposer of social hypocrisy, a misunderstanding for which Behn is partly responsible, as she 'naturalized' his maxims by setting them in the context of a society emblematic of the Restoration, with its rakes, fops, coxcombs, jilts and so forth. He was certainly pessimistic about human nature, perhaps even sceptical – although he denied it – in that he aimed at puncturing notions of virtue and honour by showing that human beings are unwittingly governed by self-love. He not only denied the Stoics' claim that the self could curb the passions, but also opposed idealism. This position could be read on one level as undermining Christian ethics, and probably explains why the publisher first included the preface by La Chapelle-Bessé, which put an Augustinian slant on La Rochefoucauld's view of life. Although it was withdrawn from all subsequent editions, La Rochefoucauld was rather worried about the reception of his text and introduced an explicitly religious maxim in the edition Behn used, which eventually asserted the possibility of Christian values.[16] Significantly, Behn expunges both the religious defence and the new maxim. Throughout the collection, she replaces the Duke's introspective drive and self-analysis with satire targeting others. The world she describes is a mundane society governed by cynicism and the will to power.

Consciously or unconsciously, she misreads several of the original maxims to make them concur with her new agenda; at the same time she often appropriates the Frenchman's impersonal maxims by making them first person. The constant shifts cannot be entirely attributed to Behn's tendency to overlook and simplify the syntactic and semantic ambiguity of the original text. They suggest that writer and translator held a differing worldview. One reflection originally reads: 'It is a well-known fact that one should not talk about one's wife in public, but one should also remember not to talk about oneself';[17] Behn drops the argument concerning the self as totally irrelevant, and for once gives the maxim a misogynist slant: 'You ought to say but little of your Wife, and less to her' (IV, p. 64). In another emblematic reflection, La Rochefoucauld denounces men's unwitting subjection to their passions: 'Man often thinks he is in control of himself whereas he is being controlled by something else . . .' Behn's version characteristically applies the maxim to social relationships, typifying the shift from self-analysis to satire: 'Men often think they govern themselves with Wisdom and conduct, when at the same time they have so blind a sight as not to perceive they are governed by others.'[18] Her reflections become a satirical anatomy of social interactions, rather than an enquiry into self-deluding mechanisms. But the vision of ethics that emerges from her collection is less pessimistic regarding the possibility of freedom and the role of reason: she in fact constantly turns a deaf ear to the passionate determinism which La Rochefoucauld saw as overbearing – to the point of claiming that free will was an illusion. In Behn's sequence, freedom is in fact achieved through the will to acquire power over others and this desire, which she often seems to equate with reason (or wit, or wisdom), allows her to downplay the idea of the self's essential powerlessness the Duke saw as inescapable. This quasi-Hobbesian vision of ethics allows Behn to emphasize the possibility of controlling one's fate through the manipulation of appearances. Her maxims thus often end up giving prescriptive advice about how to deceive, or not to be taken in, while La Rochefoucauld simply reports the pathetic ploys used by the individual in society.[19]

The Fontenelle translations

The coherence of the maxims should not be exaggerated. Behn obviously did not intend her 'translation' to serve the French text; instead, she used the original freely as a basis for her own creative maxims. But among the liberties she took with the original text, there were also a number of obvious mistakes which seem to indicate that she must have worked quickly – unless her knowledge of French was then insufficient to cope with the extraordinary complexity of La Rochefoucauld's convoluted syntax. If so, by 1688 her French must have improved dramatically, for her version of Fontenelle's *Entretiens* is, on the whole, very faithful, and her *History of Oracles* even more so. It is perhaps because the dialogic form, with which Behn obviously felt comfortable, and the learned dissertation gave her less scope for free imitation. In the preface to *Discovery of New Worlds,* she also claimed that she had 'neither health nor leisure' to give us 'the subject quite changed and made [her] own' (IV, p. 86), contrary to (one imagines) her La Rochefoucauld translation. But there is more to this than meets the eye, for the Fontenelle translations show an involvement of a different kind – Behn not only proves a first-class translator but also a scholar in her own right. In *Discovery*, she thus corrects several of Fontenelle's mistakes: she points out in the preface that she has corrected the height of the atmosphere,[20] but she also tacitly corrects other mistakes in the dialogues. In one instance, Fontenelle implies that the moon turned round the sun and on itself; Behn rectifies this misconception, dropping the reference to the sun: 'Venus turns round the Sun on her own Axis, as the moon does around the earth.'[21] But she also undertakes more than one expects from a translator in the 'dazzling display of biblical verse and chapter'[22] included in the second section of the preface. In the *History of Oracles* she also adds marginal references to the authors cited in the text and even refers to the issue of Bayle's *Journal des Savants* which reviewed the book.[23] Just when and how she was able to do the necessary reading for all this in 1687–8 remains a mystery.

Behn's readiness to engage with her various topics is perceptible throughout: she displays a remarkable empathy with her author's work and her enthusiasm for vulgarization is clearly visible in both texts. Fontenelle's plea to offer 'a middle ground where philosophy might be found suitable by everyone' significantly becomes in Behn a manifesto for 'a middle way to philosophy, such as would improve every understanding'.[24] The argument shifts from the notion of entertainment to that of education. Behn often proves very didactic: she adapts references for her English public and clarifies incomplete or confused arguments. Thus when the philosopher explains that any given point on the earth moves in and out of the light of the sun as it revolves around its axis, she adds an element overlooked by Fontenelle and, in so doing, restores the coherence of the whole argument: 'every point of the *Earth* (which is not near the South or North-Poles) loses and recovers the sight of the Sun' (IV, p. 105). She has a knack for finding the apt formulation to clarify a complex argument, often adding a concrete detail to illustrate an abstract idea. She thus compares the various layers around the sun to those of an onion (IV, p. 145) – a typically concrete (though a touch bathetic) simile that illuminates the original.

Though perhaps more discreet here than in her *Reflections*, another area of intervention concerns Behn's feminist agenda. In the *Entretiens*, the avowed aim of the gentleman-philosopher is to teach the lady how to make critical use of her reason; therefore he leads her to re-examine preconceived notions of the status of the earth and of man in the universe. Even though she complains about the Frenchman's unrealistic, unkind depiction of the lady, Behn claims in her preface that one of her reasons for translating the text is that one of the protagonists is a woman. In fact, she occasionally tones down the misogyny of some remarks, and silences passages in which Fontenelle gives the Marchioness overtly naive reactions. But by far the most spectacular correction she imposes on the text is the systematic editing of all references to men in general, which become 'men and women'.[25] Through this political act, Behn in an absolutely unprecedented way makes women feature in the philosophical discourse on an equal footing with men – no mean feat for an author claiming she was only dabbling in philosophy. Another less radical intervention can be seen in the way she occasionally corrects Fontenelle's comments about primitive peoples. Wherever possible, Behn introduces specific references to the New World where Fontenelle remained unspecific, as when 'some newly-discovered lands' becomes 'the new discovered World of America' (IV, p. 121). And it is perhaps her personal encounter with its inhabitants that leads the author of *Oroonoko* (also published in 1688) to manifest some uneasiness about the most obvious racial prejudices voiced by the Frenchman. She thus edits a clause describing the primitive races found in America as 'devoid of reason' (Fontenelle, p. 136) – although she faithfully translates the rest of the sentence which describes them as 'hardly human' (IV, p. 121). This fairly light, ambivalent, editing throws into relief the methodical corrections of 'men' into 'Men and Women', although she did not repeat this in the more impersonal *History of Oracles*.

The most interesting set of changes, however, are probably the small, paradigmatic shifts to which she submits the text, with a view to making Fontenelle's covert scepticism more radical. The main interests of the preface lie in its ambivalent critique of Fontenelle and in the partly original piece of biblical criticism that follows. Here, as in the main body of the text, Behn evinces a strategy of equivocation which allows her to radicalize her author's sceptical inferences while seemingly dissociating herself from him. First, she reproaches him with offering a caricature of natural philosophy for the sake of vulgarization. This was often invoked against him, and reminds us that Copernicanism and the plurality of worlds were still thought contentious. Although Fontenelle was careful not to engage openly with theology, his book was deemed sufficiently impious to be blacklisted by the Roman Catholic Church until the nineteenth century.

Behn's caution is therefore not surprising. But paradoxically, by referring to some of the boldest statements out of context, she makes them sound even more daring: in fact, to develop the Marchioness's critical sense, the philosopher is often led to envisage fanciful arguments, but only as temporary steps in a line of reasoning. Behn overlooks this and pretends for instance to castigate Fontenelle for imagining that 'there are thousands of worlds inhabited by animals' (IV, p. 77). More importantly, she condemns him for omitting to mention God: 'He ascribes all to Nature and says not a Word of God Almighty . . . so one would almost take him to be a Pagan' (IV, p. 77). But she refers almost in the same breath to one of the most potentially contentious arguments in the last conversation, in which Fontenelle mused on the notion of immortality. In the body of the text, she even gives to this argument a more heterodox twist. Using the fable of the rose – which, judging by its own brevity of life, might think the gardener immortal – the philosopher demonstrates the need to use one's reason rather than senses when considering subjects as important as immortality.[26] Although this fable has impious implications, Fontenelle's conclusion is deceptively modest, as he simply argues for caution. Behn increases the sceptical inference by twisting the conclusion: 'some things must have passed many Ages of Men, one after another, before any sign of Decay had appear'd in 'em' (IV, p. 164). Behn appears to negate the very possibility of immortality – a far more daring conclusion than Fontenelle's. This strategy allows her to draw attention to the potentially impious inferences of some arguments by making them more radical.

In fact, Behn often minimizes the philosopher's playfulness and irony about potentially libertine ideas, significantly altering the tone of the book. Thus she occasionally fails to translate an adverb, a conditional or modal verb which initially made a point less authoritative or more playful. In a contentious passage, Behn's philosopher is made to assert the absolute power of chance, while Fontenelle's only suggested the frequent interference of chance:[27] 'Chance of situation has decided our Fate' (IV, p. 144). The omission of a single adverb and the choice of tense significantly distort the original, ambiguous phrasing, and deflate its subtlety. In fact, Behn rids the text of much of the irony that is an integral part of Fontenelle's strategy, which could itself be called libertine as it asserts bold ideas while simultaneously appearing to withdraw or to defuse them.

As is apparent, Behn submits Fontenelle's book to a strategy similar to his own and in many instances makes the source of enunciation more complex so that the translation will serve her own agenda – whatever that may be. Nowhere is her strategy of equivocation more visible than in the last and longest section of the preface, an extraordinary complex instance of irony. After a defence of Fontenelle's Copernicanism, Behn moves on to discuss the status of scriptures in regard to scientific discourse (in astronomy, geometry, and chronology). She argues for a separation between religion and science, but also engages in the highly sensitive issues of the Bible's textuality and historicity, a debate that involved thinkers as important as Richard Simon or Newton, for instance.[28] This impressive display of biblical criticism leads to a plea against a literal reading of the scriptures, which has enabled Lisa J. Schnell to read this 'rhetorical relativism' as an attack on Whiggish, Protestant literalism, and consequently, perhaps, as an implicit defence of Stuart Catholicism.[29] But as she herself notes, Behn ends up pulling the rug from under her own feet by refusing to conclude, ironically withdrawing all certainty. Furthermore she denounces in the same sentence unbelievers, literalists, and all those who 'give the Word of God only that Meaning and Sense that pleases their own Humours, or suits best their present Purpose and Interest' (IV, p. 85). In conclusion Behn argues, in a seemingly mock serious tone, for a form of unspecified fideism: 'it is the duty of all Christians to acquiesce in the Opinion and Decrees of the Church of Christ, in whom dwells the Spirit of God, which enlightens us to Matters of Religion and Faith' (IV, p. 85). This could suggest libertine inferences, for Behn seems to argue for submission to religion as mere form rather than as a matter of faith. But this rather enigmatic formulation could also be read without contradiction as a plea for religious toleration, for it eventually obfuscates the niceties of Protestantism and Catholicism.

I would like to suggest that Behn had a consistent political agenda here: to assert, at a time of furious controversy, the need for the religious toleration she hoped James II would offer. Her translation of the *History of Oracles* gives us complementary evidence to this effect. Its dedication to one of the props of the régime, the Lord Chancellor Lord Jeffreys,[30] indicates an intention to politicize the translation, but it also raises questions: Lord Jeffreys was known for his harshness against Whigs and Protestants – he had been associated with some of the most unpopular measures taken during the reign of James II, particularly the gruesome crushing of the Monmouth Rebellion; he was definitely not an advocate of tolerance.

The original *History of Oracles* had been intended as a covert attack on religion and, more particularly, Catholicism: Van Dale was known as a fiercely anti-Catholic polemicist, although Fontenelle had toned down his most damning comments. The aim of the dissertation was to show that, contrary to what the Catholic church contended, the pagan oracles were all priestly frauds and did not simply cease with the coming of Christ. If they eventually stopped, it was because they were silenced by force. What the book intimated was that it had paradoxically been in the interest of the Church to have people believe in the oracles because it itself was based on similar frauds – an argument central to such heterodox texts as the *Treatise of the Three Impostors*.[31] In Behn's version, there are very few departures from the original, which makes the few instances where she actually introduces changes all the more significant. At one point, Fontenelle and Van Dale, musing on the popularity of oracles throughout the ages, attribute it in part to the irrepressible attraction of the marvellous ('le merveilleux'). Behn uses the word 'miraculous',[32] which Fontenelle was careful not to use because of its Christian connotation. At a second remove, sheltering behind Fontenelle, she had no qualms about using a sensitive word, which suggests her readiness to toy with heterodox ideas. But her agenda becomes perhaps clearer in her enthusiastic rendering of the defence of pagan religion. The latter is described as ideal, because it is a civil religion that does not demand faith from its citizens:

we have reason to believe that among the *Pagans*, *Religion* was a practice, the speculation of which was very indifferent. They did as others did, but believ'd what they themselves pleas'd. This principle is very extravagant; but the People who knew nothing of the impertinency of it, were content with it; and the *Philosophers* submitted to it very willingly, because it gave them freedom enough.

(IV, p. 206)

The original version was significantly less explicit about the philosophers' submission to this civil religion, and Behn probably owes more here to Hobbes than to Fontenelle or Van Dale: 'the people who saw no impertinence in [this principle], were satisfied with it, and the learned [*les gens d'esprit*] submitted to it very easily, because it was light to bear [*parce qu'il ne les gênait guère*]'.[33] This might be a key to Behn's political vision of a state that would allow liberty of conscience. She had also used the phrase, although in a playful context, in *Discovery*, and in light of her obvious interest in the issue, the allusion becomes clearer. Fontenelle's philosopher comments on what he thinks is a particularly impious passage in Ariosto: 'after all, it is a poetical licence that is only a little too fanciful'.[34] In her version, Behn introduces a significant nuance: 'But since there is a Poetical Licence, and Liberty of Conscience, it ought to pass as a Gayety' (IV, p. 118). An indirect praise of James II, this was also wishful thinking, becoming increasingly less realistic as time passed. It is nevertheless striking that she should have made a point of voicing the political ideal of a civil religion in two texts that were also considered as flirting with heresy.

These texts allow us to catch a glimpse of Behn's increasing, if muted, disillusion with a regime that found itself incapable of maintaining peace and liberty of conscience. She still believed in the necessity of religious toleration, but perhaps Catholicism no longer appeared as the best option. Her dedication to Lord Jeffreys of a text indirectly praising the liberty of conscience and casting doubt on the authority of the Church shows that she might have intended this book as her own contribution to the political debate – not as flattery, but perhaps as counsel. Yet her agenda appears to have been incredibly complex, for the choice of texts she translated also manifests her interest in heterodoxy, and perhaps even her rationalist, free-thinking inclinations, as some key paradigmatic shifts in *Discovery* have revealed. Who has never mused about Oroonoko's freethinking French master, 'a man of very little Religion', but of 'admirable Morals', to whom the hero owes his sense of morality (III, p. 81)? It would be tempting to draw a link between Behn's novella and her translations. For contrary to Cicero, whose impiety according to the *History of Oracles* was not thought shocking in his own time,[35] the mysterious Frenchman of the story was banished from his own country for his 'Heretical Notions' (III, p. 81), like the French Epicurean Saint-Évremond, exiled in London at the time Behn was writing. As has become apparent, Behn's translations from the French fully deserve to be included in her canon as original works in their own right, but they also lead us to revise our notions of the nature of translation in the seventeenth century. But, while her translations of the *précieux*, amorous works and of La Rochefoucauld's maxims show her talent in ventriloquism and free imitation, it is with the

Fontenelle translations that she made her most ambitious contributions to contemporary intellectual debates. In view of this achievement, Aphra Behn probably ought to be hailed as one of the first 'philosophes'.

NOTES

1 Janet Todd suggests that Behn might have been involved with spying activities once again. See Todd, p. 294.
2 John Dryden, 'Preface', *Ovid's Epistles* (1680), in *Essays of John Dryden*, 2 vols. (New York: Russell & Russell, 1961), I, p. 237.
3 See her complimentary poem for Thomas Creech's edition of Lucretius, which she praised because it allowed women access to a work previously denied to them (I, p. 26).
4 Elizabeth Spearing, 'Aphra Behn: The Politics of Translation', in *Aphra Behn Studies*, p. 156.
5 Paul Tallemant, *Le Voyage de l'Isle d'Amour* in *Recueil de quelques pièces nouvelles et galantes* (Cologne, 1663), and *Le Voyage de l'Isle d'Amour. A Licidas* (Paris, 1663); respectively translated as *A Voyage to the Isle of Love* in *Poems upon Several Occasions* (London, 1684) and *Lycidus: or the Lover in Fashion, together with a Miscellany of New Poems* (London, 1688). La Rochefoucauld, *Réflexions ou sentences et maximes morales* (pirated edition, The Hague, 1664; first authorized edition, Paris, 1665; definitive, fifth edition, Paris, 1678), translated as *Reflections on Morality or Seneca Unmasqued*, in *Miscellany, Being a Collection of Poems by Several Hands* (London, 1685). Balthasar de Bonnecorse, *La Montre* (Paris, 1666) translated as *La Montre: or the Lover's Watch* (London, 1686). Fontenelle, *Les Entretiens sur la pluralité des mondes* (Paris, 1686) and *Histoire des Oracles* ([Paris], 1687), translated as *A Discovery of New Worlds* and *History of Oracles* (both London, 1688).
6 An edition of the 1664 edition of La Rochefoucauld was published in 1670 by John Davies of Kidwelly (*Epictetus Junior or Maxims of Modern Morality in Two Centuries*, London). This fairly faithful translation was not known to Behn. Two new editions, both anonymous, were published in 1694. The competition was even fiercer for Fontenelle's *Entretiens*: it was translated in Dublin in 1687 by Sir W[illiam] D[onville] (*A Discourse of the Plurality of Worlds*), although this version seems to have gone unnoticed and by John Glanvill in London in 1688 (*A Plurality of Worlds*). See my 'The Translator as Critic: Aphra Behn's Translation of Fontenelle's *Entretiens sur la pluralité des mondes*', *Restoration*, 27 (Spring 2003), 23–38.
7 For the Tallemant translations in particular, see Spearing, 'Politics of Translation', in *Aphra Behn Studies*, pp. 154–77.
8 James Hindmarsh for La Rochefoucauld and William Canning for Fontenelle.
9 Behn used the fourth, 1675 edition, as Janet Todd and Bernard Dhuicq have established, but she also integrated parts of the preface by La Chapelle-Bessé for the 1665 edition. See *Works*, IV, p. xi: B. Dhuicq, 'Aphra Behn's *Reflections on Morality, or Seneca Unmasqued*', *Notes and Queries* 239 (41: 2) (1994), pp. 175–6, and 'Théorie et pratique de la traduction au XVIIe siècle', *Franco-British Studies* 10 (1990), 75–98, and my '"Aphra Behn Unmasqued": A. Behn's Translation of

La Rochefoucauld's *Réflexions*', in *Aphra Behn (1640–1689): Identity, Alterity, Ambiguity*, ed. Mary Ann O'Donnell, Bernard Dhuicq, and Guyone Leduc (Paris: L'Harmattan, 2000), pp. 13–24.

10 IV, p. 69. For Behn's ambivalence towards Monmouth, see Todd, p. 414.

11 The edition she used for her translation was anonymous, which perhaps accounts for the erratic spelling of La Rochefoucauld's name.

12 See I, p. 86.

13 Andreas Tacquet, *Opera omnia* (Antwerp, 1669); John Wilkins, *A Discourse Concerning a New World and Another Planet* (London, 1640). See note d in *Works*, IV, p. 79. There is reason to suspect that Behn used other, unidentified sources.

14 Spearing, 'Politics of Translation', in *Aphra Behn Studies*, p. 170, 167.

15 IV, p. 58. La Rochefoucauld, *Réflexions* (Paris, 1675), p. 31 (all subsequent citations refer to this edition). All translations are mine, unless specified.

16 La Rochefoucauld, *Réflexions*, p. 131: 'Humility is the real mark of Christian values.'

17 Ibid., p. 133.

18 Ibid., p. 16; *Works*, IV, p. 15.

19 See for instance *Réflexions*, p. 21, and *Works*, IV, p. 17.

20 *Works*, IV, p. 86.

21 Ibid., p. 133. See Fontenelle, *Entretiens sur la pluralité des mondes* (Paris, 1686), p. 199; all subsequent citations are taken from this edition.

22 The phrase is Janet Todd's. See Todd, p. 398.

23 *Works*, IV, p. 173, marginal note.

24 *Entretiens*, sig. ã iiii. *Works*, IV, p. 87.

25 For instance *Entretiens*, p. 136 and *Works*, IV, p. 121.

26 'A thing ought to have survived many generations added to one another for it to begin even to show signs of immortality' (*Entretiens*, p. 353).

27 'It is often the case that chance only is responsible for the success of our affairs' (*Entretiens*, p. 252).

28 See Richard H. Popkin, *The History of Scepticism from Erasmus to Spinoza* (Berkeley and Los Angeles: University of California Press, 1979), especially pp. 214–48, and my 'The Translator as Critic'.

29 See 'Parenthetical Disturbances: Aphra Behn and the Rhetoric of Relativity', *RSSI: Recherches sémiotiques, Semiotic Inquiry* 12 (1992), 107; revised as ch. 5 in Andrew Barnaby and Lisa J. Schnell, *Literate Experience: the Work of Knowing in Seventeenth-Century England* (London: Palgrave, 2002), pp. 159–95, where she gives a slightly different interpretation to the preface.

30 IV, pp. 169–71. The *Discovery* was dedicated to the Earl of Drumlangrig, who later defected to William of Orange.

31 On this, see Don Cameron Allen, *Doubt's Boundless Sea; Skepticism and Faith in the Renaissance* (Baltimore: Johns Hopkins University Press, 1964), and Françoise Charles-Daubert, *Les Libertins érudits en France au XVIIe siècle* (Paris: PUF, 1998).

32 *Works*, IV, p. 186. *Histoire des Oracles* (Paris, 1687), p. 80.

33 Ibid., p. 53.

34 Fontenelle, *Entretiens*, pp. 123–4.

35 *The History of Oracles*, IV, p. 184.

FURTHER READING

The following are among the most important and widely cited works about Aphra Behn and her literary and historical period. For a comprehensive listing of books and articles about Behn from her own time through 1985 see Mary Ann O'Donnell's *Aphra Behn: An Annotated Bibliography of Primary and Secondary Sources*, 2nd edition (Burlington: Ashgate, 2004).

Biographical studies

Beal, Peter, *Index of English Literary Manuscripts* (London: Mansel, 1987–93), vol. II.

Cameron, W. J., *New Light on Aphra Behn* (Auckland: University of Auckland Press, 1961).

Duffy, Maureen, *The Passionate Shepherdess: Aphra Behn 1640–1689* (London: Cape, 1977, repr. 2000).

Fitzmaurice, James, 'Aphra Behn and the *Abraham's Sacrifice* Case', *Huntington Library Quarterly*, 56 (1993), 319–26.

Goreau, Angeline, *Reconstructing Aphra: A Social Biography of Aphra Behn* (New York: Dial, 1980).

Hargreaves, Henry A., 'A Case for Mr Behn', *Notes and Queries*, 207 (1962), 203–5.

Hopkins, P. A., 'Aphra Behn and John Hoyle: A Contemporary Mention, and Sir Charles Sedley's Poem on His Death', *Notes & Queries*, 239 (June 1994), 176–85.

Medoff, Jes., '"Very Like a Fiction": Some Early Biographies of Aphra Behn', in *Write or Be Written: Early Modern Women Poets and Cultural Constraints*, ed. Barbara Smith and Ursula Appelt (Aldershot: Ashgate, 2001), pp. 247–69.

Mendelson, Sara Heller, *The Mental World of Stuart Women: Three Studies* (Brighton: Harvester, 1987).

O'Donnell, Mary Ann, 'A Verse Miscellany of Aphra Behn: Bodleian Library MS Firth c.16', *English Manuscript Studies*, ed. Peter Beal and Jeremy Griffiths (Oxford, 1989), vol II, pp. 189–227.

Platt, Harrison, 'Astrea and Celadon: An Untouched Portrait of Aphra Behn', *PMLA*, 49 (1934), 544–59.

'Roundtable [Bernard Dhuicq, Maureen Duffy, Germaine Greer, Mary Ann O'Donnell, Janet Todd]', in *Aphra Behn (1640–1689): Identity, Alterity,*

Ambiguity, ed. Mary Ann O'Donnell, Bernard Dhuicq, and Guyonne Leduc (Paris: L'Harmattan, 2000), pp. 277–93.

Sackville-West, Vita, *Aphra Behn: the Incomparable Astrea* (New London: Greenwood Press, 1927).

Todd, Janet, *The Secret Life of Aphra Behn* (London: André Deutsch, 1996; New Brunswick: Rutgers University Press, 1997; London: Pandora, 2000).

Woodcock, George, *The Incomparable Aphra* (London: Boardman, 1948).

Woolf, Virginia, *A Room of One's Own* (London: Hogarth Press, 1928).

Selected editions

Greer, Germaine, Susan Hastings, Jeslyn Medoff, Melinda Sanson, eds., *Kissing the Rod: An Anthology of Seventeenth-Century Women's Verse* (London: Virago, 1988).

Greer, Germaine, *The Uncollected Verse of Aphra Behn* (Stump Cross: Stump Cross Books, 1989).

Salzman, Paul, *Oroonoko and Other Writings* (Oxford: Oxford University Press, 1994).

Spencer, Jane, *'The Rover', 'The Feigned Courtesans', 'The Lucky Chance', 'The Emperor of the Moon'* (Oxford: Oxford University Press, 1995).

Summers, Montague, *The Works of Aphra Behn* (London: Heinemann, 1915).

Todd, Janet, *Oroonoko, the Rover and Other Works* (London: Penguin, 1992).
Oroonoko (London: Penguin, 2003).
The Works of Aphra Behn, 7 vols. (London: Pickering; Columbus: Ohio State University Press 1992–6).

Critical studies

Alarcon, Daniel Cooper and Stephanie Athey, *'Oroonoko*'s Gendered Economies of Honor/Horror: Reframing Colonial Discourse Studies in the Americas', *American Literature*, 65 (1993), 415–43.

Andrade, Susan Z., 'White Skin, Black Masks: Colonialism and the Sexual Politics of *Oroonoko*', *Cultural Critique* (1994), 189–214.

Aravamudan, Srinivas, *Tropicopolitans: Colonialism and Agency, 1688–1804* (Durham: Duke University Press, 1999).

Armistead, J. M., *Four Restoration Playwrights: A Reference Guide to Thomas Shadwell, Aphra Behn, Nathaniel Lee, and Thomas Otway* (Boston: G. K. Hall, 1984).

Ballaster, Ros, 'Fiction Feigning Femininity: False Counts and Pageant Kings in Aphra Behn's Popish Plot Writings', in Todd, *Aphra Behn Studies*, pp. 50–65.
'New Hystericism: Aphra Behn's *Oroonoko*: The Body, The Text, and The Feminist Critic', in *New Feminist Discourses: Critical Essays on Theories and Texts*, ed. Isobel Armstrong (London and New York: Routledge, 1992), pp. 283–95.
'Pretences of State: Aphra Behn and the Female Plot', in Hutner, *Rereading Aphra Behn*, pp. 187–211.
Seductive Forms: Women's Amatory Fiction from 1684 to 1740 (Oxford: Clarendon Press, 1992).

Barash, Carol, *English Women's Poetry, 1649–1714: Politics, Community, and Linguistic Authority* (Oxford: Clarendon Press, 1996).

Bowers, Toni O'Shaughnessy, 'Sex, Lies, and Invisibility: Amatory Fiction from the Restoration to Mid-century', in *The Columbia History of the British Novel*, ed. John Richetti (New York: Columbia University Press, 1994), pp. 50–72.

Brown, Laura, 'The Romance of Empire: *Oroonoko* and the Trade in Slaves', in *The New Eighteenth Century: Theory, Politics, English Literature*, ed. Felicity Nussbaum and Laura Brown (New York: Methuen, 1987), pp. 41–61.

Brownley, Martine Watson, 'The Narrator in *Oroonoko*', *Essays in Literature*, 4 (1977), 174–81.

Canfield, J. Douglas, *Tricksters & Estates: On the Ideology of Restoration Comedy* (Lexington: University of Kentucky Press, 1997).

Carlson, Susan, 'Aphra Behn's *The Emperor of the Moon*: Staging Seventeenth-Century Farce for Twentieth-Century Tastes', *Essays in Theatre*, 14 (1996), 117–30.

Carnell, Rachel K., 'Subverting Tragic Conventions: Aphra Behn's Turn to the Novel', *Studies in the Novel*, 31 (1999), 133–51.

Chernaik, Warren, *Sexual Freedom in Restoration Literature* (Cambridge: Cambridge University Press, 1995).

Chibka, Robert, '"Oh! Do Not Fear a Woman's Invention": Truth, Falsehood, and fiction in Aphra Behn's *Oroonoko*', *Tulsa Studies in Literature and Language*, 30 (1988), 510–37.

Copeland, Nancy, '"Once a whore and ever"? Whore and Virgin in *The Rover* and Its Antecedents', *Restoration*, 16 (1992), 20–7.

　'"Who Can . . . Her Own Wish Deny?": Female Conduct and Politics in Aphra Behn's *The City Heiress*', *Restoration and 18th Century Theatre Research*, 2nd ser., 8, 1 (1993), 27–49.

Diamond, Elin, '*Gestus* and Signature in Aphra Behn's *The Rover*', *ELH*, 56 (1989), pp. 519–41.

Davis, Lennard J., *Factual Fictions: The Origins of the English Novel* (New York: Columbia University Press, 1983).

Day, Robert Adams, 'Aphra Behn and the Works of Intellect', in *Fetter'd or Free? British Women Novelists 1670–1815*, ed. Mary Ann Schofield and Cecilia Macheski (Athens: Ohio University Press, 1986), pp. 372–82.

Donoghue, Emma, *Passions between Women: British Lesbian Culture, 1668–1801* (New York: Harper Collins, 1995).

Duyfhuizen, Bernard, '"That which I dare not name": Aphra Behn's "The Willing Mistress"', *ELH*, 58 (1991), 63–82.

Ezell, Margaret J. M., *The Patriarch's Wife: Literary Evidence and the History of the Family* (Chapel Hill: University of North Carolina Press, 1987).

　Writing Women's Literary History (Baltimore: The Johns Hopkins University Press, 1993).

Ferguson, Margaret, 'Juggling the Categories of Race, Class, and Gender: Aphra Behn's *Oroonoko*', *Women's Studies*, 19 (1991), 159–81.

　'News from the New World', in *The Production of English Renaissance Culture*, ed. David Lee Miller, Sharon O'Dair, and Harold Weber (Ithaca and London: Cornell University Press, 1994), pp. 151–89.

Ferguson, Moira, 'Oroonoko: Birth of a Paradigm', New Literary History, 23, 2 (1992), 339–59.

Finke, Laurie, 'Aphra Behn and the Ideological Construction of Restoration Literary Theory', in Hutner, Rereading Aphra Behn, pp. 17–43.

Franceschina, John, 'Shadow and Substance in Aphra Behn's The Rover: The Semiotics of Restoration Performance', Restoration, 9 (1995), 29–42.

Frohock, Richard, 'Violence and Awe: The Foundations of Government in Aphra Behn's New World Settings', Eighteenth-Century Fiction, 8 (1996), 437–52.

Gallagher, Catherine, 'Oroonoko's Blackness', in Aphra Behn Studies, pp. 235–58.

Nobody's Story: The Vanishing Acts of Women Writers in the Marketplace, 1670–1820 (Oxford: Clarendon Press, 1994).

'Who was That Masked Woman? The Prostitute and the Playwright in the Comedies of Aphra Behn', in Women's Studies, 15 (1988), 23–42.

Gardiner, Judith Kegan, 'The First English Novel: Aphra Behn's Love-Letters, the Canon, and Women's Tastes', Tulsa Studies in Women's Literature (1989), pp. 201–22.

Gautier, Gary, 'Slavery and the Fashioning of Race in Oroonoko, Robinson Crusoe, and Equiano's Life', The Eighteenth Century: Theory and Interpretation, 42 (2001), 161–79.

Greer, Germaine, Slip-Shod Sybils: Recognition, Rejection and the Woman Poet (London: Viking, 1995).

Guffey, George, Two English Novelists: Aphra Behn and Anthony Trollope (Los Angeles: Clark Library, 1975).

Guibbory, Achsah, 'Sexual Politics/ Political Sex: Seventeenth-Century Love Poetry', in Renaissance Discourses of Desire, ed. Claude J. Summers and Ted-Larry Pebworth (Columbia: University of Missouri Press, 1993), pp. 206–22.

Hendricks, Margo, 'Civility, Barbarism, and Aphra Behn's The Widow Ranter', in Women, Race and Writing in the Early Modern Period (London: Routledge, 1994), pp. 225–39.

Hobby, Elaine, Virtue of Necessity: English Women's Writing 1649–88 (London: Virago, 1988).

Hoegberg, David E., 'Caesar's Toils: Allusion and Rebellion in Oroonoko', Eighteenth-Century Fiction, 7 (1995), 237–57.

Holmesland, Oddvar, 'Aphra Behn's Oroonoko: Cultural Dialectics and the Novel', ELH, 68 (2001), 57–79.

Houston, Beverle, 'Usurpation and Dismemberment: Oedipal Tyranny in Oroonoko', Literature and Psychology, 32 (1986), 30–6.

Hughes, Derek, English Drama, 1660–1700 (Oxford: Clarendon Press, 1996).

'Race, Gender and Scholarly Practice in Aphra Behn's Oroonoko', Essays in Criticism, 52 (2002), 1–22.

The Theatre of Aphra Behn (Basingstoke: Palgrave, 2001).

Hume, Robert D., The Development of English Drama in the Late Seventeenth Century (Oxford: Clarendon Press, 1976).

ed., The London Theatre World 1660–1800 (Carbondale and Edwardsville: Southern Illinois University Press, 1980).

Hutner, Heidi, 'Aphra Behn's Oroonoko: The Politics of Gender, Race, and Class', in Living by the Pen: Early British Women Writers, ed. Dale Spender (New York and London: Teachers College Press, 1992).

ed., *Rereading Aphra Behn: History, Theory, and Criticism* (London and Charlottesville: University Press of Virginia), 1993.

'Revisioning the Female Body: Aphra Behn's *The Rover*, Parts I and II', in Hutner, *Rereading Aphra Behn*, pp. 102–20.

Iwanisziw, Susan B., 'Behn's Novel Investment in *Oroonoko*: Kingship, Slavery and Tobacco in English Colonialism', *South Atlantic Quarterly*, 6 (1998), 75–98.

Jacobs, Naomi, 'The Seduction of Aphra Behn', *Women's Studies*, 18 (1991), 395–403.

Kaul, Suvir, 'Reading Literary Symptoms: Colonial Pathologies and the *Oroonoko* Fictions of Behn, Southerne, and Hawkesworth', *Eighteenth-Century Life*, 18 (1994), 80–96.

Kavenik, Frances M., 'Aphra Behn: The Playwright as "Breeches Part"', in *Curtain Calls: British and American Women Writers and the Theater, 1660–1820*, ed. Mary Anne Schofield and Cecilia Macheski (Athens, Ohio: Ohio University Press, 1991), pp. 178–91.

Kraft, Elizabeth, 'Aphra Behn's *Oroonoko* in the Classroom: A Review of Texts', *Restoration*, 2 (1998), 79–96.

Kubek, Elizabeth Bennett, '"Night Mares of the Commonwealth": Royalist Passion and Female ambition in Aphra Behn's *The Roundheads*', *Restoration*, 17 (1993), 88–103.

Lewcock, Dawn, 'More for Seeing than Hearing: Behn and the Use of Theatre', in *Aphra Behn Studies*, pp. 66–83.

Lipking, Joanna, 'Confusing Matters: Searching the Backgrounds of *Oroonoko*', in *Aphra Behn Studies*, pp. 259–81.

Lussier, Mark, '"The Vile Merchandize of Fortune": Women, Economy, and Desire in Aphra Behn', *Women's Studies*, 18 (1990), 370–93.

MacCarthy, B. G., *The Female Pen: Women Writers Their Contribution to the English Novel 1621–1744* (Cork: Cork University Press, 1944 and 1946; repr. 1994).

MacDonald, Joyce Green, 'The Disappearing African Woman: Imoinda in *Oroonoko* after Behn', *ELH*, 66 (1999), 71–86.

'Gender, Family, and Race in Aphra Behn's *Abdelazer*', in *Aphra Behn (1640–1689): Identity, Alterity, Ambiguity*, ed. Mary Ann O'Donnell, Bernard Dhuiq, and Guyonne Leduc (Paris: L'Harmattan, 2000), pp. 67–73.

Markley, Robert and Molly Rothenburg, 'Contestations of Nature: Aphra Behn's "The Golden Age" and the Sexualizing of Politics', in Hutner, *Rereading Aphra Behn*, pp. 301–21.

Markley, Robert, '"Be Impudent, be saucy, forward, bold, touzing and leud": The Politics of Masculine Sexuality and Feminine Desire in Behn's Tory Comedies', in *Cultural Readings of Restoration and Eighteenth-Century English Theater*, ed. J. Douglas Canfield and Deborah C. Payne (Athens: University of Georgia Press, 1995), pp. 114–40.

Mermin, Dorothy, 'Women Becoming Poets: Katherine Philips, Aphra Behn, Anne Finch', *ELH*, 57 (1990), 335–56.

Munns, Jessica, 'Barton and Behn's *The Rover*: or, the Text Transpos'd', *Restoration and Eighteenth Century Theatre Research* (1988), pp. 11–22.

'"But to the touch were soft": Pleasure, Power, and Impotence in "The Disappointment" and "The Golden Age"', in Todd, *Aphra Behn Studies*, pp. 178–96.

O'Donnell, Mary Ann, 'Private Jottings, Public Utterances: Aphra Behn's Published Writings and her Commonplace Book', in Todd, *Aphra Behn Studies*, pp. 285–309.

Owen, Susan J., *Restoration Theatre in Crisis* (Oxford: Clarendon Press, 1996).

'"Suspect my loyalty when I lose my virtue": Sexual Politics and Party in Aphra Behn's plays of the Exclusion Crisis, 1678–83', *Restoration*, 18 (1994), 37–47.

Pacheco, Anita, 'Rape and the Female Subject in Aphra Behn's *The Rover*', *ELH*, 65 (1998), 323–45.

'Royalism and Honor in Aphra Behn's *Oroonoko*', *Studies in English Literature*, 34 (1994), 491–506.

Paxman, David, 'Oral and Literature Discourse in Aphra Behn's *Oroonoko*', *Restoration*, 18 (1994), 88–103.

Payne, Deborah C., '"And poets shall by patron-princes live": Aphra Behn and Patronage', in *Curtain Calls: British and American Women Writers and the Theater, 1660–1820*, ed. Mary Anne Schofield and Cecilia Macheski (Athens, Ohio: Ohio University Press, 1991), pp. 105–19.

'Reified Object or Emergent Professional? Retheorizing the Restoration Actress', in *Cultural Readings of Restoration and Eighteenth-Century English Theater*, ed. J. Douglas Canfield and Deborah C. Payne (Athens: University of Georgia Press, 1995), pp. 13–38.

Payne, Linda R., 'The Carnivalesque Regeneration of Corrupt Economies in *The Rover*', *Restoration*, 22 (1998), 40–9.

Pearson, Jacqueline, 'Gender and narrative in the fiction of Aphra Behn', *Review of English Studies*, 42 (1991), 40–56 and 179–190.

The Prostituted Muse: Images of Women and Women Dramatists 1642–1737 (Brighton: Harvester, 1988).

'Slave Princes and Lady Monsters: Gender and Ethnic Difference in the Work of Aphra Behn', in Todd, *Aphra Behn Studies*, pp. 219–34.

Pender, Patricia, 'Competing Conceptions: Rhetorics of Representation in Aphra Behn's *Oroonoko*', *Women's Writing*, 8 (2001), 457–71.

Pigg, Daniel, 'Trying to Frame the Unframable: Oroonoko as Discourse in Aphra Behn's *Oroonoko*', *Studies in Short Fiction*, 34 (1977), 105–11.

Pollak, Ellen, 'Beyond Incest: Gender and the Politics of Transgression in Aphra Behn's *Love-Letters between a Noble-Man and his Sister*', in *Rereading Aphra Behn*, pp. 151–86.

Richetti, John, '*Love-Letters Between a Noble-Man and his Sister*: Aphra Behn and Amatory Fiction', in *Augustan Subjects: Essays in Honor of Martin C. Battestin*, ed. Albert J. Rivero (Newark, DE: University of Delaware Press, 1997), pp. 13–28.

Rivero, Albert J., 'Aphra Behn's *Oroonoko* and the "Blank Spaces" of Colonial Fictions', *Studies in English Literature* 39 (1999), 443–62.

Rogers, Katharine M., 'Fact and Fiction in Aphra Behn's *Oroonoko*', *Studies in the Novel*, 20 (1988), 1–15.

Rosenthal, Laura J., 'Owning *Oroonoko*: Behn, Southerne, and the Contingencies of Property', *Renaissance Drama*, n.s. 23 (1992), 25–58.

Rubik, Margarete, 'Estranging the Familiar, Familiarizing the Strange: Self and Other in *Oroonoko* and *Widow Ranter*', in *Aphra Behn (1640–1689): Identity*,

Alterity, Ambiguity, ed: Mary Ann O'Donnell, Bernard Dhuicq, and Guyonne Leduc (Paris: L'Harmattan, 2000), pp. 33–41.

Salzman, Paul, *English Prose Fiction 1558–1700* (Oxford: Clarendon Press, 1985).

'Aphra Behn: Poetry and Masquerade', in Todd, *Aphra Behn Studies*, pp. 109–29.

Schafer, Elizabeth, 'Appropriating Aphra', *Australasian Studies*, 19 (1991), 39–49.

Shell, Alison, 'Popish Plots: *The Feign'd Curtizans* in Context', in Todd, *Aphra Behn Studies*, pp. 30–49.

Spearing, Elizabeth, 'Aphra Behn: the Politics of Translation', in Todd, *Aphra Behn Studies*, pp. 154–77.

Spencer, Jane, *Aphra Behn's Afterlife* (Oxford: Oxford University Press, 2000).

'"Deceit, Dissembling, all that's Woman": Comic Plot and Female Action in *The Feigned Courtesans*', in Hutner, *Rereading Aphra Behn*, pp. 86–101.

The Rise of the Woman Novelist: From Aphra Behn to Jane Austen (Oxford: Blackwell, 1986).

Spengemann, William C., 'The Earliest American Novel: Aphra Behn's *Oroonoko*', *Nineteenth-Century Fiction*, 38 (1984), 384–414.

Starr, G. A., 'Aphra Behn and the Genealogy of the Man of Feeling', *Modern Philology* (May 1990), pp. 362–73.

Staves, Susan, *Players' Scepters: Fictions of Authority in the Restoration* (Nebraska: University of Nebraska Press, 1979).

Stiebel, Arlene, 'Not Since Sappho: The Erotic in Poems of Katherine Philips and Aphra Behn', in *Homosexuality in Renaissance and Enlightenment England: Literary Representations in Historical Context*, ed. Claude J. Summers (New York: The Haworth Press, 1992), pp. 153–71.

'Subversive Sexuality: Masking the Erotic in Poems by Katherine Philips and Aphra Behn', in *Renaissance Discourses of Desire*, ed. Claude J. Summers and Ted-Larry Pebworth (Columbia: University of Missouri Press, 1993), 223–36.

Sullivan, David M., 'The Female will in Aphra Behn', *Women's Studies*, 22 (1993), 335–47.

Sussman, Charlotte, 'The Other Problem with Women: Reproduction and Slave Culture in Aphra Behn's *Oroonoko*', in Hutner, *Rereading Aphra Behn*, pp. 212–33.

Szigalyi, Stephen, 'The Sexual Politics of Behn's *Rover*: After Patriarchy,' *Studies in Philology*, 95 (1998), 435–55.

Thomas, Susie, 'This Thing of Darkness I Acknowledge Mine: Aphra Behn's *Abdelazer, or, The Moor's Revenge*,' *Restoration*, 22 (1998), 18–39.

Todd, Janet, ed., *Aphra Behn Studies* (Cambridge: Cambridge University Press, 1996).

The Critical Fortunes of Aphra Behn (Columbia, SC: Camden House, 1998).

The Sign of Angellica: Women, Writing and Fiction 1660–1800 (London: Virago, 1989).

'Spectacular Deaths: History and Story in Aphra Behn's *Love-Letters*, *Oroonoko* and *The Widow Ranter*', in *Gender, Art and Death* (Cambridge: Polity Press, 1993), pp. 32–62.

'Who is Silvia? What is she? Feminine Identity in Aphra Behn's *Love-Letters between a Noble-Man and his Sister*', in Todd, *Aphra Behn Studies*, pp. 199–218.

Williams, Andrew P., 'The African as Text: Ownership and Authority in Aphra Behn's *Oroonoko*', *Journal of African Travel Writing*, 5 (1998), 5–14.

Wiseman, S. J., *Aphra Behn* (Plymouth: Northcote House, 1996).

Wyrick, Laura, 'Facing up to the Other: Race and Ethics in Levinas and Behn', *The Eighteenth Century: Theory and Interpretation*, 40 (1999), 206–18.

Young, Elizabeth V., 'Aphra Behn. Gender, and Pastoral', *Studies in English Literature*, 33 (1993), 523–43.

'Aphra Behn's Elegies', *Genre*, 28 (1995), 211–36.

Zeitz, Lisa M. and Peter Thoms, 'Power, Gender, and Identity in Aphra Behn's "The Disappointment"', *Studies in English Literature*, 37 (1997), 501–16.

Zimbardo, Rose, *A Mirror to Nature: Transformations in Drama and Aesthetics, 1660–1732* (Lexington: University of Kentucky Press, 1986).

'Aphra Behn in Search of a Novel', *Studies in Eighteenth-Century Culture*, 19 (1989), 277–87.

Zook, Melinda, 'Contextualizing Aphra Behn: Plays, Politics, and Party, 1679–1689', in *Women Writers and the Early Modern British Political Tradition*, ed. Hilda L. Smith and Carole Pateman (Cambridge: Cambridge University Press, 1998), pp. 75–93.

INDEX

CAMBRIDGE COMPANIONS TO LITERATURE

CAMBRIDGE COMPANIONS TO CULTURE